Ukraine on the Road to Europe

Lutz Hoffmann · Felicitas Möllers
Editors

Ukraine on the Road to Europe

With 23 Figures
and 30 Tables

Physica-Verlag
A Springer-Verlag Company

Prof. em. Dr. Lutz Hoffmann
Former President of DIW
DIW – German Institute for Economic Research
Königin-Luise-Straße 5
14195 Berlin
Germany

Felicitas Möllers
Deutsche Bank AG
DB Research
Große Gallusstraße 10–14
60311 Frankfurt am Main
Germany

ISBN 3-7908-1369-9 Physica-Verlag Heidelberg New York

Library of Congress Cataloging-in-Publication Data
Die Deutsche Bibliothek – CIP-Einheitsaufnahme
Ukraine on the road to Europe: with 30 tables / Lutz Hoffmann; Felicitas Möllers ed. – Heidelberg; New York: Physica-Verl., 2001
ISBN 3-7908-1369-9

Physica-Verlag Heidelberg
a member of BertelsmannSpringer Science+Business Media GmbH

Cover design: Erich Kirchner, Heidelberg

SPIN 10791679 88/2202-5 4 3 2 1 0 – Printed on acid-free paper

Preface

by Viktor A. Yushchenko, Prime Minister of Ukraine

The intensification of the integration processes on our continent entirely coincides with the national interests of Ukraine, a country which is undoubtedly European both geographically and politically. What kind of Europe do we now have, and what should it be in the future? What should the role of Ukrainian society be in the economic, social, and cultural integration of the countries on the European continent? These questions are the subject of research and scientific analysis by the well-known economists whose work is contained in this book.

Let there be no doubt, the strategic goal of Ukraine's foreign policy is the active participation of our country in the European integration process. Thus, the move toward co-operation and gradual integration with the European Union was defined as one of the main priorities of the Ukrainian Government's programme "Reforms for Well-being", which is based on President Leonid Kuchma's speech "Ukraine: Steps into XXI century" and was approved by the Ukrainian Parliament. This move is not a hasty response to a new trend, but rather a pragmatic decision since the EU will define the face of Europe for the next century.

The process of globalisation in world politics and economics, and the geographic enlargement of the European Union, which will approach our borders, present additional reasons for Ukraine's active participation in the integration process. It is important to us that all people will benefit from these new developments and that Ukraine's western border will not become the eastern border of the EU.

The integration into the rest of Europe and the attaining of its levels of economic development, standards of life, private security, and guaranteed rights and freedoms are all notions of equal importance to us. These principles are guiding our work today, and will do so in our future undertakings.

The questions of how well we understand the goals and tasks before us, and how well our citizens and our foreign partners understand our actions, will define the support by the average citizen of the Government's efforts regarding accelerating Ukraine's entrance into the family of European peoples.

For us the issue of integration into the European Union is not a question of choice, but only a question of time. The road to this goal is challenging and long. But it is the way to attain sustainable economic growth, to decrease poverty, to develop an effective market economy, and to strengthen the civil society and the democratic institutions of the country. All that will be the prime focus for our country's development over the next few years and for the future.

This book contains many deep and interesting analyses of various aspects of the problem of Ukraine's integration into the European community. It presents a comprehensive overview of this process, it appraises positive accomplishments in this process, and it takes advantage of the experience of some countries which have already advanced further on their way to economic integration and thus have developed strategies which could speed up Ukraine's movement towards Europe.

It is my great pleasure to emphasise the fact that this book is one more bright example of the substantial intellectual co-operation between Ukraine and Germany within the framework of the TRANSFORM Programme.

With best regards,

Preface

by Dr. Werner Müller, Federal Minister of Economics and Technology, Federal Republic of Germany

The special interest in the Ukraine on the part of policymakers and businessmen in Germany has a real basis. After Russia, Ukraine is Europe's largest country, occupying twice the expanse of the Federal Republic of Germany. With almost 50 million inhabitants, it is the fifth most populous country on the European continent. Its location neighboring Russia and as a Black Sea state gives it strategic importance. It plays an important role as a transmitter and transit area between the European Union and Russia.

Ukraine's central function in the overall European structure was underlined by the conclusion of the partnership and cooperation agreement between the European Union and Ukraine, which went into force in March 1998. The European Council, meeting in Helsinki, adopted a "Common Strategy EU – Ukraine" on December 10, 1999. On the basis of the partnership and cooperation agreement, Ukraine is to be brought closer to the European Union. Relations are to be further developed in a systematic manner at all levels.

All of this underscores the fact that Ukraine is a European country and that it must be integrated within our European architecture. Germany emphatically supports Ukraine's pro-European orientation.

We attach particular importance to our bilateral relations with Ukraine. This is expressed in a number of ways, including the holding of official bilateral government consultations every year, with a central role being played by economic and trade questions. The last round was conducted in July and chaired by German Chancellor Schröder and President Kuchma.

The German business community continues to be strongly interested in the development of cooperation ties to partners from Ukraine.

But economic relations can only be expanded if economic policy reforms continue to be rigorously implemented so that a sustained growth process is initiated. This book provides a number of valuable hints in this regard.

Germany has a great interest in supporting Ukraine on its path toward democracy and the market economy. The Federal Republic is a committed partner in the restructuring of Ukraine's industry in the framework of the TRANSFORM Programme conducted by the German Government. In this process, the German

Advisory Group on Economic Reforms with the Ukrainian Govenment has an extremely important role to play.

Contents

Introduction

"The main task in the current phase is to build a suitable base for full membership of Ukraine in the EU, and for the development of a pro-European majority in the society."

Government of Ukraine, Programme till 2004

"All in all, those of us who take part in – or observe – the transformation process can say: We are disappointed but still committed."

Bohdan Hawrylyshyn, June 23, 2000

Lutz Hoffmann and Felicitas Möllers

1 Background

Europe – where is that? For citizens of the European Union this question seems easy to answer. For those countries that have already initiated the process of adhesion to the EU, it has been clear for a long time what their foreign policy and economic priorities are. But what for the others?

Ukraine, a nation with a long tradition inside a new state, is without doubt geographically a part of Europe. The famous battle of Peter the Great against Sweden in 1709, which allowed Russia to become one of the major European powers, was won at Poltava, a city in the eastern part of today's Ukraine. L'viv, Kyiv, the Crimea – all are places essential to European history. Economically, Ukraine once was the breadbasket of Europe, and through its middle, like an umbilical cord for energy, runs the Russian gas pipeline from Siberia to Western Europe.

And yet, in Ukraine one often hears: "You in Europe" or "We are a bridge to Europe", which could be interpreted as: "We are not part of you." The integration process into the international and European structures, which Ukraine has consistently pursued since its independence in 1991, is anchored neither in the perceptions of Ukrainians nor in that of most international observers. Even today, in the minds of most people, Ukraine is associated with Russia or the CIS or with a geo-political space called 'Eurasia'.

The German Advisory Group on Economic Reforms with the Ukrainian Government advises the Government, the Office of the President, the National Bank, and the Parliament of Ukraine on behalf of the German Government, with respect to economic reforms, and hence the way toward Europe. The Advisory Group, whose head and one member are the publishers of this book, meets about once every six weeks for consultation with leading Ukrainian politicians. Out of these consultations sprang the idea of a 'Europe Conference'. The conference, the 11th Ukrainian-German Economic Symposium, took place on 22 and 23 June 2000 in Kyiv.

When selecting the speakers – who are also the authors in this book – we tried to invite guests to Kyiv from countries which play an especially significant role on Ukraine's path to Europe, namely Poland and Russia. At the same time we tried to emphasise an interdisciplinary approach for the convention and the book. Though our focus is research and consultation concerning the economic transformation of Ukraine, we do realise that without knowledge about the historical relationships, the geo-political constraints (or perhaps options), and without an appreciation for the cultural environment, no lasting consulting effort or political action, and no integration – whether within the EU or within Europe – will be possible, other than the building of some formalised structures.

One more important aspect to this book: To many Ukrainians the way to Europe is synonymous with membership in the EU or at least with a treaty of association. We however, do not want to emphasise the development of strategies on how these goals could be attained, neither in this book nor with our consultation. Rather we hope to encourage Ukraine to persevere with its goal to promote the transformation faster and more resolutely, to open its economy, and to utilise its advantages by integrating into the world economy. Through these concrete steps Ukraine automatically gets closer to Europe, at the same time avoiding setting itself goals that for the present remain far away. Not meeting such goals could prove a discouragement and hence risk that the necessary reforms are not taken.

If Ukraine indeed follows such a path, there will be consequences for western Europe, not only based on a geographical membership, but also from an active participation of Ukraine in 'Europe'.

2 Structure of the book and key themes of the authors

2.1 Bridge or integral part? Ukraine's historical, cultural and geopolitical connection with Europe and its neighbours

Based on the above, the book is divided into three parts. *Part I* introduces the reader into the historical and political relationships between Ukraine and Europe and Ukraine and its neighbours.

In *Chapter 1*, *Bohdan Hawrylyshyn, Geneva,* researches Ukraine's options for its geo-political orientation. For him this is the central question: the "to be or not to be". Nearly three centuries as a colony of Tsarist Russia has significantly diminished Ukraine's cultural, intellectual and political potential. For Hawrylyshyn the advantages and the attractiveness of the Western option are overwhelming and obvious: security, full institutionalisation and maintenance of a pluralistic society, economic efficacy, and hopefully a social partnership between government, business, and employees. Integration into the EU is for him the true third way which in contrast to the globalisation slogan "What is good for the shareholder is good for the world" orients itself after the motto "People are the purpose, profits are the means". This approach is no mere dream; it is a vision with a good chance of being realised.

In *Chapter 2, Charles Clover, Financial Times,* continues the reflections about Ukraine's geo-political options. Though often seen by Russian intellectuals as an answer to world-wide globalisation, and evoked by Russian politicians 'Eurasia' does not present a good prospect for Ukraine. Clover comes to the conclusion that the combination of trade blocs, moves toward regional federalism, and opposition to global hegemony by the United States have combined to create a world which seems likely be dominated by three or four centres of power in the coming decades. And this is a world, which leaves Ukraine little choice but the European one.

Arkady Moshes, Institute for Europe, Moscow, explores the present relationship between Russia and Ukraine in *Chapter 3*. After centuries of 'brotherly' relations, which gave Ukraine the complex of 'always being the second', while in Moshes' view resulting in a mentality and practice of relying on Russian subsidies, the new watch word must be: "No more free lunch for Ukraine". The energy sector provides a good example – debts for purchased gas, and the unauthorised usage or theft of gas being siphoned from the pipeline passing through Ukraine's territory. Here lies one of the causes why the relations between both countries have suffered greatly. According to Moshes, if the energy question and hence the debt problem is not resolved, the situation would be a genuine catastrophe for Ukraine, making it the new 'sick person of Europe'.

In *Chapter 4, Mirosław Gronicki, Centre for Social and Economic Analysis, Warsaw*, reviews the Polish transition process towards a market economy, which is considered one of the most successful ones. He commences with a thorough review of the various stages this process has gone through in Poland, stressing in particular the important role which small private companies have played. In order to encourage the creation of such companies the Polish Government had allowed them a three-year tax holiday. By now these firms not only generate significant revenue for the Government, they have also helped to take up a significant portion of the labour force that became unemployed following the closing of the large state-owned enterprises. In addition they developed entrepreneurship and became a training ground for businessmen. Although Gronicki realises that the Polish experience cannot be applied wholesale to Ukraine, he believes that much of it could be helpful for Ukraine's continuing progress towards a market economy.

2.2 Bridges to Europe and the market economy: Aspects of a long road

Part II concerns the 'bridges' being built by Ukraine on its way to Europe, including actual economic out-looks for a rapprochement towards Europe.

In *Chapter 5, Herbert Brücker, German Institute for Economic Research, Berlin,* discusses the prospects for the convergence of per capita incomes between East and West in Europe on the background of theoretical and empirical knowledge about growth and convergence. Only some transition countries managed to realise growth rates of investment and output well above those of the developed market economies in the present EU. These developments raise the concern that the first economic divide of Europe around market and planned economies might be replaced by a second economic divide between high and low income economies. Low investment levels in economies such as Russia and the Ukraine can be largely explained by shortcomings in their institutional and macro-economic conditions, and the possibility of a poverty trap might be a real danger.

In *Chapter 6, Klaus Schneider, European Commission*, explores the concrete steps that have been taken by the EU and by Ukraine towards each other since they both signed the Partnership and Co-operation Agreement (PCA) in June 1994. Schneider notes that the PCA is far from being implemented, whereby the absence of a stable legal framework adapted to the requirements of a market economy has proved to be a key constraint to the success of economic transition in Ukraine. However, Prime Minister Yushchenko's leadership in the first half of 2000 has demonstrated a fresh determination to actually tackle long needed drastic reforms. But there is still a long way ahead. The EU cannot see itself as 'saving' Ukraine as it might be tempted to do with a smaller country. Ukraine is too big, its population too numerous, its territory too immense and its economy too vast. It must save itself.

In *Chapter 7, Wolfgang Quaisser and Volkhart Vincentz* explore the progress made by Ukraine towards integration into the world economy. Ukraine more than doubled its exports to the EU between 1992 and 1998, however the level of exports to the EU is still very low. The new Yushchenko Government's programme till 2004 states: "The main task in the current phase is to build a suitable base for full membership of Ukraine in the EU." To this end Ukraine will try "to become a member of the WTO, to start co-operation with EFTA, to begin negotiations about a free trade zone with the EU, and to get the status of a market economy from the European Commission". Indeed, there seems to be a high EU-Ukraine trade potential, even if one acknowledges the still existing trade restrictions. The realisation of this potential will very much depend on the progress of future reforms in the domestic economy. Russia and other CIS states will remain important trading partners of Ukraine, if only to prevent the deterioration of the cross-border production relationships inherited from the past.

In *Chapter 8, Dieter Biehl, Frankfurt University,* discusses the importance of infrastructure for regional development and growth. His definition of infrastructure includes not only the classical components, such as roads and rails, but also education, training and research facilities from the pre-school through the university level, libraries, museums, theatres, hospitals and sports facilities. Biehl first presents his approach within the context of a 'Regional Development Policy Approach' for some 139 regions within the EU. He then presents a brief overview of a research project that attempts to apply the same approach to Ukrainian regions. Biehl contends that the typical regional problem it is not primarily insufficient demand, but rather low competitiveness of regional supply.

Felicitas Möllers, Petra Opitz and Christian von Hirschhausen investigate Ukraine's 'potential' in *Chapter 9*, which is often invoked when discussing the future economic development of the country. At the same time, it is also said that Ukraine could be a 'bridge to Europe'. Who in practice would furnish this potential and who would build the bridge? Do different abilities and opportunities exist between the eastern and western parts of Ukraine, caused possibly by different structures and experiences made by individuals and enterprises in these two regions? Certainly, Ukraine can break out of its present isolation and become an important bridge between the whole CIS area and the western part of Europe, provided it accepts that the bridge function to Central and Western Europe is unquestioningly connected with the introduction of a capitalist, market oriented system such as practised in the other parts of Europe.

In *Chapter 10, Petra Opitz and Christian von Hirschhausen* analyse the perspectives of Ukrainian gas transit given the recent developments, and the potential repercussions on Russia and Western Europe. Ukraine continues to be an important gas transit bridge to Europe, but it has become a shaky one. It is shown that that a legal and organisational separation of the International Gas Transit System (IGTS) from the rest of the state-owned gas industry yields benefits to all parties. The entry of Belarus into the transit business can no longer be avoided; the only question being what capacities it will invest in. It is Ukraine's turn now to react quickly in order to remain the important link to Europe, which it wants to be.

In *Chapter 11, Stephan von Cramon-Taubadel and Ludwig Striewe* speculate on what impact EU accession would have on Ukraine's agriculture. While Europe is many things – and certainly more than the EU or the EU's Common Agricultural Policy (CAP) – in practical terms this CAP is one of the most important, expensive and controversial incarnations of Europe. As the main point of their analysis, von Cramon and Striewe observe that, while Ukraine should join the EU as soon as possible, 'as soon as possible' probably may not mean 'very soon'. Rather than supporting the EU in defending the CAP in coming rounds of multilateral trade negotiations, Ukrainian policy makers should recognise that the CAP represents a very significant tax on Ukrainian agriculture and that the CAP has also contributed to the disappointing performance of Ukrainian agriculture in recent years. Ukraine should add its voice to the voices of countries such as the members of the Cairns group that share an interest in a level playing field for all participants in international agricultural trade.

Iryna Akimova, Institute for Economic Research and Policy Consulting in Kyiv, analyses in *Chapter 12* the impact of export orientation (and especially orientation towards non-CIS markets), considering the impact both on the restructuring activities of Ukrainian enterprises and on their performance results. Her findings have clear policy implications: Future success with restructuring of large industrial enterprises in Ukraine is related to their increasing integration into the world economy through re-orientation towards, and production for export. Accelerating the privatisation of the remaining large industrial companies will induce them to redirect their trade towards exports and push them towards restructuring. The hardening of budget and encouraging competition between domestic and foreign producers are important driving forces for enterprise restructuring.

2.3 Aspects of financial and fiscal policy in Ukraine

Finally, *Part III* considers the financial and fiscal considerations arising out of the interplay between Europe and Ukraine; some of these aspects being unaffected by whether Ukraine actively works towards integration with the EU or continues to more or less stand by as an observer.

Poland's experience may be of some assistance to its Ukrainian neighbours and to other countries in the region. *Ryszard Kokoszczyński, National Bank of Poland,* recounts in *Chapter 13* that the Polish monetary and exchange rate policies in the 1990s have been directed towards fulfilling two important objectives at the same time: continuous and credible disinflation, and macro-economic stability. Not orthodox doctrine, but pragmatic efficiency was a major feature of both, strategy and tactics, of the Polish monetary policy, which was probably one of important reasons for the growth success of the Polish economy.

Andrew Seton from EBRD states in *Chapter 14* that at this point in time Ukraine has little need of capital 'without vision' – that is, of capital looking to make a 'fast buck' in the capital markets, or trying to derive short-term benefits from the country's assets without modernising them. What Ukraine needs today is real capital first and capital market games, a very distant second. But the 'short-term capital episode' in Ukraine's history – not to mention that in Russia's history, which met a major hiatus in mid-1998 – also led to several unfortunate consequences: continuing mutual mistrust between foreign investors, local private interests and government. It is hoped that Ukraine together with the efforts of international institutions will lead to successful privatisation, and attract long-term strategic investors to Ukraine, who bring with them the type of experience mentioned above.

In *Chapter 15, Christian Thimann, European Central Bank (ECB),* presents an evaluation of EU enlargement and its implications for Ukraine from the perspective of the ECB. The current accession process, once completed, will bring the EMU right to the doorstep of Ukraine. But even before that happens, Ukraine will be affected by the EMU and by the introduction of the Euro. This has some implications for the Ukrainian economic and monetary policies in the medium term, concerning economic and trade integration, institutional co-operation, economic policy standards, exchange rate issues, and many others.

The effects of the EMU on the Ukrainian economy are discussed by *Gerhard Krause* in *Chapter 16*. Krause believes that the over-all economic development of the Euro-zone will have a qualitatively strong influence. The legal economic policy framework within the EU – a single monetary policy, a co-ordinated economic policy, manoeuvrability limitations for fiscal policy as defined by the stability pact, the 'four freedoms' on the factor markets – force a considerable synchronisation on the economic cycles of all EMU partner states. This in turn significantly impacts on smaller open economies such as Ukraine. Increasing trade relations with the Euro-zone will strengthen the role of the Euro. Taking this tendency into account, the Euro should be regarded as being at least of equal value to the US-dollar for use as a nominal reference currency.

Ulrich Thießen asks in *Chapter 17* whether the current development in Ukraine of increasing centralisation of governmental decision making is good for Ukraine's development, or whether there may be reasons to argue for more decentralisation. In Ukraine's particular case potential theoretical arguments against fiscal decentralisation are the poor quality of the local governments and of local democracy, large income differentials between households and regions, a low degree of urbanisation, i.e. poorly diversified tax bases in the regions. However, for fiscal decentralisation to contribute to better resource allocation and economic growth the central government has to meet certain prerequisites, e.g. implementation of a consistent redistribution policy, introduction of a transparent system of tax sharing and transfers, improvements in the auditing of sub-national government budgets etc.

3 Acknowledgement

In the first place we want to thank the Ukrainian Government and all our Ukrainian partners who with their trust in us and in our work have created an atmosphere which allows us to publish this book. Foremost, we thank the Prime Minister of Ukraine, Mr. Viktor A. Yushchenko, who for the last almost six years of our consulting effort has always supported us.

We thank all the guests to the conference and the authors of this book, who have travelled the long road to Kyiv from Berlin, Brussels, Frankfurt, Geneva, London, Moscow and Warsaw in order to discuss their ideas and recommendations with a most interested and hopefully proselytising audience. May their ideas find an even greater audience through this book.

We thank the representatives of the Federal Ministry of Economics and Technology in Berlin and of the Bank for Reconstruction (Kreditanstalt für Wiederaufbau) in Frankfurt and Kyiv, who within the framework of the TRANSFORM Programme of the Federal Government follow our work with great interest, and who finance it out of moneys derived from the German taxpayer. By attempting to perform useful work with these funds, we want to express our sincere thanks to all German taxpayers, too.

We thank our collegues of the Advisory Group who should really all be mentioned as co-editors. We could not have done without anyone of them, they all formed part of the backbone of the conference and of this book. Yet, Mr. Christian von Hirschhausen's editing efforts merit special mention.

We thank Mr. Harald von Cramon-Taubadel who has paid close attention to the English version, so as to clearly reflect the messages of the various authors, and to Mrs. Antonina Guryanova who has prepared the complete Ukrainian version with equal care. With infinite patience, Mr. Kyryl Savin has collated the manuscripts in both languages out of a huge pile of paper. Of course, only the editors are responsible for any possible shortcomings or faults.

We would be glad if this book could be a small sign post on Ukraine's path toward Europe. Perhaps it will help those who want to help create this path – and those who will walk on it.

Lutz Hoffmann Felicitas Möllers

Berlin/Frankfurt/Kyiv, October 2000

PART I

BRIDGE OR INTEGRAL PART? UKRAINE'S HISTORICAL, CULTURAL AND GEOPOLITICAL CONNECTION WITH EUROPE AND ITS NEIGHBOURS

1

Ukraine between East and West, North and South: Geopolitical Options and Constraints

Bohdan Hawrylyshyn

1 Introduction

East and West options exist. North and South cannot be the primary geopolitical orientations. They can be a useful complement to the European choice of Ukraine. Choosing the right option and transforming it into reality is a vital question for Ukraine. It is a choice for the future nature of the societal architecture/order, a choice of values (Weltanschauung), of political institutions, of an economic system, of the structure of social relationships, of the role of the individual in society, of the nature and the control of power, of economic efficacy and social justice. In fact the choice may determine the very existence of Ukraine as a distinctive, sovereign, and free society. It is a question of *to be or not to be.*

2 The Eastern options: CIS and E.S.U.

1. The Commonwealth of Independent States (CIS) is not the type of entity, which is capable of acting as a genuinely integrative institution that could lead to the creation of a type of European Union, a Eurasian union comprising Eastern European, Eurasian and Central Asian states, in all 12 republics of the former Soviet Union. All but one of these countries has been conquered by force, subdued to tsarist imperial rule and later to Soviet rule, integrated politically and economically to make them indissociable. Yet, they did dissociate. CIS was seen by Ukraine as a friendly divorce procedure and not as a way to resuscitate the Soviet Union, which was dying peacefully. Ukraine is even now just an associate member of CIS. CIS can, at best, become an uncommon common market.

2. A Slavic Union: Is it an option? What are the driving forces, advantages, and constraints?

The only realistic Eastern option can thus be a Slavic Union. More correctly such an entity would have to be called *E.S.U,* i.e. *Eastern Slavic Union.* The historical Slavic Union based on Panslavism, a 19th century ideal for some Slavs, is now dead. Even Bulgarians, but certainly Czechs and Slovaks, having lived under the benevolent supervision of the 'big brother' have lost their illusions. Poles had never had them, and neither did Croats or Slovenians. Some Serbs are ambivalent about it, but they were disappointed when Russia let them down during the NATO intervention. Also, given its geographical location and its political ambitions, including the desire to hang on to Montenegro, Serbia is hardly a real candidate for a potential Eastern Slavic Union.

What then are the *driving forces behind the creation of E.S.U.?* The main ones are: President Lukashenko, big power nostalgia in Russia, some veterans, pensioners and russophiles in Ukraine. The logic for creation of E.S.U. is based on geographic proximity, cultural and linguistic similarities, fairly intertwined economies, and, of course, a common history.

2.1 Perceived advantages of E.S.U.

For Belarus: The most advantage obvious seem to be access to cheap energy and other natural resources, to a big market for its less than world quality goods and the feeling of being part of a big power.

For Russia, it would mean the return to big power status a counterweight to Western alliances, reconstitution of Mother Russia, regaining of its collective self-esteem, protection of and even assuring a privileged status for Russian minorities in all member states of E.S.U., and control over a big market with near monopoly/monopsony positions vis-à-vis Belarus and Ukraine.

For the Ukrainian side, the prospects of cheap, domestically priced energy and free access to a big market also seem tantalising. For parts of the russophone and russophile populations (there is no close overlap of these two sectors of Ukraine's population) return to the preferred status sounds attractive. Even to some russified Ukrainians the comfort of servility may be appealing.

There are however clear disadvantages to such a Union, some of which translate into constraints. These constraints are based on the credible assumption that E.S.U. would be dominated by Russia, be somewhat authoritarian, be likely an anti-Western – or at least not pro-Western – political entity, and be without a true market economy that is properly guided by laws.

For Belarus it would result in insufficient exposure to the outside world culturally, economically, intellectually and politically. The country would thus likely remain economically backward, politically under-developed with a weak civil society, and would suffer further loss of its national identity.

For Russia creation of E.S.U. would also be a step backward. Its authoritarian temptation would likely grow stronger. The joys of big power status would be diminished, not just by the military cost of it, but by the amount of leadership energy that would have to be wasted on governing of a semi-empire, instead of focusing on modernising and building of a contemporary nation state. Russia, as it is, faces some serious predicaments. The first one is the crisis of identity. Is the Russian Federation a nation state, is it still an empire, what is the common denominator, what is the root foundation of the state, what is the glue that holds the Federation together?

Another dilemma is that Russia is still a nuclear giant but an economic dwarf. Reconciling these two realities is not easy. Also, the Russian Federation is a Eurasian country, neither fully belonging to, nor excessively loved by either Europe or Asia. Finally, the Russian Federation is not only populated by orthodox Slavs. Other ethnic and religious groups might feel rather uncomfortable, rather restless in a Slavic Union.

Some of the Russian elite accepts the notion that it does not pay to be an empire in the contemporary era, that it is better to dominate other countries economically, rather than politically or territorially. Also, and this is a very important notion, *the cost of governance increases exponentially with geographical spread and cultural diversity*, which more than off-sets the economic advantage of scale. This is one of the reasons why many small and homogenous Nordic European countries, or Slovenia, have been economically successful. When I predicted the disintegration of the Soviet Union in a book published in 1980 entitled "Road Maps to the Future – toward more effective societies", which appeared later in seven other languages, the high 'overhead' cost of managing a geographically spread, culturally diverse country, was one of the factors on which my prediction was based. The present Russian Federation is still highly spread geographically, and culturally and ethnically rather diverse. Does Russia really need to add the management of a Slavic Union to the difficulty of managing the Federation?

What are the constraints *for Ukraine* arising from the creation of E.S.U.?

First, there is no strong pro-union constituency in Ukraine. A party with a clear pro-union stance failed dismally in past elections. Although some leftist leaders talk about re-unification, they do not appear too anxious to consummate a union. They would loose their present autonomy under a numerically and intellectually stronger Russian communist party. A significant part of the population, virtually everybody in Western Ukraine, many in Central Ukraine and some in the Southeast too, would oppose a reunification with Russia, even at the cost of civil war.

The main constraints for Ukraine are rooted in the common history with Russia, because it was an imposed rather than a chosen common history (Khmelnytskiy's treaty of 1654 not withstanding). The heritage from tsars and commissars has been debilitating to Ukraine and particularly to Ukrainians within Ukraine, though some minorities like the Tartars have suffered even more.

Nearly three centuries as a colony of Tsarist Russia – with political, cultural and linguistic oppression – significantly diminished Ukraine's cultural, intellectual and political potential. Seventy years of Soviet regime resulted in the destruction of the peasant class and decimated the cultural and political elites either by extermination or through a brain drain to Russia. Upon the break up of the Soviet Union, Ukraine was left:

- without any foreign currency, gold or precious metals reserves, or any part of the common Soviet assets abroad (e.g. many valuable buildings including banks), or part of the debt owed to the USSR, although there was an agreement that Ukraine should receive about 17% as its share of the common assets;
- with an economic system that had already disintegrated, and a declining GDP;
- with an economic structure that was integrated with the other republics, but mainly with Russia, based on political rather than on economic or technical criteria, and designed to maintain total interdependence controlled by Moscow;
- with over a third of the industry dedicated to the military sector. The rest of the industry was capital, energy and material intensive, included very little light consumer industry, and was technologically outdated;
- without a real banking system;
- without contemporary management know-how, or knowledge of markets;
- politically, economically, and culturally isolated from the outside world;
- with a colonial type of administration rather than a real government. 85% of Ukraine's economy had been managed directly from Moscow, the Government of the Ukrainian SSR being a branch office of that in Moscow, passing orders down and information up, often with distortions in both directions;
- with russification. All university and 70% of the secondary level education was carried out in Russian even though 75% of population was Ukrainian;
- with an exceptionally high proportion of the population on pension, including some from Russia;
- with the Chernobyl disaster with its traumatic psychological, social and financial consequences.

To conclude the review of the Eastern option, one can state that close economic relations with Russia are unavoidable and even desirable, given the economic interdependence and in particular Ukraine's dependence on Russian energy. A political union, however, would likely have catastrophic consequences. Ukraine would be condemned to economic backwardness, political subordination, and social strife. It would be deprived of an opportunity to develop into a truly free, democratic society, with an efficient economy, a strong collective self-respect, a sense of common identity, and being part of the progressive world society.

3 The Western option: Integration into the EU

The advantages and the attractiveness of this option for Ukraine are overwhelming, perhaps obvious, but worth reiterating:

Security:	Even without becoming a member of NATO Ukraine would be safe from aggression and territorial claims. Its accession to NATO would, however, be more than likely.
Governance system:	Full institutionalisation and maintenance of a pluralistic society and of individual freedom, a government of the people, for the people, and by the people, rooted in sound legislative and judicial foundations.
Economic efficacy:	Both the system and the structure would be internationally competitive, supplying and distributing quality goods and services on the domestic market with an increasing prosperity of the whole population.
Technological innovations:	Highly improved conversion of scientific knowledge into useful technologies, through the 'market pull' on the traditionally large inventory of theoretical knowledge in Ukraine for commercially useful innovations.
Social:	Access to the best educational expertise in Western Europe, adequate health care, old age security, and hopefully, a social partnership between government, business, and employees.
Cultural:	Free interchange with the Western humanist cultures, borrowing from them and contributing to them. Sharpening what is uniquely Ukrainian, yet becoming part of the global society.
A third way:	The currently dominant thought driving globalisation is: "What is good for shareholders is good for the world." There is ample proof that the single-minded pursuit of shareholder value increases the gap between rich and poor, between countries and within countries.

> Western Europe with its experience in social democracy provides a good model for reconciliation between economic efficacy and social justice. The mobilising motto could become: "People are the purpose, profits are the means." This could eliminate any nostalgia in Ukraine for an 'egalitarian' society of the Soviet kind.

Many of the benefits listed above can be achieved via the process of accession to the EU, through better technical assistance, harmonisation of standards, laws, administrative procedures, and increased trade.

Constraints on the European option: They are significant, particularly on the Ukrainian side, but not insurmountable. Among the main ones are:

- the current state of the political institutions: the legislative, the executive and particularly the judicial;
- bureaucratic barriers, and corruption;
- the economic system and structure, i.e. ownership of the means of production, nature of the markets, sectoral distribution, and poor management (in particular of state owned enterprises);
- above all, with the low level of GDP and income per capita, Ukraine would be a potential burden on the EU, particularly regarding future claims of Ukraine on the structural fund of the EU;
- a constraint of a different kind but an important one is the insufficient surface of contacts with Western Europe. These are adequate at diplomatic level, but not in the intellectual, cultural and business domains. *There is, therefore, no real pro-Ukrainian lobby in the EU.* The USA, for strategic security considerations, is advocating a Euro-Atlantic option for Ukraine, but would not likely have to deal with its costs. *Poland* is genuinely supportive but not yet a member state itself. The political leaderships of EU member states, and some of the think tanks, are well aware of the geopolitical importance of Ukraine's integration into the EU, but this awareness does not translate into any vigorous action to facilitate such integration. *Germany's* position on this issue, given its economic weight and the convergence of its national interest with Ukraine's western aspirations, will be of real importance;
- *Russia* officially cannot, and officially does not oppose the accession of Ukraine to the EU, though itself it is not a candidate. Russians, however, 'love' Ukraine too much to feel happy about Ukraine being a willing bride of the European Union. It is likely to exert some pressures on the EU and in particular on Ukraine not to be too expeditious with the integration agenda, even though Ukraine's membership in the EU would probably allow Russia to draw more benefits from its own partnership relations with the EU. Nevertheless, the EU's policy towards Ukraine has not been sufficiently

dissociated from its relations with Russia, which is one of the constraints on the European option of Ukraine.

3.1 How should Ukraine pursue this only real option?

Some rapprochement or drawing closer has already occurred as manifested by the conclusion, ratification and the first steps in the implementation of the *Partnership and Co-operation Agreement (PCA)*. The *Common Strategy of the EU* of December 1999 was a further step in the right direction.

Effective membership in the *Partnership for Peace Program (PPP)* and the *Special Charter with NATO* have also contributed to the rapprochement.

3.2 What needs to be done to transform Ukraine's European option into reality?

Ukraine must shed any ambivalence, if only implied, about its European choice. Statements that Ukraine's foreign policy is multi-vectoral or that it is neither pro-Western, nor pro-Eastern, but pro-Ukrainian may help maintain reasonably friendly relations with its Eastern neighbour, but can also confuse the Ukrainian people and raise questions in the West about Ukraine's determination to pursue its chosen Western path. The policies, pronouncements and actions of Ukraine's Government must be subordinated to its strategic, geopolitical Western choice.

To fulfil some of the key preconditions for entry into the EU, Ukraine must complete its administrative reforms and the transformation of its agriculture into a more productive and competitive one, carry out privatisation in important sectors such as energy, and achieve a higher degree of price liberalisation. Ukraine must also repair relations with the IMF, attract more direct foreign investment, in particular from Western Europe and encourage flight capital to return. This can only be achieved:

- by stabilising legislation and making it predictable;
- by the reduction of barriers to imports and of corruption;
- by the reduction of the number of taxes and tax rates;
- by the removal of special privileges for many entities;
- and by bringing more of the shadow economy into the official one.

The *EU can do much* to help Ukraine's leadership mobilise the society's energy to complete the transformation process and thus approach its long-term accession objective. The EU should:

- be less 'iffy' about future accession to membership of Ukraine;

- expand technical assistance to facilitate the harmonisation of laws and procedures;
- from its end, energetically pursue the implementation of the Partnership and Co-operation Agreement;
- grant Ukraine 'market economy' status as soon as possible, to help it with its foreign trade;
- help Ukraine to achieve associate status with the EU;
- support Ukraine's accession to the World Trade Organisation;
- open up the possibility of a free trade zone agreement.

4 Are there other options open for Ukraine?

The *Baltic-Black Sea Union* is a nice dream but it is not a reality. Improvements to the north-south transportation system are clearly desirable, but are an insufficient basis for a union.

GUUAM – has some geopolitical connotation because it represents the joint flexing of muscles by five independent countries (Georgia, Ukraine, Uzbekistan, Azerbaijan, and Moldova), without seeking the benediction of Russia. This consultative forum of five states has some fairly concrete objectives:

- the creation of a Eurasian transport corridor particularly for oil and gas;
- the peaceful settlement of conflicts and combating secession;
- military technical co-operation;
- the co-ordination of actions in international organisations;
- economic co-operation;
- the creation of a Black Sea Trade and Development Bank (headquartered in Greece).

Neither of the above arrangements are alternatives to the Western integration option. Their objectives are not constraints on Ukraine's European choice. On the contrary, their effective functioning would strengthen Ukraine's position in dealing with the EU.

5 Conclusions

Many *historical bridges* have existed between Ukraine and Western Europe. In the 11th century, four of Prince Yaroslav's children were married to Western royal courts. Anna of Kyiv became the Queen of France not just because of her beauty, but because she was the most literate at the court. Yaroslav set a sort of precedent for Western Europe by ordering a codification of laws. Western Ukraine was never fully detached from Western Europe. Even during the New Economic Policy (NEP) period in the twenties a Ukrainian literary figure from the Eastern part of Ukraine was preaching "our face to Europe and our back to Russia". This pro-Western declaration was squashed along with its author.

In reality, though, the bridges between Ukraine and Western Europe are old. They have to be rebuilt. This building should be done from both sides, the Ukrainian and the Western European. For Ukraine the objective of joining the EU is really a question of to be or not to be.

Ukraine will be a burden to the EU, but it will ultimately also be of benefit:

- It has a highly educated population, much of it with the type of education that can fit into the knowledge civilisation;
- It has a network of scientific institutions that can be revitalised;
- It has the most fertile soil in the world;
- It has established friendship treaties with all its neighbours;
- It has no imperialistic or aggressive past;
- It has achieved inter-ethnic peace, which given the historical context, is an exemplary accomplishment;
- Ukraine asserts strongly its multi-ethnic status. This is being taken rather far. The Ukrainian ethnic majority seems prepared to remain a linguistic minority for a long time in order to preserve interethnic intercultural peace.

If Ukraine were to join a Slavic Union the psychological confidence and resolve of reactionary forces in Russia to strive for big power status and create an anti-Western block, could be reborn. By joining the EU, Ukraine would lessen this danger significantly for the benefit of Russia, which could thus more readily transform itself into a normal federal nation state with peaceful relations with EU and others. The benefit of this alone would more than offset any cost of Ukraine's accession to the EU.

Am I, are we dreaming? Yes, but only partly. Do great things not start with a dream? Did the EU not come into being because of Jean Monnet's visionary dreams? At this historical juncture for Ukraine we have to dream big, transform the dreams into mobilising visions, and then work hard, pragmatically, to transform the vision into reality. This is the challenge before us.

2

Eurasia – Alternative to European Integration or the Wrong Path?

Charles Clover

> *"Yes, war did come, despite the trade agreements. But it is a fact that war did not break out between the United States and any country with which we had been able to negotiate a major trade agreement. It is also a fact that, with very few exceptions, the countries with which we signed trade agreements joined together in resisting the Axis. The political line-up followed economic line-up."*
>
> *Cordell Hull, U.S. Secretary of State, 1945*

It used to be that Ukraine's 'European Choice', the desire to integrate with European structures, was an expression of Ukraine's desire to participate in 'globalism': Opening up to unfettered trade, finance, and communication, which would link its destiny to that of the world.

Increasingly, however, this is not an accurate description. European integration is now thought of as an expression of 'regionalism', a trend, which more and more has become a substitute, rather than a compliment, to globalism.

Regionalism and globalism are similar, except for their scale: Both involve a voluntary surrender of some portion of state sovereignty in exchange for participation in multi-lateral organisations. Both involve opening up one's economy to international trade and financial flows.

It was originally theorised that regional integration was but a rung in the ladder of globalisation, an intermediate stage in the ultimate project of bringing all countries closer together. That argument still stands, but is increasingly troubled by a number of trends, such as trade diversion, regional federalism, and anti-hegemonic ideology, which seem to indicate that regionalism is the first and last stage in the project.

Ukraine's chief problem will be how it takes advantage of this increased regionalism.

Regional, as opposed to global, integration offers Ukraine many opportunities. It is conceivable that membership in the EU could be sped up by pressure to expand regionally. But there are a number of risks as well. The spectre of geopolitical competition between regions might mean that Ukraine, which has often been a pawn in super-power politics, would return to this role as some sort of buffer.

The tension between regionalism and globalism can best be demonstrated by the growth of trade blocs. Trade and finance are expanding, as per the globalist prediction, but doing so in a curious pattern: Countries trade more with each other, but only inside trade blocs, while the blocs trade less with each other.

The proponents of trading blocs say that regional deepening of trade relations is just a step, and global broadening of trade links between blocs will follow. But in the meantime, the opposite has happened, and there is little sign that the trend is reversing. The irony is that the growth of free trade in blocs threatens to cement the world in three or four autarkic economic zones, rather than a single global whole.

Parallel to the growth of regional economic integration is the growth in regional political integration, best observed in the movement towards European federalism. The catalyst for this movement, according to its advocates, is the regional expansion of the EU into Eastern Europe.

Perhaps the most interesting aspect of the new regionalism is the subtle but unmistakable criticism of the United States. Increasingly, globalism has become synonymous with the notion of a unipolar world, governed from Washington.

This point has been underlined by Zbigniew Brzezinski, the former National Security Adviser, in his book "The Grand Chessboard":

"Unlike earlier empires, this vast and complex global system is not a hierarchical pyramid. Rather, America stands at the centre of an interlocking universe, one in which power is exercised through continuous bargaining, dialogue, diffusion, and quest for formal consensus, even though that power ultimately comes from a single source, namely, Washington."

Europe's increasing concern with United States hegemony, most recently regarding the issue of anti-ballistic missile shield, is reflected in the public comments of EU officials.

For example, Chris Patten, the EU commissioner, said in June 2000 that "Europe must be a serious counterpart to the United States." The recent initiatives to build up Europe's defence industries appear to stem from a desire to wean off of dependence on the United States technology.

Although the world is still a long way from a 'balance of power' system where the lesser powers coalition against the strongest in military alliances, as was the model in 19th century Europe, there are already elements of this, which have become apparent.

For example, many conservative Russian intellectuals see globalisation as a security threat, and the answer is to create a world order based on regional 'Eurasian' counterbalance.

As late as the 1980s, for example, Moscow looked upon a united Germany, within NATO, as the worst threat imaginable. But in June 2000, Russian President Vladimir Putin, during his visit to Berlin, described such a united Germany as 'Russia's leading partner in Europe and the world.

That is a sign of how times have changed, and how the curious combination of globalisation and regionalisation, which more and more appear to be at odds with each other, change the world around Ukraine.

An expanded Europe will likely be large enough that a 'European choice' by Ukraine probably would not exclude good relations with Russia. And Russia's reaction to the processes of globalisation and regionalisation will strongly condition how Ukraine is affected, as both face much the same obstacles in their relations with Europe as they do with globalisation forces in general.

Their special challenge will be to harness the economic might of wealthier neighbours, but simultaneously avoid being sucked into a permanently subordinating pattern of economic relations, as simple suppliers of raw materials, and cheap labour.

The combination of trade blocs, moves toward regional federalism, and opposition to global hegemony by the United States have combined to create a world, which seems likely be dominated by three or four centres of power in the coming decades. And it is a world, which leaves Ukraine little choice but the European one.

3

Russia – Ukraine: Entering a New Phase[1]

Arkady Moshes

1 Introduction

At the beginning of this new decade, Russian-Ukrainian relations, rather troublesome since the very moment of the dissolution of the Soviet Union, seem to be entering a new phase and acquiring a new dynamic. In the 1990s bilateral collisions and disputes were largely rooted in the poor understanding by Russia of the substance of Ukrainian independence. Russians did not understand that for Ukrainians independence made no sense as an abstract term, but only in the sense of independence *from Russia*. Thus, Russia was genuinely surprised to see that its 'brotherly' or paternalistic behaviour, which combined a certain neglect of Ukraine's foreign policy self-perception with the will to assist 'the younger brother' economically, was not much appreciated in Ukraine. To Ukrainians, in turn, these attitudes gave birth to a desire, on the one hand, to compete with Russia wherever possible in to order to overcome a certain inferiority complex of being 'always the second', and on the other hand, to a mentality and a practice of parasitising on Russian subsidies.

At the moment, however, crucial changes take place on the Russian side and they will inevitably affect Ukrainian approaches and policies. Firstly, Russian public opinion is evolving towards a more negative attitude vis-à-vis the Ukrainian state. In sharp contrast to slogans about Slavic unity, Russia seems more inclined to support a policy of 'no more free lunches for Ukraine'. Secondly, energy exporters, unable to find a mechanism to secure payment from Ukraine for its imports, have started actively to design and build new transmission routes bypassing Ukraine. Thirdly, the new Russian administration is taking a much more pragmatic, economically driven stand concerning Ukraine, as opposed to the

---

1 This paper is a shortened, revised and updated version of an Article, prepared for the Militärwissenschaftliches Bureau of the Austrian Ministry of Defence in the spring of 2000.

rhetorical and inconsistent approaches of the previous government. If the new Russian cabinet pursues a liberal policy, aimed at a gradual decrease of subsidies inside Russia, it will be only logical for it also to dismantle the present 'donor-recipient' model of economic relations with Ukraine.

Thus, the central controversy of the new phase in Russian-Ukrainian relations will be an economic one. Other problems may have either decreasing residual impact (legal status of the Black Sea Fleet in Crimea, remaining controversies vis-à-vis further enlargement of NATO, delimitation of the inter-state border) or, on the contrary, be high-profile (humanitarian) issues – altogether forming a strong conflict potential – but the economy will be the determining factor.

This Chapter will present a brief look at the realities of Russian-Ukrainian economic relations and give a description of the above-stated trends concerning public opinion and official attitudes towards Ukraine.

2 The economic dimension

At the moment the bilateral economic relations are in a crisis. In 1999, *Russian-Ukrainian trade* fell by 17% as compared with 1998, reaching only 7.3 billion USD, which is only 300 million USD more than the trade with Belarus, the population of which is five times smaller than that of Ukraine.[2] In the period from 1996 through 1999 Russian-Ukrainian trade decreased by nearly 50%. The small increase early in 2000 cannot be considered a long-term trend as long as the basic causes that have led to the decrease have not been removed.

The explanation most often given is mutual protectionism (in Ukraine it is widely propagated as Russian protectionism). No doubt, both countries employ protectionist policies. This is unavoidable, taking into account that there are identical enterprises, unemployment in similar industries, etc. on both sides of the border. According to the Russian Ministry of Trade, Russia sent Ukraine a list of 89 complaints against trade impediments, introduced by Ukraine against Russian goods; Ukraine presented an analogous list of 8 (!).[3]

However, while this example could be used as an illustration in the discussion on which country is more protectionist, this debate is on the whole misleading. The more important reason for the falling trade is low labour productivity that makes a lot of goods non-competitive on either market. This problem cannot be solved even by means of preferential treatment. In 1998, for instance, Ukraine was entitled to sell 600 thousand metric tons of sugar tax-free on the Russian market,

2 Customs statistics. See BIKI (Bulletin of Foreign Commercial Information) (2000), No. 23, February 29, p. 3.

3 Nezavisimaya Gazeta (1999), October 26.

but it managed to sell only 15 thousand[4]; sugar being cheaper to buy on the world market.

Political implications as causes for the trade decrease with Russia are relatively insignificant. After all, Ukraine's share of Russian trade is only 7%. What is more destabilising in the economic field, is the 'donor-recipient' model that emerged between Russia and Ukraine and enabled the latter to secure the survival of an ineffective national economic mechanism. Russia is Ukraine's biggest creditor within the Paris club[5] (creditor states). Ukraine owes Russian economic actors 3.3 billion USD.[6] Most of these debts are for *energy*. The leading Russian gas trader, Gazprom, for example, claims that by February 2000 Ukraine's debt to this company only reached 1.9 billion USD[7], and is constantly growing. In 1998 Ukraine ordered fuel for nuclear power stations worth 250 million USD, but paid only 50 million (The ensuing delivery reductions were one of the major reasons for Ukraine's energy crisis in the winter of 1999-2000).[8] In early 1999 the electricity debt amounted to 135 million USD[9], which later resulted in a disconnection of the Ukrainian energy grid from the Russian one, and a complete stoppage of energy sales to Ukraine.

A consistent policy of consecutive Ukrainian Governments, including the cabinet of Viktor Yushchenko, was the main factor that politicised the issue in Russia and antagonised Russian exporters. This policy traditionally includes three components:

First, large parts of the debt are not recognised, which is made possible by a lack of transparency in Ukraine's gas market. A great deal of the confusion concerning the overall amounts of the debt comes out of Kyiv. Thus, Ukraine's Vice-Prime Minister for fuel and energy, Yulia Timoshenko, acknowledged a gas debt of 2.8 billion USD in January 2000, Viktor Yushchenko himself spoke of 1.4 billion USD in February, while the then head of the state company Naftogaz Ukrainy, Ihor Bakai, admitted a responsibility for only 911 million USD.[10] Then there is a general trend not to recognise the indebtedness of non-state importers, notwithstanding the fact that the Ukrainian gas market is for all practical purposes

---

4 See an interview with the director of the company Ukrinterzukor Evgheniy Imas in Nezavisimaya Gazeta (1999), January 30.

5 3.07 billion USD as compared to 2.58 billion of debt to the IMF, 2.02 billion to the World Bank, 330 million to the EU, 318 million to the US, and 317 million to Germany. Nezavisimaya Gazeta, July 15, 2000. However, the Russian debt is to be almost completely written off as a part of the Black Sea Fleet leasing agreement.

6 Data provided by the Ministry for CIS Affairs. Novie Izvestya (2000), March 15.

7 Vremya MN (2000), February 25.

8 Nezavisimaya Gazeta (2000), February 15.

9 Segodnya (1999), January 27.

10 Vremya MN (2000), January 24, February 25.

state-controlled, and that many deliveries to 'private' importers were made under state guarantees.

Second, Kyiv does not agree to pay back the debt with state-owned assets on Ukrainian territory, thus rejecting the only scheme, which would be acceptable for Russian exporters. This position was re-affirmed by the same Timoshenko and by Vice-Prime Minister Yuriy Yekhanurov.[11] Instead, Ukraine proposed different schemes of payment in kind, which having several weaknesses make them altogether unrealistic. Concerning payment with food products (not to mention, that this is an exchange of a first-class commodity (gas) for goods, which cannot be marketed elsewhere) Kyiv usually proposes prices that are much higher than those on the Russian retail market. Accepting the offer would be nothing else than another indirect subsidy. Concerning other proposed forms of payments in kind (strategic bombers, for example, or sums, that Ukraine spent to repair the Black Sea Fleet ships), it needs to be noted that the debt is not due to *Russia*, but to *Gazprom* and to other exporters. Other variants discourage exporters and even turn out to be detrimental to Russia's economy in general by only enriching some middlemen. In the end, all the compromises agreed to so far have never been fully implemented by Ukraine, with disastrous consequences for its credibility in Russia.

Third, large amounts of gas are simply stolen, being siphoned from the pipelines passing through Ukraine's territory. Gazprom's head, Vyakhirev, said that during the winter 1999/2000 Ukraine siphoned off 100 to 120 million cubic meters of gas every day, which by April totalled 7.1 billion cubic meters.[12] In June President Leonid Kuchma admitted to the unauthorised taking of 13 billion cubic meters.[13] To legalise the theft ('unauthorised usage', in bureaucratic language) Gazprom had to sign export contracts after the fact, otherwise the Russian export legislation would have forced the company to pay a fine of 200% of the price of the 'illegal exports'.

The Ukrainian policy was obviously based on the assumption that Russia was critically dependent on Ukrainian transit (currently 90% of the Russian gas export to Europe passes through Ukraine) and that for this reason Russia would not be able to cut off the gas deliveries. Indeed, by cutting off the supply, Russia would not only face certain technological risks (i.e. the falling pressure in the pipes could cause the collapse of the whole system), but also problems with its customers in Europe.

Until recently, Russia did not have a way out of this impasse. Now however, it is quite evident that Russia has found a way out. It is highly likely that Russia will do its best to diversify, to reorient its gas and oil exports, and to build alternative

---

11 Nezavisimaya Gazeta (2000), February 26 and Vremya MN (2000), March 3.

12 Vremya MN (2000), February 9 and Segodnya (2000), April 15.

13 Nezavisimaya Gazeta (2000), June 15.

export capacities bypassing Ukraine. Gazprom has already revealed its plans to reduce its exports through Ukraine by two thirds within six to eight years, down from the current 110 to 120 billion cubic meters.[14] For this purpose it will use the newly built pipeline through Belarus and Poland (in operation since September 1999), to which another pipeline could be added, if necessary, as well as the line on the Black Sea bed to Turkey ('Blue Stream' project to be completed in 2001). In case the construction of another line through Poland into Slovakia turns out to be impossible due to opposition in Warsaw, another alternate route via the Baltic Sea could be built. Oil exporters (Transneft Company) also seriously consider the possibility of building a new pipeline to Novorossiysk.

Contrary to allegations that purely 'neo-imperialist' attitudes drive Russian policy, in these particular matters the rationale is largely economic. The present system allowing Ukraine not to honour its contract obligations (since there is no punishment) must be stopped (a) because the exporters suffer losses, and (b) for the sake of Russia's macro-economic interests: Russia is no longer in a position to subsidise Ukraine. Furthermore, two specific arguments must be mentioned in addition to this general point. First, Ukraine's tariffs are relatively high in the post-Soviet era. For example, Ukraine nominally charges 1.09 USD for the transit of 1,000 cubic meters of gas per 100 km, while Belarus charges 55 cents for the same service.[15] Also, Ukraine's tariff for one ton of oil is 2.35 USD, while for the above-mentioned projected Russian system 0.5 USD are estimated after the first four years of exploitation, needed to pay-back investments.[16] Second, Ukraine has for many years under-invested into the maintenance of its transit facilities. Therefore, it can be expected that they will become expensive to operate and unreliable. This fact too, makes it imperative for Russia to consider alternative export routes.

Losing the income from Russian energy transit, and the consequent decrease of a free energy flow, would mean a heavy economic blow for Ukraine. For a decade now, Ukraine has tried to diversify its energy sources, but failed due to the same inability or unwillingness to pay the bills (to Turkmenistan in particular). Because of constant scandals with Russia, the image of Ukraine as a transit state is not very attractive. It failed to build the infrastructure necessary to accommodate potential exporters in the Caucasus and consumers in Europe. But even if Ukraine had succeeded, the main export route for Azeri oil would be through Turkey, not Ukraine. Under these circumstances, measures likely to be undertaken by Russian economic actors in the sphere of energy transit constitute a real challenge to Ukraine's sovereignty.

---

14 Nezavisimaya Gazeta (2000), February 26.

15 Vremya MN (1999), September 22 and 24.

16 Vremya MN (1999), October 7.

3 Perceptions and attitudes

After years of disputes over various issues, it does not come as a surprise that the attitudes in Russia towards the present Ukrainian State are becoming more negative. As far as public opinion is concerned, according to a poll, conducted in October 1999 by the 'Obshchestvennoe Mnenie' (Public Opinion) Foundation, 41% of respondents agreed with the statement that Ukraine pursued an unfriendly policy towards Russia (23% disagreed). One should not confuse these attitudes with the perception of Ukraine and of Ukrainians, which is still positive, nor should one draw any conclusions about the desire of Russians to separate from Ukraine. Only 8% of respondents would like to see Russian-Ukrainian relations based on fully protected borders, a visa regime and customs, while 31% think they should be those between independent but friendly states without borders, and 51% would support reunification. However, an economic pragmatism, based on the understanding that Russia cannot afford to subsidise Ukraine, can easily be sensed.

The attitudes of experts regarding bilateral relations show a great degree of scepticism. According to an expert poll, conducted jointly by the Ukrainian Centre for Economic and Political Studies and the Russian Public Political Centre in early 2000[17], Russian experts gave the relationship the following characteristics. 88% assessed the present state of bilateral relations negatively (30% as 'unstable', 29% as a 'declaratory partnership', 26% as 'stagnant', 3% as 'deteriorated'), only 2% assessed it positively ('progress'). The negative-positive rating of Ukraine's relations with the CIS was 91 and 9% respectively. In the hierarchy of factors most negatively affecting the relations, Russian experts mentioned the growing co-operation between Ukraine and NATO (84%), problems with the Black sea Fleet and Sevastopol (84%), control problems at the inter-state border (79%), the situation of the Russian-speaking population in Ukraine (77%), the gas debt (71%), the weakening of Ukraine's participation within the CIS (57%), an inconsistent foreign policy course of the Ukrainian leadership (55%), the negative official attitude of Ukraine towards the Union of Russia and Belarus (50%), the quality of Ukrainian goods exported to Russia (23%), the high cost of recreation in Ukraine (23%), Ukraine's participation in GUUAM (18%), and the inflow of Ukrainian guest workers into Russia (14%).

The attitudes of the Russian economic leadership have already been briefly touched upon. Seen in a positive light, they attempt to diminish Russian dependence on Ukrainian transit, and to dismantle the 'donor-recipient' relationship in general. Among the Russian political forces only the position of the Communists is of importance for Ukraine, although in post-electoral Russia it is also declining. All others – except for Moscow Mayor Luzhkov (though this does

[17] Published in Zerkalo Nedeli (2000), March 11-17.

not include his 'Fatherland' movement), who is known for speaking in favour of the Russian status of Sevastopol – do not have a platform on Ukraine at all. In the past, the Communists have been rather opportunistic. They took positions they thought would either prove them to be better 'integrationists' than Yeltsin or help their leftist allies in Ukraine (e.g., their sudden support for ratification of the political treaty in the Duma in December 1998 following the visit by the then Rada Speaker to the leftist leader Oleksandr Tkachenko). With Ukraine, and the CIS in general, ceasing to be an electoral issue in Russia, the Communists are likely to be passive and silent on this issue. However, Leonid Kuchma's attempts to crack down on leftist forces in Ukraine may rouse their Russian comrades again to become critical towards official Kyiv. Finally, since the Communists see themselves as the only true representatives of 'Russian patriotism', they have to raise their voice against any real or perceived attempts to decrease the status of the Russian language.

The views and attitudes of the new Russian administration are most difficult to describe and to forecast. On the one hand, President Putin does no longer want to pay economic subsidies to a country, which is not inclined to compromise with Russia on many important political issues. On the other hand, Putin also has to take into account that being too tough towards Ukraine may push it even more towards the West, which may have negative implications for Russia's own relationships with the latter.

Nevertheless, economic pragmatism in the approaches used by the new Russian administration is increasingly evident. In fact, in early December 1999 the Government of the then Prime Minister Putin took an unprecedented step. It imposed an oil and electricity embargo on Ukraine in order to persuade it to stop stealing gas from the pipelines. The Prime Minister sent a letter to President Kuchma protesting against Ukraine's policy.[18] Although the embargo failed – as mentioned before, Ukraine kept siphoning off gas – and in February 2000 Russia had to resume oil supplies (since for obvious reasons Russia could not discontinue this segment of its oil export), it clearly demonstrated Russia's intention to defend its business and general economic interests. During the debt negotiations with the Ukrainian authorities in January-February, and again in July 2000, Russia consistently pursued an agenda, which seemed to be well co-ordinated with the business interests, whereas previously all negotiations had ended with Ukraine making promises to pay later and with Russia's readiness to accept payment in kind.

From this point forward, the relationship may follow one of two scenarios. The positive one would include a compromise between Moscow and Kyiv, which could include among other elements (1) full payment or even full advance payment for current deliveries, possibly in exchange for lower prices, (2) end of

[18] Quoted in Nezavisimaya Gazeta (1999), December 11.

the gas theft, preferably by means of creating a joint venture with Russian participation, (3) establishing a mechanism of gas trade in Ukraine, which would allow Russian suppliers to deal directly with Ukrainian consumers without any intermediary state agencies, (4) trading the debt load partly for Ukrainian assets and partly for a large-scale restructuring. Of course, the eventual compromise may look different from the above, but it's critically important features must be (a) that it satisfies not only the Russian and Ukrainian states, but also all Russian economic actors and (b) that, once reached, it should be firmly observed; otherwise it will not be viable and will not produce the expected positive results.

The negative scenario, however, is also possible. Slow or no progress on the debt issue, attempts to 'broaden' the economic agenda (for instance, by confusing the debate on energy debts to economic actors with unsettled disputes over Soviet foreign assets), mixing economic and political issues (trading debts for a less 'energetic' policy in the sphere of language and education), blaming Russian policies as being 'neo-imperialist' domestically and internationally, etc., would quickly lead the bilateral relations to further and – as far as the economic side is concerned – irreversible deterioration.

Such a scenario is far from ideal for Russia, whose economy would be badly hurt, but for Ukraine it would be a genuine catastrophe, making it the new 'sick person of Europe', depriving it of any chance for economic revival in the foreseeable future, and postponing ad infinitum the prospects of Ukraine's integration into Europe.

4

The Significance of Poland for Ukraine: Role Model, Bordering State, Integrator?

Mirosław Gronicki

1 Introduction

During the past ten years, Poland has been one of the fastest growing transition economies. The Polish transition from a rigid centrally planned economy (CPE) to a market economy (ME) is considered a success by most observers. Economists and politicians have often used this success as proof that it is possible to make the transition smooth and without excessive welfare costs. The question is can the Polish transition to the market be imitated? Are there common factors, which Ukraine could use? There are no simple answers. Each transition economy has its own particular starting conditions and capabilities. There are many factors which influence a successful transition, and Poland was lucky to have the right ones.

The duration of the initial stage of transition depends on how flexible and how sophisticated the political and economic systems are. It was much easier in the Czech Republic and Hungary and a lot tougher in Poland. Yet, a fast and thorough initial transformation of institutions helps greatly in ensuing transition stages.

The Ukrainian transition was painful from the very beginning. First, the dissolution of the Soviet Empire and of COMECON was a serious blow to the Ukrainian economy. The demand for Ukrainian products within the CIS and central European countries declined rapidly but the management of the economy remained very much as during CPE times. Secondly, the Government was weak and disorganised. It had little experience with preparing budgets and collecting revenues, thus ending up with hyperinflation. Thirdly, the Government always thought about a 'third way' which led to the development of a shadow economy.

In all economies in transition, the initial weakness of the economic system lies in its weak regulations, mixed and often conflicting incentives, and the absence of a property law. Transition countries, which introduced reforms to overcome these weaknesses, like Hungary and Poland, are now the leaders in economic reforms.

In Ukraine, the regulatory and institutional reforms have been very slow. As a result, the micro-economic base for economic development is weak and fragile.

The vagueness of property rights, the huge state sector in industry, and the weak private sector in distribution and services (and, at the same time, the huge shadow economy) have all led to a relative separation of the institutional sectors in the economy. In the state sector, barter transactions prevail, in the private distribution and service sectors, cash transactions prevail, and in the shadow economy, hard currency (US-dollar) based transactions are the norm. Moreover, the initial hardships imposed on the citizens by the hyperinflation of 1993-94, resulted in the development of a natural economy (in agriculture and services). The most significant micro-economic impediments for consistent economic development are the lack of a proper pricing system, the absence of hard-budget constraints for state owned enterprises, and weak budget and tax laws.

The prices of energy, of basic foodstuffs and of services are controlled by the state, and reflect neither their costs nor their values to the consumer. This is a major cause for the deepening disequilibria on Ukrainian markets. It is also a major source of the implicit and explicit subsidies in the economic system which, if prolonged, may lead to a significant upward correction of prices.

In this Chapter several of the features of the Polish transition are discussed, some of which will hopefully be applicable to the Ukrainian case.

2 Stages

The Polish transition can be divided into four stages:

- The initial stage: 1988-first half of 1991.
- The take-off: second half of 1991 to first half of 1993.
- Building strong macro-economic fundamentals: second half 1993 to 1997.
- The second wave of reforms: 1998 to today.

2.1 Initial stage

2.1.1 Pre-transition

The Polish transition started before the Balcerowicz Plan of 1990. The dismantling of the old system began early in 1988, when the Government legalised hard-currency transactions and allowed for a parallel exchange rate and for limited private activity, mostly in trade and services. At the same time, the Government of the time could not cope with managing the economy and especially with balancing the state's budget. Growing imbalances and the inability to collect enough revenues caused run-away inflation. In many ways, this period was similar to the Ukrainian situation between 1993 and 1995.

In September 1989, before the new reformist government took over, the parallel US-dollar exchange rate reached a peak of more than 12,000 Zloty and several weeks later it went down to below 6,000 Zloty. At the same time, a high inflation rate changed into hyperinflation (the CPI rose more than 40% per month). The most important task of the Government now was stabilising the economy. It took only three months to devise a new economic programme (with the significant help of J. Sachs and D. Lipton). Later, this programme was called either the Balcerowicz Plan or the "shock therapy". It combined macro-economic stabilisation with elimination of the obviously absurd CPE.

2.1.2 Stabilisation programme

The stabilisation programme was based on four basic principles:

(i) *Introducing a fixed Zloty to US-dollar exchange rate.* This was the most important element of the 'shock therapy'. The exchange rate was fixed at 9,500 Zloty to the dollar, which meant a more than 50% devaluation of the Zloty (taking into account the parallel exchange rate) and became a nominal anchor of the stabilisation programme.

(ii) *Price liberalisation.* Beginning January 1, 1990 most of the previously state controlled prices were liberalised. This led to an increase of the CPI by more than 122% in the first two months of the 'shock therapy'.

(iii) *Opening up the economy.* Polish enterprises, at that time mostly state-owned, had to meet foreign competition.

(iv) *Elimination of direct subsidies to state-owned enterprises.* This was a consequence of price liberalisation. Direct subsidies to foodstuff prices were eliminated and some of the excessive turnover tax rates were cut.

The stabilisation programme pushed the inflation down (to 3-4% per month). For the first time in more than 40 years Polish enterprises faced both foreign competition and demand constraints. Initially, the very high exchange rate limited the demand constraints. This together with a very weak domestic demand pushed exports up. At the same time, the external stimulus was weaker than the shrinking domestic demand. This resulted in a decrease of the GDP. Later, due to a significant real appreciation of the Zloty and the dissolution of the COMECON, exports stagnated and domestic demand became the most significant factor in Poland's economic development.

2.2 Take-off

According to recent estimates, GDP declined until the second quarter of 1991. The economic revival or the actual take-off began in the third quarter of 1991 and since this quarter the economy has been growing without any significant interruptions. Initially growth was fuelled by a fast growing household demand. Later on, when Polish firms started generating profits, it was accompanied by a fast growing investment demand.

The rapidly growing private consumption was mostly caused by one simple decision. Balcerowicz offered all newly established small firms a 3-year tax holiday. Within several months about 2 million new small companies entered the economic system. This was the most important factor responsible for the take-off. Small firms cushioned the effect of lay-offs from the state owned plants, without them unemployment would have been much higher. Also, they became the training grounds for the new Polish businessmen. With fierce competition only the fittest could survive and grow their companies.

Due to this decision, employment in the private non-agricultural sector increased from 1.5 million to almost 4 million during the four years between 1990 and 1994. At the same time though, unemployment increased from zero to 2.9 million. This means that about 5 million people had been laid off from the state sector.

This is different from the insignificant small-enterprise sector in Ukraine (a mere 100,000 firms) mostly operating in the shadow economy. Given the weak micro-economic foundations, any piecemeal reform of the state sector in Ukraine could lead to a significant shift from hidden to open unemployment, without offering any alternative. The Polish case shows that opening of the economy for small and medium size firms even at the costs of lower revenues from direct taxes (taxes paid by these firms) might be crucial for the future success of economic reforms.

2.3 Building strong macro-economic fundamentals

The most successful aspect of the Polish development was the overhauling of the old tax system. A modern income tax and VAT system was introduced. This had a dramatic effect on both official and cross-border exports. In 1995, due to a very high surplus in the current account, official reserves increased from 6 to 15 billion USD. The net cross border trade (measured as net purchases of hard currency by Polish banks) reached 7.6 billion USD then, or about 8% of the Polish GDP.

The introduction of the new tax system helped to increase revenues. They were mostly used for the creation of a social safety net, which appeared to give the highest – relative to average wages – social benefits in the central Europe. The Ukrainian transition was different. From the very beginning weak tax regulations led to lower than expected tax revenues. At the same time, Government permitted a very weak budget discipline. Under this loose fiscal policy (the Government had high budget deficits and permitted pension increases and wage arrears in the budgetary sector), the only possible solution could have been a strict monetary policy. However, it is not possible to run such a policy mix forever, it only furnishes some short-term improvements.

Another most important feature of this period was the dynamic development of the financial and capital markets. Poland successfully coped with the problem of bad debts in the banking sector. The Polish Government implemented a special law on financial restructuring of enterprises and banks, allowing bad debt to be sold. This lowered the amount of bad debt in the banks' assets from over 30 to about 10 percent. At the same time, it helped Polish banks to renew credit actions and to move assets out of government bonds into commercial credit. Since 1994, the Polish Zloty has become a relatively strong currency, with a real appreciation rate of over 4% annually.

During this same period Poland further developed its privatisation programme. The major difference between Poland and many other transition economies was that it relied on several privatisation techniques: direct sales, management buy-outs, workers buy-outs, liquidations, vouchers etc. At the same time, the most valuable assets were sold to strategic investors (e.g. the largest Polish banks). The privatisation programme helped to develop the Warsaw stock exchange and capital markets. Analysts consider Polish banks and enterprises to be some of the most valuable assets in central Europe. However, the Polish Government kept the most valuable enterprises as a buffer for the expected costs of reforms: pension funds, health services, education and administration.

2.4 Second wave of reforms

These latest reforms were implemented at the beginning of 1999, just after the Russian financial crisis. The most remarkable feature of the Polish economy was that it could quickly recover after the initial external shock (in the first quarter of 1999 the GDP increased by only 1.5%) and at the same time accommodate the shocks related to the reforms. Economists disagree whether the reforms should be implemented simultaneously. Moreover, the reforms were not well prepared and proved to be very costly. However, the proceeds from the privatisation of the most valuable Polish assets were very helpful. They cushioned the cost effect and allowed the Government to operate without significant constraints.

2.5 Foreign capital

It took more than five years to change the opinions of foreign investors' about Poland. Until 1995, the capital inflow was small compared to the capital flows to the Czech Republic or to Hungary. The situation changed, when Poland solved most of its external debt problems and showed that the recovery and economic growth were strong. Also, a market of 38 million consumers became very tempting for potential investors. Cumulated inward FDIs reached 4.5 billion USD in 1994 and 3.7 billion in 1995, but in 1999 they attained over 29 billion USD.

Foreign capital was responsible for very high dynamics of fixed asset investments and for modernising Polish industry and services. It also helped to keep the GDP growth rates at the highest level in the region. At the same time, high inward FDI was responsible for a significant worsening of the current account. The current account deficit reached its peak in the first half of 2000 (more than 8% of GDP). It is possible that FDI will help the Polish (like the Hungarian) economy to boost exports and reverse trends in its current account in the near future.

At the present stage of Ukraine's development it will be very difficult to entice foreign investors. In Poland's case a significant inflow of FDI happened only once strong micro- and macro-economic fundamentals had been built.

3 Conclusions

Ukraine's prospects depend on how soon the Government introduces the painful but necessary reforms, especially in the state sector, in budget expenditure and in market institutions.

Other reforms should also be introduced, either simultaneously or after only a short delay. The most important would be to allow freedom of entry and exit for small and medium size enterprises. The tax structure should be switched from taxing incomes to taxing consumption. This would cause at least a partial incorporation of the shadow economy back into the official economy.

It is worth noting that the Ukrainian economy might suffer less than Poland's during the reforms of the initial period. Most of the inefficient enterprises are either closed or operate at a very low activity level. Thus, the welfare costs might be small and GDP growth only slightly effected. The most important costs might be CPI inflation. However, this price adjustment might be only due to elimination of subsidies to utilities and basic foodstuffs. Moreover, lower GDP growth does not necessarily mean proportionally lower satisfaction from consuming goods and services. Simply, goods of better quality and market value would be substituted for unwanted goods (often traded in barter). Price adjustment may cause some pain but this is necessary in order to establish proper relative pricing and to remove implicit and explicit subsidies from the economic system.

If these reforms are introduced in a consistent fashion the Ukrainian economy will take-off. Otherwise, the slow process of shrinking the state-controlled economy will be offset by a growing shadow economy. This will lead to a gradual weakening of the state with all its consequences.

PART II

BRIDGES TO EUROPE AND THE MARKET ECONOMY: ASPECTS OF A LONG ROAD

5

A Second Economic Divide in Europe?

Herbert Brücker

1 Introduction

The division of Europe in market and centrally planned economies after World War II was associated with an increasing divergence of per capita incomes. While per capita incomes of the present EU members and the other market economies in Europe have converged during the post-war period, the income gap between the market and the planned economies has increased continuously after World War II. Neither the forced accumulation of physical and human capital nor moderate market reforms such as the '*New Economic Mechanism*' in Hungary or the '*Perestroika*' under Gorbachev in the former Soviet Union did reverse this trend. The realisation of the fact that a convergence of per capita incomes to Western standards was not possible within the framework of state property and centrally planning, was one, if not the driving force behind the collapse of central planning. At the outset of transition, the population in the Central and Eastern European (CEE) countries as well as most economic experts expected that the convergence of economic systems will yield a convergence of per capita incomes. Ten years after the begin of market reforms, the record of transition and economic reforms in Central and Eastern Europe is mixed: While all transition countries experienced a deep decline in output initially, there is only a small group of countries which realised growth rates well above those of the present EU members after the end of the transitional recession. In an other group of countries the income gap to the EU has remained constant, and in a third group the transitional recession has not yet come to an end.

This mixed record raises the concern that we will face a second economic divide in Europe between a 'convergence club', which includes the present and future EU members, and sample of diverging countries, consisting of the CIS members and some other countries such as Bulgaria and Romania. However, present trends need not hold true for the future and depend heavily on economic policies. Nevertheless, the optimistic hypothesis that per capita incomes of the East will converge to Western levels in the wake of economic reforms has to be proved carefully.

In this Chapter the prospects for the convergence of per capita incomes between the East and the West in Europe are discussed on the background of our theoretical and empirical knowledge about growth and convergence. The argument is organised along the following lines: First, the theoretical arguments for the convergence and divergence of per capita incomes are briefly reviewed. Second, the empirical evidence for convergence among the market economies and divergence between the market and the planned economies in post-war Europe is proved. Third, the different developments among the transition economies after the begin of economic reforms are described and the explanations for the divergence in the post-transition period are discussed. The final Chapter summarises the main arguments and draws conclusions for the convergence process.

2 Convergence: Inferences from growth theory

Economic theory does not provide an unequivocal answer to the fundamental question whether per capita incomes of poor countries tend to converge to those of the rich ones. For a systematisation of the discussion we can distinguish four competing hypotheses (Galor, 1996; Brücker, 2000):

- *absolute convergence*: per capita incomes between poor and rich economies converge irrespective of the initial endowments and all other conditions;
- *conditional convergence*: per capita incomes between poor and rich economies converge irrespective of initial endowments if all other conditions are equal;
- *club convergence* (stratification, polarisation): per capita incomes between poor and rich economies converge if initial endowments are sufficiently similar and if all other conditions are equal;
- *divergence*: per capita incomes between poor and rich economies diverge if initial endowments and/or other conditions are unequal.

It is uncontroversial that there is neither a theoretical nor an empirical foundation for the hypothesis of *absolute convergence*: differences in institutions, technologies, the propensity of economic actors to save, etc. result in differences in the accumulation of physical and human capital, as well as in differences in levels or growth rates of factor productivity. Thus, there is no reason to expect the convergence of output and incomes between economies which differ in their institutions, macroeconomic and social conditions, technologies etc.

The hypothesis of conditional convergence can be derived from elementary neo-classical growth models which are based on one sector which produces with a production function with constant returns to scale, a constant saving rate (Solow, 1956), or endogenous savings and convex inter-temporal preferences (Ramsey, 1928; Cass, 1965; Koopmans, 1965). In those models economies tend to converge to a unique and stable growth equilibrium (*steady state*) irrespective of their initial endowments with physical or human capital. In this equilibrium, the long-run growth path is determined by the exogenous rate of technological progress. As a consequence, economies with poor initial endowments experience higher growth rates than rich economies until per capita incomes have converged, if all institutional and technological conditions and the inter-temporal preferences of the economic actors (i.e. their propensity to save) are equal.

The driving force for convergence in those models is a production function with constant returns to scale. The accumulation of physical and other forms of capital does not increase the long-run rate of economic growth, since the marginal productivity declines in the course of factor accumulation if endowments with other factors such as labour or land and technological progress remain constant. However, it is worth noting that the hypothesis of conditional convergence is not backed by all neo-classical growth models. Neo-classical growth models with constant return to scale production functions may result in multiple steady states with different income levels or the continual divergence of per capita incomes if:

- the economy possesses more than one sector and the production functions do not full-fill certain restrictive assumptions (Uzawa, 1961, 1963);
- the elasticity of substitution between the individual factors of production is low or not constant in models with overlapping generations (Galor, 1992; Galor and Ryder, 1989; Galor, 1996),
- the individuals consider a subsistence level of consumption (Brücker, 2000; Brücker and Schrettl, 1996).

Thus, initial endowments with physical or human capital matter if we relax some of the restrictive assumption of the elementary textbook models. If initial incomes or factor endowments fall below a critical level, either a subsistence level of consumption or the properties of the production function may result in a poverty trap, which prevents the convergence of per capita incomes between poor and rich economies. Even worse, in some cases investment rates may fall short of the depreciation rates until the capital stock is completely eaten-up.

Finally, endogenous growth models based on production functions which exhibit increasing returns to scale may yield persisting or increasing differences in income levels. In simple endogenous growth models with a production function which exhibits increasing returns to scale and constant returns to the accumulation of one factor (e.g. the 'AK'-model) differences in per capita income levels persist over time. However, some endogenous growth models exhibit the property of conditional convergence, for example if the production function relies on the accumulation of more than one factor of production or if the models consists of several sectors with factor accumulation. Thus, endogenous growth theory does not provide unequivocal conclusions regarding the convergence of per capita income. It is worth to note in this context that empirical evidence for the basic proposition of endogenous growth models, i.e. that production functions exhibit increasing returns to scale at least in one sector of the economy, is still missing.

So far we have considered economies in isolation. At least in the neo-classical growth models with constant return to scale production functions factor mobility tends to equalise factor prices across economies. Even if domestic savings fall short of levels necessary to extend or maintain the domestic capital stock factor mobility can therefore cause the convergence of per capita incomes (for a discussion see Mountford, 1998). Thus, it is more likely that open economies tend to converge than isolated ones.

Of course all those models of growth theory are highly abstract theoretical exercises which may or may be not relevant for real economies. However, if some of the ideas behind these models hold true, they have highly important policy implications for transition economies: First, the convergence of economic institutions and other conditions relevant for economic growth need not necessarily imply the convergence of per capita incomes. Persisting differences in income levels or, even worse, continually diverging incomes are at least a theoretical possibility. Second, a subsistence level of consumption may result in an investment rate which is too low to maintain the capital stock such that per capita incomes decline continuously. Since income and consumption levels have fallen sharply in the course of the transition recession, the case of a continuously decline of capital stocks may be real danger for some transition economies. Third, international factor mobility may be a driving force for the equalisation of factor prices and, hence, per capita incomes.

3 The first economic divide: Lessons from post-war growth

In post-war Europe we do not find an unequivocal trend for the convergence of per capita incomes. The distribution of per capita incomes is characterised by a 'twin peak' development, i.e. a convergence of per capita incomes to the upper and the lower ends of the income spectrum, while countries with medium income levels have disappeared. This development resembles largely the divide of economic systems in centrally planned and market economies. While incomes of the present EU members, and, at a lower pace, of the other European market economies have converged, the income gap between the market economies and the planned economies has increased over time. This general picture is confirmed by different measures of convergence.

3.1 How to measure convergence

The methodology to measure the convergence of per capita incomes is not uncontroversial. There exist various empirical approaches to measure the convergence of per capita incomes, which cover different aspects of convergence. The most popular measures are *cross-countries regressions*, which regress the rate of growth against initial income and a set of other explanatory variables, i.e.

$$\ln(y_T/y_0) = b \cdot \ln(y_0) + g'x \tag{5.1}$$

where y_0 and y_T is the per capita GDP at the begin and at the end of the period under investigation and x a vector of explanatory variables. A negative coefficient b on initial income is interpreted as evidence for *conditional convergence* (see e.g. Barro and Sala-i-Martin, 1991, 1992, 1995). Note that equation (5.1) is usually estimated in non-linear form, i.e. instead of the coefficient b the term $1+\exp(-\beta T)$ is estimated. The coefficient β gives the speed at which an initial differential in the log of per capita incomes declines. This type of convergence is often called 'β-convergence'. One example for those regressions follows directly from the elementary neo-classical growth model with constant savings rate (Solow, 1956):

$$\ln(y_T/y_0) = a + b_1 \cdot \ln(y_0) + b_2 \cdot \ln(s) + b_3 \cdot \ln(n + g + \partial) \tag{5.2}$$

where a is a constant, s is the average saving rate, n the rate of population growth, g the rate of technological progress, and δ the depreciation rate. A further variant considers also investment in human capital, which gives

$$\ln(y_T/y_0) = a + b_1 \cdot \ln(y_0) + b_2 \cdot \ln(s) + b_3 \cdot \ln(\text{school}) + b_4 \cdot \ln(n + g + \partial) \tag{5.3}$$

where *school* is a measure for investment in education such as school enrolment rates. A negative coefficient b_1 is again interpreted as evidence for conditional convergence (Mankiw, Romer and Weill, 1992).

This method to measure the convergence of per capita incomes has been heavily criticised, since the reversion of outliers to the mean shows up in cross country regressions as spurious evidence for convergence, while the unequal distribution of incomes between the countries within the countries may remain constant or increase (Galton's fallacy) (Quah, 1993a; Friedman, 1992). It has therefore been proposed to complement cross-country regressions by the measurement of the variance of per capita incomes over time, i.e. by

$$\sigma_t^2 = \sum_i \left(y_{it} - \bar{y}_t\right)^2 \tag{5.4}$$

where $\bar{y}_t$ denotes the sample mean. A declining value of σ^2_t over time is interpreted as evidence for convergence. Note that *σ-convergence* is a measure of absolute, not of conditional convergence.

The measurement of the variance of per capita incomes in a country sample does not allow the identification of 'convergence clubs'. If incomes converge to different income poles the variance of incomes in the total sample may remain constant or decline. The estimation of the kernel density in a sample over time allows the identification of convergence clubs (Quah, 1993a, 1993b, 1996).

Finally, unit-root tests make use of the full time series information. The convergence of incomes over time is measured here as

$$z_{t+1} = \phi \cdot z_t \tag{5.5}$$

where $z_t = y_{it} - \bar{y}_t$ and $\bar{y}_t$ denotes again the sample mean. The coefficient ϕ is a measure of convergence: If ϕ tends to one, i.e. if ϕ has a 'unit-root', the income differential remains constant. Values smaller than one are an indication for convergence, values higher than one for divergence. The null-hypothesis, that ϕ tends to one is tested by a standard Augmented Dickey Fuller-Test (ADF). The advantage of this approach is that it makes use of the full time series information. The disadvantage is that is can only test for bilateral relationships and not for tendencies in the whole sample under investigation. Moreover, it is again a measure for absolute convergence and does not allow conclusions on the economic forces behind convergence or divergence.

Beyond the measures for convergence presented here there exist several others such as sophisticated panel-estimators. See e.g. Bernard and Durlauf (1996); the contributions in the 1996 volume of the 'European Economic Review'; and Canova and Marcet (1995) and de la Fuente (1995) for surveys.

3.2 The evidence for conditional convergence

The traditional measure for conditional convergence are cross-country regressions. Our specification follows the elementary Solow (1956) model, where economic growth is a function of the saving rate, the rate of technological progress, the depreciation rate, the rate of population growth and the initial endowment with capital (see equation 5.2 in Section 3.1, Mankiw, Romer and Weill, 1992).

To analyse the impact of different economic systems we divided the European economies in three country samples: the first sample includes the present EU-15 members, the second sample the European market economies, i.e. the EU-15, Cyprus, Iceland, Malta, Norway, Switzerland and Turkey, and the last sample the European economies incl. the former planned economies (Bulgaria, Czechoslovakia, Hungary, Poland, Romania, USSR) and Yugoslavia. In all cases the PPP-GDP data and investment rates have been taken from the Penn World Tables (1995). Of course there apply a number of caveats regarding the comparison of GDP figures between planned and market economies. All results have to be interpreted therefore with caution. Nevertheless, in our opinion these problems of measurement do not affect the overall picture. The results of our estimations are reported in Table 5.1.

Table 5.1
'*β-Convergence*': Cross-country regression results

dependent variable: ln $(y_{i,1990})$ - $(y_{i,1950})$

variable	EU (15)	Western Europe (21)	total Europe (28)
		unrestricted regression	
c	**5,0492** ***	**4,1426** ***	**1,4854**
	3,531	*8,374*	*0,890*
ln $(y_{i,1950})$	**-0,5545** ***	**-0,5385** ***	**-0,4106** ***
	-12,729	*-14,208*	*-3,773*
ln (s)	**0,5101** ***	**0,6335** ***	**-0,0856**
	3,843	*6,209*	*-0,284*
ln (n+g+δ)	**-0,5025**	**-0,8305** ***	**-1,0024** *
	-0,985	*-5,013*	*-1,799*
implied ?	**0,0202**	**0,0193**	**0,0132**
R^2	0,94	0,92	0,39
		restricted regression	
c	**5,0273** ***	**4,5772** ***	**3,9626** ***
	14,726	*16,979*	*4,522*
ln $(y_{i,1950})$	**-0,5545** ***	**-0,5322**	**-0,3801** ***
	-13,324	*-14,184* ***	*-3,409*
ln (s) - ln (n+g+δ)	**0,5102** ***	**0,6846**	**0,1598**
	4,019	*7,624* ***	*0,579*
implied ?	**0,0202**	**0,0190**	**0,0120**
R^2	0,94	0,92	0,32
Wald-test for restriction			
F-statistic	0,000	1,095	2,962
p-value	0,99	0,31	0,10

t-statistics in italics. ***, **, *, significant at the 1 %, 5 %, and 10 % level, respectively.
included countries: EU = 15, European market economies = 21, total Europe = 28.
variables: y_i = PPP-GDP per capita (Heston-Summers-Dataset)
s = investment to GDP ratio (period average)
n = population growth rate (period average)
δ+g = depreciation rate and rate of technologcal progress: 0.05 p.a. by assumption

Source: Author's calculations.

The findings for the market economies are in line with the expectations of the Solow-model, and, hence, the conditional convergence hypothesis:

The negative and significant coefficient on initial GDP is an indication for the convergence of per capita incomes. However, the speed of convergence is rather moderate: The coefficient implies a convergence rate of 2% p.a., which implies that the half-life of an initial gap in per capita incomes is around 35 years. This rate of convergence resembles exactly the findings of other studies (Barro and Sala-i-Martin, 1991, 1992, 1995).

- The coefficient on physical investment in GDP has a significant positive impact on economic growth;
- The coefficient on population growth is significant negative.

Moreover, the convergence rate of the sample of the European market economies is at 1.9% slightly below that of the EU members and the significance of the coefficient on initial income is lower. This may be interpreted as an indication that the convergence trend is stronger among EU economies than in the sample of all European market economies. However, reverse causation may be at work here: The stronger the tendency to converge, the higher is the probability to become member of the club.

The speed of convergence declines significantly if we include the former planned economies and Yugoslavia in the sample. Although the coefficient on initial income is still negative, the smaller coefficient implies a convergence rate of around 1% p.a. Moreover, we find a negative, but insignificant coefficient on physical investment. This reflects the fact that that although the investment rates of the former planned economies have been well above those of the market economies, their growth rates of output have been relatively low (see below).

In a second regression we used investment in human capital as an additional variable (equation 5.3 in Section 3.1). This regression yields a positive coefficient for investment in human capital (i.e. school enrolment rates) and confirms the conditional convergence hypothesis, too. The results are available on request from the author.

3.3 The variance of per capita incomes

As is pointed out in Section 3.1, the results from cross-country regressions may suffer from spurious correlation, which is caused by the reversion of outliers to the mean. Nevertheless, our results are confirmed by other measures of convergence: Graph 5.5 displays the standard deviation of per capita incomes between 1950 and 1990 in Europe. Again, the variance of per capita incomes in the samples of the EU-15 members as well as of the European market economies declined continuously throughout the post-war period. This confirmed by a negative coefficient on the lagged standard deviation in a regression (Appendix Table 5.3). Interestingly enough, there exists a distinct gap in the level of the standard deviation between the EU members and the sample of all European market economies. This is again (weak) evidence for the hypothesis that EU membership may promote convergence.

In contrast, the standard deviation of per capita incomes did not decline in the total European sample throughout the post-war period. This fact reflects again the fact that the planned economies did not converge to the income levels of the developed market economies in Europe. Altogether, the declining variance of per capita incomes among the market economies supports the findings from the cross-country regressions.

Graph 5.1

'σ-Convergence'

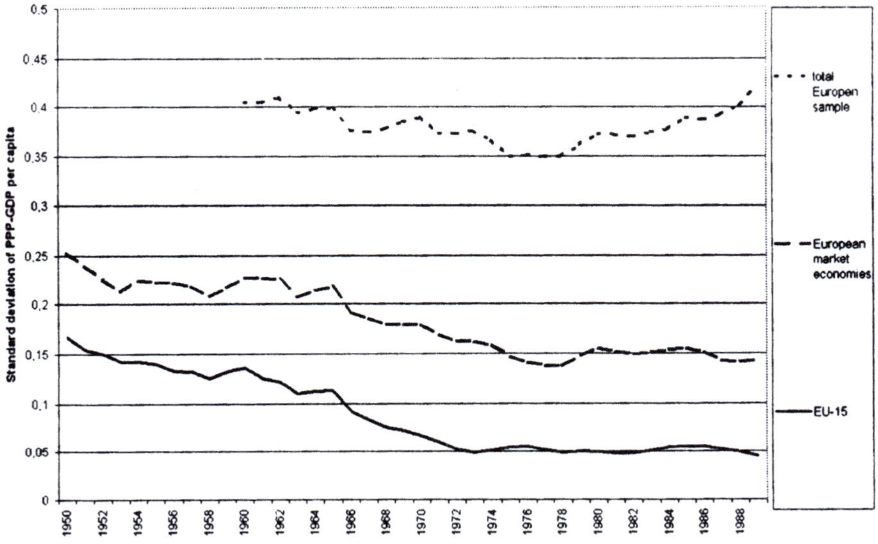

Sources: Data by Maddison (1995), author's calculations.

3.4 The polarisation of incomes

The division of the European economies into three country samples – the EU members, the other European market economies, and the total European sample – has provided evidence for the convergence in the samples of the EU and the European market economies, but not for the country sample which includes the planned economies. Our third measure of convergence provides further evidence to this general picture: The distribution of GDP across the European economies resembled a bell shaped curvature with a bias to the lower end of the income spectrum after World War II (Graph 5.2). This demonstrates that the distribution of incomes have been closed to a normal distribution at the begin of the post-war period. Some forty years later per capita GDPs have become polarised around two income poles – a lower one at around 50%, and a higher one at around 150% of the (unweighted) mean of per capita GDP in Europe (Graph 5.3).[1] The concentration of economies around the sample mean has disappeared over time. Note that this later picture resembles the global trends of income distribution (Quah, 1993a, 1993b, 1996).

Graph 5.2
Distribution of GDP in Europe 1950

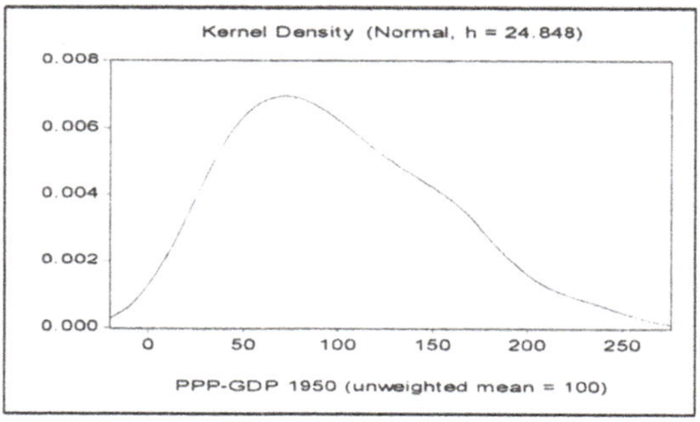

Sources: Author's estimation.

Graph 5.3
Distribution of GDP in Europe 1989

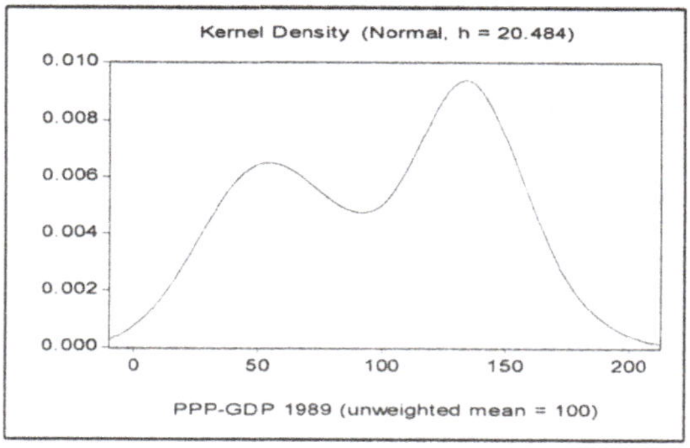

Sources: Author's estimation.

1 The country sample includes the present EU members (exc. Luxembourg), Norway, Turkey, Switzerland, Bulgaria, Czechoslovakia, Hungary, Poland, Romania, USSR, Yugoslavia. The PPP-GDP data are depicted from Angus Maddison (1995).

At first glance this picture may be interpreted as support for the hypothesis of 'club-convergence'. However, if the twin-peak distribution follows the divide of economic systems in planned and market economies it may be just a confirmation of the hypothesis of *conditional convergence*: The incomes of the planned and the market economies may have converged to different income levels.

3.5 Who converged, who diverged?

For the confirmation of our proposition that the polarisation of incomes follows the divide of Europe in market and planned economies it is interesting to know which economies have in fact converged or diverged. Graph 5.5 displays the simple correlation between initial income levels in 1950 and the average growth rate over the period 1950-1989. Low initial incomes are associated with high growth rates in almost all countries of the EU sample, the only outlier is Ireland.[2] In contrast to the EU members, the six planned economies and Yugoslavia experienced rather low growth rates of GDP relative to their low initial per capita income levels in 1950. As a consequence, their incomes have not or only slightly converged to those of market economies with higher levels throughout the post-war period. Among the non-EU market economies Turkey is an outlier, which achieved rather low growth rates relative to its low initial income in 1950.

Graph 5.4
Correlation between initial PPP-GDP and average growth 1950-1990

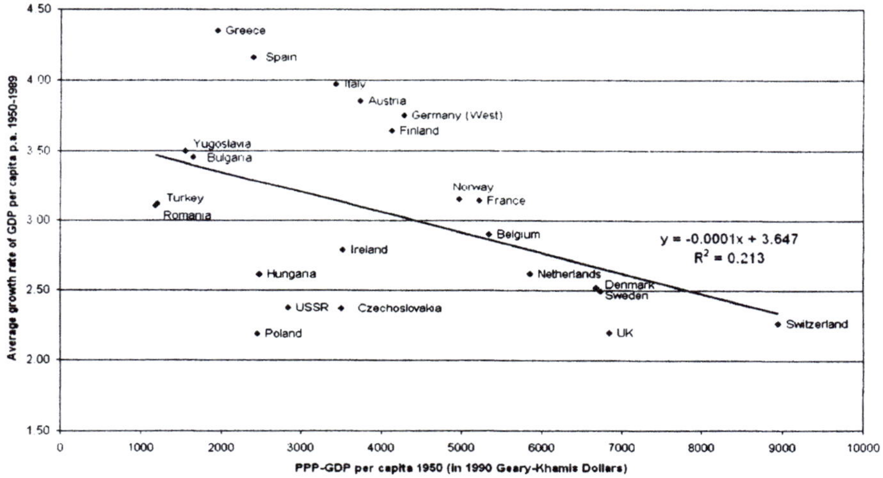

Sources: GDP-Data from Maddison (1995), author's calculations.

[2] Note that Ireland experienced a period of extraordinarily high growth rates in the nineties which are not included here.

A more sophisticated measure for the analysis of the convergence of incomes of individual countries are unit-root tests (equation 5.5 in Section 3.1). We applied unit-root tests to the difference in per capita incomes between individual European economies to the (unweigthed) sample mean of the EU-14 (exc. Luxembourg), the sample of market economies in Europe, and the total European sample. A significant negative coefficient for the lagged income differential implies the convergence of incomes between the respective economies. The results of this exercise are presented in Table 5.2 (see end of this Chapter). Although the significance and speed of convergence differs largely, the per capita incomes of most EU-14 countries converged to the mean income level of the EU. The convergence to the mean income level of the European market economies is larger. In contrast, there is no evidence for the convergence of the planned economies – neither to the mean income of the EU, nor to the mean income levels of the European economies. Positive coefficients for some planned economies (USSR, Romania) and Turkey are a weak indication that their per capita incomes have diverged (Table 5.2).

3.6 What can we learn from the post-war growth episode?

Although we applied various measures of convergence, our findings about the development of incomes in post-war Europe are rather consistent. We can draw four main conclusions from our analysis: First, the polarisation of per capita incomes around a high and a low income pole follows largely the divide of economic systems in market and centrally planned economies. In the light of the theoretical discussion in the preceding Section this trend backs the hypothesis of conditional convergence rather than the hypothesis of club convergence. The driving force behind the convergence of economies around different income poles have been the different production possibility frontiers of planned and market economies rather than initial differences in per capita incomes. This confirms the findings of other studies (e.g. Bergson, 1991; Easterley and Fischer, 1994).

Second, the strategy of forced investment, i.e. the high rates of investment in physical and human capital of the planned economies relative to the market economies, failed to achieve a convergence of per capita incomes. Although investment rates of the planned economies have been well above those of market economies, their growth rates of output declined to levels of the market economies with much higher per capita incomes at the latest in the seventies of the last century. Thus, we do not observe a significant correlation between economic growth and physical investment in the European sample (Graph 5.5). This can be interpreted as support for the neo-classical hypothesis, that the marginal returns to investment fall with capital accumulation (Weitzman, 1996). As a consequence, the strategy of forced investment could not offset the limitations of centrally planning in the CEE countries.

Table 5.2
Unit-root tests for convergence

	EU-14					Western Europe					total Europe				
	ϕ	t-statistic	lag	half-life	double-life	ϕ	t-statistic	lag	half-life	double-life	ϕ	t-statistic	lag	half-life	double-life
Austria	-0.033	-1.175	1	21	..	-0.007	-0.300	1	104	..	-0.022	-0.541	1	31	..
Belgium	-0.039	-3.617 ***	0	18	..	-0.020	-1.964 **	1	34	..	-0.068	-0.973	5	10	..
Denmark	-0.025	-2.088 **	1	27	..	-0.022	-1.732 *	1	31	..	-0.026	-0.545	6	26	..
Finland	-0.194	-2.639 ***	1	3	..	-0.091	-1.7273 *	1	7	..	-0.026	-0.869	1	27	..
France	-0.014	-2.316 **	5	48	..	-0.004	-0.794	2	170	..	0.036	0.990	1	-20	..
Germany	-0.013	-1.308	6	53	..	-0.007	-0.843	6	100	..	-0.097	-1.063	1	7	..
Italy	-0.094	-2.798 ***	1	7	..	-0.054	-2.035 **	1	13	..	-0.030	-0.985	1	23	..
Netherlands	-0.042	-3.088 ***	1	16	..	-0.030	-2.685 ***	4	23	..	-0.104	-1.295	10	6	..
Ireland	-0.007	-0.866	3	98	..	-0.051	-1.218	3	13	..	0.022	0.212	1	-31	..
Greece	-0.026	-2.174 **	3	26	..	-0.029	-2.240 **	1	23	..	-0.012	-0.794	10	55	..
Portugal	-0.017	-2.103 **	4	40	..	-0.020	-2.239 **	1	34	..	-0.022	-2.086 **	1	31	..
Spain	-0.027	-2.076 **	3	26	..	-0.031	-2.221 **	3	22	..	-0.015	-1.141	6	46	..
Sweden	-0.026	-2.900 ***	2	27	..	-0.019	-2.660 ***	1	36	..	-0.050	-1.809 *	2	13	..
UK	-0.036	-3.301 ***	1	19	..	-0.032	-3.208 ***	1	21	..	-0.074	-1.859 *	1	9	..
Norway	-0.018	-0.735	2	38	..	-0.006	-0.343	1	108		-0.059	-1.404	3	11	
Switzerland	-0.023	-3.760 ***	2	30	..	-0.019	-3.351 ***	2	36		-0.011	-0.798	3	64	
Turkey	0.004	0.901	5	..	171	0.003	0.797	5	..	202	-0.004	-0.929	1	185	
Bulgaria	-0.034	-1.098	2	20	..	..	..	..			0.004	0.682	1	..	165
Czechoslovakia	-0.033	-0.865	1	21	..	..	..	..			-0.099	-1.859	1	7	
Hungary	-0.031	-0.958	1	22	..	..	..	..			0.012	2.200	1	..	58
Poland	-0.031	-0.893	1	22	..	..	..	..			0.007	0.988	2	..	106
Romania	0.004	0.760	1	..	157	..	..	..			0.003	0.657	1	..	245
USSR	0.021	2.300	1	..	33	..	..	..			0.028	3.299	5	..	25
Yugoslavia	-0.006	-0.721	7	114	..	..	..	..			-0.003	-0.460	1	240	

Augmented Dickey-Fuller-test (ADF) for unit-roots. Lags have been choosen by the Akaike-information criteria under consideration of the Durbin-Watson Statistics. Formula: $\Delta z_t = \phi z_{t-1} + \delta_1 \Delta z_{t-1} + \delta_2 \Delta z_{t-2} + \ldots + \delta_{F-1} \Delta z_{t-F} + e_t$

McKinnon critical values for rejection of the unit-root hypothesis have been used. *** ** * indicates the significance of the rejection of the unit-root hypothesis at the 1%, 5%, and 10% level, respectively.

Source: Author's calculations.

Nevertheless, the positive coefficients on investment in physical and human capital in the cross-country regressions among the market economies support the conditional convergence hypothesis: higher investment in physical and human capital generates higher income levels if other conditions, namely the basic institutions of economic systems, are equal.

Third, the average speed of convergence among the EU members is at around 2% p.a. rather moderate. Thus, it will take generations for the transition countries to catch-up to EU income levels even if they manage to achieve a convergence in the institutional conditions.

Fourth, the speed of convergence was higher among the sample of the present EU members relative to the sample of the total European market economies. Indeed, there are several reasons to expect that EU membership enforces the convergence of per capita incomes:

- The high level of trade and factor mobility between EU countries relative to non-EU countries enforces the convergence of factor prices and endowments, and, hence, the convergence of per capita incomes;
- Income transfers by the structural and regional funds may promote the convergence of factor endowments between countries and regions of different income levels;
- The 'acquis communautaire', the joint legal framework of the EU, enforces the convergence of the institutional conditions among the EU economies.

Graph 5.5
Correlation between investment rates and GDP growth

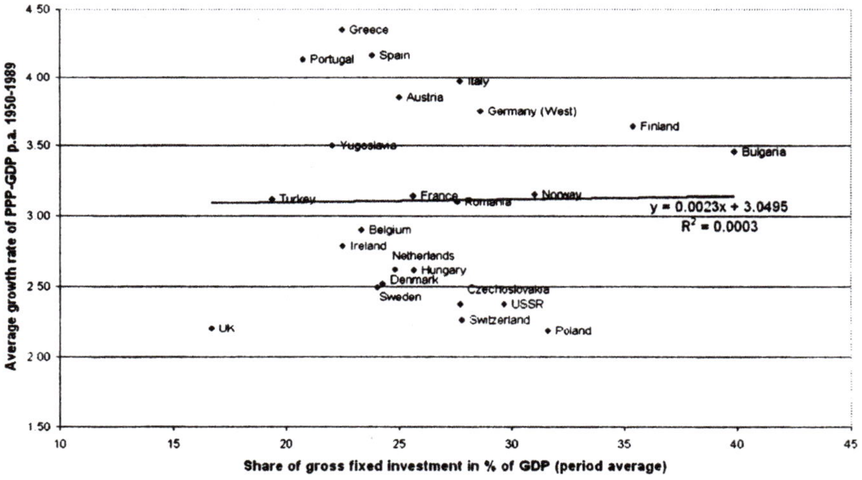

Sources: Maddison (1995), Penn World Tables (1995), author's calculations.

However, our findings are not sufficient to provide hard evidence for the thesis that EU membership promotes convergence: If a selection bias of the EU membership toward converging economies exists reverse causation may be at work. Further research is needed here.

Altogether, the historical evidence from the post-war growth episode in Europe supports the conditional convergence hypothesis. Nevertheless, one important qualification has to be made: Income differentials among the European economies after World War II have been in general lower than income differentials between the industrialised and developing countries. Moreover, some outliers such as Turkey do not fit into the picture of convergence among market economies. Thus, it might be too early to lay the hypothesis of 'club convergence' to rest.

4 Does Europe face a second economic divide?

At the outset of transition most experts predicted a rapid convergence of per capita incomes in the reforming countries. As we have seen in the preceding Sections, this prediction can be based on theoretical arguments as well as on historical experience: If the abolishment of central planning and the introduction of market institutions enhances the production possibility frontier, and that is what economic transition is supposed to do, then a transitional phase of extraordinarily high growth rates of output is expected at least under the assumptions of the conditional convergence hypothesis. The driving force behind the extraordinarily high growth rates is the high marginal productivity of physical and human capital in economies with low initial endowments. Moreover, the main lesson from the post-war growth episode in Europe is that poor economies have indeed converged *if* institutional conditions and investment rates in physical and human capital have been sufficiently similar.

Graph 5.6
Average growth of GDP 1991-99

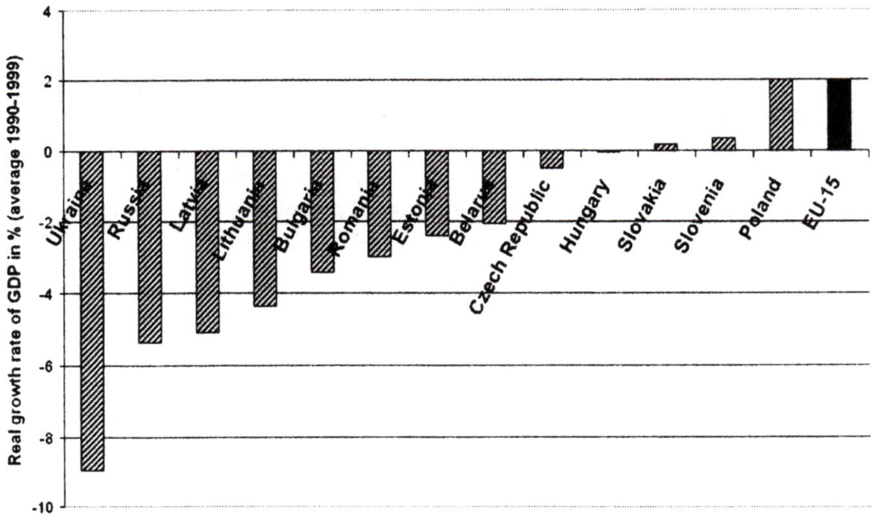

Sources: ECE (2000), author's calculations.

Graph 5.7
GDP growth since end of transition recession

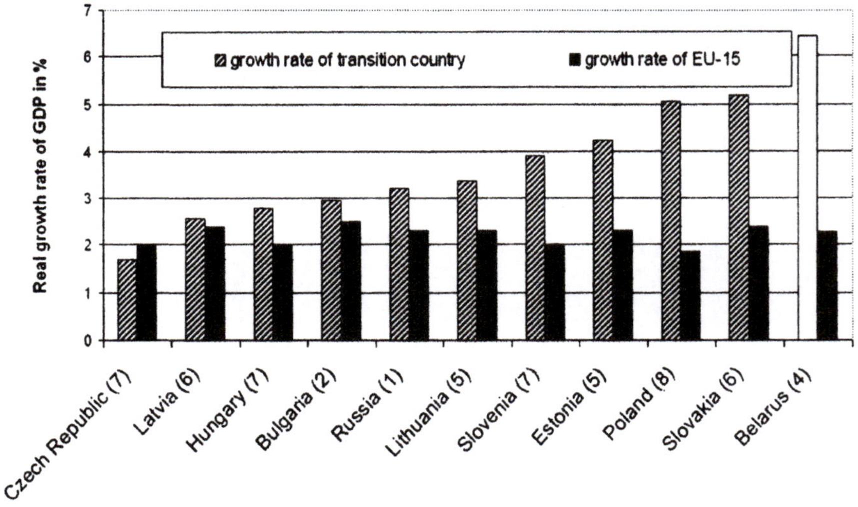

Sources: ECE (2000), author's calculations.

However, per capita incomes between the EU and the CEE countries have in fact diverged during the first decade after the begin of transition. All transition economies experienced a deep initial decline in output and only few countries have already achieved or exceeded the pre-transition output level (Poland, Slovakia, Slovenia, Hungary) (Graph 5.6). But the development has become highly differentiated between individual countries in the course of transition. We can distinguish roughly three groups of countries: In the first group we observe growth rates which corresponds to a convergence rate of 2%[3], i.e. to the average rate of convergence we found among the market economies in post-war Europe (Slovakia, Poland, Estonia and Slovenia). In another group of countries the income gap to the EU has been almost constant since the end of the transition recession (Czech Republic, Hungary, Latvia). Finally, in a third group the transition recession has not yet come to an end or it remains uncertain whether it has really ended (Bulgaria, Russia, Romania, Ukraine and most other members of the CIS).[4] Note there exists a strong *positive* correlation between initial income and GDP growth, i.e. per capita incomes have diverged and not converged among the CEE countries in the course of transition (Graph 5.8).

Graph 5.8
Correlation between initial output and GDP growth 1989-1999

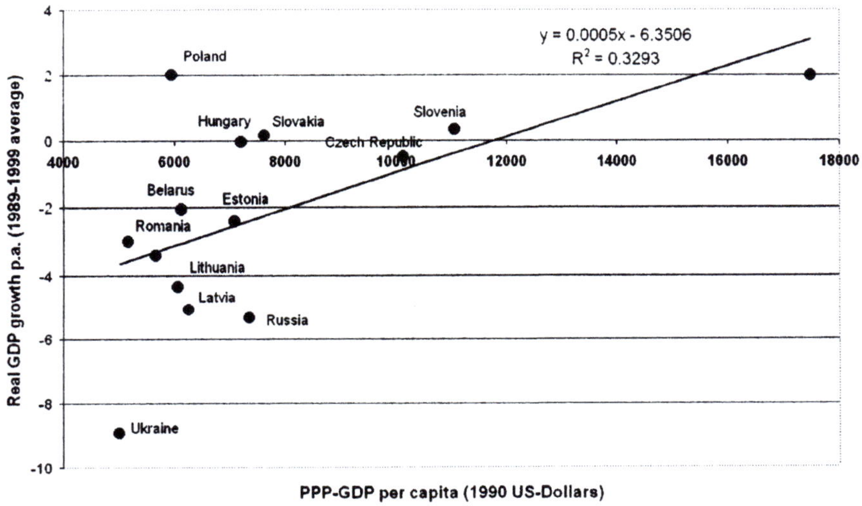

Sources: ECE (2000), author's calculations.

3 If the growth rate of the EU numbers 2%, a growth rate of 4-5% corresponds to a convergence rate of 2% for the present differential in per capita incomes between the EU and the transition countries.

4 Belarus forms an exceptional case, since it can be hardly classified as a transition country after the return to centrally planned investment policies. See below.

Graph 5.9
Gross fixed investment 1998 (Index: 1989=100)

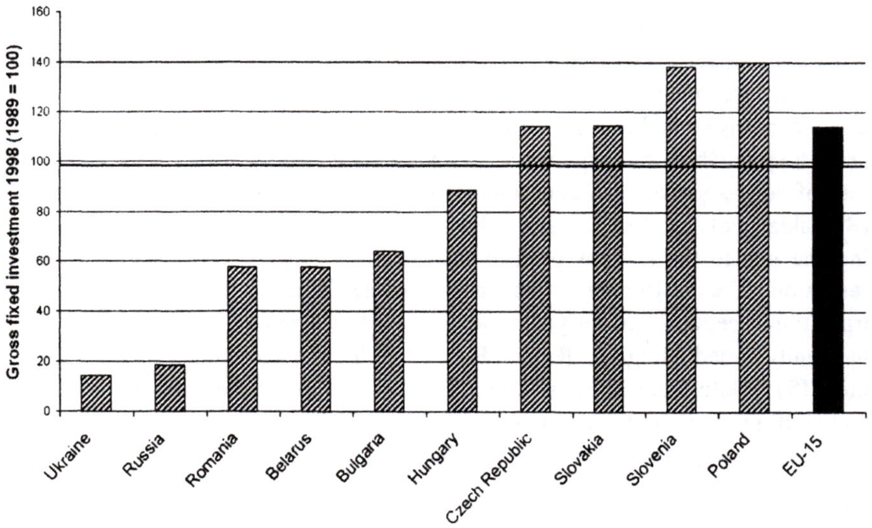

Sources: ECE (2000), author's calculations.

The transformation of systems can be understood as a decentralisation of economic decisions. One, if not the central decision for economic growth is the investment decision. Although we have seen that high investment rates can not overcome the limitations of the production possibility frontier determined by the basic institutions of economic systems, investment rates determine differences in the level of per capita income in the long-run as well as growth rates of output for a transitional period between economies if institutional conditions are equal.

In case of the transition economies, the decentralisation of the investment decisions was associated with a deep initial decline in physical investment. However, after the first shock we observe huge differences in the development of physical investment among the transition countries: In diverging countries such as Russia and the Ukraine investment in physical assets have collapsed to below one-fifth of the pre-transition level. In contrast, in converging countries such as Poland and Slovenia physical investment has increased by around 40% relative to its pre-transition level with a decade (Graph 5.9). Not surprisingly, there exist a strong positive correlation between physical investment and growth of output (Graph 5.10). Thus, investment seem to be one key for economic recovery and growth in the transition countries.

Graph 5.10
Correlation between investment and GDP growth 1989-1999

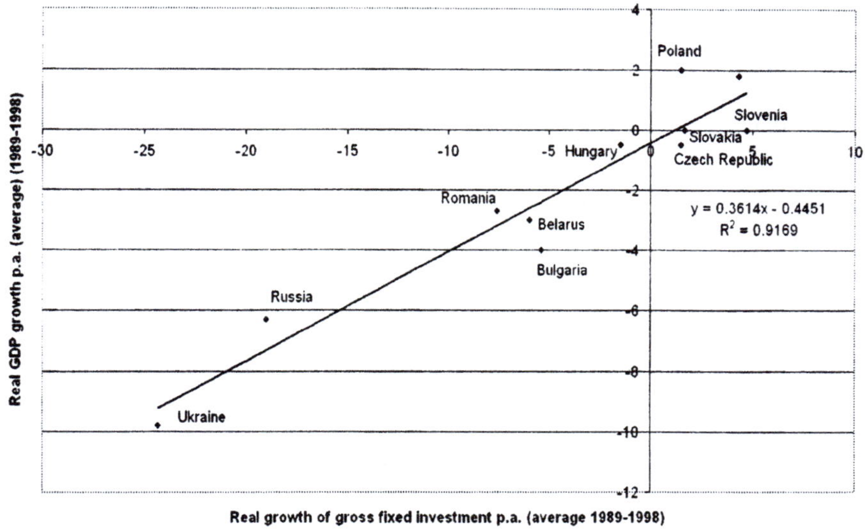

The sharp decline of investment in many transition countries is puzzling. If economic transition enhanced the production possibility frontier, marginal returns to investment in physical assets should increase. Moreover, if the shift in relative prices triggered by the transition of the institutional framework and the opening of the economies devalued some of the existing assets, returns to new investment should further increase. Indeed, low values of the Incremental Capital Output Ratio (ICOR) in the transition countries relative to the EU seem to indicate that real returns to investment are high (Appendix Table 5.4).[5] Nevertheless, in the majority of the transition countries physical investments are still well below their pre-transition levels.

The initial decline in investment and the different investment behaviour across the transition economies can be explained by a number of arguments. From the angle of growth theory, the decentralisation of decision making in the course of transition should be associated with a decline in investment, if the planers accumulated capital above optimal levels (Brücker and Schrettl, 1996). As we have seen in the preceding Section, the high investment rates of the centrally planned economies indeed generated low returns. However, this argument is less convincing if we assume that the production possibility frontier has been enhanced by economic transition. Moreover, a persisting decline in investment which effect

5 However, the ICOR can be calculated only for economies with positive growth rates of output. Thus, we have no evidence for contracting economies such as the Ukraine.

a deep decline in real consumption, which we observe in economies such as Russia and the Ukraine, can be hardly explained along these lines.

A second argument from the perspective of growth theory might be more relevant in this context: If a subsistence level of consumption is considered by economic agents, investment rates may fall short of levels to maintain the existing capital stock even if marginal returns are above the average. A deep economic shock which reduces output below a critical level may induce a continual decline of investment and capital stocks (see Section 2).

Modern investment theories stress the importance of uncertainty for irreversible investment (e.g. Dixit and Pindyck, 1995). Note that almost all investments in real assets are irreversible, i.e. they loose most of its value in other uses as those they have been planned for. If uncertainty on the real returns of investments exceeds a critical level, it may pay to wait for a later period until further information have arrived. It has been shown, that this '*option value of waiting*' drives a substantial wedge between the risk-free rate of return and the returns needed until irreversible investments are exercised even if uncertainty about the relevant economic variables is rather moderate. Economic uncertainty is in most transition economies well above those of the established market economies for several reasons: Property rights are not ill-defined and not properly enforced; corruption and other forms of criminality are high; inflation, exchange rate fluctuations and budget deficits generate uncertainty about prices, demand and other variable relevant for investment. Note that we can meanwhile observe distinct differences in the capabilities of governments in the transition countries to stabilise their institutional and macroeconomic framework. There is ample evidence that differences in investment behaviour can be traced back to those differences in governmental behaviour (see e.g. EBRD, 1999).

Finally, differences in the state of European integration may create differences in investment behaviour. European integration affects investment by various channels: First, accession to the EU demands the convergence of the institutional framework. A credible commitment to accession increases therefore the credibility of economic reform, and, hence, reduces uncertainty for foreign and domestic investors. Second, the removal of barriers to capital mobility e.g. by harmonisation in the regulation of financial markets may trigger foreign investment. Third, the removal of tariff and non-tariff barriers to trade for goods and services may increase returns in the tradable sectors and, hence, increase investment. Fourth, public capital transfers from the EU (e.g. structural and regional funds) may increase infrastructure investments and, hence, trigger complementary investment in the private sectors of the economy. We can already observe a distinct differences in foreign investment volumes between the accession candidates and other transition economies. Average FDI in the countries involved in the first-round of accession negotiations amounted to around 5% of GDP and 20% of gross fixed investment. However, there exists a selection bias:

The EU selected transition countries with a credible commitment to economic reform as accession candidates.

Note that we argued on basis of the assumption that economic systems between the East and the West tend to converge. This need not to be the case. On the background of the deep recession in many transition countries it might be tempting to re-centralise economic decisions. Belarus is such an example (see e.g. DIW, 1999). In this country investment decisions have become re-centralised by various means of governmental policy. This re-centralisation generated relatively high growth rates of output. This is not surprising, since the output level has declined in the course of transition, analogous to other CIS members, sharply. In this case the marginal productivity of capital is high even if the production possibility frontier is not enhanced relative to central planning. Thus, the re-centralisation of investment decision may result in high rates of economic growth for a limited period of time. But the historical experience discussed in the preceding Section provided strong evidence for the prediction that per capita incomes will not converge to EU levels due to the shortcomings of administrative planning.

5 Conclusions

Although economic transition started around ten years ago, it is still too early to draw conclusions about the long-run prospects for convergence and growth in the transition countries. Nevertheless, the experience of the past decade has been disappointing for a large number of countries. The income gap between the EU and the transition countries has increased. Only some transition countries managed to realise growth rates of investment and output well above those of the developed market economies in the present EU. In a large number of other countries, capital stocks and income levels continue to diverge from those of the present EU members. These developments raises concerns that the first economic divide of Europe around market and planned economies might be replaced by a second economic divide between high and low income economies.

The post-war growth episode in Europe supports the hypothesis of conditional convergence, i.e. that per capita incomes of economies with similar institutional conditions tend to converge. Although the speed of convergence has been rather moderate, this experience supports the optimistic view that the convergence of institutions in the course of transition will cause the convergence of incomes. The disperse development among the transition economies does not contradict this experience. Differences in the growth performance among the transition countries are associated with large differences in investment activity. Differences in the investment behaviour in turn can be traced back to differences in the definition and enforcement of property rights and other aspects of the institutional and macroeconomic framework. Thus, even those countries which continue to fall back may achieve extraordinarily high growth rates of investment and output if they manage to stabilise their institutional and macroeconomic framework.

Nevertheless, the chances for institutional and macroeconomic stabilisation are not equally distributed across the transition countries. The accession candidates to the EU benefit from a higher credibility of economic reform in terms of higher domestic and foreign investment. However, the membership in the EU depends on the commitment to economic reform rather than on geography. Thus, an orientation toward the EU may improve prospects for convergence.

Finally, the optimistic view that the convergence of institutions will yield the convergence of incomes has to be taken with a grain of salt. The hypothesis of conditional convergence is not uncontroversial. Economies might be convicted in a poverty trap if output falls below a critical level. Although low investment levels in economies such as Russia and the Ukraine can be largely explained by shortcomings in the institutional and macroeconomic conditions, the possibility of a poverty trap might be a real danger.

References

Barro, R.J. and X. Sala-i-Martin (1991): Convergence Across States and Regions. Brookings Papers on Economic Activity, No. 1, pp. 107-182

Barro, R.J. and X. Sala-i-Martin (1992): Convergence. In: Journal of Political Economy, Vol. 100, No. 2, pp. 223-251

Barro, R.J. and X. Sala-i-Martin (1995): Economic Growth. McGraw-Hill, New York

Bergson, A. (1991): The USSR Before the Fall: How Poor and Why? In: Journal of Economic Perspectives, Vol. 65, No. 4, pp. 29-44

Bernard, A.B. and N. Durlauf (1996): Interpreting Tests of the Convergence Hypothesis. In: Journal of Econometrics, Vol. 71, pp. 161-173

Brücker, H. (2000): Konvergenz oder Divergenz? Wachstumstheoretische Überlegungen zur wirtschaftlichen Entwicklung in den Transformationsländern Mittel- und Osteuropas. Schriftenreihe des Vereins für Socialpolitik, forthcoming

Brücker, H. and W. Schrettl (1996): Transformation, Investitionen und Wachstum: Eine theoretische Perspektive. In: Vierteljahreshefte zur Wirtschaftsforschung, Vol. 65, No. 1, pp. 5-13

Canova, F. and A. Marcet (1995): The Poor Stay Poor: Non-Convergence Across Countries and Regions. CEPR Discussion Paper No. 1265

Cass, D. (1965): Optimum Growth in an Aggregative Model of Capital Accumulation. In: Review of Economic Studies, Vol. 32, pp. 233-240

Deutsches Institut für Wirtschaftsforschung (DIW), Institut für Weltwirtschaft (IfW), Institut für Wirtschaftsforschung Halle (IWH) (1999): Die wirtschaftliche Lage der Republik Belarus. DIW-Wochenbericht, 48/99, pp. 861-880

De la Fuente, A. (1995): Catch-up, Growth and Convergence in the OECD. CEPR-Discussion Paper No. 1274

EBRD (1999): Transition Report. London

Easterley, W. and S. Fischer (1994): The Soviet Decline, Historical and Republican Data. World Bank, Policy Research Working Paper 1284, Washington D.C.

Friedman, M. (1992): Do Old Fallacies Ever Die? Journal of Economic Literature, Vol. 30, pp. 2129-2132

Galor, O. and H. Ryder (1989): Existence, Uniqueness and Stability of Equilibrium in an Overlapping Generations Model with Productive Capital. In: Journal of Economic Theory, Vol. 49, No. 2, pp. 360-375

Galor, O. (1992): A Two-Sector Overlapping Generations Model: A Global Characterization of the Dynamic System. In: Econometrica, Vol. 60, pp. 351-386

Galor, O. (1996): Convergence? Inferences from Economic Theory. In: Economic Journal, Vol. 106, pp. 1056-1069

Koopmans, T.C. (1965): On the Concept of Optimal Economic Growth. In: The Econometric Approach to Development Planning, Amsterdam

Maddison, A. (1995): Monitoring the World Economy 1820-1992. OECD, Paris

Mankiw, G., D. Romer and D. Weil (1992): A Contribution to the Empirics of Economic Growth. In: Quarterly Journal of Economics, Vol. 107, No. 2, pp. 407-438

Mountford, A. (1998): Trade, Convergence and Overtaking. In: Journal of International Economics, Vol. 46, pp. 167-182

Quah, D. (1993a): Galton's Fallacy and Tests of the Convergence Hypothesis. In: Scandinavian Journal of Economics, Vol. 95, No. 4, pp. 447-443

Quah, D. (1993b): Empirical Cross-Section Dynamics in Economic Growth. In: European Economic Review, Vol. 37, pp. 462-464

Quah, D. (1996): Twin Peaks: Growth and Convergence in Models of Distribution Dynamics. In: Economic Journal, Vol. 106, pp. 1045-1055

Penn World Tables (1995): Version 5.6 prepared by A. Heston and R. Summers, Pennsylvania University. download: http://datacentre.chass.utoronto.ca/pwt/index.html

Ramsey, F. (1928): A Mathematical Theory of Saving. In: Economic Journal, Vol. 38, pp. 543-559

Solow, R. (1956): A Contribution to the Theory of Economic Growth. In: Quarterly Journal of Economics, Vol. 70, pp. 64-90

Uzawa, H. (1961): On a Two-Sector Model of Economic Growth. In: Review of Economic Studies, Vol. 29, pp. 40-47

Uzawa, H. (1963): On a Two-Sector Model of Economic Growth II. In: Review of Economic Studies, Vol. 30, pp. 105-118

Weitzman, M. (1996): Hybridising Growth. In: American Economic Review, Vol. 86, No. 2, pp. 207-212

Appendix Tables

Table 5.3

'*σ-Convergence*': Regression results

dependent variable: s^2_t-s^2_{t-1}

Variable	Coefficient	Standard error	t-statistic	Probability	R^2
EU-14 (sample: 1950-1989, included observations: 39)					
s^2_{t-1}	-0.0326	0.0075	-4.3575	0.0001	0.082023
European market economies (sample: 1950-1989, included observations: 39)					
s^2_{t-1}	-0.0174	0.0064	-2.7291	0.0090	0.03549
total Europe (sample: 1961-1989, included observations: 28)					
s^2_{t-1}	0.0149	0.0075	1.9847	0.0561	0.0328

Source: Author's estimations.

Table 5.4
Incremental Capital Output Ratio (ICOR)

	1995	1996	1997	1998
EU-15	8.25	12.25	7.76	7.58
Austria	13.65	11.55	20.17	8.73
Belgium/Luxembourg	7.95	19.13	5.64	8.18
Denmark	5.03	7.21	6.74	7.99
Finland	4.29	4.25	2.86	4.15
France	11.06	16.82	9.05	5.66
Germany	13.18	27.13	14.27	10.00
Greece	8.86	8.12	6.18	2.20
Ireland	1.84	2.48	1.93	2.08
Italy	6.31	20.22	12.07	12.08
Netherlands	6.15	7.03	5.63	6.16
Portugal	8.31	8.17	6.32	7.86
Spain	5.95	6.55	5.76	6.96
Sweden	4.19	14.27	7.45	5.51
United Kingdom	5.82	4.72	5.14	8.31
CEE-10 countries[1)]	3.86	5.23	3.86	5.36
Bulgaria	5.28	-	-	5.50
Czech Republic	5.01	8.38	-	-
Estonia	-	7.14	2.79	7.68
Hungary	12.33	14.93	4.35	4.11
Lativa	-	5.70	2.30	-
Lithuania	6.97	4.89	3.34	5.06
Poland	2.68	3.50	3.47	5.07
Romania	3.01	5.88	-	-
Slovak Republic	4.11	5.43	5.33	7.96
Slovenia	5.13	6.39	5.06	6.12

Low values of the ICOR are an indication for a high marginal productivity of the capital stock and vice versa. Note that the ICOR can only be calculated for positive growth rates of the GDP.

1) Growing countries only. -

Sources: IMF: International Financial Statistics, various editions, Washington, D.C., World Bank: World Developement Indicators, CD-ROM, Washington, D.C. 1998.

6

The Partnership and Co-operation Agreement (PCA) between Ukraine and the EU – Idea and Reality[1]

Klaus Schneider

1 The development of contractual relations: From Trade and Co-operation Agreements to Partnership and Co-operation Agreements

After the collapse of the Soviet Union in December 1991, and when the Community and its member states recognised the new independent states (NIS) of the former USSR and established diplomatic relations, the Commission, in its Communication on January 9, 1992 to the Council, proposed to replace the Trade and Co-operation Agreement with the Soviet Union signed in December 1989. This was not only due to the fact that the identity of the Community's partners had changed. The democratisation process and the transition to market economy in the NIS called for a new approach, as compared to the 'first generation' trade and co-operation agreements.

An intermediate type of agreement was needed situated between trade and co-operation agreements and the more far-reaching Europe agreements. These new agreements should have a *common framework*.

As the disintegration of the Soviet Union had led to a severe decline in production and employment and a sharp rise in inflation, the PCA's should encourage the maintenance of a single economic area between the members of the newly created Commonwealth of Independent States (CIS) and discourage the creation of new barriers between them.

---

1 The opinions presented are those of the author and do not commit the European Commission.

Readers in the year 2000, unfamiliar with the discussions in the Community in the early months of 1992, might be perplexed with this statement. But for the Community it was important at the time to include provisions into the future PCAs about *co-operation among the NIS.* The Council's negotiating directives for the Commission later in 1992 made it clear that such provisions should figure in Title I, General Principles of the PCAs. As a result all future PCAs, including the PCA with Ukraine (Article 3) highlight "co-operation among the NIS" as a *General Principle.* With, however, one exception: the PCA with Russia. Interestingly, the Russian negotiators objected to any provision on co-operation with the other NIS from the first negotiating round, apparently considering it inappropriate that an agreement between Russia and the European Union should deal with relations with third parties. Later on in the negotiating process, Russia accepted, however, references to "regional co-operation" in the Preamble and co-operation "with the other countries of the former USSR" under Title VII, Economic co-operation.

Another objective of the PCAs would be to promote the widest possible opening of markets between the Community and the partner countries as well as co-operation in all relevant fields including financial and economic co-operation. A framework for technical assistance should be provided. Finally, the future agreements should lay emphasis on support for institution building and the strengthening of civil society and provide for a political dialogue with the Community and its member states.

In its Communication on February 26, 1992 to the Council, the Commission specified the scope of the envisaged agreements. It was stressed, inter alia, that the trade content should be based on reciprocal MFN treatment in accordance with WTO principles. Economic and financial co-operation should be emphasised in order to support the reform process. Observation of CSCE obligations should be safeguarded by a suspension clause similar to those included in the agreements with the Baltic states.

On October 5, 1992 the Council adopted directives for the Commission for the negotiation of PCAs with countries of the former Soviet Union. After exploratory talks with Russia, Ukraine, Belarus and Kazakhstan end-1992, official negotiations between the EC and the Russian Federation were opened on November 25, 1992 and with Ukraine in early 1993.

2 The Partnership and Co-operation Agreement between Ukraine and the EU

In the course of 1993 three rounds of negotiations with Ukraine were held on the basis of the negotiating directives of October 1992. On March 7, 1994 the Council agreed to alter and expand the negotiating directives in order to meet a number of Ukrainian requests, notably so as to reflect the prospect of a future free trade agreement. The enlarged mandate has enabled both sides to conclude negotiations on 23 March and to sign the agreement on June 14, 1994 in Luxembourg (signed on behalf of Ukraine by former President Leonid Kravchuk). The PCA with the Russian Federation was signed a few days later, on June 24, 1994 in Corfu.[2]

The PCA with Ukraine entered into force only on March 1, 1998 (the Russian PCA on December 1, 1997) after ratification by all the Parties, including the 15 member states of the EU. This four year delay did not in any way reflect hesitations on the part of the EU; the lengthy time interval was simply due to the need to go through the approval procedures of all the Parliaments of 15 member states.[3]

In any case, implementation of all the important *trade and trade-related provisions of the PCA* did not have to await the entry into force of the PCA in 1998. These provisions already entered into force on *February 1, 1996* via an *Interim Agreement.* It covered issues (trade and trade-related) falling within the exclusive competence of the Community without the need for lengthy ratification procedures by all member states. All the major principles of the agreed EU-Ukraine trade policy rules have, therefore, already been in force since more than four years: m-f-n rule, national treatment, the principle of protection to be granted only through the customs tariff, not through other means such as quantitative import restrictions or higher taxes on imported than on domestic goods, the standard WTO rules, concerning customs valuation of goods, concerning fees and formalities imposed on importation and checking of compatibility with technical regulations and standards, the rules on transit and so on.

3 The PCA – An evolutionary framework agreement

The PCA provides a framework for the political and economic dialogue between the EU and Ukraine. It provides reciprocal, legally binding commitments to ensure a dynamic development of two-way trade and investment flows. It lays the foundation for broad economic, financial, social and cultural co-operation.

---

2 The negotiations with Russia were highly complex and intensive, eight rounds of formal negotiations, the last one took place in Moscow on December 1-2, 1993; two revisions of the negotiating mandate, April and November 1993, numerous high-level and expert meetings between the formal rounds. The clear intention of both sides was to sign the agreement before the end of 1993. This failed mainly due to unresolved controversies in the field of trade in nuclear materials and financial services; the latter problem, the removal of limitations for some EU banks on the operation with Russian residents, was resolved only hours before the signing ceremony in Corfu.

3 The Ukraine PCA is published in the Official Journal of the European Communities (1998), L 49, Vol. 41, February 19.

The political, economic and social goals, laid down by the PCA, reflect both the political vision and the economic realities at the time. These are *practical* and *realistic* aims, articulated in such a way as to permit mutual relations between the parties to *evolve* in the light of concrete developments.

The economic realism is for example reflected in the fact that the PCA allows certain kinds of domestic state aids, that it provides phasing-in periods for some commitments such as in the field of intellectual property protection and competition rules and that it calls upon Ukraine to abide only by some of the key rules of trade policy behaviour accepted and applied by the 136 member nations of the WTO. The PCA also does not ask Ukraine to forego the right to increase its customs tariff protection for its industry and agriculture. However, with its decision to join the WTO, Ukraine accepted to observe the customary standstill in trade barriers expected from applicant countries during accession negotiations.

The provisions of the PCA are clearly designed to be only a stage in the rapprochement between Ukraine and the EU so that the evolution of the relationship would primarily depend on the way Ukraine would handle its political and economic transition to a democratic society and functioning market economy.

Ukraine's frequently declared aim is to negotiate an Association Agreement with the EU. It is useful to compare the *substance* of an Association Agreement, say the EU-Poland Association Agreement with the Ukraine PCA. Much of the contents of the Association Agreement with Poland are in line with those of the Ukraine PCA, including for example the provisions on political dialogue, provisions on establishment of companies, on movement of workers and of capital and on economic, cultural and financial co-operation. It is principally with respect to trade matters that the two types of agreements differ, as the Association Agreement with Poland is a preferential agreement, which aims at establishing a free trade area for goods covering substantially all the trade between the Parties. Although the Ukraine PCA is a non-preferential agreement, the possible evolution to a preferential agreement is clearly spelled out in Article 4. This will be discussed later on.

In short, if the evolutionary potential of the PCA is fully used, in the trade field and in many other areas, the PCA could easily be developed into an 'Association Agreement'. The rendez-vous clause of Article 5 offers an opportunity to examine this matter in the year 2001. Again, if Ukraine's aim is to achieve the *economic integration substance* of the Association/Europe Agreements, this could become a realistic, medium-term objective. The Association Agreements, concluded or under discussion with Mediterranean countries, are other examples of more advanced types of contractual relations, in particular in the field of trade.

However, if Ukraine's principal aim is rather to obtain recognition as a candidate for EU-membership (membership option) as a key political feature of an Association Agreement, as in the Europe Agreements, the perspectives of negotiating an 'Association Agreement' do not appear to be realistic in the foreseeable future.

4 The PCA – A 'road map' for gradual economic rapprochement

The institutional framework set up under the PCA has been the basis for the conduct of bilateral relations in recent years. The parties are following the 'roadmap' inscribed into the Agreement to guide and assist Ukraine in its economic policies – particularly its trade-related policies for goods and services – as well as in investment matters, competition, intellectual property protection, current payments and capital movements, all oriented to the creation of a marked-based economy.[4] The three institutions of the PCA, the Co-operation Council, the Co-operation Committee and the Parliamentary Co-operation Committee have been established and meet regularly.

Co-operation of the EU envisaged by the PCA in a considerable range of economic and social domains is now being implemented in several of the 27 specified areas of co-operation. A Joint PCA Work Programme, adopted by the first EU-Ukraine Co-operation Council in June 1998, covers 16 specific areas for co-operation, which should be given special priority in the course of 1998-2000. Active work has taken place on both sides to ensure progress in implementing the Joint PCA Work Programme.

5 The EU Common Strategy on Ukraine – Confirmation of the PCA's contractual framework of EU-Ukraine relations

The EU Common Strategy on Ukraine adopted by the European Council in Helsinki on December 10, 1999 acknowledges Ukraine's European aspirations,

---

[4] For a detailed description and interpretation of the relevant PCA provisions see the excellent "*Guide* to the implementation of the Partnership and Co-operation Agreement between Ukraine and the European Community", published by the Ukrainian Policy and Legal Advice Centre (UEPLAC) in January 1999. See also the six "Monographs" on specific PCA provisions, also published by UEPLAC in 1999 on: rules of competition, including subsidies; professional and business services; establishment and operation of companies; banking and insurance; transport services; and indirect taxation. The Guide and the monographs are available in English and Ukrainian at the Delegation of the European Commission in Kyiv.

and welcomes the country's pro-European choice. The Common Strategy (a) establishes a medium-term framework for further development of EU-Ukraine relations, taking into account the fact that through EU enlargement Ukraine will become a direct neighbour of EU; and (b) enhances coherence between EU/member states actions as well as between various EU instruments.

After recognising that a successful, stable and secure Ukraine was in the best of interests of the EU, the strategy confirms that the *legal basis of the relationship between the EU and Ukraine is the PCA, that its full implementation is a prerequisite for Ukraine's successful integration into the European economy* and that it would also help Ukraine assert its European identity.

6 Implementation of the PCA – The reality as seen from the EU side

Developments in Ukraine during the lifetime of the Interim Agreement, and even more so during the first two years after the entry into force of the full PCA created a feeling in the EU that the enthusiasm and resolve of Ukraine for implementing the PCA were at most hesitant and at times even ebbing. The record in domestic political matters, including in particular with regard to the rule of law and the freedom of the press was not evolving as well and as rapidly as anticipated when the Agreement was concluded. After all, *credibility* and trust are the key to investor confidence and to attracting those businessmen who are interested in doing long-term business in Ukraine. The *absence of a stable legal framework* adapted to the requirements of a market economy has proved to be a key constraint to the success of economic transition in Ukraine.

The EU's perception was that Ukraine's adherence to the principles of a market economy left much to be desired, that the management of the economy by the government was not being reformed and that Ukraine's deteriorating public finances were not being put in order. A succession of trade problems, most of them involving matters of observance of the PCA provisions, were souring the atmosphere of the bilateral relationship. Ukraine was in breach of virtually all key provisions on trade in goods:

- most-favoured-nation treatment (Art. 10.1);
- freedom of transit (Art. 11);
- exemption of import charges and duties on temporarily admitted goods (Art. 13);
- prohibition of quantitative restrictions on imports (Art. 14);
- national treatment (Art. 15);

- value of merchandise to be based on its actual value (Art. 16.1);
- fees and charges to reflect actual costs of services rendered (Art. 16.2);
- anti-dumping/countervailing measures to respect Art. VI of WTO (Art. 19);
- export restrictions not to constitute arbitrary discrimination/restriction (Art. 20).

In addition, Ukraine was in breach of a number of provisions on business and investment, notably those on national treatment for the establishment and operation of EC companies in Ukraine (Art. 30.2) and on access to the international maritime market and traffic on a commercial basis (Art. 39); as well as of certain provisions on competition, intellectual, industrial and commercial property protection, most importantly Art. 49 on state aids.

Of the many well documented cases of PCA-infringements, three topics will be stressed in the following.

6.1 Investment related measures in the automobile sector: The 'Daewoo' case

In early 1997, the South Korean company Daewoo negotiated a joint venture investment with the Ukrainian manufacturer AvtoZAZ. This agreement involves a commitment from the Ukrainian Government to provide a number of trading, tax and financial privileges. Counter to EU requests, a first law (535/97) "On the stimulation of automobile production" in Ukraine was passed on September 19, 1997 by the Ukrainian Parliament, granting various discriminatory fiscal advantages to the Korean investor and discriminating against car imports. A second law (482/97) "On the writing off of debt of the open joint stock company AvtoZAZ", approved by the Ukrainian Parliament on July 18, 1997, includes various fiscal privileges and officially guaranteed credits. In addition a law (217/97) "On excise duty rates and import duty for certain vehicles and tyres for them" of May 24, 1997 gives further tax advantages by exempting Daewoo from excise duty until 2007. Besides, the Cabinet of Ministers Decree 146 of February 16, 1998 prohibited imports of used cars older than five years and also stipulated a 5,000 USD minimum customs value on imported used cars.

In the view of the EC, these laws contravene the PCA (Art. 10-MFN clause, 15-non-discrimination and 49-state aids) as well as Articles I and III of the WTO. The provisions regarding the second hand car market are contrary to art 14 of the PCA. Formal consultations (under Article 97 of the PCA) in March 1998, brought no satisfactory solution, and the EC launched the dispute settlement procedure (under Article 96 of the PCA). The dispute was referred to the Co-operation Council on December 23, 1998, with a draft recommendation to be adopted by the Co-operation Council pursuant to Article 96 paragraph 2 of the PCA.

Ukraine's reply of January 29, 1999 addressed some elements requested by the Commission during previous consultations, notably local content, VAT exemption on sales, and exemption from excise duties on sales. On these points Ukraine commits itself to amend the law before the end of 2000, so as to remove the local content clause and extend VAT exemption on sales, and exemption from excise duties on sales to all cars. Other points were not addressed. A Ukrainian note verbale of April 24, 1999 following new consultations of March 19, 1999, brought nothing new to the settlement of the dispute.

The dispute settlement procedure (in accordance with Art. 96 of the PCA) was therefore pursued further, as announced at the Co-operation Council of April 26, 1999: The Council appointed a conciliator for the EU (October 20, 1999) in accordance with Art. 96 par. 3 and informed Ukraine on October 28, 1999 that it is expected to appoint its conciliator within two months. Ukraine has failed to do so.

At a Trade and Investment Sub-committee meeting of March 2000, the Ukrainian authorities announced their intention to rectify 'the mistakes' made in passing the above legislation. The minimum customs values on cars were abolished, and the export ban on second hand cars was limited to cars of eight years and over. The Government announced an Action Plan to remove the discriminatory legislation in other areas; this is currently being examined by the Commission services.

6.2 Pharmaceuticals

An order of the State Scientific and Expert Centre of medicinal products of the Ministry of Health of Ukraine of June 1999 established additional specialised expertise fees for foreign medicinal products of up to 10,000 USD per product. This regulation was introduced shortly after a similar one had been removed, following an EC request (Cabinet of Ministers of Ukraine's Resolution No. 569 of April 27, 1998 increasing registration charges for imported pharmaceutical products, eliminated 22 February 1999).

This new regulation appears to be in breach of PCA/WTO, namely Article 16 paragraph 2 of the PCA referring to WTO Article VIII, according to which fees and charges of whatever character connected with importation must be limited to the cost of the services rendered and even more importantly in breach of national treatment. Fees requested are even higher this time than under the previous legislation.

Consultations under Article 97 of the PCA were concluded in March 1999 with the removal of the original discrimination. However, this positive development was reversed by the June 1999 order. The Ukrainian side postponed further consultations without taking any other initiatives to resolve the dispute, so the Commission took preparatory steps for launching the dispute settlement procedure (to refer the matter to the Co-operation Council in accordance with Article 96, paragraph 1 of the PCA) on January 26, 2000.

On March 20, 2000 a new order of the Ministry of Health entered into force, setting out identical expertise fees to be charged by the State Scientific and Expert Centre for foreign and domestic pharmaceutical products. This removes the discrimination. Therefore the dispute settlement procedure, which was to be launched is suspended. The EC sent a letter on May 10, 2000 welcoming this development, but expressing reservations about the implementation of this order, since it establishes "boundary tariffs" (i.e. maximum fees) and provides the possibility for producers to negotiate lower fees with the State Scientific and Expert Centre. The letter also referred to other trade irritants in the pharmaceuticals sector.

6.3 Export restrictions on ferrous scrap

On May 5, 1999 Ukraine adopted a 'Law on scrap metal' aimed at "Protecting the interests of domestic metallurgy industry enterprises and securing environmental protection". The law bans the exports of non-ferrous scrap metal in non-dismantled scrap, provides restrictive requirements (including a licensing procedure) for operating in scrap metal, and empowers the Cabinet of Ministers to introduce quotas or a full ban on exports of ferrous scrap metal.

During consultations on May 19, 1999 and the Co-operation Committee of July 1999, Ukraine assured the EC that the law would not result in barriers to trade. This item was to be discussed at the relevant PCA Sub-committee scheduled for December 1999, which was cancelled at the last minute by the Ukrainian side. In a Note Verbale dated December 15, 1999, the Commission urged Ukraine to refrain from restricting bilateral trade of ferrous scrap, as required by Declaration No. 6 of the bilateral steel agreement.

On December 13, 1999, the Cabinet of Ministers of Ukraine adopted Resolution No. 1395 on the export of ferrous scrap, which provides for an export monitoring mechanism, and entitles the Ministry of Industrial Policy to take the necessary steps to ensure that domestic needs are satisfied in priority.

The Community has information suggesting that the Ukrainian Ministry of Industrial Policy concluded an agreement in December 1999 with the Ukrainian Metal Scrap Association (UMSA) defining their collaboration for the execution of the aforementioned legislation. This agreement seems to introduce export quotas for each exporter, at levels substantially below those of previous years.

The Commission services requested consultations on this matter with the Ukrainian authorities under Article 9 of the Steel Agreement in the framework of the relevant PCA Sub-committee, which was held on March 27, 2000. During this meeting, no agreement was found on the export restrictions on ferrous scrap, which the Commission considers to be a violation of the ECSC Agreement. In the subsequent meeting of the Sub-committee on Trade and Investment, the Ukrainian side undertook to remove these restrictions. This position was formally confirmed in writing on March 30, 2000.

Contrary to this commitment, the Commission has information indicating that de facto the export restrictions remain in place. The Commission will consider putting in place a system for monitoring of Ukrainian exports of ferrous scrap to the EC. If this system were to prove the existence of export restrictions, and failing an amicable resolution of the question, the EC would have to take appropriate measures under Article 102 of the PCA.

6.4 The new Yushchenko Government: New attitude

Prime Minister Yushchenko's leadership in the first half of 2000 has demonstrated a fresh determination to actually tackle long-needed drastic reforms. The adoption by the Verkhovna Rada of a budget planning for a zero deficit, the intended elimination of special privileges to certain enterprises, the drafting of a new tax code, the pledge for administrative reform and a start with streamlining the civil service are steps in the right direction. Curbing deficit spending and overhauling the public administration are among the key conditions for the nation's economic revival. *The EU, at the recent Co-operation Council of May 23, 2000, welcomed the reform programme of the Prime Minister,* which calls for deregulating business, stepping up privatisation efforts, creating a private land market, lowering taxes, improving tax collection and boosting social protection. Evidently, the problem in recent years has never been one of identifying and listing the action that had to be taken but to actually do it. If the recent decisions and the stated intentions are implemented with resolve, the disproportionate economic and political influence of some entrenched oligarchies will certainly diminish. This should benefit the whole Ukrainian economy and the living standards of the population.

The new attitude has also taken the form of welcome steps to resolve some of the festering bilateral trade conflicts with the EU and to improve upon the deficient enforcement of intellectual property rights. Two (Daewoo, pharmaceuticals) of the various positive steps were already described above.

6.5 WTO

Better observance of the trade rules of the PCA will at the same time also permit Ukraine to effectively relaunch its application to join the WTO. Indeed, in the field of economic and trade policies Ukraine's commitments under the PCA overlap in a broad range of domains with those of WTO membership. The rules of the two legal instruments are complimentary. Membership of the WTO will entitle

Ukraine to a broader range of rights and privileges and to the security provided by the rule-based world trading system. In return, Ukraine will have to undertake to open its markets, notably in the domains of customs tariffs and trade in services and to abide by a broader, more detailed and more rigorous set of trade rules. WTO membership will give Ukraine's public authorities a strengthened hand for introducing domestic reforms. It may at the same time help national policy officials to take a more balanced view of trade policy and provide them with stronger arguments to defend the nation's interests against lobbying from narrow interest groups by giving precedence to measures in the interest of everyone in the economy. The same positive effect of WTO membership has also been experienced by all other WTO members, including the EU. Thus officials of the European Commission often invoke the constraints imposed by international obligations such as those of the WTO to oppose unwelcome initiatives for protection or for unwarranted advantages.

6.6 PCA implementation against the background of structural economic reform

Continued implementation of the spirit and the letter of the PCA requires a committed and sustained policy of microeconomic reform based upon fundamental transformation of the public institutions to improve the effectiveness and efficiency with which policies are imposed, thereby removing the overbearing constraints that current implementation imposes upon business. Ukraine itself now recognises that the overarching need is to create a *level playing field* for both domestic and foreign investors that will induce the establishment and expansion of business activities; that it has to put an end to tailor made legislation that addresses only the concerns of particular investors; and that its institutions must show greater transparency in their behaviour. A civil code with an effective judiciary, laws on real private land ownership and the speeding up of effective privatisation in all sectors of the economy, particularly in agriculture where Ukraine has for years been neglecting its huge potential, are among the areas for priority action.

But it is not sufficient to adopt laws and regulations for a functioning modern market economy. What matters is how the rules and regulations are applied in practice for example in the fields of taxation and intellectual property. A concerted effort to enhance and entrench administrative and judicial reform would be an important signal for both domestic and foreign investment. It would also encourage the return of grey area activities to the official economy, which in turn would raise government revenues, increase employment opportunities and stimulate foreign trade.

6.7 Free Trade Area (FTA)

A "Joint Study on the economic feasibility, general economic impact and implications of a free trade agreement between Ukraine and the EU" has thrown interesting light on the implications for the prospective Parties of such a scheme envisaged as a possibility in Article 4 of the PCA.

For the EU, there can be no question about any free trade area with Ukraine being of the 'shallow integration' type involving simply the removal of customs duties, quantitative restrictions and other trade policy barriers at the border. In the modern economic environment only 'deep integration', that reduces the distortions created by non-border policies, can produce the economic benefits expected from trade liberalisation, as it is the only way to do away with the constraints upon the ability of foreign firms to compete in or contest markets. Individual economic actors need to be free and able to exploit the opportunities that are created by abolishing the border obstacles to free trade.

As indicated in the executive summary of the Study: "To be able to adopt and effectively implement EU compatible legislation and practices will require a significant expansion of the capacity and effectiveness of the administrative, legislative and judicial system in Ukraine." Ukraine still needs to demonstrate that it would be capable in the foreseeable future of effectively undertaking a vastly increased range of obligations in areas such as competition policy including disciplines on state aids, government procurement, technical standards and certification, customs regulations and rules of origin and in the many other fields that need to be covered by an effective free trade area. While Ukraine has made progress in reforming its economy, much still needs to be done to create an efficient, predictable and reliable institutional framework. Deep integration does indeed put heavy demands upon the legislative, administrative and judicial capacity of free trade area partners. Enlargement of the EU to Central and Eastern Europe gives Ukraine role models in its immediate vicinity. The ways of reform may prove easier to learn by for example observing neighbouring Poland.

The way forward to closer integration with the EU lies in further progress in the building up of political and democratic credibility, in the creation of a thriving market economy, in the observance of the PCA and accession to WTO. Advances in these directions will gradually increase the practicability of transition to a closer integration into the European economy, including in due course a move towards free trade.

7 Concluding remarks

The EU is committed to Ukraine's successful future. It wants to bolster Ukraine as a democracy in which the rule of law applies, as a stable and secure country with a prosperous economy, a growing middle class, a country that gradually integrates into the Euro-Atlantic community of market democracies. Ukraine can continue to count on the understanding, co-operation and support from the EU. The PCA provides a valuable instrument for developing mutual co-operation, and for support for Ukraine's transition. Its potential should not be underestimated. A demonstration of confidence in the PCA from Ukraine would be proof of Ukraine's commitment to Europe and seriousness of purpose. However, the EU cannot imagine itself 'saving' Ukraine as it might be tempted to do with small countries. Ukraine is too big, its population too numerous, its territory too immense and its economy too vast. It must save itself.

7

Integrating Ukraine into the World Economy: How, How Fast and Why?

Wolfgang Quaisser and Volkhart Vincentz

1 Introduction

Liberalisation of foreign trade has always been one of the most frequent recommendations for transition strategies in Eastern Europe. Opening up the economy promises not only material gain, but in addition it provides support and guidance to the reformers, by putting them into close contact with modern business practices in the market economies. Accession to the EU became the dominant strategic objective for many states of Eastern Europe.

Ukraine shares backwardness in the transition process with many successor states of the former Soviet Union. It took almost a decade after independence till signs of growth became visible. All this time a persistent current account deficit had to be financed mainly with official credits, because private capital flew only sparsely and intermittently into the country. The development of foreign trade in many ways reflects the lack of reform in the domestic economy. The performance of the external sector is usually a good indicator for the progress of market reform in the whole economy.

The first Section of this Chapter describes the scope and the results of trade liberalisation in Ukraine. This liberalisation is put into perspective by comparisons with more successful transition economies. In addition, we highlight the peculiarities of Ukrainian energy dependence. The second Section assesses the expected and the actual successes of opening up the economy. The third and last Section examines possible future trade strategies vis-à-vis different partner-regions.

2 The external sector: Developments and changes

The record of the development of trade at the beginning of the reforms was impressive. While production tumbled from one trough to the next, exports showed two-digit growth. However, starting in 1997 exports began to decline and continued to do so until the end of 1998. Total imports moved roughly in line with exports, however, most of the time imports exceeded exports by more than 1 billion USD per year (see Graph 7.1). During the first years, the contribution of net exports to the (negative) growth of the GDP (by expenditures) was positive, but later on expanding as well as contracting effects from the external sector could be observed – albeit each year of a different magnitude.

Graph 7.1
Quarterly foreign trade of Ukraine 1995-1999, in million USD

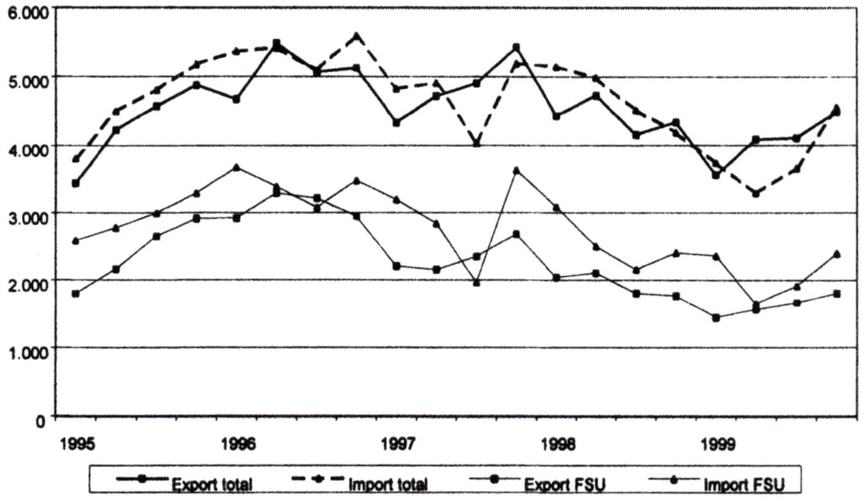

Source: Balance of payments statistics from National Bank of Ukraine.

Total exports grew, although exports to the former Soviet Union (FSU) declined, as shown in Table 7.1. The remarkable regional reorientation of trade in these years came about by re-directing export production from the former interior market of the Soviet Union to Europe and to other countries. We find this pattern typical for most transition countries, where exports grew earlier and faster than production while the share of trade with the West increased. Ukraine more than doubled its exports to the EU between 1992 and 1998, however the level of exports to the EU is still very low. In 1988 already, Poland, Hungary and the Czech and Slovak Republics (hereinafter called the EE-4 countries) each exported as much to the EU as Ukraine did in 1998. By now, any one of these advanced transition countries shows exports of 12 to 18 billion EUR, while Ukraine's export volume is only 2 billion EUR.

Table 7.1
Shares of Ukrainian exports and imports by region, in %

	1995	1996	1997	1998	1999
Exports (goods and services)					
Former Soviet Union (FSU)	56	61	49	46	40
Rest of the world	44	39	51	54	60
Imports (goods and services)					
Former Soviet Union (FSU)	64	63	61	57	55
Rest of the world	36	37	39	43	45

Source: Balance of payments statistics from National Bank of Ukraine.

2.1 The structure of Ukrainian exports to the EU

On the surface the structure of Ukrainian exports to the EU has changed a lot. Exports have become more diversified over time. However, this was mainly due to one single factor. In the early nineties Ukraine still exported large quantities of oil and oil-products, which were bought from Russia at preferential prices. As these energy subsidies from Russia were abolished, the Ukrainian exports of these goods ceased too. Since the mid-nineties Ukrainian exports to the EU consist of very few products: mainly products from ferrous metallurgy, metal scrap, clothes and oil-seeds.

A classification of Ukrainian EU-exports according to factor intensities shows that during the whole period of 1992-1998 exports of capital-intensive products dominated. Only in the mid-nineties did labour-intensive products advance to second place. This is different from the EU-exports of the EE-4 countries. In these countries labour-intensive exports overtook capital-intensive exports in 1991 already, and clearly dominated from then on (see Graphs 7.2 and 7.3). The strong position of capital-intensive exports was part of the legacy of the Soviet production structure with its emphasis on heavy industries, thus logically forming the export base at the beginning of transition. This pattern remained unchanged in Ukraine, testifying to a reluctance to adjust to comparative advantage. Furthermore, the trade balance of labour-intensive products in Ukraine was negative throughout, while the EE-4 countries – as expected – showed an increasing surplus in trade in these products. The lagging development in Ukraine also shows up in outward processing. While in the EE-4 countries this trade has started to recede again, the Ukrainian share is still on the rise. This proves the ongoing eastward shift of this extremely flexible production, and of trade arrangements, which closely follow the lowest wage costs.

A clear difference in the trade pattern between Ukraine and the EE-4 countries also emerges regarding intra-industry trade. This type of trade, where Eastern Europe delivers goods of lower quality (price) in exchange for similar goods of higher quality (vertical intra-industry trade), is significantly lower in Ukraine than in the EE-4 countries. In addition, intra-industry trade, which dominates the trade among market economies, is not on the rise in the relations between the EU and Ukraine. The strength of intra-industry trade can be taken as an indicator of how far an economy has integrated into a region. This type of trade develops as the production structures of the trade partners become more similar, and hence is a measure of the success of adjustments by eastern economies.

In conclusion, Ukraine's trade with the EU has not yet followed the changing trade pattern of the more advanced eastern reform countries. While the starting points were similar, the EE-4 countries, within two to three years after the reforms had started, accomplished such changes in the export composition as would be expected from the theory of comparative costs and the prevailing trends in trade among market economies. Few of such changes have been observed in the Ukrainian export structure vis-à-vis the EU, which still relies heavily on the inherited production systems. We take this as an indication for missing structural reforms in the country, which in turn has inhibited adjustments and the development of new products. In the EE-4 countries the large inflow of foreign direct investments also helped to smooth the path towards production of more sophisticated products.

The above is not meant to imply that Ukrainian production has not reacted at all to the stimuli of international markets, but other forces intervened. Primarily for reasons of monetary stability, Ukraine has tried to restrict the devaluation of its currency. Over the years, this has caused quite a strong real revaluation, which only ended with the financial crisis in the autumn of 1998. This development of the exchange rate made it difficult for firms to use the external market for expansion. The strong devaluation against the USD in the fall of 1998 and the subsequent real devaluation against the Russian rouble present a good example for the reaction of Ukrainian firms to drastic price changes. The results so far are mixed: On the import side, the devaluation clearly led to a drastic reduction and to an expansion of the domestic import-substituting industries. This effect was reinforced by several restrictions on the purchase of foreign exchange, which, for instance, made the prepayment of imports almost impossible. The domestic consumer-goods industries, in particular, profited from these developments. On the export side though, the reaction was less pronounced. However, in 1999 exports started to grow again after their decline since the beginning of 1997. But this recovery of exports was again driven by the traditional exporting industries mentioned above. Minerals and ferrous metals increased their share in exports from 32% in 1996 to 42% in 1999.[1] There are no signs that the devaluation was used by the Ukrainian economy to conquer new markets or to develop new products for customers abroad.

Graph 7.2
Ukrainian exports to the EU according to factor intensities

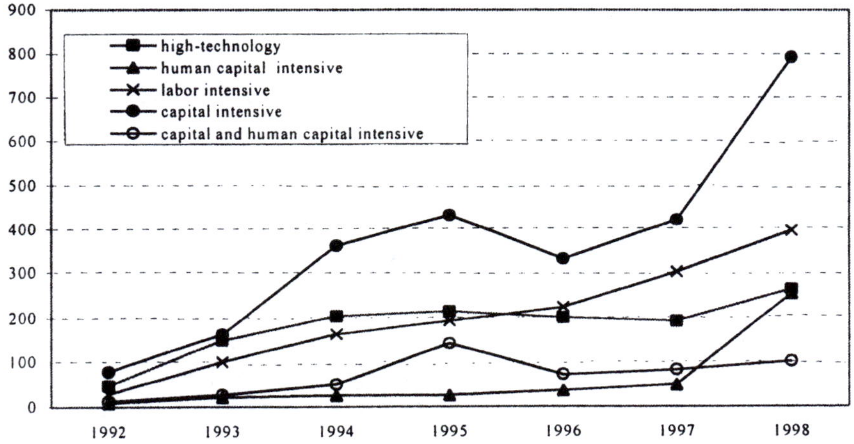

Graph 7.3
Exports of the EE-4 countries to the EU according to factor intensities

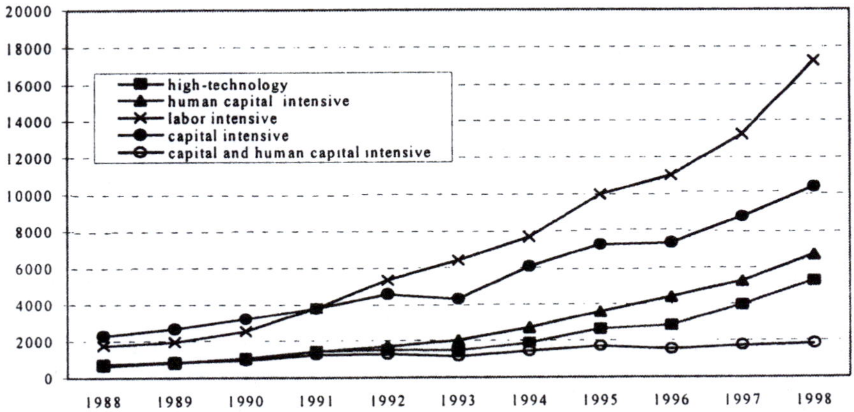

Source: Eurostat, intra- and extra-EU trade.

1 Blandinieres (2000).

2.2 Imports: Consumer goods and energy

During the ten years of transition, all advanced reform countries followed the same pattern of EU-import structure changes. At the beginning they started with a high share of consumer goods in total imports, in order to fill the needs, which the newly won consumer sovereignty had aroused. But by the mid-nineties a declining trend of these imports could be observed in all fast-reforming economies. Imports of investment related inputs began to grow faster than total imports. The role of trade changed from passive restructuring and filling immediate needs to active restructuring of production through investments.

In Ukraine this happened later and was less pronounced. The share of consumer goods in imports from the EU was rising till the mid-nineties, reaching 34%, a level significantly higher than Poland, Hungary or the Czech Republic had ever attained. Interestingly, Russia even topped the Ukrainian share with 45% in 1996 and in 1997. In 1997, and even more so in 1998, the share of consumer goods in the Ukrainian EU-imports declined drastically to 26% (for the reasons mentioned above).

Considering imports as a whole, the overwhelming importance of energy imports stands out. About 40% of all imports belong to this category. Initially Russia subsidised its energy deliveries, and when this was stopped the Ukrainian energy bill swelled to reach 6 billion USD in 1998, which has contributed substantially to the current account deficit. Ukraine has one of the highest rates of energy consumption per GDP in the world, and there is no decline visible in this trend. This is only partly a result of the inherited industry structure, which is biased towards heavy industries. More important is that reforms are lagging in the energy sector, where substantial energy savings could be brought about.

The energy sector is also at the heart of the non-payment crisis of Ukraine. For years it has become almost the norm not to pay energy bills. And yet, the central as well as local governments often forbade cutting-off non-solvent customers from the energy supply, because they feared production losses and social problems. These unceasing subsidies in the form of unpaid energy deliveries alone would spoil any interest in energy conservation. In addition, both the energy and the power industries are still mainly state-owned. The financial transactions and business deals in these areas are highly non-transparent. Domestic production, transit and distribution of gas are all managed by a single conglomerate, with cross-subsidies between the different components. Thus, it is difficult to tell which component is profitable and which is not. This again makes it impossible to select the most efficient firms, and let the losers exit the market. Since the energy and power industries consume about one third of all the energy used, their organisational structure obviously has a significant influence on Ukrainian energy demand.

Ukraine has to buy its gas from a monopoly, Russia. This is not completely true because some gas also comes from Turkmenistan, but it, too, has to be delivered via Russia. The situation is further complicated by the fact that up to now most Russian gas could only be delivered to the West via the Ukrainian transit pipeline. Thus, in a single bargaining process, both the price of the gas and the transit price are determined.[2] Both prices are linked: If the gas price rises, so will the transit price, and vice-versa. To a large extent the Government does the bargaining about these prices, although energy imports are actually the responsibility of independent Ukrainian or foreign companies, which are formally the only ones responsible for payment of the deliveries. In any case, the official import prices of 80 or 60 USD/tbm (1,000 cbm) are not the real market prices. Gas auctions usually establish prices significantly below the official import prices. The picture gets even more confused by the fact, that Russia pays for transit not with money but with gas. This gas is normally earmarked for distribution to the population at reduced – i.e. below-cost – prices.

At first sight, one would not expect that in energy-poor Ukraine most of the oligarchs started their fortune in the energy sector, same as in energy-rich Russia. Obviously, the explanation lies with the non-transparency, the many opportunities for rent-seeking (import licenses etc.), and the persistent subsidies. These have made the energy sector into an ideal starting point for the redistribution of wealth – regardless of the national endowment with natural resources.

In the medium term the burden of energy imports might even become harder to bear. Today Ukraine still enjoys a monopoly for Russian transit gas to the West. But the Russian gas export agency, Gazprom, has already started to build new pipelines bypassing Ukrainian territory, in order to break the Ukrainian monopoly. Thus, the likely perspective is a significant reduction of Ukrainian income from transit gas. Russia already started getting more insistent with respect to the accumulation of further Ukrainian gas debts. Russia also will not tolerate Ukraine to continue to tap illegally into the transit pipeline. As the Russian position in energy trade is likely to be getting stronger over time, Ukraine will have to consider the possibility of diversifying its energy sources. Same as the Czech Republic has done some years ago, Ukraine might try to strike an arrangement with Western energy suppliers for delivery of Western gas.

2 Thus, the value of Ukrainian-Russian trade can significantly fluctuate even if the volume remains almost constant. In 1996 the price for gas imports and the transit fee (export of services) were simultaneously increased and in 1998 both were reduced. Thus, in 1996 Ukrainian revenue for transit jumped by 1 billion USD, but the price for importing gas rose by about the same amount. In 1998 the opposite happened.

3 Trade liberalisation and transition in Ukraine

Most experts strongly emphasise trade liberalisation among the many transition strategies. There are many reasons why foreign trade has to be such an important aspect of the transition strategy. Firstly, foreign competition helps to fight inflation after price liberalisation. Secondly, any domestic demand contractions during recessions in the transformation period can be somewhat alleviated by the access to foreign markets. Thirdly, foreign competition can be used to break up domestic monopolies. And lastly, foreign trade is a factor of growth because of the transfer of technology that goes with it.

3.1 The results of trade liberalisation

Measured by its export or import quotas Ukraine is an extreme open economy. The share of exports and imports in GDP has fluctuated around 40% since the mid-nineties. However, this cannot be regarded as the only criterion because several restrictions, such as minimum export prices and licenses, have impeded foreign competition. The weighted tariffs have also increased over time, from 4.2% in 1995 to 7.5% in 1999. Excluding energy, the average weighted tariff even reached 12.6% in 1999. Nevertheless, the Ukrainian economy clearly felt the pressure from abroad when trying to enter foreign markets.

Did the expected benefits from opening up of the economy get realised in the Ukrainian case? As discussed above, Ukraine used the new Western markets in part to sell products that could no longer be sold within the former Soviet Union. Data on imports demonstrate the impact of foreign products especially on the consumer market. The products offered by domestic producers could clearly not satisfy the long neglected desires of the consumer. It took some time until domestic producers reacted to the flood of imported consumer goods. But slowly, especially in the fields of food and beverages, domestic producers modernised their product lines, helped by foreign competition and foreign direct investment. However, for the economy as a whole, the positive effects of liberalised foreign trade in terms of inducing modernisation and product improvements were less than one would expect. This producer passivity has several explanations. Foreign competition was stiffer than expected because of the overvalued exchange rate prior to the autumn 1998, and large losses on the domestic market stifled domestic production.

Another peculiarity of the Ukrainian economy has also helped foreign imports. Over time, the cash-strapped Ukrainian economy had developed a comprehensive system of non-monetary transactions. Barter, 'veksels' (promissory notes) and other quasi-money is heavily relied upon within the Ukrainian economy to purchase inputs and to sell outputs. In comparison to cash, payment with money surrogates is significantly more expensive. Prices in barter deals are estimated to be 20-30% higher than cash, and 'veksels' are often traded with a discount of 50% and more. Foreign competitors buy their inputs in general in cash and thus have an immediate cost advantage against Ukrainian producers. On the other hand, selling products in Ukraine is often only possible with barter, which erodes some of the cost advantages on the input side since Western firms are less familiar with the peculiarities of organising barter along the existing debt chains.

Lastly, the slow response by firms to domestic demand is, of course, related to slow reforms. After all, opening the economy to international markets looses some of its attractiveness if the economy remains highly regulated. In Ukraine the overriding concern of the government has been to prevent companies from going under. To this end a large variety of direct and indirect subsidies were used. This in turn led to close 'co-operation' between the bureaucracy and business. Foreign trade became one of the favoured areas for rent seeking, corruption and tax evasion. Because exports were one of the rare opportunities to obtain money in the form of cash, the incentives for export are huge. Due to sloppy corporate governance goods might be exported even at below-cost prices. If property rights are not clearly assigned firms will let capital assets deteriorate without replacement, i.e. they will not account fully for amortisation in the pricing of exports. Many import regions have already instituted anti-dumping procedures to combat Ukrainian below-cost sales.

An open economy with its pressures from foreign competition, on the other hand, serves as a permanent reminder to politicians to create an environment where domestic producers have incentives to take up foreign challenges.

3.2 Technology production and trade liberalisation

Great concern is being expressed within Ukraine that the country is gradually de-industrialising and that open foreign trade has contributed to this process. This is in part true, since exports, as explained above, are concentrated only on simple and standardised products. Instead, it can be argued that Ukraine should specialise on the export of modern medium and high technology products. This argument is based on Ukraine's relatively high endowment with skilled manpower, engineers, and human capital. Similar arguments had been made for most other East European countries. By and large, expectations held by some researchers at the beginning of the transformation[3], that Eastern Europe would quickly follow the

[3] "These factors abundantly suggest that among manufactures it is hi-tech goods rather than labor-intensive goods that represent Eastern Europe's area of comparative advantage." CEPR (1990) p. 11–12. "... the availability of a relatively large pool of skilled workers in combination with low wage costs will make these countries natural competitors not only with Southern Europe but with all NIEs. In a dynamic medium-term perspective, there is no reason why this competition should be limited to the lower end of the technological spectrum." ECE (1990), p. 353.

technology driven development path of some Asian countries did not come to pass. One reason might be that the present educational skills of engineers do not correspond to the skills demanded by the fast changing technology industry.

There are several ways how modern technology production and trade are linked and how these links can be shaped by policy.

In many cases, modern technology production exhibits economies of scale because of the high fixed costs involved. Plants and equipment for mass production as well as high R&D costs explain these high fixed costs. Increasing returns are an important cause of trade, as the 'new trade theory' has shown. This opens, at least in theory, possibilities for all kinds of strategic trade policies. One option would be to close the domestic market to imports, and thus to allow the domestic modern technology producer to exploit the home market without hindrance. The idea is that it would be able to lower average costs to such an extent as to become competitive on the international market. In part, many Eastern European countries applied this model when they started to develop their automobile production. In one way or another, access to the home market was temporarily restricted to help the domestic production. Ukraine too, used this approach when attracting the car producer, Daewoo. Unfortunately this venture failed very quickly despite the granted privileges. Privileges, such as tariff barriers to deter competitors, tax holidays or cash subsidies to firms in order to develop and utilise cost advantages are prone to be misused. This is particularly true in a regulated economy, such as the Ukrainian. The returns of any industrial policy here are greatly reduced because of rent seeking, corruption, and asset-stripping work against the intended purpose.

The second important link between trade and modern technology is foreign direct investments (FDI). FDI was involved in all domestic automobile production projects in Eastern Europe. Large amounts of foreign investment flowed into the EE-4 economies, upgrading equipment and improving productivity. By contrast, FDI in Ukraine still is meagre. Thus, no technological improvements can be expected from this source. Rare projects, such as 'sea launch' or a European-Ukrainian-Russian co-operation on the basis of the AN70, are in their early stages or are not even decided yet. Technological co-operation is much more demanding and generally much more long-term than the joint production for normal goods. Therefore, if the prerequisites do not even exist for normal goods, FDI with a high technology content will be so much less likely. Not many companies would employ an excellent and creative engineer, but who is unreliable. The same is true for countries: The skilful manpower available in Ukraine is unlikely to be tapped as long as legal, economic and political impediments deter FDI.

Experience in Eastern Europe shows that the pattern for improvement of the export structure is to gradually climb up the technology ladder rather than jump to the upper end immediately. A trend towards more sophisticated skill-intensive products for exports can be observed in most advanced transition countries. In this respect, Hungary is clearly leading, while Poland's exports still remain more labour-intensive. The structure of FDI helps to understand the differences in the Hungarian and Polish experience. FDI in Hungary produces to a large extent for the demanding Western export markets using the cheap and skilled Hungarian labour available, whereas FDI in Poland aims more at the Polish domestic market.

However, there is a danger that if the upgrading of industrial exports takes too much time, the initial advantages of the skill endowment get lost. Human capital quickly becomes obsolete if it is not applied. This danger is real in Ukraine, where the movement of the highly skilled labour force toward low-skill jobs is still ongoing.

4 Trade policy, past and future

Since March 1998, the Partnership and Co-operation Agreement (PCA) between Ukraine and Europe is in force. Over the past several years Ukraine has also worked towards WTO accession, although these efforts came almost to a stand-still in the last two years. Evidently, Ukraine does not yet fulfil all Articles of the PCA. Violations include preferential treatment of single investors, problems with product certification, as well as the imposition of export duties and sporadic increases of tariffs. As described above, the transformation of Ukraine to a market economy is slow and cumbersome, and still does not provide a level playing field for all enterprises. In an economy with such a high degree of non-transparency, insufficient bookkeeping and distorted pricing, it is difficult to assess the adherence to the rules of free trade.

The new Yushchenko Government promised to change this unsatisfactory situation. Under the heading 'strategic objectives', the government programme till 2004 ("Reforms for Prosperity") states: "The main task in the current phase is to build a suitable base for full membership of Ukraine in the EU and for the development of a pro-European majority in the society." To this end Ukraine will try "to become member of the WTO, to start the co-operation with EFTA, to start negotiations about a free trade zone with the EU, and to get the status of a market economy from the European Commission."

The EU is at this time not prepared to speak about Ukrainian membership. But there are several issues beyond the PCA, but short of a full EU membership, which could improve Ukrainian access to the EU market:

The treatment of Ukraine as a market economy in anti-dumping cases. At the moment, third country production cost evaluations are still used to assess dumping claims. Although Ukraine is plagued by price distortions in several areas, their frequency is probably no higher than market price deviations experienced in

Russia or China, which have already received the status of a market economies from the EU.

Despite the PCA, special agreements for import quotas for textiles and steel still exist between the EU and Ukraine, which quantitatively limit access to the EU market. Both branches are extremely important for Ukrainian exports.

In those area, which are classified by the EU as highly sensitive (textile, agriculture, iron and steel) the most favoured nations (MFN) tariffs were only reduced by 15%. For other important agricultural products as well as for products related to steel and coal, no tariff preferences were granted within the general preference system (GPS) scheme, either. Thus here too is room for concessions by the EU.

In short, the relations between the EU and Ukraine might move from a non-preferential agreement to a preferential one. Further concessions could be granted once the reform measures are in place and working in Ukraine. In the long run a free trade arrangement may be possible. But this would of course also imply more foreign competition within Ukraine, for which many domestic producers are not yet ready. Experience has shown that trade adjustments in many Central and Eastern European countries were instituted before the provisions of the free trade agreements with the EU were fully implemented.[4] In contrast with these countries, Ukrainian exports to the EU are still quite different from the average EU-import structure. Thus, there seems to be a high EU-Ukraine trade potential, even if one acknowledges the still existing trade restrictions. The realisation of this potential will very much depend on the progress of future reforms in the domestic economy.

In organising its foreign trade Ukraine needs always to be aware of its trading partners in the East, especially Russia, which, same as Ukraine, is still not a member of the WTO. Trade relations between both countries are murky, although formally a free trade arrangement is in place. Russia and other CIS states will remain important trading partners of Ukraine, if only to prevent the deterioration of the cross-border production relations inherited from the past. Geographical proximity is another factor in favour of tight trade relations, which will improve trade once the Russian economy begins to grow. But far-reaching preferential trade arrangements with the eastern neighbours, such as a payment Union[5], are less convincing. The more the CIS countries develop towards market economies, the less any single competitor, such as Ukraine, would be treated preferentially. There is no reason to assume that competition among CIS countries would be less than among Western market economies, once the bureaucratic and administrative obstacles are removed. That these markets are less demanding in terms of product quality and/or technology is at best a temporary advantage. In terms of technology transfer and opportunities arising from outsourcing, the eastern trade area is

4 Brenton (1999), p. 22.

5 The latest suggestion of this kind is by Sapir (2000).

clearly inferior to a westward orientation. Of course, the opportunities for trade within the East too, are comparative advantages in technology and factor endowment. But in this respect the Eastern countries are much more similar to each other. That means competition on the basis of low wages would be even harder. From a sales point of view is obvious that for a long time yet, the size of the western markets will exceed those in the East several times. All this suggests that Ukraine would likely experience a loss in trade growth if it would one-sidedly favour trade with the East.

References

Blandinieres, Jean-Paul (2000): Does One Swallow Make the Summer? UEPLAC-Paper, Kyiv

Brenton, Paul (1999): Analysis of Trade and Production Structures in Ukraine and the EU: Implications for a Trade Agreement. Study for the European Commission, September 9, mimeo

Brenton, Paul and Thomas Vernon (1999): Foreign Direct Investment, Technology Transfer and Economic Growth in Ukraine. Study for the European Commission, August 27, mimeo

CEPR (1990): Monitoring European Integration. The Impact of Eastern Europe, London

ECE (1990): Economic Survey of Europe 1989-1990. New York

German Advisory Group on Economic Reforms in Ukraine (2000): Wachstum in der Ukraine – Ursachen und wirtschaftspolitische Konsequenzen. Kyiv, April, mimeo

Quaisser, Wolfgang (1999): Außenhandelsentwicklung und Wettbewerbsposition der Ukraine im Handel mit der Europäischen Union. Study for the German Advisory Group on Economic Reforms in Ukraine, Kyiv, mimeo

Sapir, Jacques (2000): Developing Ukrainian Trade. Advantages of Regional Payments Union. UEPLAC-Paper, Kyiv

8

Infrastructure as an Instrument of National and Regional Development Policy in the European Union and Ukraine

Dieter Biehl

1 Introduction

The present Chapter is based on the thesis that infrastructure represents the public part of an overall capital stock that is indispensable for economic growth and sustainable development, particularly at the regional level.[1] Roads, rails, waterways, harbours, airports, telecommunication systems, energy production and distribution systems, piped water supply, sanitation and sewerage, but also education, training and research facilities from the pre-school through the university level, libraries, museums, theatres, hospitals and sports facilities are examples. That these types of facilities – though the term 'infrastructure' has been coined only after the second World War – play an important role for development and growth has often been affirmed in the literature by generations of economists from mercantilist times through the classical period up to Keynesian ones.[2]

However, quantitative econometric support for this thesis seems to have been produced since the seventies only. Since then, there exist a number of studies that shows a more or less strong correlation between infrastructure or public capital and productivity or income per capita.[3] However, some doubts still seem to remain as to whether infrastructure is the *cause* of productivity and income or their *consequence*.

I shall argue in this paper that – like in the well-known chicken and egg paradigm – both relationships are relevant, but that this does not invalidate the argument that infrastructure has to be conceived as public capital contributing to outputs similar

1 See Biehl (1975), (1986) and (1991).

2 See literature cited later on.

3 See Munnell (1990) and World Bank (1994) and the studies listed there.

to private capital. In addition, the case will be made that given the 'public' nature of infrastructure, other resources with a high degree of 'publicness' and 'capitalness', such as geographical location of a region, its agglomeration and settlement structure, and its sectoral structure, also contribute to regional productivity, income and employment. Similar arguments have been presented in the large body of literature dealing with regional development. I have called this conceptual approach the 'Potentiality Factor Approach' (PFA) and its econometrically tested version a 'Quasi-Production Function Approach' (QPFA) since it extends the well-known concept of a production function by including additional factors. Some results which have been obtained with this QPFA for regions of the European Community will be summarised in this chapter and compared with results of other studies.

In the last part of this paper, a brief overview of an ongoing research project will be given, that attempts to apply the QPFA to Ukrainian regions. The first part of this project consisted in investigating whether appropriate data are available for the Ukrainian regions, which could be compared with data from EU countries, so that they could later on be integrated into a European QPFA. Despite the difficulties with data collection for Ukraine, the first results of this project are encouraging.

2 The Regional Development Potential Approach, its bases and its main elements

The central thesis of the 'Regional Development Potential Approach' (RDPA) is that a class of resources exists that determines the development potential of a region.[4] The common characteristic of these potentiality factors is their high degree of public good properties or 'publicness'. In addition to the general institutional and socio-cultural natural resource endowment framework, those potentiality factors are geographical location, agglomeration and settlement structure, sectoral economic structure and infrastructure or public[5] capital. The particular importance of infrastructure stems from the fact that compared with the other potentiality factors and with private capital, it can be used as a direct strategy or policy instrument.

---

4 One could even argue that what is called 'comparative advantage' in the Heckscher/Ohlin theory of international and interregional trade is to a large extent determined by these potentiality factors, in particular by infrastructure. Ohlin speaks of 'specific factors' determining comparative advantage (cf. Bertil Ohlin , 1993).

5 'Public' is used here in the sense of the theory of 'public' goods; see below.

Infrastructure is sometimes defined in a narrow way and restricted to what is assumed to be directly productive or productivity oriented categories of public capital like transportation, telecommunication, energy and water, sometimes the definition is broader and comprises also educational, cultural and social facilities.[6]

Given the still existing doubts, the argument that there exists such a class of resources and that infrastructure in particular, is one of its main elements, justifies some general remarks.

As already noted, one of the basic questions is whether infrastructure represents a *cause* of output or productivity or rather the *consequence*. This is like the old chicken-and-egg paradigm. I think that both relationships are relevant – without eggs, there will be no chicken, and without chickens, no eggs. However, this does not invalidate the argument that infrastructure has to be conceived as an input needed in order to produce outputs independently of the question where the investments required to create these facilities are coming from.

It is obvious that you will never be able to maintain or to increase the number of your chickens if you eat or destroy all the eggs they produce. On the contrary, in the long run the chickens will die so that both the numbers of chickens and of eggs will fall to zero. Hence, there is general consensus in the economic community, that growth and development require savings and investment. Restricting consumption and saving some resources for future consumption is one of the basic lessons we all had to learn, living under the *cold star of scarcity* or on *spaceship earth.*

What is often forgotten is that this is the same type of argument on which the traditional theory of private capital is based, too. The astonishing experience is that not all economists who are convinced that private capital matters, are also ready to extend this idea to *all* forms of capital – private and public ones, narrowly and largely defined, material and immaterial ones.

Take for example the so-called crowding-out thesis, which can be found in many textbooks. Its essence is that debt financed public expenditure increases market interest rates that in turn 'crowd-out' private investment, and as a consequence reduce the capital stock and hence growth. However, since the overall capital stock consists not only of private, but also of public capital assets and since these assets differ from private ones, the implication is that there is something like an optimal structure of the overall capital stock.

---

6 The Report of the Infrastructure Study Group of the European Commission chaired by myself, "The Contribution of Infrastructure to Regional Development", of 1986 is based on a larger definition including educational, health, social and cultural facilities, whereas Biehl (1991) uses a smaller set of productivity oriented infrastructure categories. In its "World Development Report (1994): Infrastructure for Development", the World Bank also applies a narrow definition.

From the point of view of the extended notion of capital, the crowding-out thesis remains valid only in the case where this optimal ratio is exceeded by an excessively high a share of public capital. In this case, the marginal rate of return of private capital is higher than of the public one, and hence the net effect of increased public and decreased private investment is negative. If, however, the share of public capital is below the optimum range, the same logic implies that additional investment in public capital will increase growth despite crowding-out private investment. This time, the marginal return of public investment is higher than of the private one.

Whereas the terms public capital and infrastructure are relatively recent ones, the phenomenon as such has attracted the attention of many generations of economists, be it mercantilists, classical economists or Keynesian ones. More recently, in the late 50ies, authors like Hirschman (1958) developed the notion of 'social overhead capital'. Many others, in particular German authors, dealt intensively with the infrastructure issue in the sixties and seventies.[7] Whereas much of this literature remained conceptual and descriptive, Mera (1973) seems to have been the first to apply a production function approach and regression analysis in order to quantify the contribution of public capital to regional development in Japan. In Biehl (1975), an extended 'Quasi-Production Function Approach' (QPFA) for German regions was developed and tested.[8]

Renewed interest in the infrastructure issue can be observed during the second half of the eighties. In 1986, a two volume report, prepared by a European group of authors, chaired by myself and based on the QPFA, was published by the European Commission (Biehl, 1986), entitled "The Contribution of Infrastructure to Regional Development". This report demonstrated that there are a large number of modified Cobb-Douglas production functions and QPFAs that are statistically significant, and that support the thesis that infrastructure significantly contributes to regional productivity, income and employment. Starting towards the end of the eighties, a range of papers on the public capital issue appeared in the United States, in particular Aschauer (1989, 1990) and Munnell (1990, 1993). In 1994, The World Bank devoted its "Development Report 1994" to the infrastructure issue, asserting, however, in one place that the evidence for the causal effect of infrastructure is not yet convincing, despite the fact that only one of the 14 studies listed did not find significant econometric support.[9]

---

7 See e.g. Stohler (1965), Jochimsen (1966), Frey (1969).

8 This extended approach that includes geographical location, agglomeration and sectoral structure owes much to Johansen (1968) and Richardson (1974).

9 See World Bank (1994), Executive Summary, p. 14. Of the 14 studies cited here (among them no European ones), only one study by Holtz-Eakin (1992) is reported not to have found a significant correlation. In addition, this statement on p. 14 is not consistent with the general line of reasoning in the main part of the Report where it is argued e.g. that "good infrastructure raises productivity and lowers production cost" (p. 2). The reader may be wondering why one should make infrastructure investments

In the optimal capital stock paradigm, the notion of 'public' capital has a special meaning. A capital asset is a 'public' one, if it possesses a strong public good character or 'publicness' compared with the opposite 'privateness' property of a typical private good.[10]

Publicness implies *non-rivalries* and *non-excludability* (Musgrave, 1959).[11] A public capital good is non-rival if its capacity can be used by a large number of users without reciprocal crowding-out; and the marginal cost of an additional user up to the capacity limit is zero. Non-rivalries can be characterised by *immobility, indivisibility, non-substitutability* and *polyvalence* as opposed to *mobility, divisibility, substitutability* and *monovalence* or specialisation, the typical properties of private goods.

Non-excludability means that the cost of excluding an (additional) user is very (prohibitively) high so that exclusion in the extreme case of a pure public good is impossible. Exclusion costs include the cost for property rights and regulation together with their institutional control and sanctions on the one hand, and of exclusion technologies (e.g. toll stations and electronic devices on highways; water meters; ticket counters cashing entrance fees in museums) on the other. The consequence of a very high degree of 'publicness' is that the market fails in providing the optimal level of public capital since a private investor will not be able to obtain an adequate return for his investment.

The notion of cost has to be a broad one, comprising not only resource cost as a determinant of efficiency, but also *external* or *preference cost* perceived by political actors and voters in political decision-making (Buchanan and Tullock, 1962; Biehl, 1996).

Many types of infrastructure have important distributional effects that can be considered to be a part of the preference cost. In many countries, primary schools are public ones and require no fees; in others where they are private, where the school fees may not cover the full cost. Very often, the idea prevails that education, as a process that endows children with human capital, should not be reduced entirely to private investment decisions – in particular in poor countries where too large a proportion of the children would then be excluded from education.

---

and improve its efficiency – in particular through foreign aid in developing countries – if there is no theoretical basis for expecting positive outputs and welfare effects.

10 The issue of public goods as opposed to private ones has by now been dealt with extensively in the literature. For instance, Andel (2000) cites Adolph Wagner (1893) and Gustav Cassel (1925) who had already presented a description of the publicness issue before Paul A. Samuelson (1954) and Richard A. Musgrave (1959) presented their modern versions.

11 Musgrave, Richard A. (1959): The Theory of Public Finance. New York, pp. 8-11.

These cost aspects, however, have to be combined with the benefits that can be obtained from using the bundles of services incorporated in infrastructure capacities. They also are a function of publicness; the higher the degree of publicness, the larger the service bundle. For instance, whenever a network infrastructure capacity is increased in order to (better) connect a city with other urban centres and their hinterland, the costs are relatively high since it is not possible to add small marginal increments. But the addition to capacity is also large. Due in particular to immobility and indivisibility, a region with a large infrastructure capacity in relation to its area and inhabitants can also provide a larger bundle of services to its enterprises and private households than a less well endowed one. It is the sum of all these service bundles incorporated into the fixed infrastructure capacities that represents one of the factors determining the development potential of the region concerned.

In the real world, there exists a large body of different degrees of publicness. In general, network type infrastructure (like roads, telecommunication and energy distribution systems), due in particular to their high indivisibility, possess higher publicness and accordingly higher cost than point type infrastructure (airports, power stations, schools, local waste collection). Compared with infrastructure, private capital in the form of enterprise buildings, equipment and knowledge possesses a much lower degree of publicness and a correspondingly higher degree of privateness. In general, it can, therefore, not be considered to represent a determinant of the regional development potential. Due in particular to its higher mobility, divisibility and substitutability, it can much more easily 'emigrate' out of a region (or not immigrate). It is, however, – together with labour as the other important private production factor – indispensable in order to exploit the public service bundles incorporated in the potentiality factors.

The publicness characteristic of infrastructure also has important implications for privatisation. The major implication is that capital assets with a low degree of publicness can be more easily privatised than those with a high one. Compared with network type infrastructure, point type infrastructure, in particular local or regional public goods (e.g. primary schools, waste collection, libraries) possess a much lower degree of publicness. During the last decades, in many countries special and tailor-made solutions have been developed for these infrastructure assets, some of them with positive, others with negative results.[12]

Also, with increased publicness the institutional and public transaction cost increase. The government has to carefully design new property and regulation rights in order to prevent that a former public monopoly will become a profit-maximising private one with higher prices.[13] In addition, in particular in the

12 See the summaries of experiences in different countries in World Bank (1994).

13 One of the examples is the continuing debate in the UK as to the high profits and the high prices of the privatised former waterboards.

tradition of the European welfare state, there will be pressure to increase social transfers if prices of essential services are going up too much due to privatisation.

In summarising the preceding arguments, the following categories of resources can be considered to possess a high degree of publicness. They therefore determine the regional development potential:

- the constitutional-institutional framework of a region as a part of the respective national system;
- the socio-psychological values and preference framework of the population of a country or region;
- the natural resource endowment including climatic conditions.

These three factors represent the framework for the potentiality factors in a narrow meaning:

- the geographical location of a region and its economic distances to other regions in terms of transport and communication costs;
- agglomeration and settlement structures, i.e. the degree of spatial concentration of population and economic activities and its structural patterns;
- sectoral structure, i.e. the relationship between the three main sectors of an economy (agriculture, industry, services); and, last but not least,
- the regional infrastructure endowment or the stock of public capital of a region.

From a long-run point of view, the basic proposition of the RDPA is that productivity, income or employment of a region are the higher, the better its endowment with these potentiality factors or 'publicness' resources.

In order to transform potential into actual productivity, income and employment, the existing potentiality factors as already mentioned have to be combined with the appropriate quantities and qualities of the private production factors labour and capital. With such an optimal combination of potentiality and production factors, output can be maximised.

A given RDP can then be said to be under-utilised (over-utilised) if the private factor inputs are below (beyond) this optimum with the consequence that actual productivity, employment, and income per inhabitant are lower (higher), too. Positive and negative externalities, e.g. due to over-agglomeration, pollution, noise, and stress, can also be a cause that potential and actual figures do not necessarily coincide.

Graph 8.1
The Regional Development Potential Approach: Relationship between potentiality factor endowment, potential productivity and labour costs

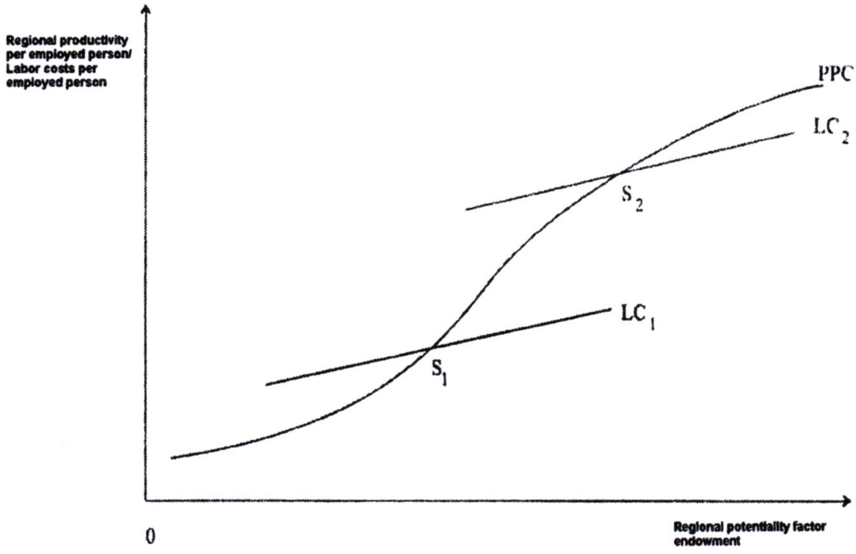

Graph 8.1 illustrates the basic proposition of the RDPA in relation to productivity: The better the endowment of a region with potentiality factors, the higher potential productivity, as reflected in curve PPC. LC1 and LC2 represent the labour cost of two countries, where the regions of country 1 have both low potentiality factor endowments and low labour costs, whereas the regions of the second country are characterised by both high resource endowments and high labour costs. As the labour cost functions in both countries are less steep than the productivity function PPC, there are regions on the left-hand side of the points of intersection S1 and S2 where labour costs are higher compared with potential productivity. As a consequence, in these regions – other things being equal – employment and income per inhabitant are lower, unemployment and/or out-migration higher than in the regions on the right-hand side of S1 and S2. Due to the higher productivity/labour cost ratio in the latter regions, they will have higher employment and higher income per capita, and in addition, lower unemployment and/or higher immigration. Accordingly, the first group of regions will show under-utilisation and the second group over-utilisation of their RDP.

3 The special role of infrastructure as a potentiality factor

Among the four potentiality factors location, agglomeration, sectoral structure, and infrastructure, only infrastructure has a strong 'strategy and policy instrument' character. It can be used by the government in order to directly influence the RDP either by increasing productivity or by decreasing cost. Infrastructure has to be conceived as a broad notion that comprises a large number of public capital stock elements:

- With the aid of transportation infrastructure (rail, road, airports, waterways, harbours) the cost for transporting products or persons can be reduced;
- Telecommunication lowers information cost;
- Energy is needed for producing and consuming goods and services, thus electricity power plants and distribution networks as well as gas and oil pipelines are other important elements of directly productive infrastructure;
- The education and research system produces both public and private human capital. 'Public' human capital represents that part of our knowledge that, once produced (e.g. through basic research), is available at zero or very low cost to anybody who wishes to use it. 'Private' human capital consists of the skills and capabilities transferred through education and professional training to children, women and men who use it in order to produce goods and services and to improve the quality of their own private consumption. Besides 'learning by doing', human capital is normally produced with the aid of the public education system, ranging from primary schools over secondary schools up to professional schools and universities. Similarly, 'public' knowledge is produced and transferred by science and engineering faculties, laboratories, research institutes, computer centres and technology transfer agencies.

Transportation, telecommunication, energy, and education infrastructure can be considered to directly contribute to productivity increase or to cost reduction.[14] Other infrastructure categories also exert a positive, but more indirect influence on productivity, income and employment: water supply, environmental infrastructure (waste deposits, incinerators, recycling centres), social infrastructure (hospitals, rehabilitation centres, homes for elderly people, kindergarten), sport and leisure facilities, cultural infrastructure (museums, libraries, theatres, concert halls, congress centres). Last but not least, natural landscape characteristics like rivers,

---

14 This reduced set of infrastructure categories is the basis for the more recent analyses in Biehl (1995).

lakes, forests can also be considered to represent quasi-infrastructure resources with high degrees of publicness.[15]

Despite the fact that infrastructure is a powerful policy instrument, an isolated infrastructure strategy is unreasonable. Firstly, as already explained, infrastructure is but one of the determinants of RDP, other potentiality factors must not be neglected. Secondly, the potentiality factor capacities must always be combined with the appropriate quantitative and qualitative inputs of labour and private capital in order to exploit their capacities. And thirdly, an optimal use of these capacities depends on favourable constitutional-institutional and behavioural conditions. If these conditions are not taken into account isolated infrastructure policies will normally be only partially successful.

This is not only a theoretical argument, but is supported by practical experiences in many countries and regions. Governments have often tried to transform a backward region with low growth into a fast growing one through massive infrastructure investments, in particular highways or waterways. But, if a new highway is built, this does not only reduce transportation cost in favour of the enterprises already located in the region concerned, but also acts like a reduction in interregional tariffs that previously restricted the access of enterprises form other regions. Efficient producers outside the backward regions also profit from the new or improved road, rail or waterway, allowing them to extend their markets. As a consequence, competitive pressures on the producers in the backward regions are increased. And as underdevelopment in general is due to too low a degree of competitiveness of the existing regional enterprises, an isolated project like a highway could in the end even undermine the competitive position of local enterprises.

A successful regional development strategy will have to be a comprehensive one, taking into account not only infrastructure, but also the other potentiality factors location, agglomeration and sectoral structure, as well as the private production factors labour and capital. A first analysis can be supplemented by a second one trying to identify serious bottlenecks that restrict the development of the region concerned. Where such bottlenecks exist, it is reasonable to concentrate on removing them with new investment.

Given this background, the RDPA provides a good basis for designing regional development strategies. They have to be region-specific in order to be able to take account of the strengths and weaknesses of an individual region. Since infrastructure is the only direct development instrument available to government, the following discussion will concentrate on this resource, but will consider this instrument in the framework of the other potentiality factors.

---

15 This larger list of infrastructure categories has been used in Biehl (1986).

4 Quantification of infrastructure capacities

4.1 The general approach

As explained, according to the RDPA the potentiality factors are the basic determinants of the regional productive capacity. They can, therefore, be considered to represent the 'inputs' in a sort of enlarged production function with the 'outputs' being productivity, income or employment. Such a function is called a 'Quasi-Production Function' (QPF) in order to distinguish it from the traditional production function approach with labour and private capital as inputs.

Both types of production functions imply that all inputs and outputs can be quantified and that the appropriate data are available. As to the traditional production function approach, this requires to measure the capital stock in monetary terms. Although this information is available in many developed countries for national totals, it does not always exist on the regional level. It does not exist at all for most developing and transition countries. In order to be able to apply the RDPA to as many countries as possible, it appears reasonable to measure the regional infrastructure endowment in physical or technical capacity terms. The basic methodological philosophy is that first, a very crude and simple indicator has to be tried in order to see if it provides a statistically significant explanation. If this is the case, it may be worthwhile later on to invest more time and effort in improving the capacity definition and in collecting more differentiated indicators including monetary aggregates for capital assets.

For instance, considering the potentiality factor *agglomeration*, the simplest and easiest way to measure it is to calculate population density. However, this indicator does not only reflect the spatial concentration of population as such, but also many other aspects linked with this spatial concentration, e.g. the localisation of private enterprises and of jobs.

Given the importance of *infrastructure* as a policy instrument, the information requirements have not been limited to this item only. The guiding idea was to identify in principle two major characteristics that can be considered to represent all *crucial bottleneck elements* of a specific category, a quantitative and a qualitative one. Taking roads as an example, their lengths have been selected as the quantitative, and their widths as the qualitative elements, after discussions with experts. Width can be considered to represent a major quality aspect since 100 kilometres of a wide highway represents a much larger transportation potential than the same length of a narrow local road. Multiplying length and width yields the surface of roads that in turn is related to the area of a region in order to obtain an indicator for regional road density. This was also followed for other network types which are related to area whereas point infrastructures (e.g. airports or universities) are related to the regional populations they serve.

The same methodology has been applied to other infrastructure categories:

- In the case of airports, the runways have been identified as the most critical bottleneck characteristic. Given the point character of airports, the runway surfaces have been divided by the regional population.
- Regarding telecommunication, the technical capacity of a cable could be measured in terms of the number of double-wire elements or in terms of optical fibre channels. However, this information is hardly ever available in a regionalised form so that second-best information has to be used. This is for instance the number of subscribers or the numbers of telephones. If a region has a high number of subscribers or telephones, then a corresponding cable network and an appropriate number of telephone exchanges must exist, too.[16]
- In the case of education, a good indicator would be the capacity of buildings in cubic metres or floor space in square metres. However, it proved to be almost impossible to obtain this information for all EU-regions. As a proxy indicator the number of students in various age groups in relation to the population has been chosen.

4.2 Definition and calculation of the infrastructure indicators retained

The original list of infrastructure categories considered in the EC-study (Biehl, 1986) for the two cross-section years 1970 and 1980 covering all ten – later on the then twelve EC member states – was based on the already mentioned comprehensive infrastructure definition and comprised 12 main categories and 27 subcategories. The main categories were transportation, telecommunication, energy supply, water distribution, environmental infrastructure, education infrastructure, health infrastructure, tourism and sports infrastructure, social infrastructure, cultural infrastructure and 'natural infrastructure'. Subcategories e.g. for transportation were roads, railways, waterways, airports and harbours.

This 1986 list of infrastructure categories, however, comprises two different groups of infrastructure, i.e. one group that could be considered to directly reduce cost or increase productivity of private production, and another group that is more relevant for the satisfaction of consumer demands, but that also influences the attractiveness of a location for enterprises, qualified labour and consumer households. In addition, it proved to be very difficult to obtain comparable capacity information for all EC regions, e.g. on environmental infrastructure, water supply, cultural infrastructure (theatres, museums, libraries) or social

---

16 In future, however, with an increasing numbers of mobile cellular phones based on radio transmission, the importance of the cable networks will presumably be reduced due to their indivisibility.

infrastructure (kindergarten, homes for children, old age homes). Very often only the number of facilities, but no information as to their capacities was available.

For the later cross-section analysis for 1985, it was, therefore, decided to concentrate on those infrastructure categories that can be considered to be more or less directly productive. The following categories were identified: *transportation, telecommunication, energy* and *education*, the latter insofar as it contributes to professional qualifications (cf. Biehl, 1991; Biehl and Ungar, 1991).

These four main categories include the following subcategories:

- Transportation: roads, railways, waterways, airports, harbours;
- Telecommunication: telephones, telex;
- Energy: electricity generating stations, high voltage electricity distribution networks, gas pipelines, oil refineries and oil pipelines;
- Education: institutions that issue certificates that are relevant to the labour market, i.e. secondary level professional schools, professional high schools, and universities.

The empirical analysis presented in this paper for the EC/EU regions is based on these 4 main and 13 subcategories of infrastructure for the mid-eighties. Since – like in the previous studies – the intention was to calculate a total infrastructure indicator as well, the indicators for these infrastructure categories had to be aggregated. This implied standardisation and normalisation of these indicators in order to get rid of the different dimensions involved like for instance road surface, rail track kilometrage, and the number of students. This has been done using the following approach:[17]

1. Depending upon whether an individual infrastructure category is of the network or point type, the absolute capacity information for each category is either divided by regional area or regional population. All infrastructures with network characteristics are classified as being space-serving (e.g. roads or electricity distribution systems), all those with point characteristics (e.g. airports, schools) as population-serving. In some cases, additional quality information is used in order to obtain weights for some subcategories. (Thus, electrified railway tracks have been weighted by 1.5 (single track) compared with 1 for non-electrified single track lines, and by 3 for double tracks. In the case of energy transmission lines, the relation between the voltage figures served as weights).
2. The indicators so obtained for every category and region are divided by the maximal ratio, i.e. the indicator for the best equipped region for each

17 A more detailed presentation will be found in Biehl (1986).

infrastructure subcategory. This yields a data series ranging from 100 (best equipped region) to close to zero (zero being a region without any equipment).

3. These normalised indicators for each infrastructure subcategory are then aggregated by calculating their arithmetic mean in order to obtain an indicator for the respective main category (e.g. transportation). These main category indicators are again divided by their maximal regional values.

4. The main indicators are then aggregated with the aid of a geometric mean in order to obtain the overall productivity-oriented infrastructure indicator, again expressed in per cent of the best equipped region.

The reasoning for choosing the arithmetic mean in order to aggregate sub-indicators and the geometric mean for aggregating the main category indicators is as follows:

- The arithmetic mean implies that all infrastructure capacity units are fully substitutable. For instance if the road infrastructure for Region A is 3 units higher (+3) and the one for rail 3 units lower (-3), all other things being equal, then the two effects can be considered to cancel each other out, and Region A will have the same average indicator value as Region B where both indicators are (assumed to be) identical. In this case, the degree of substitution can be said to be equal to 1.

- The geometric mean reacts progressively to differences between indicators. The larger the difference between two indicators, the lower will be the geometric mean compared with the arithmetic one. This implies a degree of substitution that decreases progressively with increasing indicator differences.

An alternative solution would have been to assume total non-substitutability between the main infrastructure categories. Under this assumption, the main category with the lowest capacity indicator would have been considered to be the bottleneck factor restricting regional development. Excess capacities that existed for the other three main categories could then not compensate for the deficit of the bottleneck category. Such a procedure, however, would exaggerate the importance of the bottleneck characteristic. Compared with this alternative, the procedure chosen to aggregate the four main category indicators with the aid of a geometrical mean is a less extreme assumption. It allows a certain, but decreasing substitution of a category that is in low supply by the excess capacities of another main category that is in higher supply.

In the EC-study of 1986, the full list of infrastructure categories had been used. In addition, Quasi-Production Functions had been estimated on the basis of the RDPA. Since the proposition is that the endowment with these resources or potentiality factors determines potential income, productivity and employment, we attempt to explain their interregional disparities with the RDPA. The multiple regression functions so obtained have been used in order to estimate productivity per employed person, income per capita, income density and employment for the regions of the 10 EU member countries of 1980 (see Biehl, 1986).

These studies were continued and a new cross sectional database has been created for the mid-eighties (about 1985) covering the former EC 10 plus Portugal and Spain. In addition, data for the infrastructure endowment of the 14 districts of the former German Democratic Republic were collected as well (see Biehl and Ungar, 1991). However, it has so far not been possible to include these East-German data in the econometric estimations of QPFs as no regional gross value-added figures are available. The East-German data could, therefore, only be used in order to calculate comparable infrastructure indicators for the former 14 GDR districts, and for Germany as a whole, and to integrate them into the EU-infrastructure data set.

Table 8.1 (see end of this Chapter) shows the infrastructure endowment of 153 EU regions in 1985. Despite the fact that in 1985, East Germany did not yet belong to the EU, Biehl and Ungar collected information on the infrastructure endowment of the then 14 districts of the GDR in 1990/91, i.e. after the German unification, in order to integrate them with data for the regions of the EC12 in the mid-eighties. The regions are ranked according to the value of the total infrastructure indicator INFRATOT. The best equipped region is Hamburg/Germany equal to 100. All other regions are expressed in per cent of Hamburg.

According to Table 8.1, three Greek regions have the lowest endowment with only 5.3%, 6.5% and 6.8% of Hamburg. Furthermore, infrastructure endowment of most of the East German districts is very low and some, such as Schwerin (10.8%), Neubrandenburg (11.2%) and Suhl (12.0%) are very close to some of the backward regions in southern Europe. Of the full range of 100, Germany covers almost 90 percentage points whereas the spread for EC12 as a whole is only 5 percentage points larger. Also, the quality of the East-German infrastructure seems to have been below the European average.[18]

It is plausible to assume that between 1985 and 1989, the year of German unification, the relative position of the East-German districts had not improved significantly, given the economic problems in East Germany during that period. As this information had not been available prior to issuance of the study of Biehl and Ungar in 1991, it is not surprising that at the start of German unification, the cost of improving the infrastructure endowment in the New Länder had been drastically underestimated. In the meantime, hundreds of billions of DM have been invested and today the relative position of the New Länder is certainly substantially better. Unfortunately, a new cross section analysis for 1995 is not yet finished so that more recent data are not available so far.

---

[18] See Biehl and Ungar (1991).

5 Results of the Quasi-Production Function Approach for EU-regions in 1985

Following the RDPA, in addition to the aggregated infrastructure indicator, the already mentioned indicators for location, agglomeration and sectoral structure, plus a so-called dummy-variable, which indirectly tests the influence of the general framework conditions for all regions of the same EU-member country, are used as exogenous variables. As no gross value-added figures existed for the East-German districts in 1985, they were excluded from the analysis. The number of regions was, therefore, reduced to 139.

Let us begin with the potentiality factor infrastructure and its contribution to regional productivity, income, income density, and employment. The usual procedure is to specify the full set of explanatory variables according to the theory to be tested, in our case the RDPA. However, I think it may also be interesting to present the results of the different estimations by starting with a single regression equation, containing infrastructure as the only explicitly explanatory variable, and then stepwise add the other potentiality factors. This stepwise procedure allows one to follow the changes of the regression coefficients for infrastructure, if infrastructure is so speak exposed to an increasing competition of these other exogenous variables as far as the explanation of the endogenous variables productivity, income and employment is concerned.

All regression functions are of the double-logarithmic type so that the regression coefficients represent elasticities. This allows us to interpret the coefficients in the following way: For instance, if the coefficient is 0.20, a 1% increase in infrastructure endowment would cause an increase of 0.20% in, for instance, potential productivity per employed person.

For the single variable regressions, where infrastructure is the only 'input' in order to explain the 'output', high regression coefficients for infrastructure can be expected. The reason is that infrastructure as the only explicitly specified explanatory variable, will – due to some inevitable correlations with the other potentiality factors – 'attract' a part of the explanation that, according to the RDPA, is to be attributed to these other correlated potentiality factors. As they are not explicitly present in the equations to be estimated, the high regression coefficients of infrastructure are biased due to mis-specification and tend, therefore, to exaggerate its contribution. They are nevertheless shown for illustration purposes. Adding step by step the other exogenous variables will then in general lower the contribution of infrastructure to the dependent variable, as the added explanatory variable(s) will take over some of the explanation previously attributed to infrastructure.

The analysis starts with a single variable regression function, using only infrastructure, and ends with multiple regression functions including the other potentiality factors location, agglomeration and sectoral structure. As already mentioned, the equations to be tested are called 'Quasi-Production Functions' (QPF) since they are based on the same basic idea that underlies traditional production function philosophy. However, QPFs only consider resources with a high degree of publicness as exogenous variables. This excludes private capital and labour as explicit variables from the equations, but not as production factors that need to be combined with the potentiality factors in order to transform potential productivity, income or employment into actual values. If an equation contains all potentiality factors, it is called a 'Fully Specified Quasi-Production Function' (FQPF).

In addition, country dummies are introduced in order to test for country-specific positive or negative framework effects of the overall constitutional-institutional framework, behavioural attitudes, the possible influences of (distorted) exchange rates, and other socio-economic factors. The hypothesis is that in two countries with the same potentiality factor endowment, regional productivity, employment or income will be higher in the country with 'good' overall framework conditions and lower in one where these framework conditions are less favourable. In the first case, the expected sign of the dummy is positive, in the second case negative.

The general form of such a FQPF is as follows:

$$RDP = f(I, L, A, S, D),$$

where *RDP* represents the regional development potential as the endogenous variable, and *I* infrastructure, *L* location, *A* agglomeration, *S* sectoral structure, and *D* country dummies.

The potentiality factor indicators as exogenous variables are defined as follows:

- *Infrastructure* is measured by the indicator INFRATOT (total infrastructure endowment) comprising the four main infrastructure categories transportation, communication, energy, and vocational and professional education as already explained in Section 4.2.
- *Location* is measured in terms of the sum of airline distances from one region to all other regions, taking into account geodetic properties. This variable is called DISTANCE. According to this procedure, the region with the best central location is the one for which the sum of distances to all other regions is a minimum, whereas the region with the maximal sum of distances is the most pheripherally located one.
- *Agglomeration* is simply defined as population-density (POPSPACE) or alternatively as employment-densities: EMTOSPAC (total employment density) or EMISSPAC (industry and service sectors employment density).
- *Sectoral structure* is represented by three different indicators: GVAISGVA means the share of gross value added (GVA) for the industry and service

sectors within total GVA, EMISPOP reflects the sectoral structure in terms of the ratio of employment in industry and services to population, and EMISEMTO measures the share of employment in the industry and service sectors in total employment.

In addition, two variants of a combined indicator for agglomeration and sectoral structure were considered. They are developed in order to take account of the high interrelation between sectoral structure and agglomeration. The first one, GVAISSPA, measures the sectoral income density in GVA of industry and services per unit of space (km^2); the second one, EMISSPAC, reflects the sectoral employment structure and agglomeration.

Regression functions are estimated for three dependent income variables: *productivity* (GVAEMTO: GVA per employed person), *per capita income* (GVAPOP), and *spatial income density* (GVASPACE). We also tested whether infrastructure and the other potentiality factors also contribute to *employment in industry and services in relation to population* (EMISPOP); this indicator represents a sort of specific two-sector activity rate. Another possible variable is the *total activity rate* (EMTOPOP). However, it seems as if this latter variable cannot be explained with the potentiality factor approach; the R^2s are as low as 4.07% to 35.81% and the coefficients for infrastructure are not significant.[19] A possible reason may be that the definitions for and the measurements of agricultural employment are too heterogeneous and differ substantially from those for industry and services. Hence they are not sufficiently reliable and comparable.

The different QPFs have been tested in cross-section analyses with double-logarithmic functions. Accordingly, the regression coefficients represent elasticities. The data refer to 139 regions of the EU-12 for the mid-eighties. Only statistically significant results are shown.

The estimation results concerning the contribution of infrastructure are shown in Table 8.2 (see end of this Chapter). Column (1) presents the different dependent variables tested, and column (2) the regression coefficients of infrastructure if only total infrastructure endowment (INFRATOT) is used as an explanatory variable. The contribution of INFRATOT is very high as expected, with coefficients ranging from .71 to .84. At the same time total explanation as measured by the R^2s corrected for degrees of freedom also increases from 49.84% up to 70.16%. Despite the fact that the R^2 of 49.84% for employment is low, it implies nevertheless that infrastructure alone explains about half of the observed interregional differences.

In column (3), DISTANCE or GVAISGVA are added as a second potentiality factor indicator. Column (4) shows the results for three potentiality factors, while

---

[19] In order to avoid confusion between regression coefficients and R^2s, the latter are always presented as percentages (e.g. .3581 = 35.81%).

the next two columns inform about the QPFs with four factors without and with country dummies. The beta-regression coefficients are equivalent to elasticities since they are obtained on the basis of standardised data and can, therefore, be directly compared.

Table 8.2 is based on the idea that in addition to infrastructure, those variables that perform best in the stepwise estimations and shown in the preceding columns are retained for the enlarged functions. For instance, if in the two-explanatory-variables-case INFRATOT and DISTANCE are used, these two variables are retained also in the three-variables-case and in the FQPF.[20]

If one compares the results for the QPFs with all potentiality factors plus country dummies as shown in column (6) of Table 8.2, the following results are worth highlighting:

- For all four-dependent-variables, the contribution of infrastructure decreases as expected compared with the ß-coefficients of the single regressions in column (2). The strongest reduction is observed for GVASPACE, which falls from the maximum in the single regression case of .84 to .14 in the four-explanatory-variable case with dummies. This is in line with the idea that the different potentiality factors partly compete as far as their explanatory power is concerned.
- At the same time, the R^2s increase to 75% up to 98%. This shows that despite the partial overlapping of explanations all potentiality factors make significant contributions at least at the 87.5% error significance level.
- The contribution of infrastructure to per capita income (GVAPOP) and productivity per employed person (GVAEMTO) is higher than to employment (EMISPOP) or spatial value-added density (GVASPACE). INFRATOT shows the highest ß-coefficients for productivity and income (GVAEMTO .2752; GVAPOP .2549) with almost identical R^2s of 86%.
- Whereas the R^2s increase when dummies are added (columns (6) and (7)), the infrastructure coefficients decrease. On the one hand, this is line with the general expectation previously mentioned, on the other, it supports the proposition that the national framework conditions play a significant role.

As previously noted the influence of infrastructure decreases with every added exogenous variable. This influence is very strong. Even if one compares all 20 cases of columns (1) to (6), there are only two exceptions which also seem to be influenced by the fact that in the four-variable case without dummies (column (5))

20 Some other combinations of variables may achieve better results than shown in Table 8.2 which gives a selection of fully specified quasi-production-functions with country dummies. In order to facilitate comparison only variables used in the preceding columns are shown in Table 8.2.

the sectoral structure variable GVAISGVA is not significant even at the 85% level:

- With GVAEMTO as a dependent variable, the version with three explanatory variables deviates from the general pattern (see columns (4), (5) and (6)). The value for INFRATOT is lower than in the case of the FQPF, but when the country dummies are introduced (column (6)), the general pattern reappears.
- The other exception is the FQPF with country dummies used to estimate EMISPOP, where the coefficient for INFRATOT slightly increases compared with the version without country dummies (cf. (5) and (6)).

The fact that, despite the improvement in significance for GVAISGVA, the levels of significance reached in column (6) are still only 87.5% and 90%, suggests that a certain inter-correlation between GVAISGVA and another exogenous variable exists. Inspection of the correlation matrix shows that this is the case with the agglomeration variable. By combining the indicators for agglomeration and sectoral structure into a new one (GVAISSPA) and using it together with the variables INFRATOT and DISTANCE, all variables are now significant at the 95% level and R^2 increases to 83.5% up to 98.4%. However again, this improvement is paid for by reduced coefficients for INFRATOT; they decrease to a range between an absolute minimum of .075 (GVASPACE) up to a maximum of .183 (GVAEMTO). The lowest value of .075 applies to spatial income density (GVASPACE), whereas the coefficients for the three other endogenous variables are much more consistent, having values of .136, .177 and .183.

To summarise, it can be said that the results support the RDPA in general and the proposition concerning the role of infrastructure in particular:

- Regional productivity, income and employment are determined by the region-specific potentiality factor endowment and the national framework conditions;
- Infrastructure is a significant determinant of regional employment; income, productivity and spatial value added density;
- In general, the contribution of infrastructure, measured in terms of the ß-coefficients, decreases if more potentiality factors are added, but it remains significant.

It should be noted that these results have been obtained by cross section and not time-series analyses and with crude non-monetary exogenous variables. In general, cross section regressions show lower R^2s than time series ones. This demonstrates that the explanatory power of the RDPA is high.

Given the actual problems with unemployment in almost all countries, the results of the FQPFs where employment is the endogenous variable deserve particular attention.

6 First results of the infrastructure analysis of Ukrainian regions

For a number of years now, there has been a growing interest in Ukraine in European issues and even in a possible accession to the European Union.[21]

In this context it seemed, therefore, to be interesting to conceive a study on the infrastructure endowment of various Ukrainian regions based on the RDPA. A first research project funded by the Kreditanstalt für Wiederaufbau (KfW) in Frankfurt/Main in the framework of the programme of the German Advisory Group for Ukraine aimed at checking as to whether appropriate and comparable infrastructure endowment data were available for Ukrainian regions, the oblasts. Thanks to the co-operation of the German Advisory Group and the recently founded Institute for Economic Research and Policy Consulting in Kyiv[22] and their contacts with Ukrainian authorities, it was possible to obtain a first overview and to collect a certain number of data. It is hoped that additional data will be become available in the next months, so that – at least in principle – these data can later on be integrated into the existing EU set.

Since the end of the former Soviet Union, Ukraine is an independent state. Like other parts of the Soviet Union, the country had to overcome great difficulties in the transition from a planned to a market economy. Ukraine is a large country with a surface of about 600 square kilometres and about 50 million inhabitants. It is a unitary state with a regional structure of 24 oblasts and the Autonomous Crimean Republic. These 25 regions[23] also form the basis for the infrastructure research project.

Table 8.4 (see end of this Chapter) provides a first summary of general and infrastructure indicators of the Ukrainian regions for 1985 and 1995. On the basis of this small and incomplete data set, a first preliminary analysis allows us to highlight the following characteristics:

(1) As in many other countries, Ukrainian regions differ as to spatial size, but considerably more as to population. In terms of size, the smallest region is Chernivets'ka with 8.1 thousand square kilometres, the largest one Odes'ka with 33.3. Chernivets'ka is also the smallest region in terms of inhabitants with less than 1 million in 1995, whereas Donets'ka, the largest oblast has

---

21 This is documented in some recent publications, e.g. Siedenberg and Hoffmann (1999).

22 I extend my sincere gratitude to Ulrich Thießen of the German Advisory Group on Economic Reforms (Kyiv) and to Tatyana Vakhnenko and Alexander Kobzev of the IER in Kyiv for their very valuable co-operation in contacting the Ukrainian authorities and for helping with data collection.

23 In what follows, the term 'region' comprises the oblasts and the Autonomous Republic of Crimea. The latter will not always be mentioned separately.

more than five times as many. By western standards, the population density is low, ranging from 42.3 (Chernigyvs'ka) to 196.2 (Donets'ka) inhabitants per square kilometre. Since the population density will later be used as an indicator for agglomeration, these figures already point to one of the weaknesses of Ukraine: the relatively low comparative advantage for economies of scale based on agglomeration.

(2) According to the RDPA, the transport infrastructure possesses a high degree of publicness, in particular due to the immobility and indivisibility of the networks involved. In the European studies, roads, rails, waterways, airports and harbours had been used as subcategories. In the preliminary analysis of the Ukrainian regions, only data for road and rail length are available. Given their network character, the indicators for roads and rails are defined in relation to regional area in order to obtain spatial density figures. It has not (yet) been possible to obtain information for road width as a qualitative characteristic.

Following the RDPA, the road and rail density indicators are relative ones, expressed in percentages of the best equipped region. For roads in 1985, this is Chernivets'ka (100), whereas (Khersons'ka), as the least equipped region, only reaches 47.5% of Chernivets'ka. The Ukrainian average is 70.5%. By 1995 Chernivets'ka had increased its road endowment by 8.5 percentage points up to 108.5, but lost its first rank. The best equipped oblast now became L'vivs'ka with 108.9%, which in 1985 had ranked second with 97.1%. L'vivs'ka gained almost 12 percentage points in 1995 compared with a Ukrainian average increase of roughly 9 percentage points.

On the average, rail densities seem to have remained more or less constant between 1985 and 1995 (60.5 and 60.4), but there are also remarkable differences between regions: Donets'ka is the best equipped (100% and 99.64% respectively) and Crimea the least equipped one (38.3%).

The aggregated preliminary transport indicator, calculated as the arithmetic mean based only on the length of roads and rails, shows L'vivs'ka as the best equipped region in both years (100 and 102.1), whereas the least equipped oblast in both years is Khersons'ka (38.0 and 38.8).

(3) For all other infrastructure categories, too, much information is still lacking. For telecommunication, one could estimate the number of telephones in each region based on the capacity of the telephone exchanges. As a proxy for the unavailable information on cable lengths and capacities (and given its point type character), the indicator is calculated per 1000 inhabitants. Here, the Ukrainian average increased strongly between 1985 and 1995 from roughly 90 to 140 telephones per 1000 inhabitants, and in indicator terms from 61.4 to 98.1, i.e. almost 60%. The spread around the average is reflected in the indicator values of 100 (1985) and 157.8 (1995) for Kyivs'ka (including

Kyiv) as the best equipped, and Zakarpats'ka as the least equipped oblast with only 42.0 and 63.0.

(4) In the European studies, data for students and pupils in vocational schools have been used as a proxy for not available information like buildings and equipment in order to calculate a productivity oriented education indicator. For Ukrainian regions, only the numbers of students have been used. This narrow indicator differs very much between regions. The best region is Kharkivs'ka (100 in 1985; 106.5 in 1995), the least equipped one in 1985 Zhytomyrs'ka with only 13.3 and in 1995 Zakarpats'ka with 16.0.

(5) The preliminary aggregated infrastructure indicator INFRAGG is calculated as the geometric mean from the transport, telecommunication and education indicators. As explained above (see Section 4.2), aggregation by geometric mean should reflect the fact that substitutability between main infrastructure categories like education and transport is much lower than, for instance, between road and rail, as subcategories of transport, which are aggregated by the arithmetic mean, implying full substitutability.

(6) In terms of INFRAGG, infrastructure endowment increases on the average from 68.2 to 82.5 in percent of the best equipped region, Kyivs'ka (including the national capital). Its indicator of 100 in 1985 goes up to 121.4 in 1995, i.e. more than 20%. The next best oblast is Kharkivs'ka with 97.7 in 1985 and 119.5 in 1995. The regions with the lowest values are Volyns'ka with 46.0 and Zakarpats'ka with 52.7. Volyns'ka, though, has one of the strongest increases of 40% (from 46.0 to 64.4).

As previously noted all these results are preliminary, since they are only based on a small number of quantitative indicators and no qualitative ones. It is hoped to obtain more information in the future so that the infrastructure indicators become more reliable and can be integrated in an EU indicator system, allowing for an enlarged interregional and international comparison.

7 Some policy conclusions

The preceding sections have demonstrated that the RDPA is a useful research tool in order to explain interregional differences in productivity, income and employment in the EU. As to the contribution of public capital/infrastructure to productivity, the results are also closely in line with results for Japan and the United States. The question to be dealt with briefly now is which policy conclusions can be drawn from the RDPA and its results for national and regional development policies.

(1) The term 'regional policy' has to be conceived as a large, comprehensive notion that should not be restricted to simply subsidising private activities in backward regions. What is needed is a new concept that is oriented towards the development potential of a region and the factors that determine it.

(2) From the point of view of the RDPA, a favourable constitutional, institutional and socio-economic framework is important above all. To improve this framework, more or less substantial reforms have been and still will have to be realised. Most of the EU member countries have deregulation, privatisation, tax reductions and improving the efficiency of the public administration on their agendas, though some have made more progress than others. In addition, the EU member countries created first the European Community and then the European Union in order to establish a larger common market and to find better solutions to problems that exceed national dimensions and effect them all. They understood that an institutional European framework was needed to deal with such problems. The most recent element of this framework is the Monetary Union including a European central bank system. The next very important step will be eastern enlargement.

(3) But even within a 'good' European framework and reformed national frameworks, the lesson to be drawn from the RDPA is that a low endowment with 'public' resources like location, agglomeration, sectoral structure and infrastructure restricts the productive capacity of a region and limits the levels of productivity, income and employment that the region can realise. To the extent that these levels are considered to be too low in some regions, the conclusion from the RDPA is that the regional resource endowment has to be improved, both quantitatively and qualitatively. This insight that the typical regional problem it is not primarily insufficient demand, but that the competitiveness of the regional supply is too low, took many years before being generally accepted.

On the European level, this insight has lead to the reforms of the Structural Funds, in particular of the Regional Fund. For a number of years now, it co-finances both infrastructure investments and private enterprise investments in lagging regions, selected on the basis of common European criteria. The Agricultural Guidance Fund and the Social Fund participate in restructuring agricultural investments and in improving labour qualifications. It is this investment-oriented supply-side approach that characterises the present EU regional policy.

(4) A successful regional development strategy would assume that something like an optimal relationship between public infrastructure and private capital exists. Both are elements of the overall capital stock of a country and of its regions. Improving the infrastructure endowment, and not only subsidising private business investments, is in line with the other lesson from the RDPA.

Among the four potentiality factors, infrastructure is the one that has the highest instrument character and can be used by public institutions to increase and improve the development potential of a region. Of course, this is true for all regions. On the basis of traditional cost-benefit-analyses it can often be shown that the rate of return of additional infrastructure investment is higher in already developed regions than in backward ones. This being the case, these regions should to a large extent be able to finance their own infrastructure needs. For backward regions this is, however, not possible. They have low resource endowment, which also implies a low tax capacity. Hence these regions, by themselves, are not in a position to invest substantially in order to increase their productive capacity. Thus the weight attributed to the goal of reducing interregional disparities and the funds devoted to this goal, in particular in the form of international and inter-governmental transfers (or 'Finanzausgleich') depend on political decisions.

(5) However, investing in infrastructure is not a miracle cure. It presupposes a serious in-depth and region-specific analysis of the regional resource endowment, its weaknesses and strengths, the identification of possible infrastructure bottlenecks, but also of inefficiencies in infrastructure pricing and utilisation. According to the "World Development Report 1994", annual gains from eliminating incorrect pricing and inefficiency could save almost 180 billions USD compared to a total amount of infrastructure investment of about 200 billions.[24]

(6) The crucial criterion for regional competitiveness is the ratio of productivity to labour cost, including all public sector and social insurance charges. If the factors determining productivity differ between regions, as is the case in almost all countries, and if at the same time a uniform wage policy is pursued, the situation illustrated in Graph 8.1 will arise. In those regions where the ratio is favourable, high employment, in-migration and strong growth result, whereas in other ones with an unfavourable ratio, unemployment, out-migration and low growth are the consequences. Reducing interregional disparities, therefore, cannot be done by regional policy alone, but requires also a regionally differentiated labour market and wages policy. Since in democratic mixed economies, wage policy is not a government competence, but is left to negotiations between the social partners, the trade unions and the employer associations, political influence in this field is obviously difficult.

(7) On the basis of such a comprehensive analysis, a regional development strategy can be elaborated. A major feature of this strategy is to clearly distinguish between the public policy domain and the private market domain, to improve the political framework conditions and to give sufficient leeway to private activities, but also to decentralised local and regional public ones.

---

24 See Ingram (1995), p. 24.

Within this large framework, infrastructure policy can make an important contribution.

(8) As far as Ukraine is concerned, all these considerations apply, in principle, also to this country and its regions. Given that Ukraine is still an economy in transition from the former central planning to a market system, improving the general framework conditions requires much more attention than in already established market economies. In addition, infrastructure policy within the concept of a well-balanced national and regional development strategy should be given a more prominent role. Despite the fact that from the point of view of the RDPA infrastructure is of particular importance for productivity, income and employment, it should not be forgotten that all infrastructure categories also provide direct consumer benefits. In particular the social and cultural infrastructure, that had been included in the above mentioned EC study of 1986, even if it is only indirectly contributing to productivity, has a major role to play in the development of any society. It is hoped that the infrastructure project of which the first results have been presented in this paper can make a significant contribution to a national and regional development strategy in Ukraine.

Table 8.1
Infrastructure endowment of 153 EU-regions 1985

Ranking position	Region	INFRATOT*	Ranking position	Region	INFRATOT*
1	GR - 8 Thrace	5.272%	78	IT - 8 Emilia Romagna	25.160%
2	GR - 5 Eastern Macedonia	6.495%	79	GE - 16 Koblenz	25.271%
3	GR - 4 Thessaly	6.848%	80	BE - 7 Namur	25.475%
4	IT - 17 Basilicata	7.456%	81	UK - 10 Scottland	25.686%
5	PO - 4 Alentejo	8.025%	82	GE - 22 Tübingen	25.783%
6	IT - 15 Molise	8.177%	83	GE - 27 Mittelfranken	26.116%
7	PO - 2 Centro	9.132%	84	GE - 5 Lüneburg	26.138%
8	PO - 5 Algarve	9.352%	85	GE - 15 Kassel	26.289%
9	PO - 1 Norte	9.469%	86	UK - 6 South West	26.509%
10	GR - 7 Epirous	10.034%	87	DE - 3 West For Storebaelt	27.064%
11	GR - 6 Crete	10.209%	88	NL - 2 Friesland	27.165%
12	SP – 15 Navarra	10.465%	89	UK - 2 Yorkshire/Humberside	27.171%
13	SP - 8 Castilla -La Mancha	10.549%	90	FR - 6 Basse Normandie	27.568%
14	GE - 33 Schwerin	10.756%	91	GE - 28 Unterfranken	27.639%
15	GE - 34 Neubrandenburg	11.194%	92	SP - 3 Madrid	27.699%
16	IT - 18 Calabria	11.681%	93	GE - 24 Niederbayern	27.779%
17	GE - 45 Suhl	12.032%	94	FR - 20 Languedoc	27.794%
18	SP – 11 Extremadura	12.353%	95	UK - 3 East Midlands	28.254%
19	GR - 9 Isl. of East. Agean S.	12.367%	96	GE - 21 Freiburg	28.343%
20	GE - 43 Erfurt	12.666%	97	SP - 7 Pais Vasco	28.409%
21	GR - 3 Peleponnese	13.102%	98	UK - 7 West Midlands	28.433%
22	GE - 35 Potsdam	13.376%	99	UK - 9 Wales	28.547%
23	SP – 16 Rioja	13.421%	100	NL - 5 Gelderland	29.237%
24	PO - 3 Lisboa e Tejo	13.636%	101	FR - 16 Midi-Pyrenees	29.534%
25	IT - 16 Puglia	13.963%	102	FR - 9 Lorraine	29.913%
26	SP – 17 Canarias	14.203%	103	UK - 1 North	30.137%
27	IT - 5 Trentino Alto Adige	14.431%	104	IT - 7 Friuli Venezia Giulia	30.150%
28	IT - 14 Abruzzi	14.854%	105	FR - 13 Bretagne	30.437%
29	GE - 38 Magdeburg	15.131%	106	GE - 19 Stuttgart	30.674%
30	BE - 6 Luxembourg (BE)	15.313%	107	NL - 10 Noord-Brabant	31.474%
31	SP - 5 Galicia	15.444%	108	FR - 12 Pays de la Loire	31.507%
32	SP - 1 Andalucia	15.548%	109	GE - 11 Detmold	31.534%
33	IT - 10 Umbria	15.577%	110	GE - 3 Braunschweig	31.551%
34	IT - 13 Campania	15.954%	111	NL - 4 Overijssel	31.589%
35	SP - 4 Communidad Valenciana	16.120%	112	IT - 4 Lombardia	31.981%
36	GR - 2 Central/West.Macedonia	16.185%	113	DE - 2 Oost For Storebaelt	32.022%
37	GE - 44 Gera	16.276%	114	GE - 1 Schleswig-Holstein	32.320%
38	IT - 2 Valle d' Aosta	16.900%	115	GE - 4 Hannover	33.958%

Table 8.1 (cont.)
Infrastructure endowment of 153 EU-regions 1985

Ranking position	Region	INFRATOT*	Ranking position	Region	INFRATOT*
39	UK - 11 Northern Ireland	17.198%	116	FR - 15 Aquitaine	34.689%
40	SP - 6 Castilla – Leon	17.383%	117	GE - 12 Arnsberg	35.329%
41	GR - 1 Eastern Cont. Greece	17.757%	118	GE - 18 Rheinhessen-Pfalz	35.437%
42	IR - 1 Ireland	18.192%	119	GE - 23 Oberbayern	35.933%
43	SP – 10 Asturias	18.360%	120	GE - 30 Saarland	36.106%
44	GE - 42 Chemnitz	18.763%	121	GE - 6 Weser-Ems	36.244%
45	SP – 13 Baleares	19.445%	122	GE - 13 Darmstadt	36.941%
46	SP - 9 Aragon	19.742%	123	NL - 9 Zeeland	37.356%
47	FR - 2 Champagne	19.757%	124	FR - 18 Rhone-Alpes	37.691%
48	IT – 11 Marche	19.933%	125	NL - 11 Limburg	37.793%
49	SP – 14 Cantabria	20.066%	126	BE - 3 Hainaut	38.639%
50	SP – 12 Murcia	20.166%	127	UK - 5 South East	39.182%
51	GE - 32 Rostock	20.177%	128	FR - 8 Nord	39.212%
52	GE - 36 Frankfurt(Oder)	20.351%	129	BE - 4 Liege	40.003%
53	GE - 41 Dresden	20.359%	130	FR - 21 Prov. Cote d' Azur/Corse	40.028%
54	GE –25 Oberpfalz	20.941%	131	GE - 10 Münster	40.042%
55	IT – 20 Sardegna	21.057%	132	DE - 1 Hovenstads-Regionen	42.841%
56	GE - 26 Oberfranken	21.379%	133	GE - 20 Karlsruhe	42.910%
57	NL - 3 Drenthe	21.463%	134	GE - 9 Köln	43.219%
58	FR – 14 Poitou Charentes	21.738%	135	FR - 10 Alsace	43.584%
59	IT - 9 Toscana	22.205%	136	NL - 6 Utrecht	44.531%
60	FR - 3 Picardie	22.422%	137	BE - 9 West-Vlaandern	44.548%
61	GE - 39 Halle	22.512%	138	IT - 3 Liguria	44.843%
62	SP - 2 Cataluna	23.354%	139	UK - 8 North-West	46.335%
63	FR – 19 Auvergne	23.534%	140	NL - 1 Groningen	46.712%
64	IT - 6 Veneto	23.664%	141	BE - 5 Limburg (BE)	47.583%
65	GE - 37 Cottbus	23.798%	142	NL - 7 Noord-Holland	49.505%
66	GE - 29 Schwaben	24.273%	143	BE - 8 Oost-Vlaanderen	50.154%
67	FR - 5 Centre	24.285%	144	FR - 4 Haute Normandie	51.593%
68	FR - 7 Bourgogne	24.362%	145	GE - 8 Düsseldorf	52.230%
69	GE - 17 Trier	24.459%	146	NL - 8 Zuid-Holland	53.210%
70	IT - 1 Piemonte	24.490%	147	LU - 1 Luxembourg (GD)	53.894%
71	FR – 17 Limousin	24.599%	148	BE - 2 Brabant	60.978%
72	IT – 12 Lazio	24.759%	149	FR - 1 Ile de France	64.813%
73	IT – 19 Sicilia	24.759%	150	BE - 1 Antwerpen	70.821%
74	UK – 4 East Anglia	24.886%	151	GE - 31 Berlin	71.919%
75	GE - 40 Leipzig	24.941%	152	GE - 7 Bremen	74.922%
76	FR – 11 Franche Comte	24.961%	153	GE - 2 Hamburg	100.000%
77	GE - 14 Gießen	25.077%			

Source: National and EUROSTAT data; own infrastructure data bank; own calculations.

Notes: * Total Infrastructure indicator in per cent of the best equipped region (Hamburg = 100).

Table 8.2
Single and Multiple Quasi Production Functions for 139 EC-regions for the mid-eighties

dependent variable (1)	Explanatory Variables (EV) and Dummies					
	1 EV: infrastructure (2)	2 EV: infrastructure plus 1 EV (3)	3 EV: infrastructure plus 2 EVs (4)	4 EV: fully specified QPF infrastructure + 3 EVs (5)	4 EV + Dummies: fully specified QPF with country dummies (6)	3 EV + Dummies: fully specified QPF with comb. var. and dummies (7)
EMISPOP	INFRATOT beta = .7086 t = 11.753 R^2 = 49.84%	INFRATOT, DISTANCE beta = .5126 t = 6.452 R^2 = 53.86%	INFRATOT, DISTANCE, POPSPACE beta = .2802 t = 2.562 R^2 = 56.43%	INFRATOT, DISTANCE, POPSPACE, GVAISGVA beta = .1858 t = 1.824 R^2 = 63.40%	INFRATOT, DISTANCE, POPSPACE, GVAISGVA[1)] beta = .1991 t = 2.361 R^2 = 75.16%	INFRATOT, DISTANCE, GVAISSPA beta = .1358 t = 1.783 R^2 = 83.45%
GVAEMTO	INFRATOT beta = .7619 t = 13.769 R^2 = 57.75%	INFRATOT, DISTANCE beta = .4572 t = 6.915 R^2 = 68.10%	INFRATOT, DISTANCE, GVAISGVA beta = .3719 t = 5.133 R^2 = 69.37%	INFRATOT, DISTANCE, EMISSPAC, GVAISGVA* beta = .4588 t = 4.885 R^2 = 69.61%	INFRATOT, DISTANCE, EMISSPAC, GVAISGVA[2)] beta = .2752 t = 4.146 R^2 = 86.45%	INFRATOT, DISTANCE, GVAISSPA beta = .1827 t = 2.920 R^2 = 88.53%
GVAPOP	INFRATOT beta = .7822 t = 14.696 R^2 = 60.90%	INFRATOT, DISTANCE beta = .4732 t = 7.582 R^2 = 71.53%	INFRATOT, DISTANCE, EMISSPAC[3)] beta = .4031 t = 4.467 R^2 = 71.56%	INFRATOT, DISTANCE, EMISSPAC, GVAISGVA* beta = .3833 t = 4.257 R^2 = 72.07%	INFRATOT, DISTANCE, EMISSPAC,GVAISGVA[1)] beta = .2549 t = 3.803 R^2 = 86.21%	INFRATOT, DISTANCE, GVAISSPA beta = .1768 t = 2.379 R^2 = 88.29%
GVASPACE	INFRATOT beta = .8391 t = 18.041 R^2 = 70.16%	INFRATOT, GVAISGVA beta = .7013 t = 11.250 R^2 = 72.04%	INFRATOT, POPSPACE, GVAISGVA beta = .2488 t = 8.309 R^2 = 95.58%	INFRATOT, DISTANCE, POPSPACE, GVAISGVA beta = .1512 t = 4.750 R^2 = 96.43%	INFRATOT, DISTANCE, POPSPACE, GVAISGVA beta = .1412 t = 5.046 R^2 = 97.93%	INFRATOT, DISTANCE, EMISSPAC beta = .0748 t = 3.335 R^2 = 98.40%

Explanations concerning Table 8.2:

(a) * These Quasi Production Functions contain variables that are insignificant below the 85%-level without dummies, but become significant with dummies (col. (6)) and when used with the combined sectoral structure/agglomeration variable GVAISSPA (col. (7)).

(b) All explanatory variables are significant at the 95%-level if not indicated by:

(1): significant at the 90 %-level,
(2): significant at the 87.5 %-level, or
(3): significant at the 85 %-level.

(c) Beta: regression coefficient of INFRATOT for standardised data.

(d) t: t-statistics; critical t-value for a significance at the 95%-level is 1.657; for the 90%-level 1.267, for the 87.5%-level 1.156 and for the 85%-level 1.041.

(e) R^2: Adjusted R^2 for degrees of freedom, depending on the number of explanatory variables included in the equation.

Sources: national and EUROSTAT data, own infrastructure data bank, own calculations.

Table 8.3
Comparison of infrastructure regression coefficients of different production function approaches with productivity as endogenous variable

Study/Approach	Regression coefficient
(1) Mera (1973) for Japanese regions	.20
(2) Costa/Ellson/Martin (1987) for US-States	.20
(3) Munnell (1990) for US-States	.15
(4) Munnell (1993) for US-States 1970-86	.17
(5) Munnell (1993) for US-States 1970-90	.14
QPFs for productivity per employed person	
(6) Biehl (1986) MCDPF for EC-10 Regions 1970	.14
(7) Biehl (1986) MCDPF for EC-10 Regions 1980	.27
(8) Biehl (1986) FQPF for EC-10 Regions 1970	.12
(9) Biehl (1986) FQPF for EC-10 Regions 1980	.19
(10) Biehl (1995); Biehl and Niegsch and Nimmermann (1998) FQPF for 139 EC-12 Regions 1985	**.12 - .30**

Sources: For studies (1) to (5) see Munnell (1993), p. 33; for studies (6) to (9) Biehl (1986), Tables 20 and 21; (10) is based on Biehl (1995) and Biehl,Niegsch and Nimmermann (1998). The latter source contains also additional regression results that are not reproduced in the present paper.

Explanations:

FQPF: Fully specified Quasi-Production Functions.

MCDPF: modified Cobb-Douglas production functions.

Table 8.4

Selected indicators for Ukrainian regions 1985 and 1995

Ukraine	Population		Territory	Population density		Road density		Rail density		Indicator transportation (arithm. mean road+rail)		Telephones **		Students		INFRAGG			
Oblasts and AR Crimea	in Ths.		in Ths. sq. km	inhabitants per sq. km		km hard surface roads per sq. km in % best region 1985		km rail per sq. km in % best region 1985		in % best region 1985		in % best region 1985		in % best region 1985		Aggregated Infrastructure indicator (geometric mean)		in % best region 1985	
	1985	1995	1985/95	1985	1995	1985	1995	1985	1995	1985	1995	1985	1995	1985	1995	1985	1995	1985	1995
Ukraine	**50,993.6**	**51,334.1**	**603.7**	**84.5**	**85.0**	**70.5**	**79.3**	**60.5**	**60.4**	**67.8**	**69.8**	**61.4**	**98.1**	**40.6**	**43.6**	**55.3**	**66.9**	**68.2**	**82.5**
Vinnytska	1,953.4	1,876.0	26.5	73.7	70.8	88.8	98.5	76.3	76.2	85.4	87.4	47.1	79.2	20.5	25.1	43.5	55.8	53.7	68.8
Volynska	1,031.8	1,075.2	20.2	51.1	53.2	70.0	81.9	49.2	48.7	61.7	65.3	53.9	83.2	15.5	26.2	37.3	52.2	46.0	64.4
Dnipropetrovska	3,823.9	3,852.0	31.9	119.9	120.8	72.8	83.1	79.4	79.0	78.8	81.0	61.0	97.2	49.3	44.4	61.9	70.4	76.3	86.9
Donets'ka	5,337.9	5,198.5	26.5	201.4	196.2	81.0	88.5	100.0	99.6	93.7	94.1	49.2	81.2	28.4	35.7	50.8	64.8	62.6	80.0
Zhytomyrska	1,546.6	1,480.6	29.9	51.7	49.5	74.1	80.2	60.3	60.4	69.6	70.3	57.3	96.2	13.3	17.4	37.6	49.0	46.4	60.4
Zakarpatska	1,202.6	1,288.1	12.8	94.0	100.6	65.7	75.3	79.9	79.4	75.4	77.4	42.0	63.0	17.6	16.0	38.2	42.8	47.1	52.7
Zaporizhska	2,045.3	2,077.8	27.2	75.2	76.4	65.1	72.8	58.5	58.5	64.0	65.6	74.7	118.6	35.3	42.7	55.2	69.2	68.1	85.4
Ivano-Frankivska	1,374.6	1,467.1	13.9	98.9	105.5	79.9	85.0	55.2	57.3	69.9	71.1	48.0	72.2	23.3	20.9	42.8	47.5	52.7	58.6
Kyivska (with Kyiv)	4,446.0	4,534.5	28.9	153.8	156.9	75.3	83.1	48.8	47.6	64.3	65.4	100.0	157.8	82.9	92.4	81.1	98.4	100.0	121.4
Kirovogradska	1,228.7	1,224.8	24.6	49.9	49.8	62.7	72.6	60.3	61.4	63.7	67.0	55.7	89.9	20.6	24.2	41.8	52.6	51.5	64.9
Luhanska	2,837.6	2,788.5	26.7	106.3	104.4	56.0	62.2	72.0	72.2	66.3	67.2	54.4	88.9	29.7	26.1	47.5	53.8	58.6	66.4
L'vivska	2,668.0	2,761.5	21.8	122.4	126.7	97.1	108.9	96.1	95.3	100.0	102.1	51.0	79.5	60.5	52.1	67.6	75.1	83.4	92.6
Mykolaivska	1,293.6	1,343.3	24.6	52.6	54.6	50.4	55.7	49.7	49.9	51.8	52.8	75.1	116.3	22.9	23.9	44.7	52.7	55.1	65.0
Odeska	2,612.2	2,586.5	33.3	78.4	77.7	62.1	70.1	55.4	55.4	60.9	62.7	60.9	98.7	75.7	68.5	65.4	75.2	80.7	92.7
Poltavska	1,722.4	1,739.1	28.8	59.8	60.4	74.0	89.2	47.4	47.4	62.8	68.3	58.4	93.4	32.4	29.0	49.2	57.0	60.7	70.3
Rivnenska	1,165.9	1,194.2	20.1	58.0	59.4	64.0	71.6	46.8	46.8	57.4	59.2	51.8	81.3	28.3	31.5	43.8	53.3	54.0	65.8
Sumska	1,425.4	1,397.9	23.8	59.9	58.7	66.4	78.8	55.3	56.0	63.0	67.4	54.0	88.6	16.4	28.1	38.2	55.2	47.1	68.1
Ternopilska	1,151.2	1,175.4	13.8	83.4	85.2	96.6	106.5	66.6	66.4	84.5	86.4	55.8	87.8	28.5	46.7	51.2	70.8	63.2	87.3
Kharkivska	3,146.9	3,088.4	31.4	100.2	98.4	72.3	85.5	77.7	77.4	77.7	81.5	64.0	104.7	100.0	106.5	79.2	96.9	97.7	119.5
Khersonska	1,220.0	1,265.7	28.5	42.8	44.4	47.5	52.1	25.8	25.5	38.0	38.8	65.6	101.7	28.7	32.6	41.5	50.5	51.2	62.3
Khmelnytska	1,527.7	1,508.8	20.6	74.2	73.2	90.4	100.7	57.5	57.4	76.6	79.1	56.6	92.1	24.8	28.8	47.5	59.4	58.7	73.3
Cherkaska	1,527.1	1,504.6	20.9	73.1	72.0	74.0	82.2	50.0	49.9	64.2	66.0	58.9	96.1	16.4	27.8	39.5	56.0	48.8	69.1
Chernivetska	914.1	943.6	8.1	112.9	116.5	100.0	108.5	91.1	82.6	99.0	95.6	51.5	80.2	32.4	32.7	54.9	63.0	67.7	77.8
Chernigivska	1,428.3	1,349.5	31.9	44.8	42.3	55.5	62.4	44.8	45.7	51.9	54.1	65.6	111.7	15.5	20.3	37.5	49.7	46.3	61.3
AR Crimea (with Sevastopol)	2,362.4	2,612.5	27.0	87.5	96.8	66.5	72.5	38.3	38.3	54.2	55.4	71.9	104.6	22.5	27.8	44.4	54.4	54.8	67.1

Sources: Official Ukrainian statistical data for national totals and partly for regional breakdowns by oblasts; partly supplemented by own calculations and estimates.

* Roads and Railways for common use; regional breakdown estimated.

** Estimates based on the capacity of telephone stations.

References

Aschauer, David (1989a): Is Public Expenditure Productive? In: Journal of Monetary Economics, Vol. 23, pp. 177 – 200

Aschauer, David (1989b): Does Public Capital Crowd out Private Capital? In: Journal of Monetary Economics, Vol. 23, pp. 171-188

Aschauer, David (1990): Public Investment and Private Sector Growth. Washington D.C.

Biehl, Dieter (1986): The Contribution of Infrastructure to Regional Development. Document, Commission of the European Communities, Vol. I: Final Report, Vol. II: Annex, Luxembourg, Office of Official Publications of the European Communities, pp. 395 + 73, 190

Biehl, Dieter (1991): The Role of Infrastructure in Regional Development. In: R. W. Vickerman (ed.): Infrastructure and Regional Development. European Research in Regional Science, Vol. 1, London, pp. 9-35

Biehl, Dieter (1995): Infrastruktur als Bestimmungsfaktor regionaler Entwicklungspotentiale in der Europäischen Union (Infrastructure as a Determinant of Regional Development Potential in the European Union). In: Helmut, Karl and Wilhelm Henrichsmeyer (eds.): Regionalentwicklung im Prozess der Europäischen Integration (Regional Development in the Process of European Integration). Bonner Schriften zur Integration Europas, Bd. 4, Bonn, pp. 53-86

Biehl, Dieter (1996): Economic Theory of Federalism and its Application to the European Union. In: Ritter, Ulrich Peter (ed.) (1996): Problems of Structural Change in the 21st Century. Frankfurt and Madrid, pp. 144-172

Biehl, Dieter et al. (1975): Bestimmungsgründe des regionalen Entwicklungspotentials: Infrastruktur, Agglomeration Intel sektorale Wirtschaftsstruktur (Determinants of Regional Development Potential: Infrastructure, Agglomeration and Sectoral Structure). Kieler Studien, No. 133, Tübingen

Biehl, Dieter, Claus Niegsch and Philipp Nimmermann (1999): Infrastructure from the Point of View of the Regional Development Potential Approach: A Theoretical and Empirical Analysis. Frankfurt, mimeo

Buchanan, James M. and Gordon Tullock (1962): The Calculus of Consent. Ann Arbor

Frey, René L. (1969): Infrastruktur und Wirtschaftswachstum. In: Konjunkturpolitik, Vol. 15, pp. 103-116

Frey, René L. (1970): Infrastruktur, Grundlagen der Planung öffentlicher Investitionen. Tübingen/Zürich

Hirschman, Albert O. (1958): The Strategy of Economic Development. New Haven/CT

Ingram, Gregory (1995): The Role of Infrastructure in Economic Development. In: World Infrastructure 1995. London, pp. 19-24

Jochimsen, Reimut (1966): Theorie der Infrastruktur, Grundlagen der marktwirtschaftlichen Entwicklung (Theory of Infrastructure, Bases of Market Economy Development). Tübingen

Johansen, Leif (1968): Production Functions and the Concept of Capacity. In: Recherches récentes sur la fonction de production, Ceruna

Mera, Koichi (1973): Regional Production Functions and the Social Overhead Capital: An Analysis of the Japanese Case. Regional and Urban Economics, Vol. 3, pp. 157-185

Munnell, Alicia (1990): Is There a Shortfall in Public Capital Investment? Federal Reserve Bank of Boston, Boston

Munnell, Alicia (1993): An Assessment of Trends and Economic Impacts of Infrastructure Investment. In: OECD (ed.): Infrastructure Policies for the 1990s. Paris, pp. 21-54

Ohlin, Bertil (1933): Interregional and International Trade. Cambridge/Mass

Richardson, Harry W. (1974): Agglomeration Potential: A Generalisation of the Income Potential Concept. Journal of Regional Science, Vol. 14, pp. 328-336

Samuelson, Paul A. (1954): The Pure Theory of Public Expenditure. Review of Economics and Statistics, Vol. 36, pp. 387-389

Siedenberg, Axel and Lutz Hoffmann (eds.) (1999): Ukraine at the Crossroads: Economic Reforms in International Perspective. Physica-Verl., Heidelberg New York

Stohler, Jacques (1965): Zur rationalen Planung der Infrastruktur (On Rational Planning of Infrastructure). Konjunkturpolitik, Vol. 11, pp. 279-308

World Bank (ed.) (1994): World Development Report 1994: Infrastructure for Development. New York

Appendix

A comparison with other production function approaches

As explained, the preceding results have been obtained with a variant of the production function approach where only resources with a high degree of publicness are used as inputs and which are called quasi-production functions (QPFs). It is therefore interesting to compare these QPF results with those of other studies despite the fact that they are not fully comparable.

In the study done for the European Commission for the two cross-section years 1970 and 1980 (Biehl 1986), QPFs and modified Cobb-Douglas production functions (MPFs) have been tested. However, these QPFs and MPFs are based on a partly different regional breakdown of 10 EC member states and on a more comprehensive infrastructure indicator covering 12 main categories instead of 4 as for 1985. The MPFs differ also from the traditional ones insofar far as the private capital variable was replaced by the comprehensive infrastructure variable since at that time regional private capital stock figures were not available for all countries.

A similar situation, but one where comparability is even more restricted, exists with regard to the US-American studies mentioned in the introduction, above. On the one hand, the specification of the equations is different as these studies follow the traditional production function line with labour and private capital and added public capital, on the other, the regional database consists of American States, much larger units than the EU regions. Furthermore, only productivity is used as an endogenous variable.

Despite all these differences it seems interesting to compare the US and the European results and to consider also the results of the study by Mera (1973) for Japan. As all these countries represent mixed economies insofar as they are characterised by a market sector and a public sector. Even if the latter were larger in Europe than in Japan and the US, such a comparison would appear useful.

As Table 8.3 shows, infrastructure or public capital makes an important contribution to productivity in all the countries studied. In addition, the regression coefficients representing the elasticities of infrastructure's contribution to productivity are relatively similar. The values for Japan, for the US and for the EU cover a range of .12 to .30. The bands shown for studies (6) to (10) result from alternative definitions of some potentiality factors. All coefficients from Biehl (1986) and Biehl, Niegsch and Nimmermann (1998) are significant at the 95% level and are derived from cross section regressions with R^2s between 82.6% and 95.2%. The regression results imply that a larger number of significant equations, based on alternative definitions of the potentiality factors, have been obtained.

The relatively narrow range of elasticities between .12 and .30 that have been obtained with the different theoretical approaches indicate a certain correlation could exist between infrastructure measured in terms of monetary values of public capital and the indicator INFRATOT for physical infrastructure capacities. Under this assumption it seems to be permissible to explain the outcome as an exercise where the explanatory power of infrastructure has been framed by the competition of a number of equally theoretically justified, but different other explanatory variables. From this point of view, the results seem to deserve more attention than those obtained with a single theoretical approach only. The similar results support the conclusion that infrastructure represents a powerful instrument for regional policy.

9

Are there Regional Economic Policies which Lead to 'Europe'? Voices of Ukrainian Companies in East and West

Felicitas Möllers, Petra Opitz and Christian von Hirschhausen

1 Introduction

Ukraine's 'potential' is often invoked when discussing the further economic development of the country. At the same time, it is also said that Ukraine could be a 'bridge to Europe'. Who in practice would furnish this potential and who would build the bridge? In an economic sense, Ukrainian business should play these roles. But are they ready, able and willing to do so? Do different abilities and opportunities exist, which could be based on the differing structures and experiences lived by individuals and enterprises in the eastern and western parts of Ukraine? After all, these regions were only combined into a separate state after World War II. What roles do the regional institutions and their economic policies play in the realisation of the Ukrainian 'potential'?

It is these questions, which we will discuss in this Chapter. It is based on two studies made by the authors in 1999 in consequence of visits to the two regions. They visited the areas of L'viv and Ivano-Frankivs'k in March 1999, and the oblasts Kharkiv and Donets'k in December 1999. Discussions were held with 13 western and 14 eastern Ukrainian companies and with 5 and 6 institutions respectively, all within four days in either case. In addition we held background talks with investors in Kyiv and Germany, and with Ukrainian experts. The data and general information collected do not represent statistically useful material. Nevertheless, we received so much information that it is possible to discern trends in the testimonies given. Since the administrative apparatus changes only very slowly, the replies received are still more or less valid.

The results of both studies and the trends of either 'bank of the river Dnipro', which spring from our inquiries will be juxtaposed hereafter. From them we will then proceed to draw conclusions for a regional economic policy of Ukraine, which can help to smooth the way of enterprises to Europe.

2 The endless inertia of the Ukrainian economy

West: *"This combinate is like a heavy suitcase without a handle: Too heavy to keep carrying further, yet sad to just let go."*

East: *"Optimists are those who have no idea of how our economy really functions."*

Ukrainians have reached political independence quickly, without major conflicts and setbacks. Thus, the most important goal was surprisingly quickly realised, and the most serious problems seemed quasi automatically to be solved.[1] This assumption was wrong, however. Economic independence is still a long way off. Every company and every individual wanting to invest in Ukraine today – the middle of the year 2000 – is confronted by macro-economic and institutional difficulties, which – measured by European standards – can hardly be surpassed. Overall economic growth has been regressing in the past years. Whether the slight growth observed since early 2000 will continue remains yet to be seen. The strong devaluation since the middle of 1998 has made the situation still worse. And yet, most difficulties with which companies are confronted in Eastern and Western Ukraine are home made:

Foreign trade is impeded by a multitude of administrative measures. The state's industrial policies, which consist primarily of 'plans', which cannot be financed, have failed. After the collapse of the Soviet production and distribution networks for big industry, hardly any new and more efficient net structures have evolved. Payment arrears to Ukrainian companies and to the population grow continuously. Important sectors of industry work without money, i.e. on barter.

The institutional conditions are problematic, too: Legal uncertainty, inconsistencies in the economic policies and an excessively bureaucratic administration are all words which only inadequately describe the daily labour of Sisyphus faced by the entrepreneurs whom we interviewed. With panoply of methods the state institutions constantly intervene either directly or indirectly – and often in a completely unforeseen manner – in the decision making processes of companies. They employ new tax rules (at times with retroactive force), issue special regulations, use the system of state reserves, fix prices, which do not cover costs, exert undue bureaucratic influence, use corruption, do not enforce or knowingly corrupt legal regulations and even judicial rulings (legal despotism).

---

[1] Kappeler, Andreas (1994): Kleine Geschichte der Ukraine. München, pp. 253-254

These measures, the list of which could be continued, are employed – not exclusively but primarily – by the central government offices in Kyiv – as both East and West concurred.

To this must be added that the political decision-making process is excessively centralised, a fact, which the Government and foreign advisors often do not sufficiently appreciate. Economic regions on the periphery therefore lose even more in importance vis-à-vis the centre. Most entrepreneurs, both in Western and in Eastern Ukraine, evaluate the central offices in Kyiv generally negatively. *West: "The whole effort of the President, the Government and the Parliament is directed toward the destruction of the Ukrainian economy." "Investors are afraid of us, that is not us here at the plant, but those sitting in Kyiv. You can give them everything and yet they will continue stealing." East: "What does politics mean here? As soon as something finally works, the bureaucracy will start meddling".*

Fundamentally, these problems cannot be solved at the regional level. The permissible freedom of the regional or local administrations is too limited. On the other hand, the power of the local bureaucracies is ubiquitous. Thus, our trip to Eastern Ukraine, planned for 19 to October 23, 1999, had to be rescheduled to a date after the presidential elections[2], because as we were unambiguously told, no company would openly talk about its situation and about economic conditions, fearing sanctions from the local administrations.

To these negative conditions of the institutional framework, which much impede the economic activities of industry must be added the inefficiency of the existing infrastructure. Particularly damaging is the poor electricity supply. The toleration of non-payment as well as the lacking enforcement of the legal framework concerning the power industry result in an increasingly uncertain power supply throughout Ukraine. This includes even the major industrial centres, which in theory have adequate power generation capacity.

Daily outages of power during the winter months are common. Whole city wards are dark for hours at night and people run around with flashlights. *East: "It's just like during the war."* Even companies, which regularly pay their electricity bills, are subject to outages. Some have decided to produce only during the night shift. Others try to avoid disconnections through negotiations with the local power supplier (Oblenergo). But that is rarely successful. According to their own statements, many companies suffer great economic losses through these involuntary production interruptions and idle times, which nobody will pay for.

Lastly, the few investment projects for which international financial credits had been arranged have been delayed or cancelled due to the devaluation since 1998 (e.g. the EBRD credit for a heating system in L'viv, a Czech export credit for the furnishing of a machine construction plant). Even more serious is the loss in

---

[2] Presidential elections in Ukraine were held on October 31 and November 14, 1999.

international trust, which Ukraine has suffered. *West: "We are looking for contacts in Germany, the Czech Republic, the USA. But they only say: Ukraine – where the conditions are chaotic and no laws exist?"*

3 Specific conditions for investment in Western and in Eastern Ukraine

Even though macro-economic conditions significantly influence the activities of every company, specific conditions related to the location on one or the other bank of the river Dnipro are also important. This river divides the country into an eastern and a western part, which both have quite different histories. The Ukraine of the left bank belonged for many centuries to Russia, whereas the western bank was at different times under the dominion of Lithuania, Poland and Austria. During the industrialisation of the Soviet Union, Eastern Ukraine was one of the major regions, not least because of the presence of significant raw materials. Since some of Western Ukraine only became part of the Soviet Union after 1945 and its economic and plan system, it remained from Moscow's perspective more of a border region rather than being the focus for special initiatives, except for the location of military training facilities. The economic strengths and structures of the various regions of Ukraine are, therefore, quite different and have remained so even until today. This applies too to the identification with the Ukrainian nation.[3]

When talking to people from Western Ukraine they often stressed that the region today again has a favourable geographic location, i.e. the proximity to the markets in Central and Western Europe. At the same time the companies also stated that this advantage could as yet only be minimally exploited. No good and fast road connection exists as yet between south-western Poland and the region of L'viv. Even the rail connection to Western Europe is more of a hurdle, because of the different rail gauges between Eastern and Western Europe.

Considerable transport restrictions and severely controlled oblast borders also exist, for instance on the over-night car trip to Kharkiv we were checked six times! At this time, Western Ukrainian companies concentrate therefore on their regional market. These conditions lead to a severe segmentation of the market region, which is one reason why an independent Western Ukrainian chain of gas stations could develop against very strong Eastern Ukrainian and Russian competition.

---

[3] Thus, during the independence referendum on December 1, 1991, 98% in the Western Ukrainian Ternopil voted "Yes" (highest in Ukraine, which averaged 90%), whereas in the Eastern Ukrainian Kharkiv only 75,8% (lowest result) voted that way. See: Kappeler, Andreas (1994), p. 252.

The level of education between East and West is not significantly different. Of course there remain some differences in attitudes, which are related to differences in the historical and cultural ties with Central and Western Europe: *"The idea of property is better known in the West than in the East."*

Table 9.1
Data for different Ukrainian regions, 1999

Indicator	Kharkiv	Donets'k	L'viv	Ivano-Frankivs'k
Population in mln. (total Ukraine: 49.8 mln.)	3.0	5.0	2.7	1.5
Net birth rate per 1000 inhabitants (total Ukraine: –7.0)	-8.9	-9.9	-3.2	-1.9
Gross domestic product, percentage of*	6.4	11.9	4.1	2.1
Monthly average industrial wage in UAH (Ukrainian average: 178 UAH)	184	220	152	140
Unemployment in % (total Ukraine: 11.3)*	11.5	9.2	14.9	13.7
Industrial production level Index for 1990 = 100 (total Ukraine: 51)	42	47	28	44
Foreign trade: export percentage	2.7	18.4	1.7	1.3
import percentage	5.6	5.8	1.8	0.7
Direct foreign investment, end of 1999, in mln. USD (total Ukraine: 3,247.9)	59.5	259.4	113.2	36.8
Tax revenue, percentage of	7.4	10.0	4.9	2.1

* data for 1998

Source: Statistical Yearbook of Ukraine, State Budget Commission.

Kharkiv and Donets'k are two of the most prominent of the nine oblasts on the eastern bank. After Moscow and St. Petersburg these two districts belonged to the largest industrial centres of the USSR. They were primarily characterised by hierarchically organised mega-companies with tens of thousands of employees – incarnations of industrialisation. Nearly all branches of industry, starting with mining, continuing with metallurgy and chemical plants, down to the mechanical industry (which worked up to 60% for defence) and the food industry can be found. Most of them had supra-regional significance – most plants were part of a labour-sharing network together with other plants spread throughout the whole territory of the Soviet Union. Through both districts ran major transport routes of the USSR. Both Kharkiv and Donets'k have airports. Donets'k is also linked to the sea. Kharkiv was the main hub of the southern railway. Both districts abut Russia.

There certainly exist inherited economic structures and specific geographic locations for the districts within which the companies we visited try to pursue their economic activities, although they must act within constraints, which – within all of Ukraine – are locally defined or limited. The resulting questions, which will be discussed hereafter are: How do Ukrainian companies try to operate within this framework? Are the strategies used in the East and the West different, e.g. relative to a stronger Western orientation or a tendency to re-integrate into networks with Russian companies? After 70 or 45 years of Soviet influence, are regional economic policies more defined by companies still married to planned economic thinking or by those taking the new market approach? What learning processes can be observed within companies and the regional administrations?

4 Strategies for survival during the transformation

4.1 Attempts at a new orientation since 1991

The 27 companies visited in the East and the West can be divided into two groups according to their origins: 14 (mega-)companies going back to Soviet times on one side, and 13 companies, which were founded as co-operatives in the 1980s or were created after 1991 on the other. Four of the companies of the first group belong to heavy industry (or the 'military-industrial' complex), four to infrastructure, three to chemistry and three to light industry. The companies of the second group all belonged to light industry and to the service sector.

The attempts to re-orient all these companies, even those still owned by the state, were mainly undertaken by the companies themselves, both with regards to the strategic as well as the financial aspects. "*We were left to our own devices since 1991*", even where state development plans existed, like for example early in 1994 the programme of the cabinet of ministers for the development of the automobile sector and especially of bus production in Ukraine, which defined what models were needed and who was going to produce them. This programme was only amended or scrapped in September 1998.

Of the 14 'former Soviet' companies we interviewed eight had been successful with their re-orientation. For seven of them the markets – before and after 1991 –

lay within Ukraine, or else they had already exported with success to foreign countries even prior to 1991. All eight were able to maintain their markets and their trade marks, and to stay out off red ink.

The six companies that were not successful had been strongly integrated into the labour-sharing network of the former Soviet Union. They had produced for markets, which disappeared after 1991. None of them succeeded to find new markets for their products within Ukraine or Western countries, or to develop new markets with new product lines. They operate with considerable losses and dispose of their products primarily via barter. The payment difficulties of the Ukrainian economy were given as the main reasons. This can, however, not be the only reason, since of them have Western competitors who are able to sell their products in significant quantities on the Ukrainian market.

The companies in light industry and in the service sector (15 out of the 27 interviewed) presented a ray of hope. This applies to companies founded around 1990, mostly small and medium sized companies (SMC), and to the large former Soviet companies who produce food products for domestic consumption. Most of these enterprises were able to weather the depression without having to make major investments. They can benefit directly from hoped for increased demand and the possibilities of import substitutions. Preconditions for this are, however, a customer orientation raised to a central-European level, and prices, which cover costs.

Regarding re-orientation we had expected – in line with many opinions expressed in Western Ukraine, but also in Kyiv – that many companies in the East would be 'ideologically oriented', in the sense that they were still continuing to maintain the structures of the old planned economy. But we could not find such attitudes. Of the four large former Soviet companies we visited in Kharkiv and Donets'k, three are successful and represent completely different branches (metallurgy, chemistry and food products). They look no less pragmatically at their market and profit opportunities under present conditions than do Western Ukrainian companies. The Russian market will be analysed same as any other market, completely without any emotional attachment. The reasons are (a) the difficult economical conditions in Russia (a weak demand by buyers able to make payment, and the high percentage of non-monetary payments) and (b) the trade impediments such as the regulations and the bureaucracy involved with customs duties, which have led to economic isolation rather than to the hoped for opening.[4] The companies, therefore, orient themselves toward other export markets all over the world and toward the Ukrainian market. The percentage of supplies received from Russia has been reduced sharply and is partially offset by supplies from Ukrainian sources.

---

4 Russia now even runs its southern rail transports over lines which avoid Ukrainian territory. This route, though longer, apparently results in lower overall costs, since neither transit fees nor customs duties have to be paid.

Russian companies as well as Russian regions are now competitors for markets and foreign investment.

4.2 Investment behaviour of entrepreneurs

According to information received during our interviews most investments – assuming any are made at all – derive primarily from self-generated income rather than from outside sources. Some funds were also generated through exports into hard-currency countries, or through trade in energy or the wheeling of energy. Some of the accumulation of capital goes back to the middle of the 1980s when the creation of so-called co-operative enterprises had been permitted. Holding companies often resulted from trading activities and the capital accumulation they generated. Holdings invest their capital into many regional enterprises either as strategic investors or also through the purchase of majority ownerships.

There are also some examples of investment financing via short-term bank credits. Many entrepreneurs told us that there was no problem getting credits under favourable conditions, provided the company is a proven success and has always fulfilled its obligations in the past. The problem many companies have, and the ensuing dearth of credit, is that companies do not observe contractual obligations. *East: "If we do not cheat ourselves, the others will not cheat us either."* Some credits were even raised though foreign trade partners.

State credits were of no importance, at least not in the sense that they were used for measures to improve the company's competitiveness. In the case of one foreign credit guarantied by the state significant re-payment problems occurred, whether due to corruption or a poor investment choice remains unclear. Several Eastern Ukrainian companies stated that they had benefited from funds set aside for "special investment regimes for territories with priority development status", which they themselves had helped to design and implement in the political arena.

Concerning the areas into which investments flow, a major portion is used for modernisation and product diversification by companies in the food industry. One exception is the baking of bread. Here, the state-imposed upper price limits for bread – while simultaneously the price for flour is rising – make a profitable production impossible at this time.

In the chemical, pharmaceutical and metallurgical areas, too, investments are being made. These companies are attempting to crowd out imports by using the relative advantages of lower wages, shorter transport routes, and the knowledge of consumer preferences. In the metallurgical industry costs and lower energy consumption are the main goals of modernising investments.

The only enterprises among those questioned into which few investments are made were in the mechanical and the automobile industries. These enterprises all had been part of the networking system of the integrated industry of the Soviet

Union; they had not been able to develop internationally competitive products capable to compete on Western markets. They are still waiting for improvements in the domestic markets, hoping that demand will then quasi create itself. Although management is aware of the low quality of their products, they believe that in poorly developed markets their simple products have a competitive advantage over the more sophisticated Western products. *East: "In a pinch, our motors would run on sunflower oil."* They neglect of course that once the market demand improves, the customers will also demand higher quality goods; in the transport sector this has already happened.

The attempts of some Western enterprises to start assembly operations of Western products together with Ukrainian companies have not succeeded in either part of Ukraine. The reasons given were: the size of Ukrainian companies, non-existing supervisory rights by the Western investors, and the refusal by the Ukrainian companies to stop producing their own, in-house competitive products.

4.3 The battle between local and foreign investors for ownership titles – Is this a positive sign?

A battle royal has begun for control of those companies that succeeded with their re-orientation and are now profitable. Investments play a special role, here. Since Ukrainian enterprises generally have a low market value, as measured by economic criteria (among others: a low fixed asset value, often fully depreciated production facilities, a high risk factor due to the problems within the country) but also due to the rather poorly developed stock market, third parties are in a position to acquire important ownership positions – sometimes even control – for a relatively small investment.

We noted some differences between Eastern and Western Ukraine as to the approach to this problem.

The kind of companies, which are of interest for local and foreign investors have often been created out of former state enterprise through management buy-outs or through leases ('arendnoye predpriyatiye'). In Western Ukraine, management often seemed open-minded vis-à-vis a change in ownership, especially if Western investors were involved. This was often seen as a life preserver under present circumstances. *"If I were in charge in the city, I would donate the good houses in L'viv to foreign investors, just to make sure they come."* Much criticism was heaped on the central administration in Kyiv for their arbitrary handling of foreign investors and for unforeseeable changes in laws, all of which led to restrained investment activity in Ukraine. *"The approach to foreign investment in Ukraine is not unequivocal. With us in Western Ukraine there is no doubt: We think this is the only way out of our problems. Our neighbours Poland, Hungary and the Czech Republic have shown us how."*

In Eastern Ukraine such companies reacted almost all in a rather reserved manner to foreign and even domestic investors who were not local people. They didn't seem to be interested in an ownership change after a long period of restructuring and the building of income generating systems. Hostile take-overs threaten medium size companies particularly when there are taxes outstanding or when they have violated laws (e.g. barter payments). These things are typical for most companies, but are not always their own fault (e.g. when state enterprises do not pay for deliveries, although the company is obliged to make deliveries[5]). It also happens that the interested investor has good connections to important central state institutions (access to the required information and the ability to prevail). With financially strong holding companies one could also observe an attitude of great self-assurance (growing out of the advantage of being better informed about regional and national markets and having good relations to the political power structure) vis-à-vis foreign capital.

4.4 The structural heritage of Eastern Ukraine – Blessing or curse?

Industrial clusters can create a high demand for suppliers and companies in the service sector. This holds true in Western market economies whenever the core companies of these clusters show growth and rely substantially on supplies and services of third parties. For a number of small and medium sized enterprises (SME), often created as joint ventures, the existing dense industrial structure of the Kharkiv and Donets'k regions was indeed a deciding factor for choosing their locations.

To-date, structural changes made by the existing large companies were mostly limited to reducing staff as well as to disconnecting large segments of the social infrastructure and its transfer to the municipalities. The expected restructuring of these companies (disentanglement from and disposition of non-core businesses or of sectors, which are unprofitable) has hardly happened so far. Therefore any new demand for which the newly founded SMEs had hoped did not materialise on any significant scale. The large companies try to employ present employees for all the new tasks with which they are confronted. Only for specialised jobs (e.g. financial management) are persons hired from the outside.

Clinging to the old, strong vertical integration structures (at least as far as companies are concerned, which are profitable and make investments) can be seen as strategy of reducing risk vis-à-vis the major uncertainties of the present contractual relations situation (supply and payment delays, legal arbitrariness). That is to say, that the transaction costs of networks and the barter relationships

5 Such obligations are often of an indirect nature, i.e. they cannot be judicially pursued but state institutions posses many opportunities for sanctions.

are valued higher than possible efficiency gains due to the avoidance of the less satisfactory internal cost structures. Thus, the overall economic uncertainties prevent the creation of new, more efficient structures, in the specific case the co-operation between large companies and SMEs.

It was mentioned several times that this absence of restructuring of large state owned companies also scares foreign investors away from direct co-operation. The leader of a very large plant, which had not been privatised nor restructured because of its status as a 'strategical enterprise' stated pointedly: *"Do we have any advantage being a state enterprise? No, not at all, rather the opposite is true."*

The continuance of SMEs is partially endangered. According to an Eastern Ukrainian company, the number of small enterprises founded after 1998 in his oblast has shrunk to a tenth of its original number. The medium size enterprises in the food or construction sectors, or those, which have found market niches (e.g. special supplies and services for the new upper class), are somewhat better of. They do not rely on the restructuring of large companies, but profit from the advantages of a heavily industrialised area.

4.5 Is there a feeling of belonging to an eastern or a western region, and what does that mean to the companies?

The strongest 'vision' that companies and administrative units of Western Ukraine appear to have of themselves is that of being a bridge between Western Europe and the 'East', which begins at the Dnipro. This concept was brought up in all discussions in L'viv and Ivano-Frankivs'k whenever the question was asked whether there was a Western Ukrainian region and what its characteristics would be. The goal of any regional and central economic policy must be, they said, to build the bridge to Europe, or rather to make Western Ukraine into a part of (Western) Europe also in the economic sense.

In Eastern Ukraine, too, 'Europe' and the way leading to it were often seen as a desirable goal for Ukrainian policy, even though for export oriented companies Europe, Asia and Russia were seen as equal potential markets without any preferences. Ukraine's function of a 'bridge' between Europe and Russia was being proposed as a goal of Ukrainian foreign and economical policy, same as in Western Ukraine. Eastern Ukraine, however, believes all of Ukraine should become this bridge between Eastern and Western Europe.

The enterprises on the eastern side of the Dnipro saw themselves as part of Ukraine and its independence, and acknowledged the need to disengage from Russia more strongly than we expected – and as was assumed in Western Ukraine. They frequently stressed the need of – and their willingness to work for – closer economic ties with the western part of the country. No mention was made of an economic or a territorial Eastern Ukrainian identity, whether in the sense of differences vis-à-vis Western Ukraine or having stronger cultural ties to Russia.

Many saw the political stability of Ukraine – as distinct from Russia, and Eastern Ukraine being a part of the whole Ukraine – as an identity-creating factor. This, they noted was an advantage for sitting in Ukraine as compared to Russia. Western Ukrainian enterprises had a tendency to compare themselves to Poland. They deplored that history had cut them off from the more positive developments on the other (western) side of the border.

5 Possibilities and limits for a regional economic policy

West: "Local powers did what they could, but they could not do much."

East: "One must never go to see a government office without money."

5.1 Is the best regional policy no policy at all?

This provocative thesis can certainly be accepted for developed capitalistic market economies. Where markets do not fail, and where competition between regions works well enough ('voting with ones feet'), no steering activities by the state are needed to improve a region's attractiveness. Rather, the regions will flourish with competitive enterprises, where employment is being created, and which will in the end become crystallisation points for regional production networks. Enterprises, which purchase and sell all over the world, which have free access to labour and capital markets, and which are not excessively burdened with regulations and taxes, require no regional policies.[6]

The situation in Ukraine, and in Russia and Belarus too, is somewhat different. Under the post-Soviet institutional framework – as discussed in Section 2 above – an unimpeded entrepreneurial activity is very difficult to realise. Rather, as regularly stressed by the interviewees, there is much intermingling of state regulation and state interference with economic activity. Bottlenecks in the infrastructure lead to further regionalisation of economic life. It therefore becomes necessary to regionally influence the development processes in these post-Soviet countries.

6 See: Hirschhausen, Christian von and Jürgen Bitzer (2000): The Globalization of Industry and Innovation in Eastern Europe: From Post-socialist Restructuring to International Competitiveness. Cheltenham.

5.2 Does the separation of powers between the centre and the regions work?

Its basic function to create a stable overall economic environment has so far only inadequately been fulfilled by the Central Government in Kyiv. *West: "To let a country flourish takes very little, namely a foundation in the form of a proper judicial system. But in our country it's not working that's forbidden but to live."* Some companies would even deny to the state the power to create such a framework: *East: "There is neither a central nor a regional power. Those who are in power cannot be seen on TV."*

Although, the control function of the state exercised over enterprises has been greatly reduced as a consequence of privatisation, direct or indirect dependence on central institutions still continues for privatised and for private (newly founded) companies (for instance due to contracts with the state, through the establishment of prices and tariffs for certain goods, when special taxation rules are granted, through the enforcement of court judgements, etc.).

Where the central state power has been abolished or has disappeared, the regional administrations have often jumped in the breach. Sometimes they attempt to help companies in their regions to prevail with central institutions (multi-faceted forms of lobbying) and they try to gain control functions within companies (e.g. by the region demanding to administer the state's share of the enterprise). Sometimes the Central Government intentionally transfers control functions to the region, without however, providing the necessary resources. For example, this might concern the determination of privileges for certain user groups, without permitting that additional funds could remain in the region. Hence, the regional administrations demand greater authority over the taxes raised in their respective regions. Some also demand a bi-cameral system, similar to that in Russia, to give the regions a stronger voice.[7]

5.3 Forms of regional policies

East: *"The less the 'chinovniki' (civil servants) have to distribute, the better for the economy."*

West: *"We must have clear rules of the game. They must not be changed all the time – and then even retroactively. We can succeed everywhere, provided we are not interfered with."*

---

7 A proposal to that effect received an overwhelming plurality of votes in the referendum of April 16, 2000.

Most enterprises were of the opinion that the oblasts and the cities attempt to pursue regional policies. The forms in which these expressed themselves often did not meet with approval.[8]

Regional policies at this time is concerned with the following items:

i) Special economic zones (SEZ): 'Free' or 'special economic zones', according to an opinion held throughout Ukraine, provide particular opportunities to attract investments and to further a good investment climate. Investors in these zones receive special privileges, such as elimination or reduction of customs duties, corporate and value-added taxes, luxury tax and social taxes; they may benefit from advantages when purchasing land and for raw material supplies.

SEZ Yavoriv in Western Ukraine is an example. During Soviet times the area had the disadvantage of being on the border to Poland. Today this location is a potential advantage for Western companies, which, for reasons of cost savings (wage costs) want to move their production from Central to Eastern Europe, but want to stay as close as possible Western Europe. Up to February 27, 1999, the day Parliament granted Yavoriv the status of SEZ, this area could not benefit from its potential advantages because of the general economic and institutional uncertainties within Ukraine.[9]

A slightly different approach to insulate oneself from the general economic situation is being taken by Eastern Ukraine. After attempts to establish an SEZ in the region bordering Russia had failed, and only two small SEZs were established in the Donets'k region, the two regions were able to persuade the Verchovna Rada (Parliament) to enact two laws, one for Donets'k (as of 1999) and one for Kharkiv (as of January 1, 2000), allowing for implementation of a special investment regime for territories requiring priority in development. Investments in certain 'priority' branches – which however de facto comprise all branches, excepting trade – are promoted under this special regime. These special investment regimes, which are not based on territory like SEZs, but rather on production, are meant primarily to further restructuring of the enterprises and to attract outside investments. In contrast to the SEZs, which are mainly oriented towards improved import and export custom duties, the emphasis of the special investment regimes is mainly on reduced capital gains taxation for the investments.

According to administration data, 65 applications for subventions in accordance with the special investment regime have been approved in the Donets'k region, totalling 539 million USD, of which 59% were foreign investments. Admittedly it

---

8 It is interesting that regional policies was often seen as a negative thing in the West, i.e. as "*Lobbying in Kyiv*". It was said, that more subventions were flowing into the eastern part of the country, since the western regions did not have as big a lobby in Parliament as the east (the difference in lobby effort was said to be about 1:10).

9 Prior to February 1999 only about 15 million USD in foreign investments entered the region.

cannot be established with certainty whether the introduction of the regime was the cause for the investments, or whether it simply created a windfall for investments, which would have taken place without. However, some investors, when questioned, mentioned the investment regime as a positive factor among the selection criteria.

The flood of applications for special advantages can be seen as a reaction to the excessive centralisation of the Ukrainian economy. After all, all exemptions permitted to investors are exemptions to regulations enacted by the central authorities. And yet, the efficacy of such zones is being questioned. They may well provide a short-term corrective by creating, within a small sphere, conditions, which insulate it from the desolate general conditions in the country. Yet it is doubtful whether the regions in question will really profit from this special status. The laws for the SEZs, for instance, again contain elements of over-regulation and possible state intervention.[10] In addition, there are by now so many zones having a special investment status, that the usefulness for any one given area is wasted.

ii) Policies concerning good order: In Western Ukraine these policies were mainly seen in the context of an external, non-interfering framework. For instance, the non-interventionist regional policies of the L'viv oblast were judged positively as well as neutral and negatively: *"They do not trouble us." "It was positive that no measures were taken. They only observe." "The oblast helps us by not interfering. But it is not able to change laws, which are hostile to investment."* The concept 'policy' was thus instinctively equated with 'intervention' or 'interference', and that both in the West and in the East. Non-interference in L'viv oblast was judged positively concerning tax collection *("The oblast budget covers its needs, this reduces corruption.")* and also concerning the acquisition of foreign investments *("They [the responsible ministry in Kyiv] supported us by not having interfered.").*

In Eastern Ukraine, supporting non-interference was more the wish of companies than the reality. Here, the regional politicians act mainly in the interest of the large enterprises. They undervalue the importance of law and order and protection from administrative arbitrariness, which are of critical importance to small and medium sized companies. The dependence upon the regional administration and its good will (rights can be withdrawn, pretexts can always be found) was frequently mentioned by companies in Kharkiv and Donets'k. They noted that personal contacts to the authorities were of crucial importance. *"Only if you can reach an agreement based personal acquaintance will you be left in peace."* These relationships are connected with significant transaction costs. *"It is impossible to resolve anything by phone or fax."*

---

[10] See also German Advisory Group on Economic Reforms in Ukraine (1998): Sonderwirtschaftszonen als Mittel der Investitionsförderung? Kyiv, June, mimeo.

iii) Fiscal policies: The local administrations can play a certain positive role with regards to tax assessments and collection. Some fields of taxation are entirely within their domain, such as real taxation (in one case bankruptcy of a company was avoided by waiving the taxation of its realty). The regional authorities can also use some latitude, for instance, regarding delays of payment of tax arrears. This competency regards not only regional, but also central taxation. (*West: "The mortgaging of our company was deferred because the regional administration prorogued our tax arrears."*) It was frequently mentioned that more money (taxes) should stay in the region, i.e. that financial equalisation should define the responsibilities of the various levels of government. This happens in Ukraine every year, so that great uncertainty exists with respect to the income situation of the regions.

In this sense, the regional authorities do not as yet make full use of their powers; sometimes they may even make the situation for an enterprise more difficult. Small and medium sized enterprises, especially in Eastern Ukraine, often suffer under permanent stress caused by the regional tax offices. They receive no support from the regional authorities, for instance, when it comes to the remission of value-added taxes in the case of exports, or to the recognition of their favoured tax status as joint ventures. On the contrary, even legal judgements of higher courts are often not recognised by the regional authorities. The significant delays in the payment of remissions appear to be desired for budgetary reasons. The political weight of small and medium sized enterprises is small and their importance to economic life is still being undervalued, and so they seem to be chosen to make up for the regional budgetary difficulties concerning revenues. The regional administrations use all means, even unfair ones, in order to raise the revenues for the regional budgets, and this especially prior to presidential elections. *East: "A cash difference of 10 UAH, evidently provoked and caused by local officials, resulted in a fine of 3,800 UAH."*

iv) Credit policies: Cities and regional administrations posses means of investment financing in spite of a poorly developed fiscal federalism. For instance, cities can issue treasury notes (even though there have already been painful experiences).[11] Furthermore, securities can be given in the form of real property and buildings. To some of the visited enterprises, especially those serving the community's infrastructure, the cities distribute direct subventions to keep the production process going.

v) Information policies: The transmission of information is very important, but does not need to be done by the state. At this time, most transmitters of information are occupied with circumventing bureaucratic obstacles. Their activity, primarily in foreign trade, is lucrative. (*West: "Every chamber of*

---

11 However, for investments above a certain value, this should only happen under strict conditions, with the agreement of the ministry of finance, and in domestic currency.

commerce and industry has its area of expertise. L'viv is particularly knowledgeable in the certification and distribution of codes. Chernihiv has specialised on brokering at the border, and Dnipropetrovs'k on the certification of metal exports.") The chambers of commerce and industry, both of L'viv and Ivano-Frankivs'k, are good examples that these tasks can be efficiently executed.

vi) Policies concerning the infrastructure: This field offers many possibilities, which depend primarily on price policies. There are significant degrees of freedom regarding the fixing of prices for community services. For instance, it would be possible to raise all tariffs within a region step by step up to a level, which would cover costs, and to remove existing reduced tariffs (which are now used by over 50% of all users), since they have to be paid out of the regional budget. Not only community services, but also adult education and middle-class policies are part of the infrastructure in the wider sense. For example, some very positive experiences had been made in one Western Ukrainian city with very small credit programmes financed by foreigners. Positive results are also experienced with immediate building and modernisation programmes (For instance: A railway branch line was laid up to a plant being built, hotels meeting Western standards were built, railway stations were renovated). Educational programmes (university level training courses for small and medium sized enterprises) and programmes supporting the introduction of international technical and quality standards, also showed very positive results. The authorities are also helpful when it comes to the transfer to the communities of the social infrastructure belonging to companies. Most of the interviewed companies did not have any social infrastructure left in their systems.

However, political goals concerning infrastructure often collide with goals of social politics, which is a particularly sensitive part of regional politics. Most of the people who have been hurt by the reforms blame local politics for their misfortune. From this perspective, one can understand that some cities have maintained the socialist symbiosis between companies and the social sphere. *West: "We are the city: Our power plant maintains the whole social sphere, builds, provides recreational possibilities, etc., etc., and even furnishes the tomatoes, which you are eating at this moment."* In another context, they even keep a certain minimum of (value destroying) production going in order to justify the survival of the social sphere. *West: "While production stops during the winter, the social sphere continues (polyclinic, kindergarten, residences). This assures employment for some 300 to 400 people (out of a total of 5,000) who maintain the infrastructure."* One extreme case of social politics consisted in forcing the whole social sphere onto an investor who only wanted take over a small portion of a large company. *West: "The regional administrators, pointing to the contract, ordered the paying of all 17,000 members of the company by the investor."*

6 Bridges to Europe that could be built

Ukraine can break out of its present isolation and become an important bridge between the whole CIS room and the western part of Europe, provided it accepts that the bridge function to Central and Western Europe is unquestioningly connected with the introduction of a capitalist, market oriented system such as practised in the other parts of Europe.

However at this time, Ukraine presents itself to the visitor as a wall rather than a bridge to Western Europe: There is a border, which takes much time (and money) to get across, there are impediments to transport (narrow/wide rail gauge), there are language and communication problems, etc. Western Ukraine has not been able to get over its role as a 'border region' of the CIS, and Eastern Ukraine is confronted with a partially reducing willingness to co-operate by Russia, which is building its own bridges to Western Europe by re-building the gas pipeline and by attempting to found special economic zones such as Kaliningrad.

Its Central European neighbours, too, have up to now recognised Ukraine only partially as one of their own. Only a short time ago had the Polish President taken the initiative and publicly addressed to what extent the west-orientation of his country will touch his Ukrainian neighbours, and declared this to be a political integration challenge. The fact that the summit of Central and East European heads of state took place in L'viv in May 1999, may well be a consequence of this recognition.

Ukraine must make every effort to build its own bridges if it wants to avoid the danger of being isolated from both East and West. After all, Russia doesn't need Ukraine anymore, and its Central European neighbours concentrate on Western Europe, which demands a closing, rather than an opening of the borders. The time of waiting for Ukraine to be discovered or needed has long since passed.

The following measures could represent starting points for such bridge functions:

- expansion of the Western Ukrainian network of gas station in a western direction. A first co-operative venture with a Lithuanian refinery is working well so far. The markets in south-western Poland, eastern Slovakia, eastern Hungary and north-western Romania are but a few kilometres away (whereas the large user markets of Ukraine are at least 500 km further off). A precondition for this bridge function is the liberalisation of foreign trade with raw materials and oil products. Also, Western Ukrainian consumers would have to accept Central European petroleum prices;
- re-opening of the product pipeline between Kalush (Ivano-Frankivs'k region) and Tiszavasvari (eastern Hungary). Caused by increased demand in Central Europe and in consequence of the modernisation of the mega-companies, one can observe a move to intensify the co-operation between Ukraine and Hungary in the fields of olefins, poly-olifins and vinyl chloride. Additional

members of this common 'bridge' enterprise could be Ukrainian, Russian and Western European trade partners. The preconditions for such a co-operation are that world market prices form the basis of the trade relationships and that international norms will be respected (product quality, law and order, respecting credit contracts);

- connection of Western Ukraine to the oil pipeline between the Black Sea and Central Europe. The project of an oil pipeline between Odessa and Brody (100 km east of L'viv) has at this time and under the present economic and energy conditions no hope of being financed. It would, however, be immediately realisable as soon as those refineries in Central Europe, which would profit from it, would engage themselves financially and institutionally (e.g. Borsa, Szazhalombatta, Tiszavasvari, Strazske, Glinic, Jaslo, Jedlice, Plock);
- an early completion of *one* high-speed highway connection between south-western Poland and the L'viv area. The connection Przemysl (Poland) with Mostiska (Ukraine) had been identified during the trans-European traffic network negotiations in Crete (1993). Now however, it appears as if Ukraine prefers the connection Radymno (Poland) with Yavoriv (Ukraine).[12] Should the high-speed road connections really be primarily project-financed, then it would be possible to select the better corridor on the basis of competition. If not, then the region should try to avoid unnecessary expense by selecting one specific road. More important, however, than any road improvements is the acceleration and simplification of customs and passport formalities. Only in this way can the present 'wall' between Poland and Ukraine be turned into a bridge;
- harmonising the railway transit between Central Europe and L'viv. With the East and West European rail gauges being different, the project of lengthening the western-gauge rail line from Mostiska to L'viv could take on an historic bridge function in the context of a trans-European corridor. Improvements to the L'viv cargo terminal and to the central hotels should also be considered in this context. Preconditions are higher prices for cargo and passenger tariffs and for all related services;
- construction of a linkage system between the post-Soviet (IPS) and the Central-Western European power grids. Two project compete with each other: (a) Modernisation of the direct-current connection system of the Burshtyn station (and in parallel: Dobro Dvir) in the direction of Slovakia and Hungary, expansion to 800 MW with the possibility of connecting the whole system ('island solution'). This solution presupposes the disconnection of the

---

[12] This is suggested by the improvements being made to the border station at Krakovets, as well as by the concession proposal for improving the high-speed highway between Krakovets and L'viv (see Presidential Decree No. 739/98 of July 7, 1998).

Western Ukrainian grid from that of the rest of the country. (b) Connection of the two large grids via a direct-current linkage ('back-to-back station'). No matter which solution is eventually chosen, this power linkage would exert significant pressure for general modernisation on the Ukrainian electricity system;

- raising the standard of wastewater treatment to European levels in all medium size and large cities of Western Ukraine. At this time no adequate treatment capacities exist; industrial and household waste effluents enter the rivers (Bystrica, Dnestr, Prut) without treatment and in large quantities. As a result downstream areas (Moldova, Odessa, Black Sea) are also badly polluted. The introduction of Central European standards and technologies into Ukraine could be supported through pilot projects in the western areas. This region, because of its geographical location and its natural riches, has a particular interest in maintaining minimal ecological standards. A first example could be the project of the city of Ivano-Frankivs'k, which is being implemented with Western help;
- raising the tourism infrastructure in the Carpathian Mountains in Ukraine to European standards. The Ukrainian part of the Carpathians is often called the most beautiful. Its tourism potential is high: The Yeremcha-Varokhta National Park, Truskavets, the ski and hiking region of Slavsky. Whereas Romania, Slovakia and Poland have developed their parts of the Carpathians into internationally recognised tourist areas, the services available in Western Ukraine have, with few exceptions, remained at the post-Soviet level. Any existing tourist capacities would have to be privatised and the opportunities for new facilities would have to be improved (e.g. Hotel Roksolana in Ivano-Frankivs'k);
- development of foreign language skills for specialists working for infrastructure projects, which require a high degree of co-ordination. To be able to function as a bridge requires an ability to communicate. A striking example is the requirement foreseen for personnel in the Ukrainian dispatch centre once it will be hooked up with the Central European electricity grid: The only two permitted languages will be English and German;
- increased use of telecommunications with Western Europe. At this time, Ukraine is connected to the world primarily through an overlay network. This system works well, but it is costly and has a low capacity. As soon as prices are in line, this bridge function will be easy to fulfil. The normal net should be brought up to an international level;
- payment of Ukraine's debts for energy supplies in order to ease the relations with Russia. Otherwise the danger exists that Ukraine's position as a gas transfer partner will be seriously weakened. The consumption of energy without paying for them should be stopped, and energy selling prices should be introduced, which cover costs. This would also create incentives for saving

energy, a factor that could greatly ease the payment balance for energy imports.

7 Conclusions

The regions can contribute a lot to change the potential bridges to Europe into real ones. The regional authorities should most strongly emphasise law and order, and protection from arbitrary decision making. The creation of special structures for enterprises already established in the region does not change the basic existing framework. The dependence on the responsible administration, in this case the regional one, and on their 'good will' remains. Rights must be enforceable independent of personal relations. Furthermore, the dominance of personal dependence makes real competition between regions impossible.

Meaningful regional politics should aim for the stabilisation of the principles of distribution of tax revenues, i.e. the introduction of financial equalisation principles. Parliamentarians, who want to serve their oblasts, should not lobby for specific branches or companies, but should work together with their peers, across party boundaries, to establish conditions allowing for stable financial planning within their oblasts. This would create certainty in the regional planing processes and assure an active, not sporadic, fiscal policy.

Regions could also become information transmitters, e.g. via a capable chamber of commerce and industry. This would also help to reduce the dependency of enterprises on personal relations with state organisations. Transparent associations of entrepreneurs (which are non-discriminatory and do not depend on personal relationships) should be founded to push the economic interests of their members, and to replace non-transparent and discriminating existing structures between the industrial and political spheres.

This makes it clear, that regional policies of this type will result in furthering the investment climate throughout Ukraine. The central authorities should embrace and support these ideas; they should not undermine the development of a uniform market in Ukraine by insisting on extreme centralist policies. After all, no region will be able to hold on to an investor if the climate within the country is not friendly toward investors. A whole series of basic problems concerned with efficient economic activity (the right to purchase real estate, price fixing by the state, tax rates) must therefore be solved at the level of the Central Government. Attempts by the regions to solve these problems at the regional level – in view of the lack of action at the centre – raise the possible danger of using the region for enforcing special (private) economic interests.

The argument that capital was lacking for financing investments is a myth. Projects with the promise of gain have found financing, even though learning processes had to be gone through. Diversification strategies, investment activities and changes in the senior management prove to point. The personal relations factor remains a deciding factor at this time, a fact that can be clearly demonstrated, when two companies of similar size, and working in the same sector, achieve different results.

In spite of the laudable and necessary efforts to attract foreign investors, their role is being greatly over-valued. Any regional economic development depends primarily on local investments. The experience in other transformation countries proves this: For instance Poland, where about 250 billion USD have been invested between 1993 and 1998, 'only' about 20 billion USD (or 4%) came from foreign sources. Special treatment of foreign investors can therefore not be justified. The competitiveness of Ukraine with respect to wages also does not justify special tax treatment. Ukrainian holding companies and banks are waiting for reasonable investment conditions.

10

Ukraine as the Gas Bridge to Europe? Economic and Geopolitical Considerations

Petra Opitz and Christian von Hirschhausen[1]

1 Introduction

Gas transit is a sensitive issue, particularly in a crisis-prone region such as the former Soviet Union. Strategic power games and geopolitical issues seem to dominate 'pure' economic theory when it comes to determining transit fees, capacities, investment projects, and the like. Privatisation and deregulation become highly sensitive issues as well. It may have come as a surprise, therefore, that amidst the political, economic and social upheaval of the post-Soviet transformation crisis, the transit of Russian gas to Central and Western Europe has continued smoothly, and even expanded. Indeed, recent contracts and economic forecasts seem to foresee an increasing role of Russian gas on the expanding Western European market.

Ukraine is a strategic link in this relationship. Until recently, it exercised monopolistic power for gas transit from Russia to Central and Western Europe and the Balkans, influencing prices and quantities. Gas also plays a dominant role in the development of the Ukrainian economy, transit revenues representing almost 10% of total exports. However, the quick fortunes to be made in this sector also contribute to the general political climate of rent-seeking and corruption, making the state reluctant to let go of this windfall and to introduce efficient corporate governance. While few changes have occurred in the gas sector during the first decade of independence, the pressure on Ukraine to modify the functioning of its gas transit activities is increasing:

- The technical state of the pipeline is said to be very poor. Indeed the under-investment of the last ten years is now beginning to show, be it in increasing

1 With research assistance from Igor Kalapun, Tatyana Vakhnenko, Uta Kreibig, Wolfgang Härle and Berit Meinhart. The usual disclaimers apply.

compressor fuel consumption, or with corrosion problems. Estimates of investment requirements for the transit system alone vary between 0.5-2.0 billion USD;

- The issue of Ukrainian debt towards Russia stemming from unpaid energy bills is increasingly challenging the country's independence, and thus the gas sector's independence. As of late 2000, unpaid bills to Russia have reached about 1.4 and 2.0 billion USD. Russia is intensifying its lobbying efforts towards debt-equity deals, seeking ownership of the transit pipeline and of two strategic underground storage facilities;
- After several fruitless attempts to increase the transparency within the vertically integrated state owned gas monopoly Naftogaz Ukrainy (formerly Ukrgazprom), the Government is now seeking solutions to reduce the information asymmetry and extract more of the company's rent. Several options are being considered, such as privatising Ukrtransgaz, which is actually a subsidiary of Naftogaz, or offering a long-term concession for the operation of the transit pipeline (most likely to a foreign company);
- The Northern connection from Russia through Belarus into the European Union, after having progressed slowly, now seems to be picking up speed, the new Yamal-1 pipeline linking Belarus (Minsk- Nesvizh) to Poland (Kondratki-Wloclawek) having been finished in November 1999. Its present capacity of 10 bcm (billion cubic meters), it is supposed to reach 28 bcm within 3 years and 56 bcm at a later date. The next step to bypass Ukraine would be the Yamal-2 pipeline connecting Kondratki (Poland) to Velke Kapusany (Slovakia) and thus to join the central corridor (the Brotherhood pipeline, see Graph 10.1). These developments put even more pressure on Ukraine's negotiating power, and thus the profits resulting from gas transit.

This Chapter analyses the perspectives of Ukrainian gas transit given the recent developments, and potential repercussions on Russia and Western Europe. Our hypothesis is that unless Ukraine quickly puts in place a stable and reliable framework for gas transit, it will loose a large part of its current market share and profits from gas transit between Russia and Central/Western Europe.

The Chapter is structured as follows: Section 2 presents the current status of the Ukrainian transit pipeline system, both from a technical/economic and a political perspective. We discuss costs, spare capacity, investment requirements, and estimate the profits from the monopolistic gas transit in 1999. Section 3 provides an analytical framework for a concession of the International Gas Transit System of Ukraine (IGTS) to a Ukrainian or a foreign operator, currently under debate. Keeping in mind the negative experience with management contracts in Kazakhstan, some proposals for the design of a concession are laid out. The critical issue is the value of the pipeline for which we provide quantitative estimates. Finally in Section 4, we discuss options for external coalitions for the

Ukrainian gas industry, including the role of Belarus as a competitor in the 'market' for transit. Conclusions are formulated in Section 5.

2 The state of the Ukrainian International Gas Transit System (IGTS)

2.1 Overview

The IGTS currently consists of four main corridors: the *Belarus* (Torshok-Dolyna), *Progress* (Yelets-Ushgorod), *Soyus* (Novopskov-Ushgorod) and the *Balkan* (Yelets-Izmail, see Graph 10.1). The total transit capacity to Central/Western Europe and the Balkans is estimated at 150 bcm, with a maximum capacity to Central/Western Europe of about 110 bcm. The length of the transit pipelines is 5,492 km, the volume-weighted length of haul for transit gas to Europe being 1,150 km (IEA, 1996, 148). In the 1990s, over 95% of Russia's gas export to Europe transited through Ukraine (the remainder passing through a low-pressure pipeline between Kobrin (Belarus) and Warsaw (Poland)). The IGTS transit system is not separated from the domestic high-pressure system. As a consequence, Russia is essentially unable to secure payment for gas supplied to the Ukrainian market by cutting the supply, since most large Ukrainian industrial gas consumers are hooked directly into the transit pipelines.

The main transit volumes are flowing to Central/Western Europe (about 102.8 bcm in 1999), other volumes are flowing through the Southern 'Balkan' line to Moldova, Bulgaria, Rumania and Turkey (about 19.9 bcm in 1999) and via Eastern parts of the high pressure system to Russian territories (about 11.8 bcm) (see Table 10.1). In addition, every year considerable volumes are pumped into and extracted from large underground storage systems, which are mainly situated near the Ukrainian border with the West (about 16.2 bcm in 1999).[2]

---

2 There is also a small amount of official Ukrainian natural gas exports, amounting to about 63 million USD in 1999. These exports created several conflicts with Gazprom, which accused Ukraine of illegal re-exports of Russian gas, related to the outstanding debt for gas imports from Russia.

Graph 10.1
Gas transit pipelines from Russia to Central/Western Europe through Ukraine and Belarus

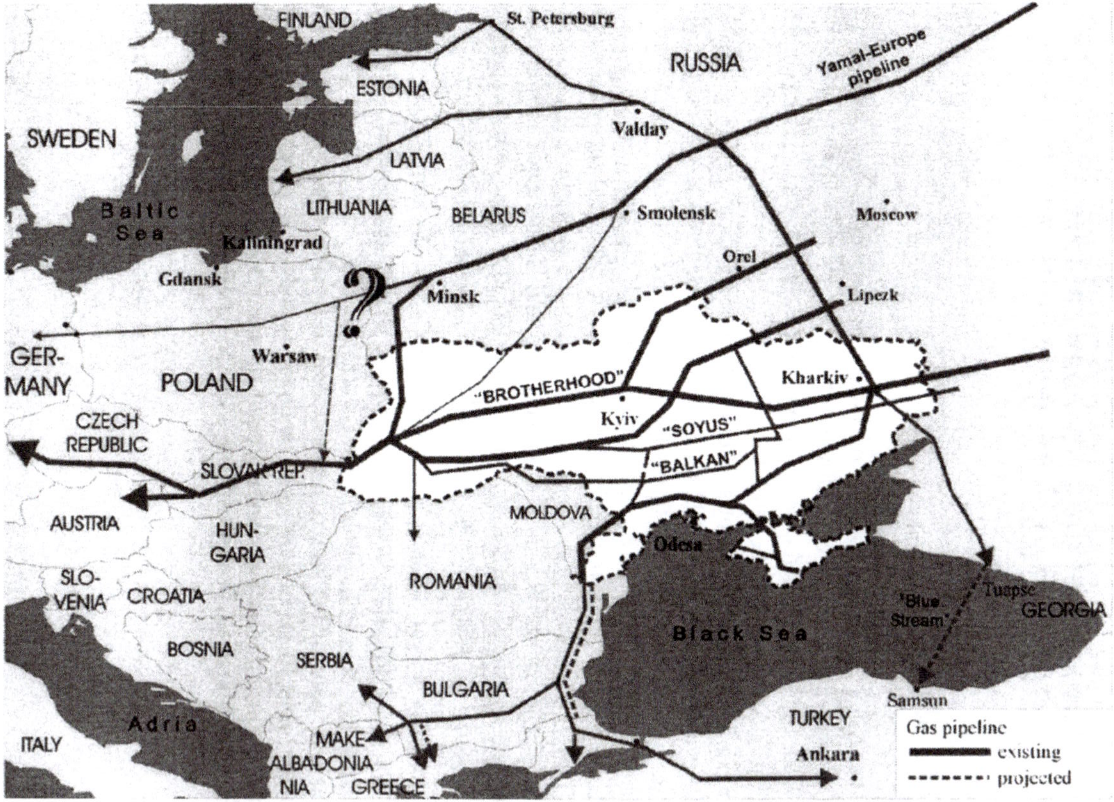

Table 10.1
Gas transit through Ukraine, 1992-1999

	Units	1994	1995	1996	1997	1998	1999
Total volume of gas transported through high pressure pipelines*	bcm	n.a.	n.a.	n.a.	239.3	241.5	226.8
Of which total transit	bcm	133.6	136.5	140.5	134.5	141.7	134.5
Of which:							
to Central/Western Europe		106.8	110.5	118.0	110.5	115.5	115.5
to South Eastern Europe							17.1
to NIS and Russia		26.8	26.0	22.5	24.0	26.2	14.6
Price of transit**	bcm	n.a.	n.a.	n.a.	30.0	n.a.	34.7
Negotiated transit fee	USD/tcm/ 100km	0.65	0.65	1.75	1.75	1.09	1.09

Source: Ministry of Economy of Ukraine.

* Transit pipelines are considered part of the high-pressure system, but not all high-pressure pipelines are considered transit pipelines.

** Here calculated as the volume of gas delivered to Ukraine in payment for the gas transited.

2.2 Technical description

The transit pipeline needs considerable investment for modernisation and maintenance. About 17% of the pipelines have already exceeded their estimated lifetime of 33 years. One third of them is about 14 to 23 years old and only about 40% was built during the last 13 years. For nearly 50% the anti-corrosion isolation is considered insufficient or broken.[3] Although the compressor stations are generally in good condition, many of them need to be modernised, and some need replacement in order to upgrade efficiency. According to expert assessments, the amount of natural gas required for operation of the pipeline system itself could be reduced from 7.1 bcm to 5.6 bcm. Given an average gas price of 35 USD per thousand cubic meters (USD/tcm), this would represent a saving of about 52.5 million USD a year.

3 Kyivskie Vedomosti (1998), December 19, p. 6.

The transit pipeline is considered to be run at its maximum capacity at this point in time. This is linked to the almost simultaneous increase of demand by Ukrainian and by Western customers during the winter months. Due to expected increases in demand in South Eastern Europe, especially in Turkey, capacity extension of the Balkan pipeline from Tal'noye to Izmail is under way, carried out by a Russian-Ukrainian joint venture. As this extension would lower the capacity of the Western part of the Soyus pipeline, capacity extension is planned for the Torshok-Dolyna pipeline by adding some compressor stations. For the near future this seems to be the only extension needed.

2.3 Perspectives for gas exports

Until 2010, the European market expects an increase of natural gas imports up to a total of about 270 bcm (compared to about 140 bcm in 1995), meaning that Europe would increasingly rely on gas imports from non-European countries.[4] Russia is estimating to on increase its gas exports to non-CIS countries by about 160 bcm by that same time.[5]

Concerning gas issues, Ukraine presently has to deal with two major Russian companies. While transit concerns Gazprom only, Ukrainian gas imports from Russia are at this time being realised by Itera, an international offshore company founded in 1992. The company, recently registered as a company residing in Moscow, became an important player on the East European and Middle Asian natural gas markets in 1999. Unlike Gazprom, which seems to set its priority on Western European markets, Itera manages an increasing share of the CIS (Commonwealth of Independent States) market, with its commercial difficulties related to the non-payment problem. Maintaining a close relationship with Gazprom, Itera is a totally privately owned company operating like a 'normal' Western company with little need to consider political issues, which Gazprom often has to take into account.

Thus, the idea, at present being discussed in Kyiv, of creating a joint venture between Itera and Naftogaz Ukrainy with the responsibility for managing the transit gas pipeline inside Ukraine, might be a plausible and acceptable solution for Ukraine. Involving a private foreign company would allow it to put more pressure on increasing the payment discipline of Ukrainian customers, but would also allow the Ukrainian State to maintain control over revenues. Concerning security of gas transits, the close relationship between Itera and Gazprom would be a kind of guarantee, without involving Gazprom directly.

---

4 European Commission (2000): European Union Energy Outlook to 2010. The Shared Analysis Project. Brussels, pp. 46-48.

5 Ekspert (2000), No. 11, p. 28.

2.4 Transit volumes, prices and costs

Gas transit through Ukraine has steadily increased throughout the 1990s (see Table 10.1). The transit fee is negotiated yearly between Gazprom (and eventually other trading companies such as Itera) and the Ukrainian state holding company Naftogaz Ukrainy, depending on the negotiated gas price. The transit fee is not paid in cash but as a gas equivalent: In 1999, Russia delivered 34.7 bcm of gas for 119.9 bcm of gas transited by Ukraine to Central and Southern Europe. Thus, the nominal transit fee is of anecdotal interest only, what counts is the economic value of the gas. In 1999, this was estimated at an average 35 USD/tcm.

According to business estimates, total costs for operating the transit system in 1999 were 2,575 million UAH (about 515 million USD).[6] Variable costs include the compressor station gas (1,440 million UAH) and about 90% of the electricity consumption (i.e. 90% of 202 million UAH = 182 million UAH). Given a transit volume of 119.9 bcm and an average haulage of 1,150 km, this yields a marginal transport cost of 0.235 USD/tcm/100 km.[7] The fixed costs amount to 953 mln. UAH (191 mln. USD), including capital costs, maintenance, personnel, and other expenses.

The revenue side, too, can be calculated in two ways:

- using the official transit fee of 1.09 USD/tcm /100 km, the total revenue is 1,504 million USD;
- using the monetary value of the 34.7 bcm of transit gas and the gas price of 35 USD/tcm, the revenue calculates as 1,215 billion, or 0.88 USD/tcm/100 km, which is somewhat less than the official figure. In the following calculations, we shall retain this latter revenue estimate, as it seems to correspond more closely to reality.

The transit price of 0.88 USD/tcm/100 km is clearly above the marginal costs of 0.235 USD/100km/tcm. This can be explained by Ukraine's monopoly situation: It sets the fee by equating marginal revenue with marginal costs.[8]

Yearly profits before taxes can now be calculated as Π = revenues – costs = (1,215–515) million USD = 700 million USD.

---

6 This and the subsequent calculations are based on data published in Energobusiness, Kyiv, various issues. We use an average exchange rate of 5 UAH/USD.

7 An alternative way to calculate the marginal costs is to use the figure for compressor station gas (7.2 bcm) and monetise it with 35 USD/tcm: marginal costs c = [7.2 bcm x 35 USD/tcm] / [1,150 km x 119.9 bcm] = 0.183 USD/tcm/100 km; this is somewhat below the figures used above.

8 Grais, Watin and Kangbin Zheng (1996): Strategic Interdependence in European East-West Gas Trade: A Hierarchical Stackelberg Game Approach. In: Energy Journal, Vol. 17, No. 3, pp. 61-84.

Three types of taxes have to be paid:

- tax to the budget: 1.8 billion UAH = 360 million USD;
- value-added-tax of 20%, here backward calculated as 16.67% on the profit reduced by the tax to the budget: VAT: 16.67% x (700 – 360) million USD = 57 million USD;
- profits tax of 30% on the remaining 284 million USD = 85 million USD.

The profits after taxes thus amount to: (700 – 360 – 57 – 85) million USD = 198 million USD, i.e. the effective tax rate is as high as 72%.

The pre-tax profit of 700 million USD represents no less than 2.4% of the country's GDP. However, the problem is that the Government does not see much of this manna. In 1999, payments of the transit tax were as low as 200 million UAH, and in the first months of 2000, the tax payment ratio was as low as 8%. This is where the idea of a concession comes into play.

3 Concession as a compromise between the status quo and privatisation

Under present conditions, a concession of the gas transit pipeline to one or more experienced industrial operators looks like a promising way out of the dilemma. Concessions are used world-wide in order to attract private capital and know-how. However, one recent experience with a large-scale concession has demonstrated the complexity of private-public partnerships and the risks to private investors in such institutions, linked to commercial risk and to blackmail.[9] Kazakhstan is an example on how *not* to do it.

3.1 Experiences with infrastructure management contracts in Kazakhstan

During the last decade the Kazakh Government concluded a large number of so-called management contracts with foreign companies, some of them concerning network-linked industries like the power and the gas sectors. This was due to the worsening of the financial and technical situation of Kazakh state-owned companies. These companies might otherwise have had to be closed, on the one

---

9 Just think of the first privately financed highway in Hungary, which was expropriated by the state soon after completion; or the Channel Tunnel project linking Great Britain and France, the financial collapse of which was avoided only be direct and indirect state subsidies.

hand because of lacking operating capital, and on the other because public sentiment did not support privatisation (though the Government did). By concluding management contracts, the Government wanted to attract foreign investment and management know-how rapidly, without having to wait for a change in public opinion in favour of privatisation.

Although there is not much information available about the actual contract conditions, because they had been concluded under the special supervision of the Kazakh President, the basic conditions can be summarised as follows:

a) Rights of the foreign management:

- limited time period for operating the assets;
- profit sharing;
- right to have first call when privatisation would be decided.

b) Obligations of the foreign management:

- provision of operating capital and credits;
- redemption of debts (i.e. of unpaid wages);
- investment required to maintain production;
- employment guarantees.

Over time, some conflicts arose concerning the management contracts in the power and the gas sectors. These seem to have developed because of changed economic conditions and of violations of the agreed-to conditions of the contracts.

The case of the management of the natural gas pipeline: In 1997 the Belgian company Tractebel had been selected from among other bidders (Gaz de France, Enron) to operate the Kazakh part of the Middle Asia–Center natural gas transport pipeline[10] and the Northern and the Southern Kazakh gas distribution lines. The operating license was issued by the Kazakh Government for a 20 year term and included among other things the obligation of Tractebel to build a 156 km gas pipeline to ensure gas supply to Almaty.

As a result of the new management approach Tractebel cancelled the gas swap agreement with Gazprom. This required the supply of Russian regions close to the Kazakh border from the Karachaganak field, and in exchange for this the supply of the Kazakh regions of Aktyubinsk and Kostanay from Russian fields. According to micro-economic considerations the company also raised transport and distribution tariffs resulting in conflicts with Kazakh institutions. After Swiss and Belgian prosecutors had started to examine Tractebel's behaviour, who was blamed by the mass media for having paid bribes in order to obtain the licenses,

10 At present this is the only pipeline for exporting gas from the Middle Asian fields.

the Kazakh Government cancelled the license contract with Tractebel. The Kazakh Government then created a state pipeline company named KazTransGaz in March 2000. Participation of Gazprom in managing the Kazakh pipeline system is under discussion.

The case of the management of power sector assets: Among the management contracts concerning the power sector, the best known to the public is with Almaty Power Consolidated (APC), a subsidiary of Tractebel. APC had the license for operating the generating facilities as well as the distribution network for the Almaty region.

Conflicts arose between APC, the city's administration and the Kazakh monopoly regulation institution about tariff policy. Referring to changes in taxation, the huge number of unpaid electricity bills, losses from illegal siphoning-off of electricity and the devaluation of the Tenge, APC considered increased tariffs necessary in order to cover the losses and to reach the planned profit rates. In addition APC deplored distortions of the framework for competition, accusing the Kazakh Government with favouring Kazakh companies over foreign ones. While foreign companies would have to pay taxes and wages regularly, tax and wage delays (debts) of national companies would be tolerated. As result, APC reduced investments and the security of supply deteriorated.

From the viewpoint of the Kazakh administration, APC's commercial losses were the result of insufficient investment (i.e. technological losses due to lack of needed investment for maintenance and modernisation) and from extraordinary high salaries for the foreign managers. In addition, the administration expected that foreign companies would learn to 'adjust' to Kazakh business practices, and accept the high proportion of barter payments and tax offsets. But behind the conflicts, one can also discern a political game. Raising tariffs is the responsibility of the administration, while APC is seen as culpable for any insecurity in the electricity supply.

When summarising the Kazakh experience it becomes obvious that basic conditions for efficiently functioning management contracts or licenses would be:

- transparency for all contract conditions;
- public tenders for contracts;
- precise risk assessment with the goal of risk prevention, taking into account possible changes of the conditions under which the contract would be realised (e.g. allowing for tariff adjustments and sanctions if agreements are broken);
- periodical audit of operation by international auditors.

3.2 Design of a concession contract for the IGTS

In order to design an efficient concession contract for the IGTS, and avoid the Kazakh experience, Ukraine needs to prepare itself well. The first issue is a purely political one. Ukraine needs to have a general political consensus in favour of contracting-out the gas transit pipeline operation, one of the most sensitive issues in the entire economy. One argument to be used could be that a concession of the IGTS to an external operator is a compromise between the current, unsatisfactory status quo, and full-scale privatisation, which is politically unfeasible and forbidden by law, anyway. In fact, from a theoretical point of view at least, all players in the game, except for the current management of Naftogaz Ukrainy, stand to win from a concession:

- The Government reaps a share of the profits that Naftogaz currently dissimulates among unpaid bills and private coffers. It would also be assured regular tax payments. The information asymmetry between the Government and the gas industry could be somewhat reduced.
- By creating stable conditions, the Government would incite the concession company to undertake long-term investments, which Naftogaz is neglecting at present. Indeed the short-term vision of the Naftogaz management ("who knows what tomorrow will bring?") has prevented the company from pursuing a medium-term investment strategy. According to industry estimates, investments between 0.5-2.0 billion USD would have a medium-term payback, mainly by reducing compressor station gas consumption.[11] In this way, the value of the concession would also improve.
- The gas industries of the upstream and downstream countries stand to gain from increased reliability of the Ukrainian transit system, induced by foreign participation (Russian and/or Western). Increased confidence in supply security of Russian gas increases Russia's market share in Central/Western European markets. This in turn strengthens the bargaining position of Ukraine and improves profitability.[12]

Once political support is assured, the most important issues of the concession contract are the following:

---

11 According to Grais and Zheng (1996), reducing fixed costs of transit by 1% leads to a 0.12% increase in profits for the transiter. Should variable costs be cut by 1%, profits would even rise by 0.3%. Assuming that the concessionaire succeeds in reducing fixed and variable costs by 10%, the resulting extra profit would be about 35 million USD annually.

12 Grais and Zheng (1996, 1979) estimate than a 1% increase in Russia's market share increases the transiter's profit by 0.71% (Russia's profit increasing by 0.93%). As long as Ukraine retains the transit monopoly, a 10% increase in Russia's market share would increase profits of the Ukrainian transit company by about 60 million USD.

i) *Contract duration*: The duration of the concession contract generally depends upon the amount of sunk investments (i.e. costs that the concessionaire is not able to recover at the end of the contract). Contrary to other large concessions, e.g. the Channel Tunnel, the ratio of sunk costs (0.5-2.0 billion USD) to expected annual profits is relatively small. Indeed it is expected that investments can be fully financed out of current earning, no investment borrowing being necessary. Thus the concession period can be short, e.g. in the range of 20 years.[13]

ii) *Risks* should be borne by the party best able to assess them. *Economic* risks such as the variation of transit volumes, price changes (e.g. occurring due to a modification of Russia's market share in Central/Western Europe) or increased competition by Belarus, should be born by the concessionaire.[14] He also has more information regarding *technical* risks (such as unexpected expenses for repair and maintenance, replacement of compressor stations, etc.), and is thus better suited to bear them than the Government. By contrast, the Government is responsible for minimising the *political* risk. In particular, a reform-oriented Government should include barriers against expropriation or non-compliance by subsequent governments. One element of such a strategy would be to make instalment payments for the concession, spread over the entire duration of the concession.

iii) *Investment requirements*: It has been proposed to include a fixed investment obligation into the concession contract. However, this would be counterproductive, if one assumes (as we do) that the concessionaire has an information advantage over the Government. Should this be so, why should the Government decide on the required investment and its allocation? It is the concessionaire who has a vested interest in proceeding with those investments that he deems profitable in the long-term (up to the concession duration), and who will proceed with them out as long as the marginal productivity of the investment is higher than the marginal costs. The only technical problem to be resolved, then, is to define the technical state of the transit system once it will be returned to the Government after the concession ends, say in 2020 (current state vs. state of the art in 2020).

---

13 The initial concession period for the Channel Tunnel consortium was 55 years, for the Hungarian highway project 35 years.

14 This assumes risk neutrality by the concessionaire and the Ukrainian government. Should the concessionaire be more risk averse than the government, he will not accept the full commercial risk; in this case, a risk-sharing agreement is necessary.

3.3 How to calculate the value of the concession

There is a heated debate going on over one critical issue of the concession contract, namely its price. Current estimates vary with assumptions, expected revenues, and discount rates. The final price should ideally be established in an open auction, and thus should not be fixed by administrative procedures. However, it is useful to have a rough estimate of the most likely order of the price range. In the following, we present – for the first time – various transparent scenarios for determining an appropriate concession price. For the sake of simplicity, the calculations are based on real 1999 data. Also, we assume transit volumes to be constant over the concession period (a discussion of the 'Belarus' effect follows in the next Section).

The value of the concession is the discounted net present value of the expected turnover and of the expenditures over the concession period.[15] We assume the value of one thousand cubic meters (tcm) of gas in Ukraine to be 35 USD, this corresponds both to the current wholesale price level in Ukraine, and the import price of the EU (net of transit fees). In line with current government thinking which favours lowering taxes, we expect that the effective tax rate will be reduced from the current 72% to 60%, and assume this in our calculations.

The *discount rate* is considered by some foreign investors to be as high as 25%, whereas Ukrainian economists evaluate it at about 20%. If one takes the country risk as the relevant discount rate (which is what time-pressed investment bankers usually do), an even lower figure might be appropriate (given that the country risk is gradually approaching Russia's, where Eurobonds have a coupon somewhere below 20%). Discount rate scenarios of 15%, 20%, and 25% seem to reflect likely outcomes adequately.

Finally, the *transit fee* may also be subject to variation, be it through market changes in Central/Western Europe, or intensified competition by Belarus. We calculate scenarios using transit fees of 0.7, 0.88 (the real present fee), and 1.09 (the present official fee) per tcm and 100 km, respectively.

Graph 10.2 shows scenarios for the value of a 20-year concession for different discount rates and transit fees. Assuming the real present fee of 0.88 USD/100 km/tcm and a discount rate of 20%, the value of the concession would be 1,379 million USD. Given the high discount rates, extending the concession to 40 years hardly changes the result, the respective value being 1,425 million USD.

---

15 This valuation does not take into account the issue of gas storage, which is an additional Ukrainian asset.

Graph 10.2
Concession Value of the Ukrainian International Gas Transit System (IGTS), (20 year term, tax rate = 60%)

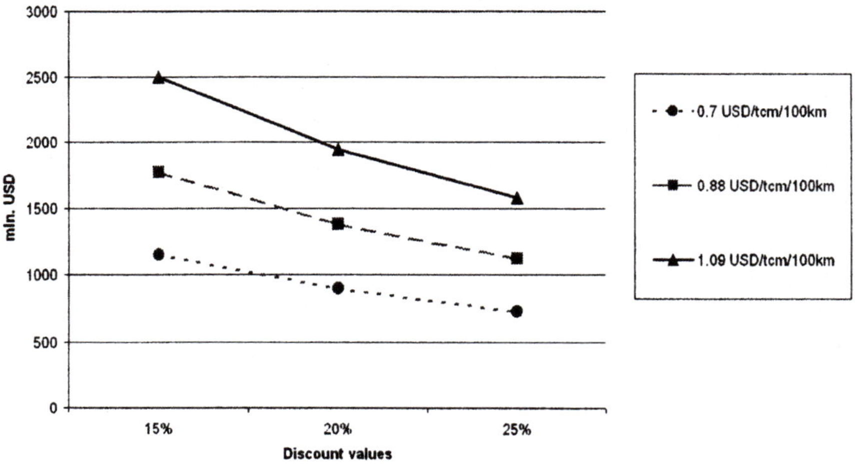

Source: Author's calculations.

4 Effects of the transit pipeline construction in Belarus

The picture changes drastically once the possibility of a second transit trunk between Russia and Central/Western Europe is taken into account. This scenario of duopolistic competition has become more definitive with the opening, in the fall of 1999, of the first pipeline connection between the 'Northern Lights' and Poland, concretely speaking, the 56''-pipeline between Nesvizh (Belarus) and Kondratki-Wloclawek (Poland), called 'Yamal-1' (see Graph 10.1 above).

The market entry of Belarus significantly weakens the bargaining position of Ukraine. Once a monopoly, it will now have to take into account the pricing policies of Belarus in its future negotiations with Russia over transit fees. In this Section, we analyse the outcomes of different possible approaches between

Ukraine and Belarus (the transit countries), Russia, and the Central/Western European consumers (see Graph 10.3):[16]

I. The profit maximising solution for Ukraine is an East-West co-operation with Russia as the gas supplier, and the Western European gas industry as the end customer. Belarus might join this coalition, eventually. This solution corresponds to the above mentioned concession solution. Increased reliability of gas transit would improve the market share of Russian gas. Internal marginal cost pricing for transit would furthermore increase the competitiveness of Russian gas on the European market. The optimal solution is thus not an either-or solution, but one where Ukraine orients its efforts both towards the East and the West.

II. & III. Should the concession or some other form of contract between all concerned parties not come about, an alliance of the gas producing country (Russia) and the transit country (Ukraine, or: the transit countries Ukraine and Belarus) would be the next best profit maximising strategy. Once again, the transit country would only charge marginal costs, and thus increase total exports and total profits; a profit-sharing agreement would have to be concluded between Russia and Ukraine (and eventually, Belarus).[17]

IV. A fourth option is a coalition between the two transit countries Ukraine and Belarus, imposing monopolist transit prices on the gas exporter, Russia. In the case of any further market entry by Belarus, Ukraine would loose quantities but at least maintain the present price level. However, given the distribution of political forces between Russia, Ukraine and Belarus, this option seems quite unrealistic.

V. Belarus and Russia could decide to co-operate, in order to spoil the monopoly rent of Ukraine. This is the worst case scenario for Ukraine, but it is a very realistic one, given that Russia has reached the end of its patience with Ukraine, and given the present political reconciliation between Russia and Belarus. In this case, transit capacity through Belarus would significantly increase over the next years, from the current 10 bcm to 28 bcm, 42 bcm, 56 bcm or even more. Russia would shift a maximum of gas transit to the new, Northern pipeline. The ultimate outcome could be the construction of pipelines bypassing Ukraine altogether, with Ukraine loosing *all* transit activities. The co-operation with Belarus would allow marginal cost pricing, these marginal costs most likely being lower than Ukraine's due to the more modern technical state of the Belarus pipeline.

Thus, even though an East-West co-operation would be most beneficial to Ukraine, political factors rather point to a constellation in which Ukraine stands to loose both market share and marginal profits.

---

16 At this point, the analysis is only a verbal one; it is planned to quantify the effects of the different scenarios at a later stage.

17 Indeed a vertical integration between the Russian and Ukrainian gas industry has been proposed recently by the Vice-Prime Minister of Energy of Ukraine, but this definitely is a politically sensitive issue.

Graph 10.3
Ukraine's external options for economic cooperation in the gas sector

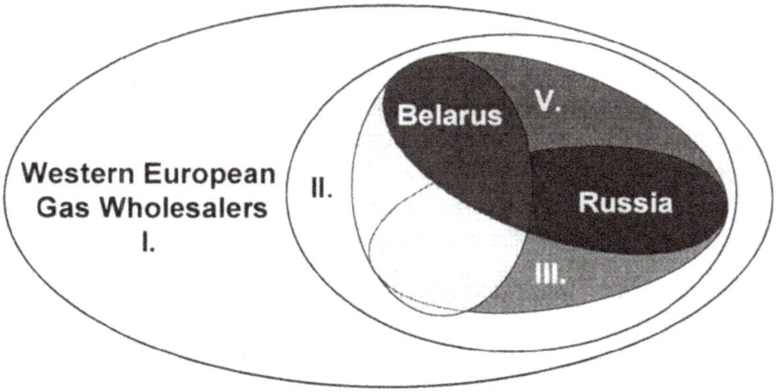

5 Conclusions

Ukraine continues to be an important gas transit bridge to Europe, but it has become a shaky one. Permanent discontent by Russia and the Western European gas industry over the political, technical and economic reliability of Ukrainian transit services have favoured the development of the competing pipeline linking Russia and Central/Western Europe through Belarus. This puts pressure on both the volume of the gas transit through Ukraine and the (formerly monopolistic) margins. The likely macro-economic effects for Ukraine are considerable, a potential reduction of pre-tax profits in the range of several hundreds of million USD per year, or 3 to 5 billion USD in discounted profits.

The Ukrainian Government and the gas industry need to react rapidly if they want to avoid a significant loss of income and the political leverage of being a bridge to Europe. In this Article, we have shown that a legal and organisational separation of the International Gas Transit System (IGTS) from the rest of the state-owned gas industry yields benefits to all parties: To the Ukrainian industry itself (since investment in the spin-off company is made possible), to the Ukrainian Government (since its real tax revenues will increase), and to the Russian and Western European gas industries (because the standing of Ukraine as a reliable gas transit country is increased). One way of organising this separation is to tender a long-term concession for the IGTS. If procedures are open and transparent, and the concession period sufficiently long (e.g. 20 years), then investment decisions and economic risk could be borne by the concessionaire, who has an information advantage over the Government.

The entry of Belarus into the transit business can no longer be avoided, the only question being what capacities it will invest in. Ukraine still has the possibility to influence this decision, by reducing its transit fees and/or expanding its own pipeline capacities and by improving the day-to-day operation of the IGTS. Ukraine's optimal external option, in terms of strategic co-operation, consists in an East-West coalition including both Russia and the Western gas industry, e.g. in the form of the proposed concession. Should this not come about, an alliance with Russia would allow marginal cost pricing for Ukrainian gas transit, which would increase the Russian market share in Western Europe, and thus total profits; the most sensitive issue with this kind of co-operation will be the profit-sharing agreement. An adverse coalition stands to emerge in reality, however, between Russia and Belarus, which would not only spoil a part of Ukraine's current monopoly rent but – in the long run – could deprive Ukraine totally of one of its most important source of revenue. It is Ukraine's turn now to react quickly in order to remain the important link to Europe, which it wants to be.

11

Reform of the EU's Common Agricultural Policy and Agricultural Policy's Strategies for Ukraine

Stephan von Cramon-Taubadel and Ludwig Striewe

1 Introduction

Talk of Ukraine's membership in the European Union is often couched in terms of dreams and visions.[1] Agriculture, all mud and manure, is not necessarily the stuff of dreams and visions. But while Europe is many things – and certainly more than the EU or the EU's Common Agricultural Policy (CAP) – in practical terms this CAP is one of the most important, expensive and controversial incarnations of Europe. It is still true that spending on the CAP accounts for roughly one half of the entire EU budget. If the EU's regional policy expenditures in rural areas are included, this share increases considerably. At the same time, agriculture remains an important sector of the Ukrainian economy, both in terms of its share of GNP and its share of total employment. For these reasons, agriculture and agricultural policy in the EU and Ukraine are likely to play a major role in any attempt to foster Ukraine's European integration. The central and at times debilitating role that agriculture is playing in the current negotiations between the EU and the potential new members in Central and Eastern Europe (CEE) foreshadows what might be expected in analogous negotiations with Ukraine. In the following Section we begin by speculating what impact EU accession would have on Ukraine's agriculture. Based on this speculation and projections of how EU and Ukrainian agriculture might be expected to develop between now and the date of some future accession, we then consider implications for the design of agricultural policy in Ukraine.

---

[1] See for example Bohdan Hawrylyshyn's opening contribution to this volume.

2 What could Ukraine expect from the CAP if it were an EU member today?

To accurately estimate the impact that the CAP would have on Ukraine, it would be necessary to construct a complex empirical model of Ukrainian agriculture. Constructing such a model would require both data and parameter estimates that are difficult to collect, especially in the case of a country like Ukraine where reliable statistics are rare and the economy is in turmoil. Sometimes it is possible, using back-of-the-envelope calculations, to produce estimates that are almost as reliable as those that might result from a complex model, but at a fraction of the cost. We hope that this is true of the results of the back-of-the-envelope calculations presented in Table 11.1.

Table 11.1
Estimated Common Agricultural Policy spending in Ukraine (basis year 1999)

Product	CAP spending 1999 (mln. Euro)	EU production 1999 (mln. t)	CAP spending per tonne (Euro/t)	Ukrainian production 1999 (mln. t)	Hypoth. spending in Ukraine (mln. Euro)
Grain & oilseed	17,866	199.5	90	27.4	2,466
Sugar	2,113	17.6	120	15.5	1,860
Fruit & vegs.	1,454	80.5	18	7.2	130
Wine	615	16.6	37	0.07	2.7
Tobacco	910	0.3	2,627	0.003	7.9
Rice	165	2.7	62	0.071	4.4
Milk	2,501	120.7	21	13.4	277
Beef	4,579	5.0	921	0.93	857
Sheepmeat	1,894	0.8	2,493	0.002	50
Pork	327	11.7	28	0.18	5.1
Eggs & poultry	111	14.2	8	0.66	5.3
Total	32,534				5,665

Sources: EU Commission (2000); State Committee of Statistics of Ukraine (annual); own calculations.

Note: The figure for grain and oilseed production in Ukraine includes 24.5 million t of grain and 2.9 million t of sunflower seeds and rape seeds.

The first column in Table 11.1 contains information on CAP spending in 1999 by agricultural product or product group. Total CAP spending in 1999 amounted to 36,169 billion EUR which is somewhat larger than the sum presented in Table 11.1; this discrepancy can be explained by the fact that Table 11.1 does not include information on some products, such as olive oil, that are not produced in

Ukraine. The second column of Table 11.1 lists EU production of the products in question in 1999, and the combination of the information in this column with the information on CAP spending in the first column makes it possible to calculate CAP spending per ton of EU production in the third column. Multiplying CAP spending per ton in column 3 with Ukrainian production of the products in question in column 4 generates column 5, in which hypothetical CAP spending in Ukraine in 1999 is listed in million EUR.

These calculations show that if Ukraine had been an EU member in 1999, it might have expected to benefit from CAP spending of roughly 5.7 billion EUR. Before we continue to discuss and analyse the implications of this amount for Ukraine and Ukrainian agricultural policy, several comments and caveats are in order.

First, it is important to recognise that there is a difference between the net budgetary transfers that would accompany CAP membership on the one hand and the net economic welfare effects of CAP membership for Ukraine on the other. This key distinction between budgetary transfers and economic costs and benefits from the point of view of an individual EU member was first explicitly discussed in the context of the CAP by Koester (1977). It is complicated by the fact that EU expenditure is jointly financed by all member states in proportion to their economic size (roughly GNP). Without the use of a complex empirical model it is not possible to generate estimates of the total welfare effects of CAP membership for Ukraine. However, since Ukraine is a relatively poor country, it would have to contribute very little to the common financing of EU expenditure. Moreover, since Ukraine would probably be a net exporter of agricultural products, it is reasonable to expect that the net welfare effects of the CAP for Ukraine would be positive and of the same order of magnitude as the net budget inflows estimated in Table 11.1. However, behind this magnitude, there would be winners and losers in Ukraine. While farmers would benefit from increased agricultural prices and other forms of support, consumers in Ukraine would be taxed by increased prices for food. Taxpayers would also lose but, as outlined above, to a limited extent in the case of Ukraine.[2]

Second, there are two major uncertainties that should be kept in mind when evaluating the results of the calculations in Table 11.1. The first of these concerns is the volume of agricultural production in Ukraine. The amount of CAP spending that a country receives is, ceteris paribus, a function of the volume of its agricultural production. It is well documented that agricultural production in Ukraine has fallen to very low levels in recent years. Furthermore, there is ample evidence that membership in the EU and, hence, participation in the CAP can have a very stimulating effect on agricultural production. Graph 11.1 illustrates how agricultural production in Denmark, after having remained more or less constant

---

2 It is important to make no mistake: the CAP may be good for farmers in EU but it definitely makes the EU as a whole considerably poorer.

in the 1960s and early 1970s, increased very rapidly following accession to the EU in 1973.

Graph 11.1
Agricultural production in Denmark before and after accession to the EU (1989-1991=100)

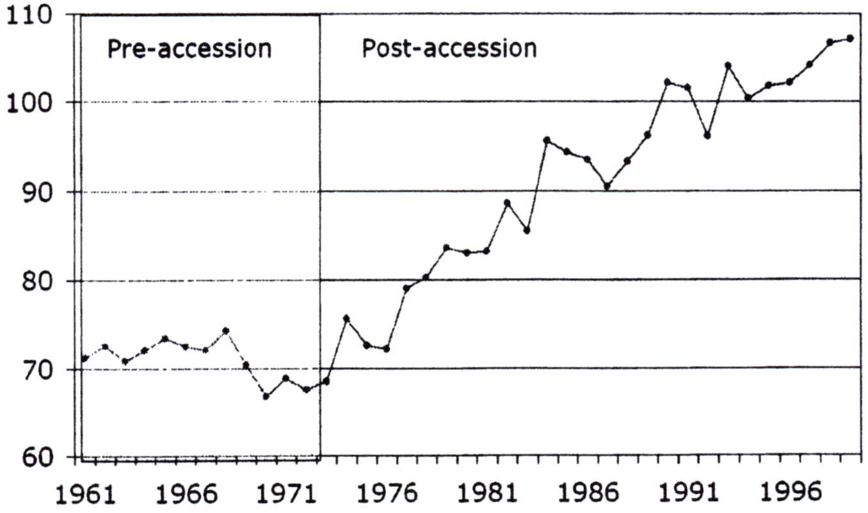

Source: FAO.

Taken together, these facts suggest that agricultural production in Ukraine, and with it the amount of CAP spending that Ukraine could expect to benefit from, could very rapidly increase beyond the levels indicated in columns 4 and 5 of Table 11.1 respectively.

While this suggests that the estimates in Table 11.1 underestimate the amounts that Ukraine might expect to receive from the CAP, the second major uncertainty alluded to above dampens expectations somewhat. A glance at Table 11.1 reveals that grains and oilseeds account for roughly half of the EU's 1999 CAP spending. Since the implementation of the so-called MacSharry reforms beginning in 1993, EU farmers receive a fixed payment per hectare that varies between member states and regions roughly in proportion to grain yields. These direct payments currently amount to 54.34 EUR/t which, given typical yields, translates into roughly 600 DM/ha in Germany.[3] These hectare payments account for a major part of the 17.9

3 These payments are given to farmers to compensate for 30% reductions in support prices for grain that were phased in between 1993 and 1996. As a result of the so-called Agenda 2000 reforms, support prices for grain will be reduced by a further 15% in 2000 and 2001 (7.5% per year) and the hectare payments increased to 63 EUR/t (BMELF (2000), p. 51).

billion EUR of grain and oilseed expenditure in the EU in 1999, and unlike much CAP expenditure, they are not directly linked to the volume of production.[4] Therefore, a significant proportion of the expenditure listed in Table 11.1 can be considered fixed and would not increase as Ukrainian agricultural production recovered and began to increase.

Furthermore, it is far from certain that these hectare payments would be available to farmers in Ukraine. Currently, the question of whether or not hectare payments will be extended to farmers in the candidates for EU enlargement in CEE (e.g. Poland, Hungary etc.) is one of the most controversial aspects of the accession negotiations. The EU argues that these payments were granted to farmers in the EU as compensation for the effect of reductions in support prices that were implemented between 1993 and 1996 as part of the MacSharry reforms. The EU argues that since farmers in Eastern Europe did not suffer from these price reductions – indeed upon joining the EU they will more likely benefit from price increases – there is no reason why they should be eligible for compensation in the form of hectare payments. Farmers and policy makers in the CEE accession countries, on the other hand, argue that not making hectare payments available in these countries would distort competition within the EU and be discriminatory (see Nagy, 1998). To understand this point of view one only need to imagine the perverse situation that would arise if farmers on the west bank of the Oder River continued to receive over 600 DM/ha of land in so-called compensation payments, while much poorer and less competitive farmers on the east bank in the new member state Poland received nothing. In recent months the EU appears to have softened its position and Agriculture Commissioner Fischler has suggested that it may not be feasible to exclude new member states in CEE completely from the hectare payments when they join the EU (Anon., 2000). One way or another, CAP spending on cereals and oilseeds in Table 11.1 is to a large extent due to hectare payments that may not be available to new members in Eastern Europe. Hence, the corresponding estimates of hypothetical CAP spending in Ukraine in Table 11.1 may be exaggerated.

In summary, therefore, the estimates in Table 11.1 are very rough and there are reasons to believe that they overestimate some portions of the EU budget expenditures that might flow and underestimate others. These potential inaccuracies notwithstanding, there can be little doubt that EU membership and the resulting stream of transfers from the CAP appear most enticing from the Ukrainian point of view. Whether the correct figure is 3 or 5.7 billion EUR, this

---

4 These payments are linked to production in that they provide farmers with an incentive to continue cultivating land. However, they do not themselves grow as a function of production.

would represent a huge flow of resources into Ukrainian agriculture and the Ukrainian economy as a whole.[5]

3 Policy implications for Ukraine

If membership in the EU can be expected to generate such huge benefits for Ukraine in the form of CAP spending, then the implications for Ukraine's policy makers would appear, at first glance, to be very clear. These implications might be summarised in three main points as follows:

1. Join the EU as soon as possible to benefit from the CAP;
2. Adjust Ukrainian agricultural policy to converge with CAP;
3. Support the EU in defending the CAP in the Millennium Round of WTO negotiations.

In the following paragraphs we would like to argue that the implications for policy makers in Ukraine are not as clear as they might seem at first glance and that Ukraine would be ill-advised to design and implement a policy along the lines of the three points just listed above. Let us consider these three points one after the other.

The *first policy implication* is that Ukraine should endeavour to join the EU as soon as possible to benefit from the CAP. In the beginning it is important to realise that 'as soon as possible' will not be 'very soon' in the case of Ukrainian EU accession. As agricultural economists we can only speculate on the broader economic and political forces that will shape the evolution and growth of the EU in the coming years. However, it appears quite reasonable to assume that it will be at least a decade before EU membership becomes a concrete possibility for Ukraine. In a nutshell, the EU will simply be too busy in the coming years with the ten CEE countries[6] that are currently regarded as front-runners for accession, and with the various internal policy and decision making reforms that it will have to implement in order to make this accession manageable. The ten CEE accession candidates have a combined agricultural potential that exceeds that of Ukraine and, of course, these countries too expect to benefit considerably from transfers induced by the CAP. Using an agricultural market model, Weber et al. (2000, p.

---

5 5.6 billion EUR correspond to 27.3 billion UAH at current exchange rates. This corresponds to 21.5% of total Ukrainian GDP in 1999 and almost twice the estimated Ukrainian agricultural GDP of 15.3 billion UAH (Ukrainian Economic Trends (2000); Zorya and von Cramon-Taubadel (2000), p. 19).

6 Bulgaria, the Czech Republic, Estonia, Hungary, Latvia, Lithuania, Poland, Romania, Slovakia and Slovenia.

12) estimate that the accession of these ten countries to the EU would increase EU CAP expenditure by roughly 7.5 billion EUR by 2007. All of the issues that were raised in the previous Section – such as the question of whether CEE farmers should be eligible for hectare payments, and the question of the production response that might be elicited by EU membership – are currently at the forefront of negotiations between the EU and the prospective new members. At the same time, it is clear that the EU's cumbersome decision making structures will have to be reformed as the EU moves from 15 to perhaps as many as 25 members in the near future.[7] All of these issues will have to be solved in the period leading up to accession, and it appears likely that accession itself will be followed by a period of transition that permits old and new members to adapt to changing conditions and the EU as a whole to come to grips with its growing pains. The challenge of enlarging to include states in CEE is immense and is likely to keep the EU fully occupied for many years to come.

The *second policy implication* suggested above is that Ukrainian policy makers should adjust their agriculture policy to converge with the CAP. This recommendation might make sense if there was a real prospect of Ukraine becoming an EU member in the near future. As argued above, however, this is not likely to be the case. By the time Ukraine could become a member of the EU, it is likely that the CAP will have changed considerably.

The CAP has already changed considerably in the last ten years due to major reforms such as the MacSharry and the Agenda 2000 reforms. There are two main reasons why the CAP can be expected to continue to change. The first of these has to do with budgetary limitations. As illustrated in Graph 11.2, CAP expenditure has increased dramatically over the last 30 years but has stagnated since the mid-1990s and is projected to remain more or less constant, even decreasing slightly, through to the middle of the current decade.

CAP spending is slated to stop growing and remain more or less constant because EU policy makers have committed themselves to reducing the share of the total EU budget that is dedicated to agriculture, thus freeing up funds for structural and regional development programmes as well as pre- and post-accession aid to the prospective new members in CEE. If CAP spending is to remain within the limits projected in Graph 11.2, the CAP will have to be reformed. And any such reform – whether it involves a reduction in support prices for agricultural products or a reduction in the hectare payments provided to farmers – would reduce the benefits that Ukraine might expect to receive as an EU member. It is safe to assume that budgetary limitations in conjunction with the enlargement of the EU to include countries in CEE will lead to significant pressure to reform the CAP.

---

7 In this regard, recall the point made by Bohdan Hawrylyshyn in his opening chapter to this book that the cost of governance increases exponentially with size and ethnic diversity.

Graph 11.2
Expenditure on the Common Agricultural Policy: 1971-2006 (in billion EUR)

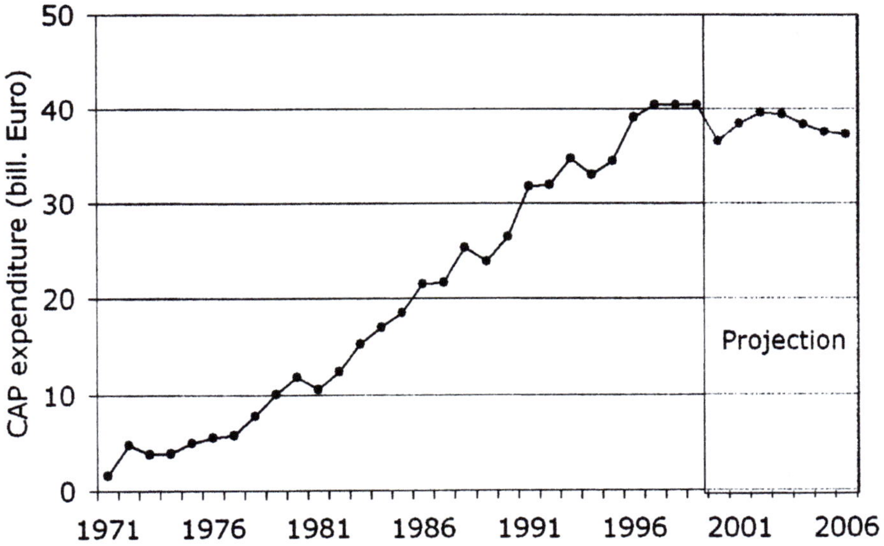

Source: European Commission (a); European Commission (b, various issues).

Note: The Euro came into existence in 1999, replacing the ECU which had been in use since 1979 and which, itself, had succeeded the European Unit of Account.

While EU policy makers maintain that the most recent set of CAP reforms (the Agenda 2000 package) will suffice to make accession financially feasible, there are many indications that this assessment is too optimistic. For example, while Weber et al. (2000, p. 12) calculate that enlargement to include only the first round of prospective EU members in Central and Eastern Europe (the Czech Republic, Estonia, Hungary, Poland and Slovenia) will result in additional CAP expenditure of over 4.3 billion EUR per year by the middle of this decade, the EU's financial perspectives for the year 2006 only provide for 3.4 billion EUR of additional agricultural expenditure for accession (Anon., 1999).

The other reason why it is reasonable to expect that the CAP will change considerably in the coming years is the Millennium Round of WTO trade negotiations. The members of the WTO succeeded for the first time at the end of the Uruguay Round of negotiations in 1992 in subjecting agricultural policies to disciplines designed to reduce the distortion of international agricultural markets and trade. One of the most important disciplines in this regard are limitations on the use of export subsidies. Since the EU is a net exporter of agricultural products and since the CAP supports agricultural prices in the EU at levels that are higher than world market prices, it is not possible for the EU to export agricultural products without the use of export subsidies. At the end of the Uruguay Round the WTO members agreed to reduce expenditure on export subsidies by 36%, and to reduce the volume of subsidised exports by 20% by the year 2000 (Zorya and von Cramon-Taubadel, 2000).

Graph 11.3
World grain trade: Will the EU participate?

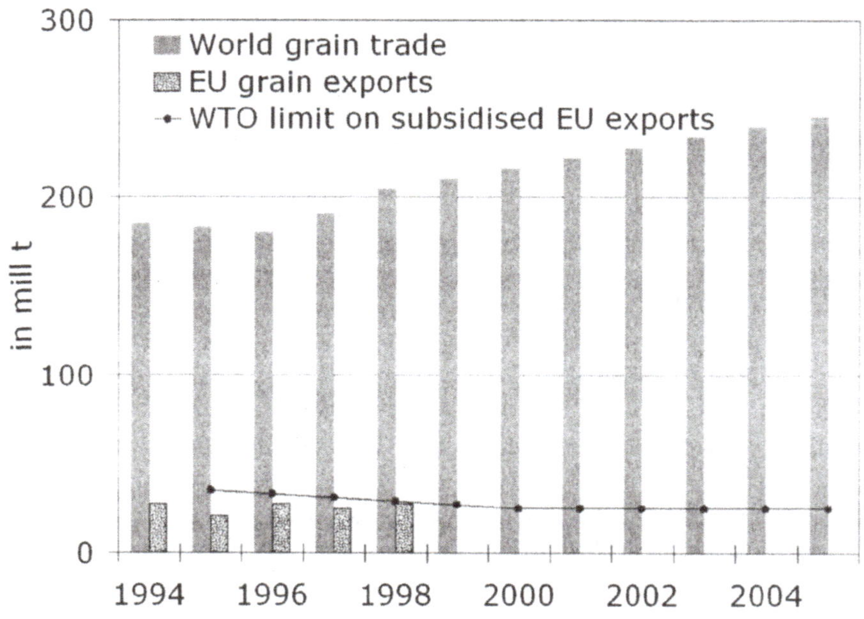

Source: Tangermann (1999), p. 20.

Graph 11.3 illustrates what impact these limitations on the use of export subsidies could have on agriculture in the EU. Graph 11.3 presents information on the projected growth of world grain trade through to the year 2005, as well as data on past EU grain exports and the WTO limit on the use of export subsidies by the EU. We see that the gap between the EU's grain exports and the WTO limit on the use of subsidised exports by the EU has been closing since the mid-1990s. Thus, it is anticipated that the WTO limits on subsidised EU exports of grains will be binding in future years. This implies that if the EU insists on maintaining its current agricultural policy and supporting domestic prices above world market levels, the resulting need to use subsidies to dispose of surplus production will limit the EU to a small and shrinking share of world grain trade. In other words, without agricultural reform the EU will not be able to participate in growing world grain markets.

It is for this reason that EU policy makers have decided to further reduce support prices for grain as a part of the Agenda 2000 reform package (see Footnote 3). At the moment it is not clear whether this reduction in prices will suffice to completely eliminate the need for export subsidies which would, in turn, enable the EU to export as much grain as it wishes without limitation.[8] However, many observers are convinced that the Agenda 2000 price reductions for grain will not suffice (see, for example, Manegold (2000), p. 6), especially when one takes into consideration that the US-dollar is currently very strong vis-à-vis the Euro which has the effect of increasing world market prices in Euro terms and thus reducing nominal rates of protection in the EU.

Be that as it may for grains, neither the MacSharry nor the Agenda 2000 reforms have addressed similar problems in the areas of milk and dairy products and sugar. Here, too, WTO restrictions on the use of export subsidies are beginning to bind and will force the EU to consider major reform of the CAP. Finally, beyond dealing with the limitations and disciplines imposed by the last round of WTO negotiations, the EU will also have to come to grips with whatever new disciplines are agreed to in the course of the Millennium Round which is expected to gain momentum in the coming months. Some of the proposals that have been suggested for this new round of WTO negotiations, such as the complete elimination of all export subsidies in agriculture, would add to the already considerable pressure on the EU to reform the CAP.

There are, broadly speaking, two strategies that the EU could pursue in dealing with this pressure. On the one hand it could, in the tradition of the MacSharry and Agenda 2000 reforms, continue and accelerate the process of liberalisation. This would entail further reduction of domestic support prices, and in particular the reduction of protection for products such as milk and sugar that have been largely excluded from the reform process so far. This would also entail a major overhaul of the hectare payment system, especially with a view to making it affordable to extend this system in some form to new member states in CEE. Note, however, that if the EU were to follow this strategy, the benefits of the CAP for Ukraine would fall below the levels estimated in Table 11.1. Note as well that further liberalisation on the part of the EU would likely include the elimination of the intervention systems for grains, and the elimination of production quotas for milk and perhaps even sugar. In this case, however, the argument that Ukraine should implement such policy tools in order to adapt its agricultural policy to the CAP would no longer make sense.

The other strategy that the EU might pursue in response to the pressure exerted by past and future rounds of WTO negotiations would be to turn inward, by withdrawing from world markets for agricultural products and pursuing a policy

---

8 As a matter of fact currently EU-intervention prices are very close to world market prices, but this appears due to exceptional circumstances.

of autarky. It is conceivable that the EU's partners in the WTO would be willing to tolerate continued protection of agricultural production in the EU, provided the EU agrees to stop using export subsidies. If the EU chose to pursue this strategy, then the CAP-related benefits of EU membership for Ukraine would also be significantly reduced. In particular, Ukraine would sacrifice significant growth potential in agriculture by joining such an EU. This is because the EU would not be in a position to support agricultural commodities produced in Ukraine with export subsidies. The EU as a whole, and with it Ukraine, would not be able to participate in world agricultural trade (recall Graph 11.3). Hence, Ukrainian agriculture would be limited to producing for domestic Ukrainian consumption as well as some export to the rest of the EU, although it is clear that the EU already produces more than enough food for itself and there would be little potential for absorbing additional surpluses from Ukraine.

Convergence between Ukrainian agricultural policy and the CAP, therefore, will be very difficult to manage because the CAP is changing rapidly and is likely to continue to change in the future. It is not clear exactly how the CAP will evolve, although of the two scenarios discussed above, the continued liberalisation scenario is perhaps most likely. But it is clear that however the CAP evolves, it is likely to become less attractive from a Ukrainian perspective. Either the CAP will evolve in the direction of less protection, which implies less financial transfers to Ukraine, or it will evolve in the direction of autarky and withdrawal from world markets, which would limit Ukraine's ability as a member of the EU to develop a sector in which it has considerably comparative advantage.

Recall as well that EU membership will likely take a long time. If Ukrainian policy makers decide to implement a CAP-like policy in the meantime, they must recognise that the costs of this policy will have to be born by Ukraine alone in the meantime. The CAP is enticing from a Ukrainian perspective because as a country with a large agricultural potential Ukraine would stand to benefit from considerable inflows of money (as outlined in Table 11.1), while as a country with a low level of per capita GDP, it would not have to pay. On its own, however, Ukraine would have to pay for the costs of a CAP-like policy alone. It is an illusion to believe that Ukraine is in a position to do so. Simply increasing grain price levels in Ukraine by 10 USD/t (which would represent a nominal rate of protection of roughly 10% given current world market prices) would, given production in the neighbourhood of 25 million tons, cost 250 million USD or 1,36 billion UAH, which amounts to roughly 1% of the nominal GDP in 1999. Extending similar protection to livestock products, oilseeds and sugar could easily triple or quadruple this cost. Consumers and taxpayers in Ukraine are not in a position to finance costs of this magnitude.

Moreover, since EU membership is probably a medium to long-term perspective, it is quite likely that Ukraine will become a member of the WTO before it becomes a member of the EU. Certainly, it is a stated priority of the Ukrainian Government's economic policy that Ukraine will become a WTO member, and in recent months efforts to secure Ukraine's accession to the WTO have been strengthened. As a WTO member, however, Ukraine would also be subject to limitations on the use of export subsidies and other agricultural policy tools. The amount of export subsidies that a country is allowed to use under WTO regulations (for example, the limit on the use of grain export subsidies by the EU in Graph 11.3) is determined on the basis of the historical use of export subsidies in a basis period (in the case of the EU this period was 1986 to 1990). Since Ukraine has not used export subsidies at all in the past, it would, as a new WTO member, probably be granted a very low or zero limit on the use of such subsidies. This implies, however, that Ukraine would not be able to support the prices of any agricultural products for which it is more than 100% self-sufficient above world market price levels. After all, what trader would be willing to buy agricultural products at supported prices in Ukraine and sell them for less money on the world market, if he or she did not receive export subsidies as compensation?

In summary, the implementation of a CAP-like policy in Ukraine can not be justified by the argument that it is necessary to help Ukraine adjust its policies in preparation for EU membership. Furthermore, the costs of implementing such a policy would greatly exceed what Ukraine is able to pay, and WTO membership, which is a priority goal of economic policy in Ukraine, would preclude the implementation of such a policy in the first place.

The *third and final policy implication* derived above is that Ukraine should, in the interests of maximising the benefit it will later receive from the CAP, support the EU in defending the CAP in the Millennium Round of WTO negotiations. The EU expects that the ten CEE countries that are currently negotiating accession will support the EU in defending the CAP in coming rounds of multilateral trade negotiations. However, for the reasons discussed above, Ukraine would be ill-advised to add its support. As a country that is not a member of the EU and that is unlikely to become one in the near future, Ukraine's agricultural interests are diametrically opposed of those of the EU. Ukraine is a typical 'Cairns group' country. The Cairns group is named after a city in Australia where a group of agricultural exporting countries first met to co-ordinate their strategies in the last Uruguay Round of WTO negotiations. The Cairns group includes countries such as Argentina, Australia and Canada that have a comparative advantage in agriculture and export significant quantities of agricultural goods but are not in a position to subsidise their agricultural sectors as heavily as the EU or the US. These countries want increased access to protected markets especially in the EU for their agricultural products, and they are calling for a reduction in the use of export subsidies by 'big players', such as the EU and the US, because these subsidies distort world markets, reduce world market prices, and give the EU and the US an unfair advantage in competition for export markets.

Ukraine is in a very similar position. It is a small country with a comparative advantage in agriculture that cannot, as has been argued above, afford to protect its agricultural sector. From a Ukrainian perspective, the subsidisation of agriculture in the EU and the US represents a direct tax. Estimates of the magnitude of this tax vary and are difficult to calculate (for a discussion of the modelling approaches that can be used and their strengths and weaknesses see Gohin et al., 1999). Even if we make the conservative assumption that agricultural protection in the EU and the US depresses world market prices for agricultural products by 5-10 %, it is quickly apparent that the impact on Ukraine is significant.[9]

4 Conclusions

In view of the discussion in the previous Section we would suggest that the policy implications for Ukraine presented above must be modified as follows:

1. Join the EU as soon as possible to benefit from ~~the CAP~~ European integration.
2. ~~Adjust~~ Liberalise Ukrainian agricultural policy to ~~converge with the CAP~~ create conditions for growth.
3. ~~Support~~ Pressure the EU ~~in defending~~ to reform the CAP in the Millennium Round of WTO negotiations.

First, while Ukraine should join the EU as soon as possible, it must recognise that 'as soon as possible' probably does not mean 'very soon'. Furthermore, it should not be interested in joining the EU simply to benefit from a free lunch in the form of the CAP spending but rather to benefit from European integration and all of the advantages in terms of enhanced political and economic growth and stability that this would bring.

Second, rather than attempting to adjust its agricultural policy to converge with the CAP, the Government of Ukraine should endeavour to liberalise Ukrainian agricultural policy to create conditions for agricultural growth. While Ukrainian agricultural policy may appear quite liberal in a formal sense, effective liberalisation lags far behind official liberalisation (see von Cramon-Taubadel and Koester, 1997). Zorya and von Cramon-Taubadel (2000) demonstrate that Ukrainian agriculture still receives large and highly distorting subsidies and von Cramon-Taubadel and Striewe (1999, Chapters 3 and 6) argue that Government intervention has made a significant contribution to the disappointing performance of the Ukrainian agriculture since independence in 1991.

---

9 5% of a current world market grain price of roughly 100 USD/t is equivalent to 5 USD/t and this corresponds to a reduction in the value of Ukraine's approximately 25 million tons of grain production of 125 million USD/year. It is widely accepted that the combined effect of EU and US agricultural policies on the world market prices for example of sugar are much larger than 5-10%.

Third, rather than supporting the EU in defending the CAP in coming rounds of multilateral trade negotiations, Ukrainian policy makers should recognise that the CAP represents a very significant tax on Ukrainian agriculture and that the CAP has also contributed to the disappointing performance of Ukrainian agriculture in recent years. Ukraine should add its voice to the voices of countries such as the members of the Cairns group that share an interest in a level playing field for all participants in international agricultural trade.

References

Anon. (2000): Reform of Direct Aid Scheme Pre-accession? In: Agra Europe, No. 1897, April 20, p. EP/1.

Anon. (1999): EU Budget System Reformed. In: Agra Europe, No. 1842, March 26, p. EP/5

Bundesministerium für Ernährung, Landwirtschaft und Forsten (BMELF) (2000): Agrarbericht der Bundesregierung 2000. Bonn

Cramon-Taubadel, S. von and U. Koester (1997): Official and Effective Liberalisation in the FSU: The Example of Ukrainian Agriculture. Contributed Paper, XXIII Conference of the International Association of Agricultural Economists, Sacramento, August

Cramon-Taubadel, S. von and L. Striewe (eds.) (1999): Die Transformation der Landwirtschaft in der Ukraine: Ein weites Feld. Vauk-Verl., Kiel

European Commission (a) (2000): Vorschlag der Kommission für die Festsetzung der Agrarpreise 2000/20001. Brussels, March 23, Anhang 1 und Anhang 2

European Commission (b): Die Lage der Landwirtschaft in der Gemeinschaft. Brussels, annual

FAO (Food and Agricultural Organisation) (2000): FAOSTAT Online Statistical Database, June

Gohin, A., H. Guyomard and C. Le Mouël (1999): L'analyse des politiques agricoles: l'apport de l'équilibre général calculable. In: Èconomie Rurale 251, Mai-June, pp. 4-10

Koester, U. (1977): EG-Agrarpolitik in der Sackgasse – Divergierende nationale Interessen bei der Verwirklichung der EWG-Agrarpolitik. Baden-Baden

Manegold, D. (2000): Die landwirtschaftlichen Märkte an der Jahreswende 1999/2000 – Aspekte gemeinsamer Agrarpolitik 1999. In: Agrarwirtschaft, Bd. 49, Nr. 1, pp. 2-14

Nagy, Frigyes (Minister für Landwirtschaft der Republik Ungarn) (1998): Beitrag zur Podiumsdiskussion. 5. Ost-West-Agrarforum: Europäische Landwirtschaft zwischen Mangel und Überfluß – Agrarpolitische Strategien für 2000 und danach – Dokumentation. Bonn, Berlin, pp. 33-34

State Committee of Statistics of Ukraine (annual): Agriculture of Ukraine, Statistical Yearbook. Kyiv

Tangermann, S. (1999): The European Union Perspective on Agricultural Trade Liberalisation in the WTO. Department of Agricultural Economics and Business, University of Guelph, Ontario, Canada, February

Ukrainian Economic Trends (2000): Quarterly Issue, March

Weber, G., O. Wahl and E. Meinlschmidt (2000): Auswirkungen einer EU-Osterweiterung im Bereich der Agrarpolitik auf den EU-Haushalt. IAMO/Institut für Agrarentwicklung in Mittel- und Osteuropa, Discussion Paper No. 26, Halle

Zorya, S. and S. von Cramon-Taubadel (2000): Agricultural Aspects of Ukrainian Membership in the World Trade Organisation. German Advisory Group on Economic Reforms in Ukraine, Kyiv, May, mimeo

12

Export Orientation and Its Impact on Enterprise Restructuring in Ukraine

Iryna Akimova

1 Introduction

On the micro-economic level international integration means that enterprises should move in a direction, which is characteristic for companies participating in a market economy, i.e. they should undertake the necessary restructuring measures and participate in international trade. The involvement in export and import activities provides an enterprise with better access to international markets, and facilitates the introduction of international standards regarding product quality, product innovation, cost levels and marketing strategies. In fact, in developed countries, export-oriented enterprises usually demonstrate better performance compared to firms that operate only within the domestic market. In the transitional context, export orientation should be expected to play an important role in encouraging enterprises to restructure. However, most recent empirical literature on restructuring of large industrial enterprises, following their privatisation, has focused only on the role of privatisation and on hardening of budget constraints. At times competition and human capital aspects were also included. Some studies on trade re-orientation of enterprise in transition economies have found little evidence for a relationship between the enterprises' export orientation and conventional measures of performance (Peters and Claessens, 1996). This might be due to a time lag between a change in export orientation and the related effect on performance results.

In the first place, we will focus our attention in this Chapter on an analysis of the impact of *export orientation* (and especially orientation towards non-CIS markets) *both on the restructuring activities of Ukrainian enterprises and on their performance results*. We will consider the export orientation of a firm as a proxy for economic openness and international integration at the micro-economic level. Next, we will test the hypothesis that a higher level of export orientation (particularly towards non-CIS markets) will be associated with a higher probability of undertaking restructuring measures (and strategic activities in particular), which should eventually result in better performance.

Our second research aim is to investigate *what forces drive companies to orient their trade towards exports*. We expect that an increased percentage of export sales and a re-orientation of sales towards non-CIS markets are associated with private ownership, increased competition, hardening of budget constraints and improved managerial quality.

The Chapter is structured as follows: Section 2 briefly outlines the present Ukrainian economic environment. Section 3 discusses the links between restructuring and its driving forces (namely export orientation, ownership changes, hardening of budget constraints, increasing competition, and changes in human capital). It also develops various hypotheses, which will then be tested. Section 4 describes the data used in the analysis. Section 5 presents the equations, which will be used, and describes the variables employed in the analysis. Section 6 discusses the regression results, and Section 7 presents the policy implications derived from the foregoing.

2 The Ukrainian economy: Background for restructuring

Since 1992, the economic environment in Ukraine has been described as a continuous fight for the implementation of privatisation programmes, macro-economic stabilisation and trade liberalisation. Trade liberalisation has been initiated in 1994, and by 1996, all quantitative restrictions on exports had been abolished and many tariff rates reduced. After the Russian crisis in 1998, some trade and exchange restrictions (e.g. indicative prices, foreign exchange controls) were re-introduced and tariff rates grew. Though the Ukrainian economy is relatively open (the GDP share of exports has always been above 30% since 1996, and the GDP share of imports has constituted about 40% between 1996 and 1999), Ukraine's integration into the world economy has not taken place so far. Foreign trade continued to be dependent on countries of the Commonwealth of Independent States (CIS). During 1995-1996 the share of total exports to the former Soviet Union (FSU) was 57%, and imports from the FSU accounted for 65%. Some re-orientation towards non-CIS markets has occurred since 1997, though. However, the total volumes of both exports and imports have been declining since 1996. Intermediary goods held a dominant position in the export structure, while energy and fuel constituted the main imports.

The privatisation process in Ukraine was initiated in 1992 when there existed around 18,000 medium and large state-owned enterprises and some 45,000 state-owned small enterprises. Almost two-thirds of these companies were transferred to private owners using non-competitive methods (buy-outs and leases with buy-out), which led to a dominance of insider ownership. Privatisation in Ukraine has proceeded unevenly with numerous adjustments to the legislative base and to the methods of implementation. All this has created a lot of uncertainty and has impeded the restructuring process (Leshenko and Revenko, 1999). By the time of my survey (summer of 1998) about 57,000 enterprises had been privatised (including over 7,800 medium-sized and large companies).

The development of the enterprise sector was constrained by the limited ability to attract sufficient outside capital, by the lack of financial discipline and by the failure of enforcing bankruptcy laws. The continuing economic crisis resulted in decreasing profitability of Ukrainian enterprises, more than 50% reported losses between 1995 and 1999. The lack of clarity and stability of the legal environment and of governmental policy has negatively effected the flow of foreign direct investment. Ukraine's banking sector was small and undercapitalised. Credits to the private sector were scarce and loans were mainly short term. Though state subsidies were considerably reduced during the last four years, soft budget constraints have remained in the form of arrears and of barter trade (accounting for more than 40% of industrial sales).

As a result, Ukraine has occupied a place in the last quartile in the ranking of East European countries according to progress made in privatisation and restructuring of the large enterprises, and to the quality of governance (Transition Report, 1999).

3 Conceptual framework

3.1 Enterprise restructuring

Pohl, Anderson, Claessens and Djankov (1997) define *Enterprise restructuring* during the transition from centrally planned to market economies as a complex process of maintaining profitability in the face of a changing economic environment, technological progress and competition from other firms. The restructuring process starts with redefining the goal of the firm (from rent-seeking to value maximisation) and with re-orienting the overall strategy of the firm's management (from fulfilling central plan requirements to customer satisfaction). It then proceeds to the implementation of changes to its basic company structure. Restructuring includes taking reactive (passive or defensive) and active (strategic or deep) measures.

Reactive restructuring is forced upon enterprises in transitional economies as a consequence of the decline in the demand for their products, market liberalisation and the imposition of harder budget constraints. Reactive restructuring includes labour force reductions, cutting of real wages and maintaining them at a low level, reduction in social and unused production assets, closing of unprofitable product lines, and switching to cheaper inputs. Reactive restructuring is unrelated to ownership structure (Carlin and Aghion, 1996).

Active or deep restructuring measures aim at a long-run improvement of the viability and performance of the firm in a competitive environment. It is the consequence of a radical change in the company's goals and strategic outlook towards value maximisation and market orientation, respectively. Deep restructuring is typically accompanied by investment in new and up-to-date equipment and technology, by the development of new products and new markets, by increasing attention to product quality, by structural changes to the labour force, by improvements to the organisational structure, by creation of new distribution channels, and by the preparation of strategic business and marketing plans.

Strategic restructuring of the enterprise should eventually result in its successful adjustment to a new market environment and in *improved performance*. While in the long run this relationship is not in doubt, in the short run it is not so obvious. In the Ukrainian case, performance variables may not yet vary significantly between firms, which undertook steps towards strategic restructuring and enterprises, which just muddled through by means of vast barter operations. Moreover, some strategic measures like product innovations require additional costs and, in the short run, might even negatively influence performance indicators (for example, profitability). Therefore, given the slow transformation of the Ukrainian economy, *measuring restructuring by using both performance indicators and indicators for restructuring activities makes sense.*

3.2 Export orientation

As suggested in the endogenous growth literature, external trade is an important driving force behind economic growth. Trade liberalisation opens the economy to international competition and, at the same time, provides domestic producers with greater access to global markets for designs, equipment, and for intermediate and final products. From the perspective of an individual firm, the intensity of international competition in the final product market should be a powerful force inducing efforts to restructure and to improving productive efficiency. International competitive pressure introduces international standards in terms of product quality and product innovation, cost level and marketing strategy.

Maintaining or increasing the percentage of exports relative to total sales is an indicator of the international competitiveness of the firm and its integration into the international market. Therefore, it can be expected that export-oriented enterprises are more actively involved in restructuring and are better performers than firms that operate exclusively within the domestic market. Export-oriented firms in developed economies, as compared to non-exporters were found to have better opportunities to buy intermediates and up-to-date equipment, thus allowing them to improve their productivity (Feenstra, Markusen and Zeile, 1992).

The evidence concerning the impact of exports on the performance of companies in transition economies is limited and rather contradictory. Djankov and Hoekman (1996) found that re-orientation of export production towards global markets was positively correlated with total factor productivity for Bulgarian firms. At the same time, Estrin and Takla (1995) and Peters and Claessens (1996) found no correlation between pre-reform export shares of sales of Bulgarian firms and changes in their performances. Besides possible measurement problems, this could also be connected with a time lag between the change in export operations and the resulting performance effects. For example, re-orientating exports towards Western markets might affect profits negatively in the short run, since it requires additional expenditures to develop a proper product policy, marketing and financial systems. In such a case, it is necessary to also look *at the range of restructuring activities undertaken by the enterprises.*

In this paper, we consider the level of export orientation of a firm as a proxy for economic openness and international integration on the micro-economic level, and investigate its impact *both on the restructuring activities of the enterprises and on its performance results.* In order to determine whether restructuring causes better export performance, or vice-versa, we try to correlate the level of export orientation in the year *before major restructuring measures were undertaken* with the actual restructuring that occurred *afterwards. If the level of export orientation (measured as a percentage of total export sales) had been high – especially towards non-CIS countries – prior to any restructuring, then we expect it to be very likely that actual restructuring – and strategic activities in particular – will be undertaken.*

In the case of performance indicators, a positive association between the changes in efficiency indicators and a change in the export share of total sales (as well as the share of non-CIS exports) might turn to be insignificant in the short-run because of the time lag.

In the literature on transition economies, a change in export orientation is considered not only as a *driving force* for the enterprise's restructuring efforts, but also as an *indicator* of the restructuring itself (e.g. Pohl, Anderson, Claessens and Djankov, 1997). On one hand, we try to incorporate this approach into our analysis by investigating the *relationship between the re-orientation of the firm towards international markets as measured by the change in the export share of total sales as well as by the change in the non-CIS export share of total sales. On the other hand, we will investigate the forces, which drive restructuring, namely, ownership structure, level of competition, the hardness of budget constraints, and changes in the managerial human capital.*

There is general agreement in the literature that market liberalisation and deregulation constitute the pre-requisite of successful restructuring, while changes in ownership structure, increasing competition, hardening budget constraints, and changes in the managerial human capital are considered to be the driving forces behind restructuring.

3.3 Ownership structure

Privatisation is seen as the most important element in the process of de-politicisation of the economy (Boycko, Shleifer and Vishny, 1995), sometimes also as a key to industrial restructuring in general (Pohl, Anderson, Claessens and Djankov, 1997), and to reactive restructuring in particular (Carlin and Aghion, 1996). Economic theory suggests that concentrated private ownership (and concentrated outside ownership in particular) will improve the chances for active restructuring, since it reduces the effects of agency problems generated by diffuse ownership (Aghion and Blanchard, 1998).

On the other hand, as far as the early stages of transition – and in particular within slowly reforming economies – are concerned, various empirical inquiries have cast doubt on a strong and positive relationship between changes in ownership structure and restructuring or performance (see, for example, Earle and Estrin, 1997; Jones, 1998). In any case, the short period of time for which records are available for privatised firms in Ukraine, makes it unlikely that a significant positive correlation between restructuring indicators and performance indicators can be developed. However, it is expected that variables representing ownership structure (if they have an impact at all) will affect restructuring and performance indicators differently.

3.4 Hardening budget constraints

The hardening of budget constraints is a necessary condition for restructuring as it imposes discipline from outside sources of finance and forces the enterprise to increase the efficiency of operations under threat of bankruptcy. In most studies, the hardening of budget constraints is measured by dummies for government subsidies. However, there are off-budget sources of softness of budget constraints like the extensive reliance on barter arrangements by firms, which are approaching the limits to accumulating further payments arrears.

We include in our analysis the reduction in barter operations and subsidies as proxies for hardening budget constraints. We expect a positive effect of hardening budget constraints on the enterprise restructuring activity and performance.

3.5 Competition

Elimination of soft budget constraints creates preconditions for functioning competitive markets. It is generally agreed that competition is the main force behind efficiency and innovation. However, empirical tests of its effects in transitional economies are limited (Earl and Estrin,1998). It has also been pointed out that, in the short-run, strong competition might negatively affect enterprise adjustment if adjustment costs are high (Earl and Estrin, 1998). Our hypothesis is that increasing competition has a positive effect on the level of restructuring activity and performance.

3.6 Human capital

Another important determinant of restructuring is human capital. The domination of insider ownership means that the management's competence and its motivation for restructuring become crucial to the company's success in the market. Yet, most managers of the former state-owned enterprises lack entrepreneurial spirit, marketing skills and the ability to raise outside investment funds, i.e. a change in the top management is needed.

In the case of Ukraine, the inflow of new human capital with superior knowledge and skills is extremely limited. There is almost no infusion of western managers. A new generation of market-oriented local management talent does not yet exist. The market for general managers is weak and underdeveloped. For this reason, simply changing the top management of a Ukrainian firm, at this point in time, will not necessarily promote its restructuring. This suggests that management training is an important step towards improving the quality of human capital (Djankov, 1997).

From our point of view, the positive impact of management training on enterprise restructuring can be attributed to two factors. One factor concerns the accumulation of managerial knowledge and skills during the training process. The other factor relates to the fact that those managers who undergo training programmes are showing much more initiative than those who do not get involved. Participation in training programmes is a self-selection procedure. Therefore, it can be expected that those managers who enrol in training programmes are highly motivated to improve their business, are entrepreneurial and interested in acquiring new skills. We consider this entrepreneurial component of management training to be at least as important as the accumulation of new knowledge and skills, and expect training of senior management to have a positive impact on the restructuring activity of companies and their performances. On the other hand, just exchanging one set of managers for another might not turn out to be significant.

4 The data

We analysed the data of 174 replies received from Ukrainian industrial enterprises with more than 1,000 employees (no newly created private firms were included) that was conducted in the fall of 1998. The survey sample of 500 firms had been selected from a complete list of Ukrainian industrial enterprises drawn up in 1990. The selection made, insured a good cross-sectional representation by region and industry.

The questionnaire was mailed to the top management of the companies in June 1998. One month later 174 replies had been received, representing a response rate of 34.6%. The characteristics of the final sample are presented in Table 12.5 in the Appendix. Although the sample is not perfectly representative, it covers a range of industries broad enough to allow us to draw meaningful conclusions about corporate behaviour of large industrial enterprises in Ukraine. 36.5% of the enterprises in the sample were state-owned, and 63.5% were in private hands. More than half of the non-state enterprises had been privatised between 1995 and 1996 (the rest in 1994).

In the questionnaire, we have asked management to report on the geographical distribution of sales for 1995 and for 1997. The statistics for the geographical sales distribution in 1995 and in 1997 are shown in Table 12.2 in the Appendix. Although the export structure of sales has changed in favour of non-CIS countries, the share of exports to Western Europe and to the rest of the world has remained quite low in absolute terms. From 1995 to 1997 the number of exporting firms had slightly decreased from 144 (82.2%) to 140 (81%). Similarly, the number of firms with exports to non-CIS countries has reduced from 98 (56.3%) in 1995 to 95 (55.2%) in 1997.

5 Variables used for analysis and in the estimation procedure

5.1 Restructuring

We use 16 qualitative restructuring indicators that can plausibly be assumed to signal moves towards market orientation. Six indicators – selling/leasing of excess equipment, closure of old product lines, switching to less costly raw materials, reduction of social assets, maintaining low real wages, and employee layoffs – represent passive measures directed, mainly, at cutting costs and adjusting to the conditions of declining demand. Another ten indicators represent strategic measures aimed at the long-term improvement in the firm's viability and performance. They include changing to new suppliers, increasing the share of qualified labour, purchasing new technology, increasing quality control, acquiring new equipment, changing the organisational structure, making product innovations, obtaining international certification of products, creating new distribution channels, and developing a strategic marketing plan.[1]

The management of the surveyed enterprises was asked whether they had employed any of the listed restructuring measures following the firm's privatisation (or during last three years in the case of a state-owned enterprise). Their answers were converted into a set of dummy variables defined as equal to 1 whenever a measure had been adopted.

5.2 Performance

We use five measures of performance, namely changes in profitability, labour productivity (sales per employee), production volume, sales volume, and market share, and constructed five performance dummies (INCREASED PROFITABILITY, INCREASED LABOUR PRODUCTIVITY, INCREASED SALES VOLUME, INCREASED PRODUCTION VOLUME, INCREASED MARKET SHARE). These were set equal to 1 whenever management reported an increase in an indicator between 1997 and 1995.

5.3 Export orientation

Two variables are used to capture the effect of export orientation on enterprise restructuring: EXPORT95 and EXPORTnon-CIS95. EXPORT95 measures the share of exports relative to total sales of the firm in 1995, and EXPORTnon-CIS95 measures the share of exports to non-CIS countries in total sales in 1995. In the performance equations, we use the variables INCEXP and INCEXPnon-CIS to measure the effect of changes in export share on changes in performance. INCEXP is a dummy variable that equals 1 whenever the firm's export share relative to total sales has increased between 1997 and 1995. Similarly, INCEXPnon-CIS is a dummy variable that equals 1 whenever the firm's share of non-CIS exports relative to total sales has increased. Finally, in the export orientation equations, we use the absolute change in export share, and in the share of exports to non-CIS countries, as dependent variables.

---

1 Descriptive statistics for restructuring indicators is presented in: Akimova, I. (2000): Export Orientation and Enterprise Restructuring in Ukraine. Working Paper No. 2, Institute for Economic Research and Policy Consulting/German Advisory Group on Economic Reforms in Ukraine, Kyiv, October (http://www.ier.kiev.ua).

5.4 Privatisation and ownership structure

The effect of privatisation is captured by the variable PRIV that is equal to 1 if private parties hold more than 50% of the company's equity capital, and it is equal to 0 otherwise.

5.5 Hard budget constraints

For gauging the hardness of a firm's budget constraints we employ two indicators: state subsidisation and share of barter operations in total sales. State subsidisation (SUBSIDY) is a dummy variable that is equal to 1 if the firm has reported receiving state subsidies after its privatisation (or in the past three years in the case of state-owned enterprises), and 0 otherwise. The share of barter in total sales (BARTER) is an interval variable measured on an 11-point scale (1 = no state orders, 2 = the share of state orders was less than 10% of total sales, 11 = the share of state orders was more than 90% of total sales).

5.6 Competition

In the absence of information on sales concentration ratios for Ukraine, we use two subjective measures for the degree of competition. We define DOMCOMP as the level of competitive pressure exerted by domestic (Ukrainian) competitors on the surveyed firm. DOMCOMP is equal to 1 if the firm has reported a high level of domestic competitive pressure. We define INTCOMP as the level of competitive pressure produced by foreign (non-CIS) competitors. INTCOMP is equal to 1 if this level was reported to be high.

5.7 Human capital

Two dummy variables are used to measure management personnel turnover and training. CHANGE is equal to 1 if the firm has reported a change in its senior management after privatisation. The senior management turnover rate between 1995 and 1998 in our sample is 61.5%.

TRAINING is a dummy variable that is equal to 1 if any senior manager of the enterprise has participated in a training programme after privatisation. The participation in training programmes for senior management in the sample is 52.9%.

5.8 Control variables

In order to allow for differences in company performance prior to privatisation, we use a variable (INIPOS), which subjectively rates the firm's overall position prior to privatisation (or three years before the date of our survey, in the case of state firms) as reported by management. INIPOS is an interval variable measured on a 5-point Likert scale (5 = much better than the average in a particular branch, 3 = average, 1 = much less than the average). We also use industry (IND) and region (REG) dummies in order to control for the differences related to product market structure, growth rates of particular industries, and peculiarities of regional policies.

5.9 Estimation procedure

The final estimation equations are the following:

$$R = a + \sum_i b_i IND + \sum_j c_j REG + dEXP + ePRIV + fCOMP + \sum_m g_m HBC + hHCAP + \varphi \tag{12.1}$$

$$P = a + a_0 INIP + \sum_i b_i IND + \sum_j c_j REG + dINCEXP + + ePRIV + fCOMP + \sum_m g_m HBC + hHCAP + \varepsilon \tag{12.2}$$

$$E = a + a_0 INIP + \sum_i b_i IND + \sum_j c_j REG + dEXP95 + + ePRIV + fCOMP + \sum_m g_m HBC + hHCAP + \varepsilon \tag{12.3}$$

These equations allow to separate the effects of transition (or marketisation), export orientation, ownership, competition, hardening budget constraints, and human capital. In all equations, $ePRIV + \varepsilon_2$ measures the ownership effect on performance *P*, on restructuring activity *R*, and on the change in export orientation E. Following the approach by Frydman, Gray, Hessel and Rapaczynski (1997), we interpret $t_c = a + a_0 INIPOS + \sum_i b_i IND + \sum_i c_j REG$ as a transition effect that is a performance element common to all firms. It consists of several components: The mean component of a transitional effect *a*, the initial position effect $a_0 INIPOS$, the industry effect $\sum_i b_i IND$ and the region effect $\sum_i c_j REG$. In the *R*estructuring equation, $dEXP + \varepsilon_2$ measures the effect of export orientation, in the *P*erformance equation, $dINCEXP + \varepsilon_2$ measures the effect of the change in the export share of total sales, and in the equation for the change in *E*xport orientation, $dEXP95 + \varepsilon_2$ measures the effect of the initial export share in total sales. In all equations, $fCOMP + \varepsilon_3$ measures the competition effect, and $\sum_m g_m HBC + \varepsilon_4$ measures the effect of hardening budget constraints. Finally, *hHCAP* captures the effect of human capital.

6 Regression results

The estimates of the logistic regressions (those which turn out to be statistically significant) for restructuring activity dummies with EXPORT95 and EXPORT non-CIS95 specifications are presented in Table 12.1 and Table 12.2 (see end of this Chapter). *The basic conclusion we can draw from our analysis is that the joint impact of export orientation, privatisation, competition, hardening of budget constraints and changes in human capital on the restructuring activity is rather different from that on performance.*

As far as the propensity of large industrial firms to engage in restructuring activities is concerned, *export orientation of the firms, and orientation of sales towards non-CIS markets in particular, represents an important driving force for restructuring.*

The analysis of the regression coefficients for export orientation variables shows that, first, general export orientation has a statistically significant positive effect *on both passive and strategic restructuring activities*, while orientation towards non-CIS markets mainly influences *strategic restructuring activities.* One possible explanation for this phenomenon is that the firms, which are more oriented towards non-CIS markets, have undertaken some passive cost-cutting restructuring measures at an earlier time compared to firms where exports are mainly directed towards CIS countries. Enterprises with non-CIS exports concentrate their main efforts on strategic restructuring. The absolute values of the regression coefficients for EXPORTnon-CIS variables are high, they vary from 0.57 to 1.17. *This suggests that orientation of sales towards non-CIS markets is very important for strategic restructuring.*

Ownership does not correlate in any significant way with the various performance indicators, except the one for changing suppliers. We have tried to refine the ownership category by breaking it into different dominant owner groups, and re-run the estimation equations with PRIV variables (the dummy for enterprises with dominant private owners) for three alternative groups: dominant inside owners, dominant concentrated outside owners, and dispersed owners. However, for all three groups the differences between the regression models have turned out to be statistically insignificant. The lack of importance of ownership status can – at least partly – be explained by Ukraine still being at an early stage in the transition when formal ownership changes have not yet had a chance to bring about improved corporate governance and restructuring. Also, the slow pace of economic reforms has not provided potential investors with attractive business opportunities. Another explanation is that outsiders may not be able to impose effective corporate governance on Ukrainian firms because of weak capital markets (Estrin and Rosevear, 1999). We expect an increasing influence of outside and concentrated ownership on strategic restructuring activity of the enterprises in the later stages of transition.

Our results show that, apart from export orientation, *changes in managerial human capital, the hardening of budget constraints, and increased competitive pressure* (especially from foreign producers) represent the other driving forces behind enterprise restructuring in Ukraine. The evidence suggests that *management training has a strong positive impact on restructuring activities (both passive and strategic) of Ukrainian firms.* This effect is related to the more entrepreneurial nature of those managers who selected themselves for participation in training programmes. Relative to the other determinants for restructuring, the effect of accumulation of human capital (i.e. management training) appears to be the strongest one in the short-run. This seems to be quite different from the findings of numerous studies on restructuring of East European countries, which point out the primary importance of ownership structures. It shows that in a slowly reforming economy, *the relative importance of restructuring determinants can differ from that in faster developing transitional countries*

The effect of a change in senior management on the restructuring activity was found to be positive, but is significant mainly for the passive measures. This supports our hypothesis that under the conditions of imperfect labour markets for top management and a very limited inflow of human capital from outside, a simple change in senior management can not promote strategic restructuring unless it is accompanied by entrepreneurial abilities and the development of better business skills.

Our results suggest *a strong negative effect of soft budget constraints* (in particular, state subsidies received after privatisation) *on the restructuring activities* (both passive and active) of enterprises. Noteworthy are high absolute values (with negative signs) of the coefficients for SUBSIDY and BARTER in the equations for 'hard' strategic restructuring measures like buying of new equipment, product innovation, and international certification of products. This suggests that the hardening of budget constraints is very important for accelerating major *strategic innovations.*

We have found a positive significant relationship between restructuring activity and competitive pressure, in particular from foreign producers. The coefficients for FORCOMP are positive and significant in five strategic activity equations including equations for international certification of products, creation of new distribution channels, selling of unused equipment, closing of old product lines, and reduction of social assets. High levels of domestic competition was found to be significant for product innovation and international certification of products, while it turns out to be insignificant for passive restructuring measures.

Among the control variables, only the indicator of initial position of the enterprise has turned to be of significant importance in the majority of equations for strategic measures. This suggests that those enterprises, which had some advantages with respect to their financial or technological position within the industry in the past, tend to be better at restructuring.

Our results also suggest that *the general climate for restructuring during the first years after large-scale privatisation had not been favourable.* The constant in all logistic regressions is consistently negative and, most of the time, statistically significant. Moreover this general transition effect is of such a size – that even under the most favourable circumstances with respect to ownership, competition and hard budget constraints – a probability of above-average restructuring activity is obtained that is at best equal to the complementary probability.

The estimation of the *performance equations* has produced results that are somehow different from those for the restructuring indicators. The regression models turn out to be statistically significant only for two performance indicators out of five (namely, the increases in market share and in labour productivity from 1995 to 1997). These estimations are presented in Table 12.3 (see end of this Chapter). In neither case did *we find any evidence of a positive effect on improved performance of the enterprises by an increase in the share of exports in total sales, or by a reorientation of exports towards non-CIS markets.* For both performance equations, the coefficients for INCEXP and INCEXPnon-CIS are statistically insignificant. One possible explanation concerning the weak relationship between the restructuring activity and performance results, may be that we are at an early stage of transition in a slowly reforming country (see Akimova and Schwödiauer, 2000). In other words, the restructuring efforts induced by export orientation and re-orientation might not yet have translated into better performance. However, in the long run we expect export orientation (including re-orientation towards non-CIS markets) to show more pronounced positive effects on performance, providing Ukraine succeeds in accelerating market reforms.

Another explanation may be connected with the fact that the re-orientation of exports, during the time period under analysis, has occurred due to changes in the international environment and is not directly linked to restructuring efforts of the enterprises. The worsening of the trading relations with Russia (the major CIS partner of Ukraine), with imposition of tariff and non-tariff barriers on both sides, has resulted in the redirection of Ukrainian exports towards non-CIS markets in 1995 to 1997. This may explain (at least partly) why we fail to find a positive correlation between the export reorientation and performance outcomes. It should be taken into account that this shift to non-CIS markets might have occurred under unfavourable terms of trade, i.e. companies might have been pushed to sell their products at very low (or dumping) prices in order to be able to export. Therefore, in the short run the re-orientation of exports towards non-CIS countries has not resulted in an improvement in performance, while in the long run this could still be expected.

Similar to the case of restructuring measures, *ownership changes turn out to be insignificant in explaining differences in performance results*. This result is quite consistent with other recent studies on Ukrainian and Russian restructuring (see Estrin and Rosevear, 1999; Akimova and Schwödiauer, 2000), which show that in the early years of transition, the multifaceted restructuring activities of companies are not directly associated with performance improvements.

Our results suggest that the *main driving force behind performance improvements for Ukrainian industrial firms between 1995 and 1997 is high competitive pressure from domestic and, in particular, from foreign producers*. This supports the conclusions of some empirical findings suggesting that competition should be the leading force for performance improvements (Earle and Estrin, 1998). The coefficients for hard-budget-constraints variables have predicted negative signs, but are statistically insignificant. The changes in managerial human capital measured by *participation in management training programmes have a strong positive impact on the increase in market share of the firm*. Evidence of a significant impact of management turnover on performance results was not found.

Concerning control variables, the industry effect has a significant impact on the propensity of a firm to increase its market share. Finally, the overall transitional effect (represented by the regression constant*) has been found to be negative for enterprise performance*.

What then are the main factors that influence companies to *reorient their sales towards exports*? In Table 12.4 (see end of this Chapter), we present our estimates of changes in the export share relative to total sales. Our results suggest that *private ownership and improvements to the quality of managerial human capital (both management turnover and training) have a clear strong positive impact on the change, both to the share of total and of non-CIS exports*. Firms with dominant private owners, have, on the average, increased their export share of total sales by 4.2 percentage points more than the enterprises where the state is the dominant owner. For the shares of non-CIS exports of total sales, this difference is even higher, reaching 5.2 percentage points. Very likely, private ownership influences restructuring activity of the enterprises indirectly by inducing export reorientation.

Our findings suggest that *soft budget constraints measured as the share of barter in total sales negatively influence the change in export orientation of enterprises*. No evidence was found concerning significant competition, industry, regional and initial position effects. The former share of exports in total sales was found to be negatively correlated to the change in trade orientation towards exports. This shows that enterprises with a lower export share in the past have experienced a higher growth in export share between 1995 and 1997.

7 Implications

Our findings have clear *policy implications*.

First, future success with restructuring of large industrial enterprises in Ukraine is related to their increasing integration into the world economy through re-orientation towards, and production for export. This applies particularly to exports into non-CIS markets. On the macro-economic level this requires the promotion of openness and transparency of trade policy, implementation of such measures as elimination of all remaining export barriers, adoption and mutual recognition of internationally accepted norms, standards and certification procedures, elimination of all restrictions on the use of foreign exchange.[2] Joining the WTO is an important step in enhancing and ensuring trade liberalisation.

Second, accelerating the privatisation of the remaining large industrial companies will induce them to redirect their trade towards exports and push them towards restructuring.

Third, the hardening of budget constraints is a necessary pre-condition for restructuring and improving the performance of enterprises. State subsidisation should be considerably reduced, and any future subsidies should be subject to regular status reports and performance reviews. Serious attention should be paid to re-monetisation of the economy, i.e. to the reduction of barter operations, which are still used by many unprofitable firms as an instrument of survival.

Fourth, encouraging competition between domestic and foreign producers is an important driving force for enterprise restructuring. This requires implementation of a well-developed anti-monopoly policy, the creation of a favourable business environment for the establishment of new private firms, and ending the practice of import protection.

Fifth, enterprise restructuring will never work effectively in an unstable and investment-discouraging business environment. Enforcement of contracts, protection of property rights, stability of the legal framework, together with simple and clear tax legislation, are pre-conditions for the success of enterprise restructuring and for economic growth.

---

2 German Advisory Group on Economic Reforms in Ukraine (1999), pp. 43-44.

Table 12.1
Logistic regressions with EXPORT95 variable, dependent variables, and passive and strategic restructuring dummies (standard errors in parentheses)

	Change in suppliers	Buying new technology	Buying new equipment	Product innovation	Internatio-nal certifi-cation of products	New distribu-tion channels
EXPORT 95	0.005	0.007	0.01**	0.03**	0.02**	0.01*
	(0.007)	(0.007)	(0.001)	(0.01)	(0.009)	(0.007)
Ownership						
PRIV	1.0** (0.4)	0.11 (0.42)	0.10 (0.4)	0.66 (0.50)	0.60 (0.68)	0.43 (0.41)
Competition						
DOMCOMP	-0.52 (0.4)	0.27 (0.4)	0.10 (0.38)	1.04**	1.29**	0.02
				(0.5)	(0.5)	(0.03)
FORCOMP	0.10 (0.47)	0.57 (0.54)	-0.07 (0.4)	0.33 (0.6)	0.7* (0.39)	1.2** (0.4)
Hardening budget constraints						
SUBSIDY	-0.19 (0.6)	0.20 (0.7)	-1.03*	-2.7**	-7.6 (18.1)	-0.7 (0.5)
			(0.5)	(0.8)		
BARTER	0.08 (0.06)	0.02 (0.07)	-0.15**	0.02	-0.20**	0.01 (0.06)
			(0.06)	(0.08)	(0.08)	
Human capital						
TRAINING	0.33 (0.36)	1.4** (0.4)	1.5**	0.80**	0.84**	0.84**
	0.73**		(0.39)	(0.4)	(0.47)	(0.36)
CHANGE	(0.37)	0.57 (0.3)	0.20 (037)	0.48 (0.40)	0.36 (0.48)	0.61*
						(0.37)
Control variables						
REG	Y	Y		Y	Y	Y
IND	Y	Y	Y	Y	Y	Y
INIPOS	-0.18 (0.4)	0.42*	Y	0.70**	0.53**	0.22 (0.22)
		(0.21)	0.40*	(0.30)	(0.31)	
Constant	0.81 (1.0)	-3.81**	(0.23)	-3.0**	-5.5**	-2.1**
		(1.3)	-2.1**	(1.4)	(1.7)	(1.08)
Chi sq.	21.3**	25.5**	(1.08)	67.2**	38.9**	29.3**
Correct percent	74	74	25.4**	87	83	69
N	165	165	73	165	164	160
			163			

*significant at p<0.1, **significant at p<0.05; Y – industry and regional dummies included.

Table 12.1 (cont.)
Logistic regressions with EXPORT95 variable, dependent variables, and passive and strategic restructuring dummies (standard errors in parentheses)

	Sell/lease equipment	Close old product lines	Switch to cheaper raw materials	Reduction of social assets	Maintain low real wages	Employee layoffs
EXPORT 95	0.002** (0.007)	0.02** (0.008)	0.01* (0.006)	0.01* (0.007)	0.018** (0.008)	0.02** (0.01)
<u>Ownership</u>						
PRIV	-0.36 (0.39)	-0.11 (0.4)	0.02 (0.4)	-0.87 (0.79)	-0.51 (0.47)	-0.72 (0.53)
<u>Competition</u>						
DOMCOMP	-0.23 (0.39)	-0.06 (0.4)	0.38 (0.38)	0.46 (0.38)	0.04 (0.04)	-0.14 (0.5)
FORCOMP	1.1** (0.50)	1.5** (0.50)	0.43 (0.45)	1.16** (0.5)	0.10 (0.4)	0.54 (0.6)
<u>Hardening budget constraints</u>						
SUBSIDY	-2.5** (0.80)	-1.3** (0.7)	-0.72 (0.50)	-1.4** (0.65)	-1.12 (0.7)	-0.22 (0.8)
BARTER	0.08(0.06)	0.06(0.07)	-0.17** (0.06)	0.17** (0.07)	0.009 (0.6)	0.11(0.9)
<u>Human capital</u>						
TRAINING	0.66** (0.37)	0.76** (0.38)	0.49 (0.36)	0.81** (0.38)	-0.13 (0.4)	-0.87** (0.52)
CHANGE	0.77** (0.38)	0.46 (0.39)	0.35 (0.31)	0.69** (0.38)	0.66* (0.39)	0.90** (0.49)
<u>Control variables</u>						
REG	Y	Y	Y	Y	Y	Y
IND	Y	Y	Y	Y	Y	Y
INIPOS	-0.21 (0.27)	0.40* (0.24)	0.05* (0.02)	0.01 (0.02)	0.08 (0.2)	0.25 (0.28)
Constant	-1.5 (1.1)	-4.0 (1.2)	0.14 (1.0)	-2.41** (1.1)	-1.0(1.1)	0.88(1.3)
Chi sq.	44.3**	49.2**	20.6**	44.8**	20.5**	25.5**
Correct percent	72	72	71	72	70	85
N	165	167	159	166	159	168

*significant at p<0.1, **significant at p<0.05; Y – industry and regional dummies included.

Source: Author's calculations.

Table 12.2
Logistic regressions with EXPORT non-CIS 95 variable, dependent variables, and passive and strategic restructuring dummies (standard errors in parentheses)

	Change to new suppliers	Buying new technology	Buying new equipment	Product innovations
EXPORT non-CIS 95	0.01	1.0** (0.49)	0.57* (0.36)	0.57* (0.34)
Ownership				
PRIV	1.0** (0.4)	0.36 (0.4)	0.24 (0.4)	0.69 (0.65)
Competition				
DOMCOMP	-0.15 (0.4)	-0.09 (0.4)	0.35 (0.46)	0.30 (059)
FORCOMP	0.36 (0.5)	0.25 (0.6)	0.07 (0.6)	0.13 (0.8)
Hardening budget constraints				
SUBSIDY	-0.26 (1.0)	1.3 (1.0)	0.64 (0.9)	-2.1** (0.96)
BARTER	0.04 (0.07)	0.05 (0.05)	-0.14** (0.07)	-0.08 (0.1)
Human capital				
TRAINING	0.38 (0.42)	1.4** (0.4)	1.7** (0.47)	0.97** (0.55)
CHANGE	1.3** (0.43)	-0.3 (0.4)	0.15 (0.4)	0.18 (0.5)
Control variables				
REG	Y	Y	Y	Y
IND	Y	Y	Y	Y
INIPOS	-0.08 (0.2)	0.74** (0.32)	0.38 (0.3)	0.74** (0.37)
Constant	-0.22 (1.3)	-5.3** (1.6)	-3.7** (1.5)	-0.68 (1.8)
Chi sq.	24.8**	25.1**	27.6**	18.5*
Correct percent	72	72	70	86
N	124	124	120	121

*significant at p<0.1, **significant at p<0.05; Y – industry and regional dummies included.

Table 12.2 (cont.)
Logistic regressions with EXPORTnon-CIS95 variable, dependent variables, and passive and strategic restructuring dummies (standard errors in parentheses)

	International certification of products	Development of marketing plan	Selling/ leasing excess equipment	Maintaining low real wages
EXPORT non-CIS 95	1.17** (0.62)	1.02** (0.4)	-0.005 (0.4)	-0.63 (0.44)
Ownership				
PRIV	-0.08 (0.50)	0.44 (0.40)	-0.50 (0.40)	-0.82** (0.42)
Competition				
DOMCOMP	1.11** (0.50)	0.42 (0.40)	-0.73** (0.40)	-0.04 (0.43)
FORCOMP	0.29 (0.70)	0.92** (0.50)	0.96** (0.50)	0.73 (0.57)
Hardening budget constraints				
SUBSIDY	-7.6 (20.1)	0.51 (0.80)	-3.0** (1.1)	-0.21 (0.90)
BARTER	-0.24** (0.09)	0.07 (0.07)	-0.01 (0.007)	0.17*(0.07)
Human capital				
TRAINING	0.89* (0.50)	0.41 (0.38)	0.64 (0.40)	0.85** (0.4)
CHANGE	0.31 (0.50)	0.36 (0.40)	0.88** (0.40)	0.53 (0.40)
Control variables				
REG	Y	Y	Y	Y
IND	Y	Y	Y	Y
INIPOS	0.50 (0.34)	0.26 (0.26)	-0.13 (0.20)	-0.21 (0.27)
Constant	-5.4** (1.8)	-3.9** (1.4)	0.07 (1.3)	0.34 (0.30)
Chi sq.	31.6**	18.5*	27.9**	22.0**
Correct percent	87	69	73	70
N	122	122	127	125

*significant at p<0.1, **significant at p<0.05; Y – industry and regional dummies included.

Source: Author's calculations.

Table 12.3
Logistic regressions, dependent variables: Improvement in performance indicators (standard errors presented in brackets)

Independents	Increase in market share, 1995-1997	Increase in labour productivity, 1995-1997
Ownership		
PRIV	0.94 (0.63)	0.66 (0.49)
Competition		
DOMCOMP	1.27* (0.73)	1.23** (0.57)
FORCOMP	1.34 (0.99)	1.56**(0.81)
Hardening budget constraints		
SUBSIDY		
BARTER	-6.9 (28.7)	-0.38 (1.14)
	-0.14 (0.10)	-0.07 (0.08)
Human capital		
MANTRAIN		
MANCHANGE	1.06** (0.54)	0.17 (0.49)
	0.13 (0.62)	0.81 (0.51)
Control variables		
REG		
IND	Y	Y
INIPOS	Y*	Y
INCEXP	0.73 (0.48)	0.57 (0.37)
INCEXP non-CIS	-0.22 (0.74)	0.45 (0.60)
	1.03 (0.78)	-0.34 (0.61)
Constant		
Chi	-2.87** (1.5)	-3.6**(1.7)
Correct percent	20.8**	20.1**
N	79.3	78.4
	92	92

*significant at p<0.1, **significant at p<0.05; Y – industry and regional dummies included.

Source: Author's calculations.

Table 12.4
Linear regressions, dependent variable change in the share of exports in total sales between 1995 and 1997

Independents	Change in export share, 1995-1997	Change in non-CIS export share, 1995-1997
Ownership		
PRIV	4.28** (2.5)	5.3** (2.59)
Competition		
DOMCOMP	-0.25 (2.5)	0.54 (2.5)
FORCOMP	(3.4)	0.58 (3.5)
Hardening budget constraints		
SUBSIDY		
BARTER	6.1 (5.8)	6.8 (6.0)
	-1.5** (0.45)	-1.25** (0.45)
Human capital		
MANTRAIN		
MANCHANGE	5.8** (2.3)	6.2** (2.45)
	2.7 (2.4)	3.0 (2.16)
Control variables		
REG		
IND	Y	Y
INIPOS	Y	Y
EXP95	2.3 (1.5)	1.9 (1.5)
	-0.1** (0.05)	-0.04 (0.05)
Constant		
Adj R sq	-7.4 (7.9)	-11.8 (7.8)
F	0.116	0.10
N	2.58**	2.24**
	132	90

*p<0.1, **p<0.05, standard errors are presented in brackets; Y- regional and industry dummies are included.

Source: Author's calculations.

References

Akimova, Iryna and Gerhard Schwödiauer (2000): Restructuring of Ukrainian Enterprises After Privatization: Does Ownership Structure Matter? In: Atlantic Economic Journal, March

Aghion, Philippe and Olivier Blanchard (1998): On Privatisation Methods in Eastern Europe and Their Implications. In: Economics of Transition, Vol. 6, No. 1, pp. 87-99

Boycko, M., A. Shleifer and R. Vishny (1995): Privatising Russia. MIT Press, Cambridge/Mass.

Carlin, Wendy and Philippe Aghion (1996): Restructuring Outcomes and the Evolution of Ownership Patterns in Central and Eastern Europe. In: Economics of Transition, Vol. 4, No. 2, pp. 371-388

Claessens, Stijn and R. K. Peters (1997): State Enterprise Performance and Soft Budget Constraints: The Case of Bulgaria. The World Bank, mimeo

Djankov, Simeon (1997): On the Determinants of Enterprise Adjustment: Evidence from Moldavia. World Bank, October, mimeo

Djankov, Simeon (1998): Ownership Structure and Enterprise Restructuring in the Commonwealth of Independent States. World Bank, July, mimeo

Djankov, Simeon and Bernard Hoekman (1996): Trade Reorientation and Post-Reform Productivity Growth in Bulgarian Enterprises. CEPR Discussion Paper, November

Djankov, Simeon and Gerhard Pohl (1998): Restructuring of Large Firms in Slovak Republic. In: Economics of Transition, Vol. 6, No. 1, pp. 667-685

Earle, John S. and Saul Estrin (1998): Privatisation, Competition, and Budget Constraints: Disciplining Enterprises in Russia. Stockholm School of Economics, SITE Working Paper No. 128

EBRD (1999): Transitional Report, London

Estrin, Saul and Adam Rosevear (1999): Enterprise Performance and Ownership: The Case of Ukraine. In: European Economic Review, Vol. 43, pp. 1125-1136

Estrin, Saul and Lina Takla (1995): Enterprise Adjustment in Transition: Does History Matter? London Business School, mimeo

Feenstra, Robert, James Markusen and William Zeile (1992): Accounting for Growth with New Inputs: Theory and Evidence. In: American Economic Association Papers and Proceedings, Vol. 82, pp. 415-421

Frydman, Roman, Cheryl Gray, Marek Hessel and Andrzej Rapaczynski (1997): Private Ownership and Corporate Performance: Some Lessons from Transitional Economies: Research Report 97-28, C.V.Starr Centre for Applied Economics, New York University, July

German Advisory Group on Economic Reforms in Ukraine (1999): The Next 1000 Days: An Economic Reform Agenda for Ukraine. Kyiv, November

Jones, Derek S. (1998): The Economic Effects of Privatisation: Evidence from a Russian Panel. Comparative Economic Studies, Vol. XXXX, No. 2 (Summer), pp. 75-102

Leshchenko, Larisa and Valerij Ravenko (1999): Privatisation and Restructuring in Ukraine. In: Paul Hare, Judy Batt, Martine Cave and Saul Estrin: Reconstituting the Market: The Political Economy of Microeconomic Transformation. London: Harwood Academic press

Pohl, Gerhard, Robert E. Anderson, Stijn Claessens and Simeon Djankov (1997): Privatisation and Restructuring in Central and Eastern Europe: Evidence and Policy Options. World Bank Technical Paper No. 368, The World Bank, Washington D.C.

Shleifer, Andrei and Robert Vishny (1996): A Theory of Privatisation. In: Economic Journal, Vol. 106, pp. 309-319

Appendix

Table 12.5
Sample characteristics

	Number of the firms (%)
Branch	
Energy and fuel	29 (16.8%)
Machine building	77 (44.5%)
Chemicals	18 (10.4%)
Metallurgy	15 (8.7%)
Production of consumer goods	12 (6.9%)
Communications and electronics	13 (7.5%)
Other industrial production	9 (5.2%)
Size (number of employees)	
1000-3000	100 (57.3%)
>3000	73 (42.2%)
Type of ownership enterprise	
State enterprise	61 (36.5%)
Privatised enterprise,	112 (63.5%)
Including privatised by more than 50%	56 (31.7%)

Table 12.6
Descriptive statistics for the geographical distribution of sales in 1995 and in 1997

Distribution of sales	Mean values in 1995	Std deviation	Mean values in 1997	Std deviation
Region where the firm is situated	21.9	28.4	21.8	28.5
Other regions of Ukraine	43.5	27.6	45.6	28.8
CIS countries	22.5	21.9	18.3	21.0
Eastern Europe	2.5	5.87	2.6	7.0
Western Europe	4.4	13.1	5.4	15.5
Rest of the world	5.37	14.9	7.8	24.3

Source: Authors's calculations.

PART III

ASPECTS OF FINANCIAL AND FISCAL POLICY IN UKRAINE

13

Monetary and Exchange Rate Policy During Transformation: Experience and Recommendations

Ryszard Kokoszczyński

1 Introduction

Many Central and East European countries started the process of transforming their economies at the beginning of the 1990s. This start was very difficult. Inflation was high, the domestic currency was not respected, and therefore stabilisation was the most important short-term target for macro-economic policy. On the other hand, the transformation process meant much more: creating a market economy. That was a challenge going far beyond macro-economic stabilisation. Promoting entrepreneurship, building the legal and systemic infrastructures required for effectively functioning markets, privatising of state-owned enterprises and stimulating the competitiveness of domestic industries – these were the all encompassing goals for general government policies. The ultimate objective for all these countries could be described with a single phrase: 'catching-up with the West'. Permanent economic growth that was sustainable in the long run was an important pre-condition. This common policy objective notwithstanding, ways to reach it were as diverse as the countries involved. These differences can clearly be demonstrated in the area of monetary policy, where every transition country adopted a different strategy and used its own distinctive means of implementation.

This Chapter is meant to present the Polish monetary policy in the 1990s, with the major emphasis given to exchange rate policies. I hope that our experience may be of some assistance to our Ukrainian hosts and to other countries in the region. The next Section of this Chapter describes the initial conditions at the beginning of the decade, and the joint efforts undertaken by the Government and the Central Bank (CB) in shaping monetary policy at that time. The following Section covers the evolution of monetary policy strategies during the period of 1990 to 1998, and of the changes in the CB's legal and institutional frameworks – an important factor influencing the efficiency of its activities. This is followed by a Section, which covers the most recent experience – implementing direct inflation targeting as a strategy for monetary policy in Poland. In the last Section conclusions are presented.

2 Monetary policy during the initial transformation period

Some important features of the Polish economic situation were common to all countries in Central and Eastern Europe, i.e. underdeveloped financial markets, lack of institutional independence of the central banks, monetisation of a major part of the budget deficit, etc. Hyperinflation, however, was not a phenomenon present in all transforming economies at the beginning of the transition process. In Poland, average annual inflation went way beyond 500%, hence eliminating hyper-inflation was the most important goal – not only for the National Bank of Poland, but also for the Government. Price liberalisation, international convertibility of the domestic currency, a positive real interest rate policy, wage controls, tax rates, and a fixed exchange rate – all of them were parts of the initial stabilisation package.

The exchange rate policy played a crucial role in achieving disinflation at that time. The fixed exchange rate in 1990-1991, being a nominal anchor, initially meant a fixed rate of the Zloty to the US-dollar, and later to a basket of five currencies (USD, DM, GBP, FRF, and CHF). Its outcome was a substantial real appreciation of the Zloty, compensated for with two discrete devaluations versus the basket. These devaluations notwithstanding, the fixed exchange rate made it possible to bring inflation down to approximately 70% in 1992.

At that time, disinflation would probably have progressed faster, had the budget deficit not largely been financed by direct credits from the CB. That approach was partly justified by the lack of a developed financial market. CB independence, including the prohibition of this kind of financing, was introduced gradually, and only the new Polish constitution of 1997 and the new central bank law of the same year practically completed this process. Only then did price stabilisation, the primary goal of monetary policy, finally become a pivotal part of this new legal framework. On the other hand, this gradual approach to eliminating the possibility of monetisation of the budget deficits greatly reduced the direct social costs, which a more rapid approach would have entailed at the beginning of transformation.

3 Choosing an adequate strategy for monetary policy

The National Bank of Poland had to choose an adequate monetary policy strategy (i.e. a set of formalised rules required to meet the strategic goals of monetary policy for the long run) at the very beginning of the transformation process already. Hyperinflation made it relatively easy – disinflation was a natural choice target for Polish monetary policy. This decision meant that the monetary authorities unambiguously declined to adopt other possible targets, such as an external equilibrium or a nominal GDP level. An external equilibrium would have been a premature choice as a target in a situation of limited convertibility of the Zloty. On the other hand, a policy by the CB designed to influence the level of economic activity might surely have found a lot of public support during this period of GDP decline and unemployment growth. Under the conditions in Poland at that time, this kind of strategy would, however, have promoted more inflation in the longer run.

There is a need here, to remind ourselves of a well known, though often overlooked, issue. A necessary pre-condition for success of this kind of a monetary policy strategy is the role of monetary factors in shaping inflationary processes. Inflation is always a monetary phenomenon in the long run. Nevertheless, monetary policy in a country like Poland at the beginning of the 1990s had frequently been assessed from a short-term point of view. Using this kind of perspective, non-monetary factors were often seen to be much more important for explaining the inflationary process. There are two major reasons for this. First, thanks to the growing ratio of foreign trade in the GDP, the Polish economy's degree of openness increased, and Poland was more and more becoming a typical small open economy. This resulted in its greater vulnerability to various external shocks, influencing strongly the dynamics of the inflationary processes. This has clearly been proven by the strong impacts that the Russian crisis (a typical demand shock) and the oil price increase (a typical supply shock) had on the rate of change of the consumer price index (CPI) in Poland in 1999. Second, another important non-monetary factor is the administrative pricing system applying to some parts of the Polish economy. Utilities and some other goods and services, being outputs of monopolised and state-dominated sectors, still have prices decided on or limited by the Government. The relative importance of that second factor has been rapidly declining recently, however, due to the openness of the Polish economy, which continues to increase. That means there is a growing exposure to various kind of external shocks with their impact on domestic inflation. This, in turn, requires some flexibility in defining monetary policy targets – inflexibility may either make monetary policy ineffective or very expensive or both.

These conditions notwithstanding, i.e. taking into account the large influences of non-monetary factors on inflation, it seems here the right place to remember that Poland's disinflation policy has managed to maintain a continuous course of declining inflation between 1990 and 1998, when the CPI dropped to a single-digit figure for the first time this decade. Unhappily, this trend was interrupted in 1999, due to a great many reasons, of which some were just the factors noted above.

3.1 Intermediate targets and the effectiveness of monetary policy

In the period between 1990 and 1998 the monetary policy strategy of the National Bank of Poland (NBP) had the orthodox design of the three-tier system: operational goal – intermediate target – ultimate objective. An operational goal in this period – with the exception of 1996 and 1997 – was the level of short-term interest rates in the money market. An intermediate target was a projected increase in money supply (M2) on an annual basis. It is worth noting that adoption of an intermediate target defined in this way is justified only if there is a relatively stable relationship between the money supply and the average price level in the economy. The quantitative projections concerning an increase in the money supply were at that period, excluding 1993, systematically exceeded, among other reasons, due to incomplete sterilisation by the NBP of foreign capital inflows to Poland. However, the exceeded monetary projections were accompanied by a growing monetary policy effectiveness, manifesting itself in systematically decreasing deviations of the annual inflation rate from the target set by the NBP. It seems that the main reason of the then existing discrepancies between the degrees of implementation of monetary and inflationary targets was the increase in money demand resulting from a growing confidence in the Zloty, dynamic developments in the financial system, and substantial and hardly predictable changes in economic activity. Under such circumstances it was difficult to put the money demand into a formalised framework, so helpful when quantitative targets for monetary policy are being set.

One of the most important lessons of the monetary policy conducted in Poland in the 1990s seems to be that it is difficult to create a stable money demand function and at the same time project how it will change. The significance of the growing money demand cannot be overestimated since it absorbed surplus money supply, enabling a systematic slowing down of inflationary dynamics in accordance with the projections made. It helped to maintain and even to increase the credibility of the monetary authorities, which is usually adversely affected when quantitative monetary policy goals, including intermediate ones, are exceeded.

3.2 Freedom of capital flows and exchange rate policy

The quick decline of inflation in the first years of the transformation made it possible in 1991 to replace the fixed exchange rate regime with a crawling peg Zloty devaluation versus the basket of currencies. Since then, the main targets of the exchange rate policy were stabilisation of the real Zloty exchange rate, and creating favourable conditions for export-oriented enterprises. Quite quickly, the exchange rate policy ceased to be an anti-inflationary policy instrument, becoming instead more an instrument of general economic policy rather than of monetary policy. In spite of a relatively quick liberalisation of the availability of short-term treasury securities to foreign investors (which took place from 1991 to 1993) the change in the exchange rate regime did not have a significant effect on the possibilities for the NBP of controlling money supply. Due to Poland's relatively low investment credibility, resulting from the fact that our country had not regulated its debt status in accordance with the requirements of the London Club, Poland did not experience substantial portfolio capital inflows. The situation changed entirely upon signing of the agreement with the London Club at the end of 1994 when Poland's investment credibility increased considerably. It led to a substantial speculative capital inflow accompanied by a growth in foreign direct investment in Poland.

Trying to maintain control over the monetary processes the monetary authorities decided in 1995 to re-orient the exchange rate policy by implementing the so-called crawling band system. The band, limiting the range of possible Zloty exchange rate fluctuations around the central parity, in fact determined the exchange rate risk incurred by foreign investors. It was a preventive instrument giving more autonomy to monetary policy. The modified exchange rate regime preserved its characteristic, which was a relative stabilisation of the real exchange rate. In subsequent years, due to a systematic decline in the rate of inflation and the need to increase the exchange rate risk, the pace of the crawling devaluation was systematically decreased and the exchange rate fluctuation band widened. A decision to fully float the Zloty exchange rate, taken in April 2000, completed the evolution of the exchange rate regime, which had started in Poland in 1990.

Looking back on the crawling band system in force in the second half of the 1990s, we can evaluate it positively. When taking the decision for the above-mentioned modification to the exchange rate system, the monetary authorities resisted the temptation to implement a fixed exchange rate regime. Such a policy, undoubtedly socially attractive, would only have appeared to facilitate the CB's struggle with inflation. Given the substantially higher inflation in Poland than for Poland's major trading partners, a fixed rate regime would have led to a quick real Zloty appreciation, followed by a growing speculative capital inflow and soon thereafter by its sudden outflow as a result of devaluation expectations. Exactly this scenario materialised in 1997 in the Czech Republic, where an early implementation of a fixed exchange rate regime brought about such a sequence of events. On the other hand, maintaining the crawling peg Zloty devaluation would have meant the necessity of greater sterilisation of portfolio capital inflows with potentially inflationary effects, than in the case of a crawling band. However, the possibilities of a sterilised intervention are substantially limited due to its cost. A moderate real Zloty appreciation, being a result of the crawling band regime, was a sensible compromise between the need to maintain export competitiveness and the necessity to conduct an anti-inflationary monetary policy.

3.3 Implementing institutional independence for the monetary authority

Independence of the monetary authority is one of the most important premises for its credibility. In turn, the CB's credibility influences the effectiveness of its monetary policy, and is of key significance to all countries undergoing economic transformation. In these countries the experience of hyperinflation or of high inflation is firmly rooted in the consciousness of its households and its enterprises, i.e. inflationary expectations are formulated mainly on the basis of the past inflation rates. This is also the case in Poland where we witness adaptive inflationary expectations, which as a result are of an instinctive nature. Greater credibility of the monetary authority helps to change these expectations at lower social cost, thus increasing monetary policy effectiveness.

Although the majority of policy-makers and economic experts were aware of the need to give full autonomy to the monetary authority from the beginning of the decade, in practice this postulate was implemented only after the Polish Constitution was adopted in 1997. Maintaining price stability as a basic objective of the NBP monetary policy was raised to a constitutional level, and prohibiting the financing of budget deficits by the CB was also included in the constitution. The need to have implemented this regulation is becoming obvious when taking into account that between 1990 and 1997 the NBP financed part of the budget deficit, which adversely affected the Polish monetary authority's credibility. The Monetary Policy Council (MPC) – a constitutional and independent organ responsible for shaping monetary policy – has also become a new authority in Polish economic life. Adoption of the constitution has given the monetary authorities the autonomy indispensable for creating the conditions favourable for altering the monetary policy strategies implemented so far.

4 The direct inflation target (DIT) strategy: Initial experiences

The strategy of a direct inflation target adopted by the Monetary Policy Council in 1998 specifies that the monetary authorities take into account changes in all the economic parameters, which might have an impact on the inflation rate when making their decisions on shaping monetary policy. In practice, implementation of the above strategy means appropriate control of interest rates by the NBP to achieve short- and medium-term inflationary objectives. The MPC adopted the

DIT strategy having in mind the following factors. First, direct inflation strategy means that there are to be no more intermediate targets for monetary policy, whether an exchange rate, money supply growth, or other. Considering earlier noted difficulties in implementing quantitative monetary targets and the need to maintain the autonomy of monetary policy, the lack of intermediate targets seems to be one of the major advantages of the DIT strategy. Second, direct inflation targeting is a more transparent strategy, which facilitates the communication between the CB and market participants and other economic agents. That means that the CB can more effectively influence the level of inflation expectations, which increases monetary policy effectiveness. Third, DIT enables the CB to adjust in a flexible manner to unexpected changes in the dynamics of the monetary processes. This feature of the DIT strategy is especially important in Poland where non-monetary factors are responsible for a substantial part of inflation.

One has to emphasise that direct inflation targeting can be an efficient monetary policy strategy only if the monetary authorities' analytical capabilities are sufficiently developed to prepare short- and medium-term inflation forecasts, and if the monetary transmission mechanism is well researched and is not subject to too many distortions. Neither condition is as yet fully met in Poland. Short time series are a major factor responsible for the relatively poor quality of longer-term inflation forecasts and the structurally high liquidity of the Polish banking system is an important distortion in the monetary transmission mechanism. For that reason, both the speed and the strength of the reaction by commercial banks to changes in the CB's interest rates can only be imprecisely estimated. Thus it is correct to say that the decision of the MPC to adopt a new monetary policy strategy presented the risk of having a new monetary policy framework without any substantial increase in monetary policy effectiveness. Overshooting the inflation target in 1999 can be interpreted as proof. An important contrary argument, however, is that the disinflation trend reversal of 1999 was mostly a result of a fiscal policy, which was much less restrictive than had been envisaged, together with an external supply shock (i.e. the world-wide oil price increase). Both factors were beyond the CB's sphere of influence. Also, these two impulses materialised too late in the year to make it possible for monetary policy to counteract them strongly enough to have an impact on that year's CPI figure (the average lag between interest rates and inflation is four to six quarters). In my opinion it is still too early to evaluate whether the direct inflation targeting strategy is a successful tool for Poland.

4.1 Inflation target definition and central bank credibility

Direct inflation targeting as a monetary policy strategy means that the inflation rate and its deviation from the target are de facto the sole indicators of monetary policy effectiveness. Defining an inflation target therefore becomes an important factor of the CB's credibility. It is not a choice without problems – in the Polish case the major dilemma was whether to use the concept of core inflation or the traditional consumer price index (CPI) as the measure of inflation.

Core inflation is a very popular concept in countries implementing direct inflation targeting. However, the general public in Poland expresses its traditional distrust when statistical measures of inflation differ too much from living cost changes perceived by households. Also, the important role of non-monetary factors shaping inflationary processes made it practically impossible to give core inflation a dominant role in the DIT strategy. Core inflation plays an important role in research and in communication with the public, the inflation target is however defined in terms of CPI.

4.2 Floating exchange rate: An indispensable part of direct inflation targeting as a monetary policy strategy in Poland

A floating exchange rate regime maximising the exchange rate risk increases the effectiveness of Polish monetary policy. Still, the relatively high inflation rate in Poland requires us to maintain a restrictive stance in monetary policy. That means maintaining a substantial interest rate disparity between Poland and other countries. A disparity of that kind causes portfolio capital inflows, which appreciate the Zloty, and are partly responsible for the current account deficit. The current account deficit, in turn, increases the risk of capital flow reversals and a resulting weakening of the domestic currency. These developments could be a major obstacle for a successful disinflation policy in the medium and long term. A floating exchange rate regime as a risk factor for speculative portfolio inflows is therefore a disincentive for excessive capital inflow growth; on the other hand, the same regime increases prohibitively the potential cost of speculative attacks against the Zloty. Under the current conditions of the Polish economy, i.e. the high level of the current account deficit, we highly value these inhibitory features of floating exchange rates.

Another reason for introducing a floating exchange rate regime in Poland is our long-term goal to become members of the EMU. Joining the EMU, as is widely known, requires as a pre-condition a minimum period of two years' stability for the exchange rates, with the benchmark being a fixed parity of the country's currency versus Euro. To maintain a floating regime means that the potential parity level will be defined mostly by market forces and by administrative decisions. This may increase the probability of maintaining successfully a stable exchange rate in the period of ERM membership, which Poland faces in some years from now.

5 Conclusions

The Polish monetary and exchange rate policies in the 1990s have been directed towards fulfilling two important objectives at the same time: continuous and credible disinflation, and macro-economic stability. These priorities constitute important premises for long-run sustainable economic growth in Poland. Disinflation had always been an ultimate objective of the CB's policy but its implementation was always put in a long-run perspective. No orthodox doctrine but pragmatic efficiency was a major feature of both, strategy and tactics, of the Polish monetary policy, which was probably one of important reasons for the growth success of the Polish economy. The exchange rate policy has always been an important part of this approach – its flexibility has been defined mostly by the need to adjust to capital flows and make the Polish economy less vulnerable to their potential reversals.

In a similar manner, direct inflation targeting – a monetary policy strategy has been implemented since 1999. The ultimate medium-term goal of the National Bank of Poland is to reach and to maintain price stability. This will facilitate further growth of the Polish economy and bring us closer to completing the decade-old process of economic transformation.

14

The Role of Long-term Capital for a European Ukraine

Andrew Seton

The prime objective of the European Bank for Reconstruction and Development (EBRD) is to assist its member countries in their transitions to market economies. All these countries are eager to go through this transition in order to become part of the family of countries with functioning markets. This, of course, is something that cannot be achieved within a short period of time.

Ukraine is a member country of the EBRD, and one of its largest clients. It should become an even larger partner in the future. Last year, the EBRD signed nearly 250 million USD of new commitments, the largest amount since its involvement with Ukraine began seven years ago. Overall, the EBRD has signed more than 800 million USD of commitments to Ukraine since Independence – which makes it the biggest and most diversified foreign investor of Ukraine, by far. The EBRD continues to enhance its presence in Kyiv in order to do even more. Much of its work focuses on the banking sector and on providing support for small and medium size private businesses. Although I wouldn't want to belittle the role of the EBRD in these areas, I want to place the emphasis of this presentation on long-term finance, and on overhauling the country's infrastructure and thus bringing it into closer rapport with that of its European neighbours.

Based on my twenty years of involvement with and travel in the countries of the former Soviet Union (though less in Ukraine), let me start with some comments about what I know is *not* needed, especially in view of some of the important lessons learned from the Russian crisis of 1998.

At this point in time Ukraine has little need of capital 'without vision' – that is, of capital looking to make a 'fast buck' in the capital markets, or trying to derive short-term benefits from the country's assets without modernising them. As a former investment banker with an interest in emerging markets, I know what the obvious appeal of countries like Russia and Ukraine was in the early-mid 1990s. Then, you could buy shares in companies very cheaply, or you could enjoy making money out of the huge volatility of treasury bonds. The risks were high, but everyone thought that one could rely on the low prices going up, at which time one would find an opportune moment to sell without first having to add value to the assets. It was a great game. The trouble is, everyone knew there would be a limit to that kind of fun – and indeed there was a limit. Obviously, what Ukraine needs today is *real capital first* and *capital market games*, a very distant *second.*

The 'short-term capital episode' in Ukraine's history – not to mention that in Russia's history, which met a major hiatus in mid-1998 – also led to another unfortunate consequence: Continuing mutual mistrust between foreign investors, local private interests and Government. The foreign investor is now normally perceived as having no more interest in adding value to the assets he had acquired than do most of his local private counterparts. Short-term greed is generally assumed to be the prime motive of the foreigner, perhaps all the more so since foreign interests were not offered much incentive to invest for the long term. Unfortunately this perception does little to discourage the predatory tendencies of some officials in Ukraine – something most of the few foreign strategic investors in the country are complaining about. The presence of foreign capital in a Ukrainian town has on occasions been seen as an irresistible temptation by the local authorities to exact special taxes to finance quite unrelated local needs. The potentially *positive* role of foreign capital as a creator of new jobs, payer of taxes, provider of opportunities for local suppliers and of general prosperity for a region or city, seems altogether forgotten. So far, this vicious circle has not been broken, at least not on a national scale. Nevertheless, we also know of some genuinely positive cases of co-operation between foreign companies and the Government, as well as private interests, in this country. But as a whole, Ukraine has not yet experienced enough foreign investment to know and to trust what it can really do for the country. Foreign investors, for their part, have not received sufficient encouragement to give the country a try, they are often deterred by the experiences of those who are already here. These and similar sentiments have been expressed as recently as at the June 2000 meeting of the Foreign Investment Advisory Council with President Kuchma, which included some of the largest foreign strategic investors in Ukraine.

Some of Ukraine's underlying structural problems since independence have grown, not diminished. Much of the country's essential infrastructure is in worse shape now, than it was in 1991. No business, regardless of the sector it operates in, can function without a healthy infrastructure. In addition, Ukraine needs a smoothly functioning energy sector to sustain and to grow businesses, and to serve domestic needs. But all infrastructure assets and the power distribution companies are out-of-date and out-of-cash. They run at only a fraction of their original capacity and depend heavily on external sources of fuel at international prices over which Ukraine has no control. Continuing to operate infrastructure assets in this manner has contributed to the economic crisis in this country, and will slow or even prevent Ukraine's integration with the market economies further West. This is already happening.

To make its transition along the difficult road to the market, and in order to overhaul its infrastructure, Ukraine badly needs *committed capital from strategic investors*. Nowhere is this more apparent today than in the electricity sector. This 'committed capital' should be capable of playing a number of roles, both in this key sector and elsewhere in the economy:

- It should bring with it long years of experience of operating within a market environment;
- It should bring the financial strength and vision to modernise and re-structure large companies, to help them face up to the market, and effect cost and energy savings;
- It should bring with it a firm instinct for acting commercially and transparently in relations with other companies and customers;
- It should bring knowledge of, and an ability to access, financial tools from around the world;
- And it should bring experience of *self-discipline* rather than experience of *avoiding or evading harsh discipline*.

This last point is an important one if we are to break the vicious circle of mistrust, mentioned earlier. It is a hopeful sign that we are now witnessing some practical progress towards making the 'rules of the game' in the energy sector more transparent for those who operate in it, as the Government prepares for privatisation of the distribution companies and their sale to strategic investors. If the rules of the market are really clear to everyone, self-discipline can more easily be perceived as the right way for the private sector to operate. Officialdom will have less scope, let alone need, to behave arbitrarily and outside the scope of work laid down for it as the sector regulator.

The EBRD has the mandate, as described earlier, to function as a long-term capital provider. Together with the International Financial Institution and donor partners, the EBRD is spending much time on contributing ideas about the structure of Ukraine's future energy sector. It is hoped that these efforts will lead to successful privatisation, and attract long-term strategic investors to Ukraine, who bring with them the type of experience mentioned above. Hopefully this effort will lead to a new era of private strategic investment and soon thereafter to opportunities for more project financing in Ukraine.

Project financing is even more a prime function of the EBRD than privatisation. It really is its raison d'être, rather than a means to an end. The EBRD will put its technical expertise, legal teams and experience of particular sectors to work in any area where it can assist the transition process, but, being a bank, the EBRD ultimately wants to put its balance sheet to use on bankable projects.

The energy sector and other vital utility sectors, such as telecommunications, must undergo those regulatory changes that will bring Ukraine closer to European norms. More rational tariff-setting, more independent regulation, more transparency and less government interference in the utilities and in the operations of strategic investors, would provide a much sounder base for the EBRD's own future operations. The EBRD will indeed only be able to take forward major national project financings (such as the K2R4 nuclear power completion project) when there is more cash flowing into the energy sector from enhanced cash collections, and when structural reform is truly underway. The EBRD will also be able to demand fewer sovereign guarantees once municipal utilities have the opportunity to build self-financing capacity. This should be achieved through full costs recovery tariffs, with cost saving incentives, and an effective system of 'addressed' subsidies to low-income families. The EBRD also looks forward to a time when fiscal relations between the local and central authorities are a lot clearer than they are today. And most importantly for the EBRD's overall mandate, it will be able to find more projects in the private sector if and when, encouraged by high-profile privatisations, strong new sponsors enter the Ukrainian market with robust cash flow projections for their projects, and once a less arbitrary regulatory environment will permit bankable transactions.

Potentially there is an enormous scope for EBRD's long-term financing approach in Ukraine. Several promising opportunities in the power sector have been identified, some involving alternative low-cost energy techniques, some concerning the export of power from Ukraine. These could one day be undertaken on the basis of structures involving private sector participation, provided sector reform takes place as described above. The EBRD has already commenced financing of municipal infrastructure project in Ukraine, e.g. a major water project at Zaporizhzhia. There are many other potential projects under consideration in other cities, concerning water and waste management and district heating. It would be in everyone's interests if these projects could one day be financed with less involvement from the centre, as a result of more rational, consistent tariff-setting and clear fiscal relations between the central and local authorities.

Having just returned from a fascinating whistle-stop tour of western Ukraine, I have seen some large businesses, including power stations and chemical plants, where the need for a long-term approach is self-evident, and where there are cases of heavy indebtedness. The absence of long-term capital in these large establishments has led in some instances to what one can only call short-term solutions, such as multiple small joint-ventures, which produce a variety of 'downstream' goods requiring to be sold in markets, which differ completely from the core business. However, the root of the problem remains unsolved. In another instance though, it was heartening to see how EBRD's capital, and that of our Polish partners, the Polish Credit Bank, invested in the Western Ukrainian

Commercial Bank has provided a stimulus to entrepreneurism in smaller companies.

In conclusion, let me sum up the role the EBRD wants to play as a provider of long-term finance:

- Firstly, the EBRD wants to encourage the Government of Ukraine and the country as a whole to welcome foreign strategic investors in key industries and, in the process, to finish the job, now started, of vital sector reform;
- Secondly, with a new climate thus created and real improvements in the financial health of the key utility sectors, the EBRD expects to be better able to bring more of its own 'long-term capital' into play and act more boldly as a project financier in infrastructure.

The EBRD dislikes using the expression 'helping Ukraine' as much as anyone in Ukraine dislikes it. Rather, the EBRD believes that its key function and that of any long-term capital in Ukraine is actually *to provide support for Ukraine to pay for itself.* That way, I suggest, Ukraine will certainly feel more comfortable as a European nation.

15

EU Enlargement and Implications for Ukraine: A View from the European Central Bank

Christian Thimann[1]

1 Introduction

After having focused on Western Europe for decades, the institutions of the European Union (EU) are now increasingly looking eastward. The process of EU enlargement, which may ultimately imply membership of up to a dozen or more new members, will profoundly change the policies and the institutions of the EU.

The European Central Bank (ECB) is one of the EU institutions, born out of the Treaty establishing the European Community (the Maastricht Treaty). While it obviously focuses on the current Euro-area, it is also one of the European institutions, which is increasingly looking towards the East. It does this, because the process of EU enlargement – or, as it is often called, EU accession – is ultimately also a process of accession to the Euro-area. The European Union has decided that there will be no opting-out with regard to Monetary Union, so that all prospective EU members are expected eventually to join the Monetary Union and to adopt the Euro.

But this direction of causality does not only point from the EU to the Euro, it also works in the other direction: At the Copenhagen Council meeting in June 1993, the EU decided that only those countries, which intend to adhere to the Economic and Monetary Union will be admitted to the EU in the first place. This means that the ability ultimately to adopt the Euro is part of the requirements for joining the EU in the first place. Therefore, the ECB, which will be involved in assessing the ability of every applicant country to adopt the Euro, is already involved indirectly

1 The author is grateful to Boris Kisselevsky for useful input and to Pierre van der Haegen for helpful comments. The views expressed are those of the author and do not necessarily represent those of the European Central Bank.

in assessing EU accession strategies, including pre-EU accession monetary and economic policies, in the countries concerned.

As the ECB looks east, however, it does not stop at the accession countries. The ECB also follows developments in countries further to the East, such as Ukraine and Russia, in addition to countries in south-eastern Europe and to the south of Europe. It does so because the countries in these regions, being on or close to the European continent, have a special link with the EU and the Euro-area that encompasses historical, political, economic and also monetary dimensions.

For many of these countries – such as countries in the Balkans, the Mediterranean region, the Middle East or Northern Africa – the Euro-area and hence the Euro are particular focal points for their monetary and exchange rate policies. For these countries, the European Union is the most important partner for real economic and financial flows, and is also the counterpart for most external assets and liabilities. As a result of these close economic and financial ties, information and co-operation on real economic, financial and economic policy developments is valuable for improving economic efficiency and welfare. It is particularly important to prevent losses arising from possible disruptions and crises, both for the countries themselves as well as for the Euro-area.

The Russian crisis, for example, has been costly for the Euro-area in terms of losses in asset values for Euro-area banks, corporations and shareholders. It also had implications for monetary policy in many industrial countries and has triggered many changes in the key institutions within the international monetary and financial system. The ECB, which is an important institution in the latter system, has been closely involved in these developments.

The following remarks are aimed at providing some reflections on the process of EU accession and developments in Eastern Europe, especially in Ukraine, as seen from the perspective of the European Central Bank.

2 The EU enlargement process

The ECB itself does not define the accession process but applies it as an institution of the European Union.[2] According to the Treaty establishing the European Community, any country in Europe may apply for EU membership. Currently, the applications of 13 countries have been formally recognised and accession negotiations have started with 12 of them (the 13th country, Turkey, has not yet met certain conditions to allow negotiations to start).

---

[2] For a discussion of the co-operation framework between the ECB and accession countries see ECB (2000).

This enlargement is by no means the first – rather it is the fifth. It follows the accession of Austria, Finland and Sweden in 1995, the accession of Portugal and Spain in 1986, and two earlier waves of accession. Thus, for almost 30 years, 'accession' has been part of the process of shaping European policies. Furthermore, the current accession countries are again likely to enter at different points in time, given the highly divergent political and economic starting conditions and the different paths towards convergence with the EU in economic policies and structures.

Still, the current process of enlargement is also a very significant one for monetary and economic policies within the EU, owing to the large number of applicants and to the fact that most of them still have very different economic structures and income levels compared to the present EU members states. The 12 accession countries together have a population equal to 36% of that of the present Euro-area, but only the equivalent of 6% of the Euro-area GDP. This means, that while altogether they have the potential to become a significant portion of the Euro-area, their current economic impact is small.

In fact, with the exception of Poland, every country's current output is less than 1% of the Euro-area GDP, and in many cases less than 0.5%. With relatively higher rates of economic growth many of these countries will gradually catch-up with the Euro-area average income level, but since the current gap is quite large – the simple unweighted average of per capita GDP levels in these countries is equivalent to 22% of the Euro-area average at current exchange rates and to 44% based on purchasing power parity – reaching the Euro-area average will take decades. However it should also be noted, that the per capita GDP of some accession countries, for instance the Czech Republic and Slovenia, has already reached levels comparable to those of certain EU countries.

Most of the economies in the region are highly open and – with the exception of the Baltic countries whose main trading partner remains Russia – the main trading partner is the Euro-area. Therefore, they would benefit from closer integration with the Euro-area and the positive impacts on real and financial flows created by the introduction of the Euro.

3 The ECB's monitoring of the EU accession process

The ECB's monitoring of the accession process can be summarised under six major headings: nominal and real convergence, exchange rate arrangements, banking and financial sector soundness, monetary policy strategies and conduct, capital account liberalisation, and central banking institution and infrastructure issues.[3] In this Chapter I shall only focus on the first three of these issues.

3.1 Nominal and real convergence

Nominal and real economic convergence with the Euro-area is important, since Euro-area membership implies a single monetary policy. Since January 1999, there is only one monetary policy in the 11 states of the Euro-area – implemented by the Eurosystem – with a single monetary policy regarding interest rates applying for the entire area. Furthermore, Euro-area membership implies being an integral part of the European Union, which presumes common fiscal and other economic policies. In the case of fiscal policy, the Maastricht criteria and the Stability and Growth Pact have strongly influenced the shape of fiscal policy strategies and conduct throughout the European Union. Other economic policies have been harmonised significantly within the Union, based on a large number of EU Directives.

Monetary, fiscal and other economic policies are to some extent determined by the income levels of the countries concerned. For example, in lower income countries that are heavily involved in a catching-up process, fiscal and economic policies may have different priorities than those in high-income countries. Here they will focus on building-up, rather than merely maintaining physical infrastructure or social security systems. The relative level of real incomes also has implications for nominal variables, that is, prices. It is one of the basic facts of international economics that price levels are lower in countries with lower real incomes.[4] Therefore, real and nominal convergence in any economy is reflected in price dynamics and has important consequences both for the strategy as well as the conduct of monetary policy.

The convergence of real incomes and prices is particularly relevant for economies in transition, where profound structural changes, external opening and market liberalisation are all likely to have a significant impact on price dynamics in addition to the conduct of the monetary, fiscal and economic policies themselves.

For accession countries – and probably also for Ukraine – the first step towards convergence has to be the establishment of a functioning market economy, including the setting-up of relevant institutions and regulations. This generally means replacing direct government influence on economic decision making and on price setting, with government policies that focus on providing the conditions

---

3 The latter area comprises institutional issues such as central bank independence, strategy, and operational framework, and it also comprises infrastructure issues related to financial market functioning, including payment systems.

4 The so-called Balassa-Samuelson effect (see Balassa, 1964).

for the development of market forces within a framework of social protection and the desired degree of income redistribution. The ground for this has been laid in most of the accession countries. The next step consists in improving economic income levels by benefiting from market forces and international integration. Here, the authorities' main task is to make the economy robust and flexible so as to cope with competitive pressure and external shocks. This process, which is already well advanced in some accession countries, implies the pursuit of macro-economic policies, which foster economic growth and stability. For monetary policy this implies a focus on price stability, while recognising the need for relative and absolute price adjustments vis-à-vis the prices of the main trading partners. These adjustments imply that during the catch-up period, inflation rates can be expected to be somewhat higher than those of the main trading partners and those within the Euro-area. When monitoring the accession process, this phenomenon has to be carefully considered in the context of price dynamics in accession countries.

3.2 Exchange rate arrangements[5]

While policy approaches concerning a number of arrangements and policies are broadly similar for all accession countries, there are remarkable differences in exchange rate arrangements. They cover the whole spectrum from free floats to currency boards. Of the 12 accession countries, the currencies of five float within free or managed floating regimes, three operate pegs with or without fluctuation bands, one operates a crawling peg and three operate a currency board. Even within a certain category, there are marked differences. For example with regard to currency orientation, Bulgaria and Estonia operate currency boards linked to the Euro, while Lithuania operates one linked to the US-dollar.

It may surprise that all these economies, which share the goal of joining a common currency area, have chosen such different currency regimes. One reason lies in the different starting positions for the transition processes, and in different economic experiences – resulting from different external shocks and different policy successes and failures – which have induced different authorities to adopt different exchange rate regimes. Another reason is that there is no clear-cut answer to the question of what the best exchange rate regime for any given economy would be. Discussions about appropriate exchange rate regimes following the Asian crisis of 1997-1998 amply testify to the difficulties within the international community to agree on an appropriate exchange rate regime.

The ECB is well aware of these issues – both the different conditions within accession countries, and the difficulties in deciding on the optimal exchange rate

---

5 The IMF published several studies on the issue of exchange rate regimes of Central and Eastern European countries (see Kopits and Masson, 1999).

regime – and has therefore accepted that a variety of exchange rate arrangements may be compatible with preparation for EU accession. In particular, the ECB has recognised that even currency boards – if based on the Euro – may be compatible with the requirement of two years' membership in the Exchange Rate Mechanism (ERM II), as stated in the Treaty. Currency boards will be assessed on a case-by-case basis. While they will be no substitute for the requirement of participating for two years in ERM II, the ECB recognises that accession countries, which have operated a Euro-based currency board arrangement (CBA) deemed to be sustainable, might not be required to go through a second ERM II stage to qualify for membership. Thus such countries may participate in ERM II with a CBA as a unilateral commitment augmenting the discipline within ERM II. The ECB requires, however, that a common accord be reached on the central parity against the Euro.[6]

Despite marked differences in arrangements, there have been some moves in the exchange rate strategies of a number of accession countries that have gone in a broadly similar direction over the past few years. This trend has mostly taken place in the form of an increasing weight of the Euro in the target basket, but considerations have also related to focusing existing exchange rate arrangements more clearly on the Euro. This is in line with the increasing integration of trade and financial flows with the Euro-area, as well as the fact that the counterparts of most external assets and liabilities are Euro-area residents. This trend is expected to continue as trade with the Euro-area intensifies further and the aim of accession to the EU and ERM II draws closer.

3.3 Banking and financial sector soundness[7]

In view of the fact that integration into the EU will entail increased competition for banks and other financial institutions, the ECB and the national central banks of the Euro-area also have a vital interest in keeping the banking and financial sector developments in accession countries under close scrutiny. Maintaining the stability of the financial system is of particular importance in this context.

In the context of compliance with EU legal and institutional requirements, the accession countries will be expected to adopt EU legislation in the area of financial services, including those related to banking, insurance and investment firms. Against the background of the Copenhagen Criteria set in 1993, they will also have to meet the broader set of structural and institutional requirements necessary for their banking sector to cope with competitive pressure.

---

6 The Governing Council of the ECB addressed the issue of currency board arrangements, and issued a statement regarding their conformance with the accession process (see Duisenberg and Noyer, 2000).

7 See Duisenberg (1999).

Furthermore, sound and efficient banking, financial and payment systems are an essential requirement for the appropriate conduct of monetary policy, and therefore for successful participation in the Euro-area. The following reasons are worth mentioning in this respect.

First, the creation of deep and liquid capital markets is a necessary step if market based instruments involving a number of counterparts are to be used for the conduct of monetary policy. Second, without sufficiently developed capital markets it might be difficult to prevent governments from having privileged access to the financial system. Third, structural weaknesses in the financial system could also have implications for the monetary policy transmission mechanisms, since poor competition and soft budget constraints may affect the responsiveness of banks to changes in the monetary policy situation.

4 Effects of EMU and EU enlargements on Ukraine

At first sight, enlargements of the European Monetary Union (EMU) and the EU seem not to have significant effects on Ukraine, given that the latter is obviously not an accession country and EMU is far away, in time and in geographical distance. Both may change, however. The current accession process, once completed, will bring the EMU right to the doorstep of Ukraine. But even before that happens, Ukraine will be affected by the EMU and by the introduction of the Euro. These effects may have some implications for Ukrainian economic and monetary policies in the medium term. The following points elaborate on this.

4.1 Economic and trade integration

The creation of the EMU has merged together a number of important Western European partners of Ukraine into a single entity, which is now Ukraine's second largest trading partner, and its most important source and destination of foreign direct investment and other capital flows. Over the longer term, accession will increase the weight of the Euro-area as more countries, including those of today's 'EU 15', which are not yet part of the Euro-area, join the area. It is not inconceivable that in 10 years' time, the Euro-area will consist of today's 15 EU member states and several accession countries. By then, if not earlier, the Euro-area will be Ukraine's most important trading partner. Once all of today's accession countries have joined the Euro-area – no doubt a development, which still lies far in the future – four out of Ukraine's seven neighbours would be Euro-area member states.

Trade links between Ukraine and the Euro-area have recently intensified. In the aftermath of the Asian and Russian crises of 1997 and 1998, Ukraine's terms of trade have indeed been significantly re-oriented towards the Euro-area, which represents roughly one quarter of Ukraine's external trade. This trend is still ongoing and it can be expected that the share of the Euro-area will continue on its increasing trend for the foreseeable future.

Economic developments in the Euro-area affect the economies of third countries, which have significant links with the Euro-area through three major channels: *Firstly*, via an impact on growth through existing trade links, *secondly*, through more highly integrated, liquid and efficient markets in Euro, which facilitates access to international financing by non Euro-area governments, banks and corporations, and *thirdly*, through price and exchange rate stability for the countries using the Euro as a nominal anchor. Regarding Ukraine specifically, the first channel is likely to be the most important. With regard to the second channel, its impact on Ukraine is limited by existing restrictions on capital movements and the low level of Ukraine's Euro-denominated debt. Finally, since the Hryvnia is floating the Euro plays only a limited role in Ukraine's exchange rate regime.

One of the main positive effects of the advent of the Euro on all countries of the European continent runs through trade relations. The introduction of the Euro benefits the world economy insofar as it contributes to higher growth in the Euro-area and to the maintenance of low inflation and interest rates.

4.2 EU-Ukraine institutional co-operation

The financial relationships between the EU and Ukraine have developed significantly during the past few years. Ukraine is a beneficiary of EU assistance programmes and has received grants for a total of about 500 million EUR. In July 1999 the EU also granted a macro-financial assistance loan of 150 million EUR, while EU grants in 1994 and 1995 together amounted to almost EUR 300. Moreover, in December 1999 the Helsinki European Council approved a common strategy for Ukraine, which includes, among other things, commitments in terms of economic policy advice and technical assistance.

4.3 Maastricht economic policy standards

The Treaty of Maastricht is Europe's monetary constitution.[8] In a way, the Maastricht process provides an example for the rest of Europe. The Maastricht Treaty – even though its ratification initially caused enormous economic and political turbulence, which Tommaso Padoa-Schioppa has labelled a "ratification storm"[9] – has become a benchmark for the adaptation of institutional frameworks

8 See Padoa-Schioppa (1999).

9 Padoa-Schioppa (1994), p. 9 f.

and the conduct of macro-economic policies. The general trend towards independent central banks and the primacy of price stability for monetary policy has been induced by Maastricht and the EMU. Both elements now go beyond the Euro-area, as the statutes of the central banks of several accession countries have been amended to strengthen their independence and focus their monetary policy objectives on price stability. This means that a number of central banks of Ukraine's western neighbours are beginning to think about their monetary policy in terms of the Maastricht Treaty, which is bound to become the European standard over the longer term and could eventually also serve as a guide for some elements of monetary policy strategy and conduct in Ukraine.

As for fiscal policies, the medium-term orientation of fiscal policies within the Euro-area, together with the quantitative criteria for the fiscal deficit – the 3% of GDP threshold – and for public debt – the 60% of GDP threshold – have served as catalysts for other European countries' fiscal and structural reforms. The significance of these criteria has gone far beyond the borders of the European Union and they too have become guides for many other countries.

4.4 Exchange rate issues

With regard to exchange rate issues, European countries pursue a variety of strategies, with the Euro gaining increasing importance. After having been pegged to the US-dollar, the Hryvnia has been floating since February 2000 with the central bank not excluding the possibility of intervening in the market from time to time, if necessary. The depth of integration with the Euro-area in terms of trade, capital flows and movement of workers is probably the most crucial factor for Ukraine's choice of the new exchange rate regime. The deeper the integration between the Euro-area and Ukraine, the larger will be the role of the Euro in economic and financial exchanges, and the greater will become the need to increase the importance of the Euro in Ukraine's exchange rate strategy. Of course, the need for closer links between the Euro-area and Ukraine does not only depend on a number of objective parameters that are exogenous for policy-makers, it also depends fundamentally on the willingness to carry out a process of regional integration. In this framework, the ECB stands ready to provide closer institutional co-operation in the form of a mutual and frank exchange of information on developments and policies.

5 Conclusion

The process of EU enlargement will profoundly affect EU policies and institutions. Enlargement is an integral element of the EU, having taken place already in a number of waves in past decades and having led to a larger and larger

Union. The European Union has also become deeper, with a single monetary policy and a common understanding on fiscal and other economic policies. This has promoted growth and stability in Europe and for its trading partners. EU enlargement is also linked to Euro-area enlargement, as all new EU countries are committed to ultimately adopt the Euro. The European Central Bank will contribute within its area of competence to insure that this process occurs in an orderly fashion and does not dilute the standards and principles of the Euro-area.

The ongoing enlargement process will bring the EMU to Ukraine's doorstep and make the Euro-area its largest trading partner, with a population of over 400 million people and the largest GDP in the world. Even though these developments still lie well in the future, it may be worthwhile to take them into consideration for Ukraine's future development and integration with Western and Central Europe. The European Central Bank stands ready to assist this process now.

References

Balassa, B. (1964): The Purchasing Power Parity Doctrine: A Reappraisal. In: Journal of Political Economy, December

Duisenberg, W. F. (1999): EU Enlargement: Some Views from the ECB. Zolotas Lecture, Bank of Greece, October 15

Duisenberg, W. F. and C. Noyer (2000): Introductory Statement. ECB Press Conference, April 13

European Central Bank (2000): The Eurosystem and the EU Enlargement Process. Monthly Bulletin, February

Kopits, G. (1999): Implications of EMU for Exchange Rate Policy in Central and Eastern Europe. IMF Working Paper No. 99/9, January

Masson, P. (1999): Monetary and Exchange Rate Policy of Transition Economies of Central and Eastern Europe After the Launch of EMU. IMF Policy Discussion Paper No. 99/5, July

Padoa-Schioppa, T. (1994): The Road to Monetary Union in Europe: The Emperor, the Kings and the Genies. Oxford University Press

Padoa-Schioppa, T. (1999): The Euro: Significance for Europe and Beyond. Committee on Financial Affairs of the House of Counsellors, Tokyo, March 9

16

Effects of the European Monetary Union (EMU) on the Ukrainian Economy

Gerhard Krause

1 Introduction

The introduction of the Euro is not only an important milestone for European integration, but has some important consequences even for Ukraine and other third countries. The EMU creates an economic zone, which is of the same size and potential as that of the USA. It will force structural changes in the financial world. Aside from the positive implications of a common currency, an integrated financial market will be the result, through which it will be possible to generate additional gains in wealth via an efficient allocation mechanism.

The future largest single market will influence the economic policies of third countries, including Ukraine, through many transmission mechanisms. The common currency has stimulated economic growth in the states participating in the currency union, and, in this way, induced an increased demand for imports by EMU countries. The increasingly synchronised market cycles in the EMU states will be of importance to third countries, aside from the transmission channel presented by international trade. These cycles will become an increasingly important criterion in economic decision-making, especially concerning monetary and exchange rate policies. Political considerations, aside from economic reasons, may encourage third countries to use the Euro, at least in part, as their reference currency. Ukraine, too, in view of its trade connections and political ambitions, will not be able stay aloof from this process. With this background in mind, this Chapter will try, within the first paragraphs of each Section, to define the newly created economic sphere with respect to its role in the world economy and its potential influence on third countries, using several indicators. As a second step, these characteristics will be considered within the Ukrainian situation. In the centre of our interest will not only be the effects of the EMU on monetary and exchange rate policies but also to related policy areas.

2 The new economic heavy weight furthers growth

With creation of the Euro-zone in 1999, a new player has appeared on the world economic stage, which is, at least in some respects, equal to the US economy. The gross domestic product (GDP) of the Euro-zone in 1999 was 6,511 billion USD, compared to 9,300 billion USD for the USA. Thus, with 20.3% of world GDP the Euro-zone took second place just behind the USA (29%), but rather significantly ahead of Japan (with 4,400 billion USD and 13.7% of world GDP). Comparing foreign trade figures makes Europe look even better. For 1999, the percentage for the Euro-zone of world foreign trade was 16.1, for the USA 16.2% and for Japan 6.2%.

The introduction of the Euro has caused significant structural changes with respect to the degree of openness of the Euro-zone and the EU. Prior to 1999, the EU consisted of many small and medium sized economies, each exhibiting a medium to high degree of openness. Now the picture has changed. Excluding inter-EU exports, the foreign trade openness (exports as a percentage of GDP) of the Euro-zone for 1999 attained 13.5%, well ahead of the USA with 7.5% and Japan with 8.9%. In its totality the Euro-zone presents the picture of a large, and relative to its external trade relations, rather closed economy.

The third EMU phase not only creates a greater GDP volume, but also positively effects the economic dynamics within the EU. Two major categories[1] of factors can be noted:

- Micro-economic efficiency gains are being realised with the elimination of uncertainties and with the avoidance of transaction costs connected with flexible exchange rates. On the whole, the thus increased efficiency of the allocation mechanism causes a permanent increase of GDP and of real incomes, whereby the transition to the higher economic level is realised through stronger economic growth.
- The elimination of the exchange rate volatility and the greater monetary and fiscal discipline insisted on by EMU regulations, minimise interest rate related risk premiums within the Euro-zone.[2] This interest rate reduction induces additional investment, which also manifests itself through greater economic growth.

Depending on the extent of their trade relationships, third countries, including Ukraine, will profit from this Euro-induced economic dynamism; they may, in fact, already profit from an additional growth impulse. Though some of the 'trade-generating' effects will be diminished somewhat by the re-orienting of trade – (a) no transaction costs, and (b) the absence of exchange rate risks will induce EMU

---

1 Bekx (1998).

2 De Grauwe (1997).

members to trade with other EMU members – , but the net effect should, no doubt, be positive for third countries. The additional growth effect on Ukraine caused by the EMU could not be demonstrated by an econometric model, because of a lack of data. It had to be estimated on the basis of a quantitative analysis of structural variables (degree of openness, percentage of Euro-zone to total exports, product composition of the exports) as compared to other transformation and development countries. In addition to general cyclical impulses (see Section 3), we expect an induced growth of 0.2 to 0.3% for each percent of GDP growth in the EMU. The sensitivity of the Ukrainian economy to external growth signals should increase significantly, once the new Ukrainian Government's increased reforming and restructuring efforts bear fruit.

At this point, it is perhaps important to underline, that the growth rates shown in the Table 16.1 are based on a fairly positive attitude by European politicians vis-à-vis reforms in the fields of product and labour markets. Should the EMU prove to be a catalyst for structural reforms within its members, then third countries should profit significantly from higher GDP growth rates and lower interest rates within the Euro-zone. On the other hand, the transfer effects would reverse should there be signs of 'Eurosclerosis' and no taste for reforms within the European economic system.

Table 16.1
Impact of EMU on economic growth (in addition to baseline scenario)

	2000	2001	2002	2003
EMU members	0.20	0.90	1.00	2.90
Non-European G-7	-0.10	0.00	0.00	0.10
Other industrial countries	-0.10	0.10	0.10	0.20
Developing countries	0.00	0.10	0.20	0.30
Ukraine*	0.00	0.1 - 0.3	0.2 - 0.3	0.5 - 0.8

Source: International Monetary Fund (1997/1998), German Advisory Group on Economic Reforms in Ukraine.

* Values for Ukraine are derived from a qualitative assessment of Ukraine's direction and composition of trade and its openness relative to other developing countries.

3 Stronger spill-over effects through synchronisation of the individual economic cycles

Whereas the economies of several European countries, especially the hard currency countries led by Germany, had already achieved a certain equal level during the 1980s, in the 1990s the economic cycles of the remaining European countries, too, started to behave in synchronous fashion. Initially, the deciding factor was the increased trade volume[3]: In the period from 1950 to 1997 world GDP rose 5.5 times, whereas world trade volume rose 16 times (!) in the same time period. When, at the beginning of the 1990s, liberalisation measures concerning capital flows were first introduced as part of the first phase of the EMU, increasing interconnection of the financial markets aided to develop this equalisation of the economic cycles. Finally, as of the middle of the 1990s, the forced convergence of the various national economies, required by the Maastricht criteria, added a third incentive to the other two. The legal framework for economic policies within the EU – single monetary policy, co-ordinated economic policies, restricted manoeuvring room for fiscal policies as defined by the stability pact, the four freedoms of the factor markets (unhindered traffic for goods, services, people and capital) – permits even now the prognosis that the three factors mentioned will, together with the new unitary money policies, continue to act as the driving force for the synchronisation of the economic cycles in coming years. The more the economic cycles of the European member states converge, the stronger the economic cycles in the Euro-zone will transmit themselves, via the following three channels, to third countries.

3.1 Transmission of growth impulses via trade links

The tighter the trade links, the closer the third country is to the Euro-zone and the smaller the third country's economy, the more intense will be the influences of European economic cycles. The growth forecasts for the Euro-zone and the turning points in its economic cycles will become increasingly relevant considerations in the decision-making processes of third countries, Ukraine included. These will, in the final analysis, largely determine their monetary and exchange rate policies. The strength of transmission of the growth signals are being increased by the creation of the EMU, since the latter, as discussed above, led to an increased synchronisation of the economic cycles of the member states. The incompleteness of the data available as well as the small number of samples, unfortunately, does not yet allow us to make an econometric estimation of the export demand function for Ukraine. However, conclusions can be drawn from studies of advanced Central and Eastern European countries (CEEC). Table 16.2[4] shows the effects of a growth impulse of one percent on three regions, which are close to the EU in a geographic and/or an economic sense:

---

3 German Advisory Group on Economic Reforms in Ukraine (1999): The Next 1000 Days: An Economic Reform Agenda for Ukraine. Chapter IV, Kyiv, November.

4 Desruelle, Kahn and Nord (1998).

Table 16.2
Impact of a 1% GDP increase in the Euro-zone

	GDP change, %	Export change, %	Exports to Eurozone, % of GDP	Manufactured exports, % of total exports
CEE countries	0.6	1.5	17	80
Mediterranean countries	0.3	1.0	10	53
CFA franc zone members	0.2	0.6	16	17
Ukraine	0.2 - 0.3*	0.8 - 1.0*	9	33**

Sources: IMF staff estimates (MULTIMOD), Direction of trade statistics, Ukrainian Statistical Office, German Advisory Group. Ukrainian data refers to 1999, other data to 1998.

* These values are derived from a qualitative assessment of Ukraine's direction and composition of trade in comparison with the results from the IMF forecasting exercise.

** For Ukraine this value refers to manufactured exports without the highly subsidised metal exports. The latter represents about 42% of total exports.

On the basis of structural factors – the degree of openness of the Ukrainian economy, the composition of exports and services, and the geographical directions the exports take – one can roughly evaluate the effects of growth signals from the Euro-zone. Ukraine is high ranking among Central and Eastern European transformation countries as far as degree of openness is concerned (see Table 16.5 and Graph 16.1), only Estonia and Malta rank higher. However, the re-orienting of trade flows has not yet reached the level as in the other CEEC states. Graph 16.2 shows that since the second half of 1996 a re-direction of exports out of the CIS (Commonwealth of Independent States) has taken place, namely to non-CIS states. Of these about two thirds went into the Euro-zone. But this re-orientation process is very slow as compared to other Eastern European states. About one fifth of all exports are being sent into the Euro-zone at this time. Thus, the export content of the Euro-zone is just over 10%, which is comparable with that of the states bordering the Mediterranean or of Latvia and Lithuania. The low percentage of manufactured goods can be explained by the high percentage of metal and steel exports. At this time, the growth impulses transmitted by trade flows are best compared to those of the states bordering the Mediterranean and not those of the CEEC states. Our rough and qualitative estimates indicate that a growth of one percent in the Euro-zone would result in a growth impulse of 0.2 to 0.3% of GDP in Ukraine, which should cause an increase in exports of 0.8 to 1.0%. Similar results have also been estimated for Albania, Bulgaria, Macedonia and Romania[5].

[5] Feldman and Temprano-Arroyo (1998).

Graph 16.1
Degree of openness of Ukraine

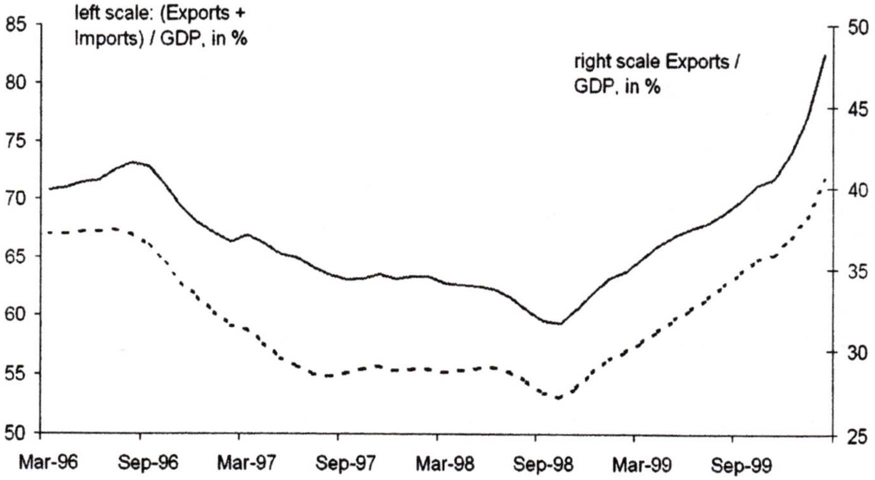

Source: Ukrainian Statistical Office, German Advisory Group calculation.

Graph 16.2
Direction of Ukrainian Exports of Goods and Services

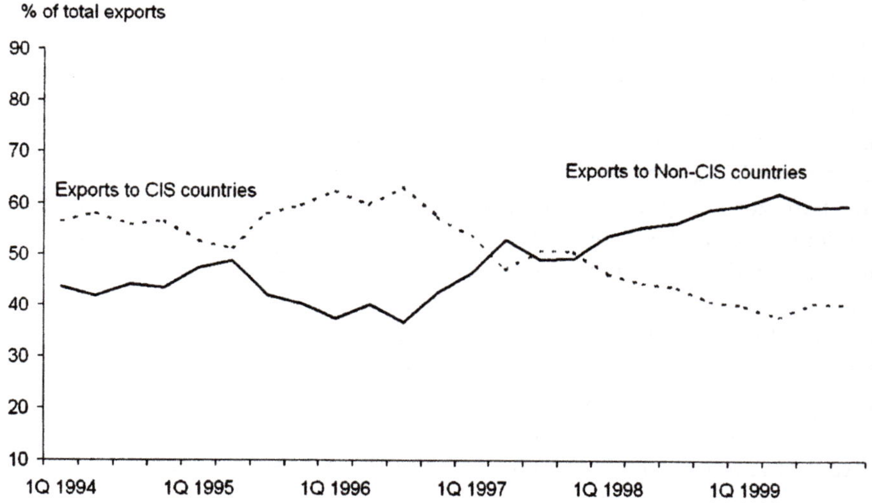

Source: Ukrainian Statistical Office, National Bank of Ukraine, German Advisory Group calculation.

Table 16.2 represents only a momentary picture and does not make any statement about the great potential effects EU economic cycles might have on the Ukrainian economy in the future. Assuming (a) that the remaining four EU members will join the Euro-zone, (b) that most Eastern European neighbours of Ukraine will join the EU (EMU) eventually, and (c) that the trade re-direction towards the Euro-zone will continue, we would estimate that the present export percentage of Ukrainian GDP going into the Euro-zone of nearly 10% will rise to 20% by the year 2010. Increased exports from the manufacturing sector to the detriment of energy-intensive (and still subsidised) metal and steel products, should be the result of increased serious budget restraints in the public sector and continuing re-structuring in industry. With respect to growth transmission effects, Ukraine should at the end of this decade be approximately where the Czech Republic, Slovenia, Hungary and Poland are now. A one percent growth within the Euro-zone should result in a two thirds (0.6-0.7) percent increase in Ukraine, inducing an export growth of 1.5 to 2.0%.

3.2 Effect on Ukraine of decisions concerning interest rate levels within the Euro-zone

The more third countries use the Euro as the nominal anchor for their currency exchange systems (see Section 4), and the less capital movement is restricted, the more the interest rate policies of the European Central Bank (ECB) will have an influence on these countries. Studies concerning this second transmission mechanism, made by the International Monetary Fund (IMF), have confirmed the existence of spill-over effects from interest rate changes within the Euro-zone upon geographical border regions.[6] An interest rate channel is said to exist, when interest rate changes in the Euro-zone cause interest rate changes in third countries, which in turn result in changes to economic activities, to debt service schedules and to currency exchange rate movements. Factors that will support the efficiency of this transmission channel are the financial integration into the world economy, and as already stated, the monetary and currency regimes in existence.

---

[6] Actually, separate individual transmission channels do not exist, since prices, interest rates, currency rates and export volumes are determined endogenously.

Table 16.3
Impact of a 1% interest rate increase in the Euro-zone

	GDP change, in %	Change in debt service, in %	Net Capital Inflows*, % of GDP	External debt stock in EU currencies at variable IR, % of total exports
CEE countries	-0.2	0.5	5.4	5.2
Mediterranean Countries	-0.1/ 0.0	0.6	3.9	3.2
CFA franc zone members	0.05	...	3.7	...
Ukraine	-0.1/ 0.0***		-0.1**	???

Sources: IMF staff estimates (1997/1998), Global Development Finance database, NBU, German Advisory Group.

* Net capital inflows are defined as the balance on the financial account of the balance of payment, excluding changes in international reserves, plus net errors and omissions

** 1998 figure. The respective 1997 figure amounted to 4.1%

*** Qualitative assessment taking into account Ukraine's dirty floating FX regime vs. USD and the current low exposure to private capital flows, the underdeveloped banking system as well as the low degree of capital account liberalisation

Although the results[7] (see Table 16.3) show significant spill-over effects of interest rate decisions in the Euro-zone on the economic growth in Eastern Europe – a 1% interest rate increase reduces the GDP of this region[8] on the average by 0.2% -, these effects are likely to be quite limited in Ukraine's case. The present financial integration into the world financial system is low, as demonstrated by low net capital inflows. Considerable restrictions still exist on capital accounts, and even restrictions on foreign currency activities related to transactions of the current account have not been completely removed since the Russian crisis. In addition, the present monetary and exchange rate regime – dirty floating with the USD as reference currency – hinders (first round) transmission effects of interest rate changes. Only once the exchange rate system becomes a fixed rate system vis-à-vis the Euro, or at least a dirty floating system with the Euro as reference currency, will domestic interest rates and hence domestic demand, be directly influenced[9] to a higher degree. But even in this scenario remains (see Sections 4.1 and 4.2), the impact of interest rate signals out of the Euro-zone will on the

7 Desruelle, Kahn and Nord (1998).

8 The negative growth effect – higher interest rates reduce local demand – exceeds possible positive ones – lower growth reduces import demand and positively influences the trade balance.

9 The more strongly the currency is linked to the Euro, the lower is monetary independence.

Ukrainian economy limited in the short term. This is because the banking system is still underdeveloped. Interest rates in Ukraine are generally defined by the fragmented institutional infrastructure of the domestic financial market.[10] High risk premiums for the desolate banking system, and for the generally low trust in the Ukrainian economy and thus in the stability of currency exchange rates, result in a big interest rate differential compared to more highly developed capital markets. In addition to the low relevance of external factors for determining interest rates is added the relatively high interest in-elasticity of investment demand. This is because the most common financing source remains internal cash flow, and because the banking system isn't as yet able to play its proper role as financier of the economy[11]. Based on this assessment, there is a high degree of probability that no (0.0%) GDP reduction results from an interest rate hike of percentage point in the Euro-zone; at best a small negative influence of around – 0.1% might show up.

Interest rate changes within the Euro-zone influence not only economic growth, but also the position of third countries vis-à-vis the debt payments they have to make and their fiscal policies, and hence they indirectly influence the economic cycle. In the rule, the higher the portion of EUR denominated foreign debt and the higher its variable interest rate portion, the stronger is this effect[12]. The following equation[13] shows these relationships:

$$\Delta DSR = \Delta i_{eur} * \frac{S_{EMU}}{100} * \frac{S_{SV}}{100} * \frac{D/GDP}{X/GDP} \qquad (16.1)$$

The direct effects of an interest rate increase in the Euro-zone are relatively minor in the case of Ukraine, in view of the low level of the EUR denominated foreign debt. Nevertheless, the Ukrainian economy is subject to some significant indirect effects, which are introduced via the EUR/USD exchange rate. They will be discussed in the following Section.

10 Gros and Steinherr (1999).

11 Papaphilippou (1998).

12 Estimates show that the negative effects of an interest rise on the debt service – raising the re-financing costs – will exceed the positive ones – an interest rise reduces, through reduced domestic demand, the import demand and thus new indebtedness.

13 ΔSDR is the change, expressed in percentage points, in the country's debt service ratio; Δi_{eur} is the percentage point change in the interest rate of the Euro; S_{EMU} is the share of Euro-denominated debt in total foreign debt; S_{SV} is the share of short term plus variable medium- and long-term debt in foreign debt; D/GDP and X/GDP are the shares of foreign debt to GDP and exports to GDP, respectively.

3.3 Changes in the EUR/USD ratio seriously effect Ukrainian economic policies.

Graph 16.3
Real exchange rates of the UAH vs. USD & EUR

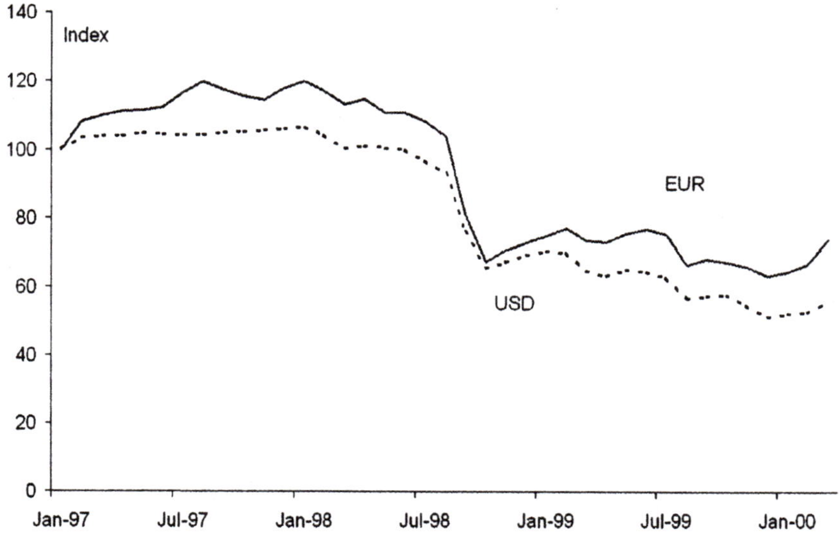

Source: National Bank of Ukraine, UEPLAC, Bloomberg, Ukrainian Statistical Office, German Advisory Group calculation.

Interest rate changes or expectations about future interest rates in the Euro-zone, relative to those in the USA, significantly influence the development of the EUR/USD currency rate. Those countries which do most of their trade with the Euro-zone, and which peg their exchange rates to the USD or to other third countries, are particularly interested in the interest rate policies of the Euro, and its development relative to other currencies, especially vis-à-vis the USD. Ukraine is no exception to this. Changes in the value of the Euro vis-à-vis the USD are reflected in the exchange rate of the Hryvnia (UAH) to the Euro. An assessment of the state of the economy with emphasis on future EUR/USD development is therefore important for forecasting the real exchange rate for the UAH, and becomes a significant determinant for the direction economy growth and inflation will take. With its present 'dirty floating' exchange rate system linked to the USD, any USD upward revaluation vis-à-vis the EUR will be reflected in a higher real value of the trade weighted Ukrainian currency. Though this imports price stability on account of the high degree of opening of Ukraine, the real upward evaluation will lead to a divergence of the export and import patterns. Should this revaluation not be equalised by productivity increases at the enterprise level, this divergence might easily lead to a current account deficit problem and a currency crisis. As shown by Graph 16.3, the 20 to 25% decrease in value of the single European currency vis-à-vis the USD since the beginning of 1999, has already led to rather pronounced different developments of the bilateral real exchange rates of the UAH versus the USD and the EUR. Whereas the real UAH/USD exchange rate dropped by about 20 to 23% during this period, the real UAH/EUR rate increased by 2 to 5%. In the opposite direction, a potential upward re-evaluation of the EUR compared to the USD would cause a devaluation of the UAH vis-à-vis the EUR, bringing with it increased export demand and higher economic growth in Ukraine. The negative effect would be that the domestic price stability would be endangered due to rising import prices.

In Section 3.2 we already noted the relatively small direct effects of a rise in the interest rate on the Ukrainian debt service. However, we also mentioned the substantial indirect effects, caused by EUR/USD exchange rate changes. The denominator of the equation given in Section 3.2 contains a relatively large Euro-component, since more and more goods and services are being exported into the Euro-zone. Foreign debt, however, is mostly denominated in USD. Interest rate changes or expectations about future interest rates in the European and United States economies significantly influence the development of the EUR/USD exchange rate and thereby also the debt service ratio of Ukraine.

Table 16.4
Sensitivity analysis of Ukraine's debt service ratio[14]

Debt service ratio in 2000, % of exports	Exports to the Eurozone, in %	Change of EUR/USD (negative sign denotes depreciation of the EUR)								
		20%	15%	10%	5%	0%	-5%	-10%	-15%	-20%
	25	19.2	19.4	19.7	20.0	20.2	20.4	20.7	21.0	21.3
	33	18.9	19.2	19.6	19.9	20.2	20.5	20.9	21.3	21.6
20.2	40	18.7	19.1	19.4	19.8	20.2	20.6	21.0	21.5	22.0
	50	18.4	18.8	19.2	19.7	20.2	20.7	21.3	21.8	22.4
	66	17.8	18.4	18.9	19.6	20.2	20.9	21.6	22.4	23.3

Source: German Advisory Group calculations.

With a devaluation of the EUR vis-à-vis the USD, as it was the case from January 1999 to May 2000 – market participants expect relatively higher interest rates in the USA compared to the Euro-zone – the debt service ratio of Ukraine will automatically get worse.

With an estimated 20 to 25 percent of exports going into the Euro-zone, the debt service ratio of Ukraine would increase by a further 1.1% (to rise from 20.2 to 21.3%) should the Euro devaluate another 20% vis-à-vis the USD. Should the percentage of exports into the Euro-zone increase to an optimistic, but also

14 The debt service ratio of 20.2% for 2000 was taken from Vakhnenko (2000).

realistic 50%, relative to the other exports, then the debt service ratio would increase by another 0.8%.

In this example we have not yet taken into consideration the indirect (second round) effects of a devaluation of the EUR compared to the USD. In the wake of the USD, the Ukrainian currency would also increase in value vis-à-vis the EUR, which would negatively effect the export volume into the Euro-zone, and thus further impact the denominator of the said equation in a negative way. Forward transactions may represent good short-term solutions for safeguarding future debt repayment streams. In the medium to long term, however, a change in denomination of the debt portfolio would be better, with the EUR providing a greater percentage of the debt portfolio.

4 The EMU will induce changes in the Ukrainian exchange rate system over the long term

The attractiveness of the Euro as the reference currency for third countries is much greater than that of the previously used reference currencies (DEM, FRF, SDR). At the time when the Euro was being introduced, 34 countries of the Central European time zone already used an exchange rate system[15] of which the Euro was the explicit or implicit component. The choices used ranged from 'currency boards' and an informal use of the EUR (DEM), to exchange rate ties, to baskets which included at least one EU country's currency, to 'managed floating' systems informally using the Euro as reference currency.

Aside from economic reasons, political considerations, too, play an increasingly important role in inducing third countries to consider the Euro as their reference currency. The European integration process has a strong attraction, way beyond the borders of the present EU. Up to now, 13 Central and Eastern European states have been given the status of membership candidate, and membership negotiations have already started with 12 of them. The EMU is a part of the 'acquis communautaire', and an opting-out clause such as Great Britain and Denmark have received, is not being envisioned for these on-going membership negotiations. Accession to the EU irrevocably entails introduction of the Euro, sooner or later.

---

15 Noyer (2000).

4.1 Advantages and disadvantages of the single currency

The Article 'A Theory of Optimal Currency Areas'[16] presents the theoretical arguments why it would be advantageous to replace one's own currency with the Euro, or to consider a fixed parity with the Euro (within system II of the European Monetary System, EMS II). According to this paper, the advantage of the new currency is that a substantial part of the trade and capital flows, especially in Eastern European countries, but also in some African states, are transacted in this currency. Reduced transaction and information costs would result in increased efficiencies and in the improved allocation of production factors.[17] The exchange rate induced interest rate risk premiums would also be significantly reduced. In case of 'only' a strong dirty floating vis-à-vis the Euro, the lower currency volatility, and the ability to roughly estimate the future development of the exchange rate, will widen the planing horizon of participants in import and export trading and raise the quality of planing. In sum, this interplay of factors, as already demonstrated in Table 16.1, will result in a permanent increase in trade, in investments, in employment, and in economic growth. Disadvantages[18] may result from the appearance of possible asymmetrical shocks which, assuming low mobility in the labour market and low nominal wage flexibility, could potentially cause high adaptation costs. Stresses in the different parts of the new currency zone could also be caused by differences in the labour market institutions and the fiscal systems.

In principle, the higher the degree of openness toward the Euro-zone, the lower the export diversification of the economy in question, the smaller the country is relative to the Euro-zone, the more similar the economic structure of the country compared to the Euro-zone, and the higher public indebtedness, the stronger will be the advantages[19] of making the EUR the reference currency.

Transferring these thoughts to the Ukrainian situation not much can (as yet) be said in favour of an EMU membership, considering the present situation. The degree of openness toward the Euro-zone has continuously grown in the past years, but still remains at a rather low level in an Eastern European context. Exports into the Euro-zone represent 20 to 25% of total Ukrainian exports. Imports are at about the same level. Only Cyprus, of all membership candidates, has lower ratios. However, the greatest difficulty at this time surely is the different economic structure, which makes Ukraine very susceptible to asymmetric shocks.

---

16 Mundell (1961).

17 De Grauwe (1997).

18 European Commission (1990).

19 Kopits (1999).

Table 16.5
Accession countries & Ukraine: Structural indicators

	Population (millions)	GDP in ECU (% of Euro area GDP)	GDP in PPP terms (% of Euro area GDP)	Per capita GDP in ECU (% of Euro-zone per capita GDP)	Per capita GDP (PPP) (% of Euro-zone per capita GDP)	Share of industry in GDP* (%)	Share of agriculture in GDP** (%)	Degree of openess***	Exports to Euro-area (% of total exports)
Bulgaria	8.3	0.2	0.6	6.6	22.8	22.2	18.7	45.7	38.7
Cyprus	0.7	0.1	0.2	60.8	78.8	13.4	4.4	47.3	13.1
Czech Republic	10.3	0.9	2.1	24.3	60.1	32.2	4.2	60.7	58.5
Estonia	1.5	0.1	0.2	16.0	36.4	18.2	5.6	85.3	30.4
Hungary	10.1	0.7	1.7	20.6	47.7	24.9	5.2	45.7	67.7
Latvia	2.4	0.1	0.2	11.6	27.2	21.1	4.1	54.3	27.6
Lithuania	3.7	0.2	0.4	12.9	30.5	21.1	9.1	53.2	27.8
Malta	0.4	0.1	...	40.4	...	...	...	90.7	34.1
Poland	38.7	2.4	4.7	18.1	35.9	24.4	4.2	26.2	58.8
Romania	22.5	0.6	2.1	7.5	27.0	31.7	16.0	29.9	57.7
Slovak Republic	5.4	0.3	0.8	16.8	45.8	26.7	4.4	69.3	52.9
Slovenia	2.0	0.3	0.5	43.9	67.8	28.1	3.4	57.4	61.9
Ukraine****	50.1	0.6	2.7	2.6	15.9	24.6	11.4	70.9	21.0

Sources: Eurostat; IMF (exports to the Euro-zone and all Malta data). ECB calculations

* Industry, including energy and excluding construction. Data for Hungary refer to 1997. Data for Ukraine is from the EBRD's 1999 transition report

** Agriculture, hunting and forestry; fish business. Data for Ukraine is from the EBRD's 1999 transition report

*** Average of exports and imports of goods and services as a share of GDP. Data for Hungary refer to 1997

**** Data refer to 1998 and is taken from Ukrainian statistical office, WIIW, NBU, EBRD, IMF Direction of Trade Statistics, UEPLAC and German Advisory Group

Furthermore important parts of the Ukrainian economy, due to the slow progress with transformation, are not yet in a position to withstand international competition. Please note that the exchange rate as a policy instrument would not be available anymore once Ukraine is inside the Euro-zone. Although the criteria of Maastricht[20] only refer to nominal convergence and do not mention structural standards, yet both the European Commission and the ECB[21] strongly underline the importance of real convergence in the context of eastward expansion

This implies a fast and comprehensive continuation of the transformation process in the direction of a market economy.[22] Also, aside from the implementation of a corresponding legal framework, this comprises structural changes in nearly all areas of the economy. Ukraine's susceptibility to shocks could be observed during the Russian crisis in the autumn of 1997. A currency exchange system which was not based on trade linkages, and entrepreneurial sector marked by lacking ability to adapt and compete, inevitably allowed the costs of the fixed rate system to rise above its benefits. This is a situation, which would re-occur at this time if the Euro or a fixed rate system with the Euro as reference was introduced (see Section 4.2.1).

4.2 The path of economic policies leading to EMU

The exchange rate policy path can be divided into three steps[23] for all countries that are interested in joining the EU and eventually the EMU:

1. the period prior to EU membership;
2. the period starting with joining the EU and lasting up to the two-year-period, which must precede EMU accession;
3. the two-year-period, during which the Maastricht criteria are applied in the country in question.

Since Ukraine has not as yet attained the status of membership candidate, let us – at this point – concentrate on the monetary and exchange rate options[24] of Ukraine prior to a potential EU accession (Step 1). These we will just simply divide into

---

20 The criteria of Maastricht were developed for the EU states. Their degree of real convergence is or was at that time quite similar. Therefore there was no need to design further criteria related to real convergence.

21 ECB (2000).

22 The so-called 'EU membership criteria' were developed at the Copenhagen summit; they strongly emphasise real convergence. Although they are not directly related to EMU membership, yet since EMU membership would follow EU membership, they are still relevant for the way toward the EMU.

23 Bofinger and Wollmershäuser (2000).

24 Masson (1999).

fixed rate systems (including currency board) and nominally flexible exchange rates (crawling peg, dirty floating). Neither the EU Commission nor the ECB recommend one particular currency exchange system or another. Membership candidates and potential applicants have complete freedom of decision. The ECB explicitly quotes in the final conference[25] of the Helsinki seminar:

> "...no common path should be prescribed to all 12 accession countries with regard to the orientation of their exchange rate policies prior to accession, the inclusion of their currencies in ERM II or the latter adoption of the Euro. Against the background of different starting points for the economic reform process and the difficulty of ascertaining the lead-time for further headway towards nominal and real convergence, a plurality of approaches should be feasible without compromising equality of treatment..."

4.2.1 Arguments against an early tie-in with the Euro

Over the long term, a fixed rate regime for Ukraine only makes sense if the inflation differential between the domestic inflation and the price rises in the more stable region (Euro-zone, US-dollar-zone) can be reduced to zero within a short period of time or can be compensated by higher productivity gains. This goal was not attained in Ukraine during the last stabilisation period (January 1994 to August 1998), due to inertia of the price increase rates. Yet, the international competitiveness was not being improved through comprehensive restructuring at the company level, in parallel to this real upward revaluation. Thus, the resulting external imbalance made the currency vulnerable.

The Central Bank requires adequate currency reserves[26] to defend a fixed parity. This, to our mind, very important precondition is, at this point in time, not met by Ukraine. Granted, the currency reserves have improved to 1.0 billion USD between the first quarters of 1999 and May 2000, but with an import cover of only 0.9 months and a ratio of only 25% to M2 money supply, Ukraine is still far away from a situation which could guarantee a fixed parity for a stable currency.

The situation in the autumn of 1998 clearly demonstrated the susceptibility of Ukraine to real external shocks, though the country of the reference currency was not affected. This negative shock asymmetry of the fixed rate system will remain with Ukraine for several years yet, being caused by the Russian economy's instability and susceptibility to crises. The low absorption capacity, caused by lacking flexibility of product prices and nominal wages and by the limited reactivity of Ukrainian fiscal policies, also argue for having available the exchange rate tool in the case of a strong external demand change.

---

25 ECB (1999).

26 Zettermeyer (1995).

A variant of the fixed rate system is the currency board. Here a law stipulates that either the cash component of the money supply (soft currency board) or the complete currency supply[27] (hard currency board) will be covered 100% through foreign currency reserves. Because of the legal obligations, the criteria listed when discussing the general fixed rate system must be much more strongly enforced with currency boards. Assuming a currency board being in existence, and assuming a completed restructuring of foreign debt and a normalisation with the IMF, the National Bank would, under current conditions, need to hold at least 2.3 to 2.6 billion USD in currency reserves. Furthermore, a currency board demands strict fiscal policy discipline, and, as a principle, excludes central bank credits[28] to domestic state institutions. This appears to be a condition, which would be difficult to fulfil, given, that present indicators – in particular, the enactment of the law concerning the National Bank – point in the opposite direction.

In general, implementation[29] of a currency board or a fixed rate system is recommended during hyperinflation, when the arguments for stabilising expectations, for fighting inflation and for improving the confidence of market participants are of prime importance. A situation which does not pertain at this time, thanks to the disciplined (restrictive) monetary policies[30] of the Ukrainian National Bank.

4.2.2 The advantages of a flexible, nominal currency exchange rate system for Ukraine, especially of a crawling peg system.

After careful consideration of all the relevant criteria in the Ukrainian economic context we arrived at the conclusion, that a more flexible nominal exchange rate represents, under present economic and political conditions, the best strategy for Ukraine until an eventual accession to the EU, at least for the next few years. Among the choices available in this category, we want especially to underline the advantages of the crawling peg system[31] vis-à-vis dirty floating. Both exchange rate systems, however, combine the advantages[32] of fixed rate systems with completely flexible exchange rates and are recommended for Ukraine mainly for the following reasons:

- A relatively flexible exchange rate system rather than a fixed rate system will be better suited to attain real exchange rate stability and maintain international competitiveness, which are so important to Ukraine today. The crawling peg

---

27 Bredenkamp (1993).

28 Balino (1997).

29 Rosati (1996).

30 German Advisory Group (1999a).

31 German Advisory Group (1999c).

32 Nuti (1996).

system, especially, would counteract the popular temptation to maintain the nominal exchange rate (of the flexible system) unchanged.

- A flexible exchange rate system permits immediate adaptation to internal or external shocks, and replaces the only minimally developed mobility of labour and the insufficient nominal wage and price flexibilities in Ukraine. In addition, domestic monetary policies gain a certain freedom of action.
- As opposed to a completely free exchange rate system, the status of the USD and/or EUR as the nominal reference currency remains safeguarded, an important feature for the stability of expectations and the building of confidence[33], which are as much in demand now as ever. Under these conditions, the crawling peg system with scheduled devaluation steps would seem to be more advantageous.
- The difficulty of estimating the equilibrium exchange rate[34] for a fixed rate system in a transformation country does not present itself. Actual imbalances or changes in the equilibrium exchange rate, due to structural reforms made during the transformation phase, can be made less harsh by discretionary adaptations under ,'dirty floating', or by changes in the devaluation rate in the case of a crawling peg system.

We would consider it advisable that Ukrainian decision-makers look at the EUR more favourably when choosing a reference currency, and not to continue to orient themselves exclusively towards the USD. A possibility would be a basket composed to 50% of USD and 50% of EUR. In favour of the Euro is the increasing importance of the EU as a trade partner, as well as the likely introduction of the Euro[35] in the western neighbour countries of Hungary, Poland and the Slovak Republic by 2010. The influence of the USD is based less on trade patterns, as on the high degree of dollarisation, the dollar denominated foreign debt, the relatively strong dependence on petroleum and natural gas imports, and the USD orientation of the exchange rate systems of the eastern neighbours. Concerning the present degree of dollarisation and foreign indebtedness, other EMU induced arguments (see Sections 6.2 and 6.3) should also argue for stronger weighting of the Euro.

---

33 Helpman a.o. (1994), pp. 259-306, show on the basis of tests that such systems mixing flexible and fixed exchange rates cause neither loss of trust nor raise the fear of inflation.

34 Fry and Nuti (1996).

35 We consider the potential for Slovakia's catching up to be very great, so that its EMU accession by 2010 can also be assumed.

5 Summary

The discussions in this Chapter show that the largest unitary market of the future already influences Ukraine's economic activity through a great number of mechanisms, and will do so more strongly yet in the future. Economic growth in Ukraine will profit, though minimally, from the impulses induced by the single currency. We believe that the over-all economic development of the Euro-zone will have a qualitatively stronger influence. The legal economic policy framework within the EU – a single monetary policy, a co-ordinated economic policy, manoeuvrability limitations for fiscal policy as defined by the stability pact, the four freedoms on the factor markets – force a considerable synchronisation on the economic cycles of all EMU partner states. This in turn significantly impacts on smaller open economies such as Ukraine. Furthermore, we consider the development of the EUR/USD ratio to be very important, since it can lead to a relatively significant change in the debt service of Ukraine, aside from changes in the real trade weighted UAH exchange rate. On the other hand, we believe the direct first-round effects of interest policy signals from the Euro-zone on Ukraine to be small. The limited integration into the international financial market, the under-developed banking system, and the present exchange rate system (dirty floating with the USD), reduce the effectiveness of the transmission mechanism.

Concerning the Ukrainian currency system, the discussion of the traditional 'theory of optimal economic areas' shows that a fixed rate system vis-à-vis the EUR (also vis-à-vis the USD) would entail more costs than advantages. Nonetheless, increasing trade relations with the Euro-zone will strengthen the role of the Euro. Taking this tendency into account, the Euro should at least be regarded as being of equal value with the USD for use as a nominal reference currency (see Section 4.2). Within the category of flexible nominal exchange rates (dirty floating, crawling peg) we prefer, under the present economic conditions, the crawling peg to start off on the path towards eventual EU/EMU accession.

References

Balino, Tomas J. and Charles Enoch (1997): Currency Board Arrangements: Issues and Experiences. IMF Occasional Paper, Washington D.C.

Balino, Tomas J., Adam G. Bennett and Eduardo R. Borensztein (1999): Monetary Policy in Dollarized Economies. IMF Occasional Paper, Washington D.C.

Bekx, Peter (1998): The Implication of the Introduction of the Euro for Non-EU Countries. European Commission, Euro Papers, Brussels, July

Berthold, Norbert, Rainer Fehn and Eric Thode (1999): Real Wage Rigidities, Fiscal Policy, and the Stability of EMU in the Transition Phase. IMF Working Paper, Washington D.C., June

Bofinger, Peter and Timo Wollmershäuser (2000): Options for the Exchange Rate Policies of the EU Accession Countries (and other emerging market economies). Würzburg Economic Papers, Würzburg, January

Bredenkamp, Hugh (1993): Conducting Monetary and Credit Policy in Countries of the Former Soviet Union: Some Issues and Options. IMF Working Paper, Washington D.C.

Chauffour, Jean-Pierre and Loukas Stemitsiotis (1998): The Impact of the Euro on Mediterranean Partner Countries. Euro Papers, Brussels, June

De Grauwe, Paul (1997): The Economics of Monetary Integration. Oxford University Press, New York

Detken, Carsten and Philipp Hartmann (2000): The Euro and International Capital Markets. ECB Working Paper No. 18, Frankfurt am Main, April

Dornbusch, Rudi and Francesco Giavazzi (1999): Hard Currency and Sound Credit: A Financial Agenda for Central Europe. EIB Working Paper, Vol. 4, No. 2, Luxembourg

Duisenberg, W.F. (1999): EU Enlargement: Some Views from the ECB. Zolotas Lecture, Bank of Greece, Athens, October 15

ECB (1999): Helsinki Seminar on the Accession Process. ECB Press Release, Frankfurt am Main, November

ECB (2000): The Eurosystem and the EU Enlargement Process. ECB Monthly Bulletin, Frankfurt am Main, February

European Commission Staff (1997): External Aspects of Economic and Monetary Union. Commission Staff Working Paper, Brussels, April

European Commission (1990): One Market, One Money: An Evaluation of the Potential Benefits and Costs of Forming an Economic and Monetary Union. European Economy, No. 44, Brussels, October

Feldman, Robert A., Karim Nashashibi, Roger Nord, Peter Allum, Dominique Desruelle, Klaus Enders, Robert Kahn and Heliodoro Temprano-Arroyo (1998): Impact of EMU on Selected Country Groups. In: Feldman et al.: Impact of EMU on Selected Non-European Union Countries. IMF Occasional Paper, Washington D.C.

Feldman, Robert A. and Heliodoro Temprano-Arroyo (1998): Trade and Financial Effects of EMU on Selected Transition and Mediterranean Countries. In: Feldman et al.: Impact of EMU on Selected Non-European Union Countries. IMF Occasional Paper, Washington D.C.

Fry, Maxwell J. and Domenico M. Nuti (1996): Monetary and Exchange Rate Policies During Eastern Europe's Transition. In: Oxford Review of Economic Policy, Vol. 8, No.1, Oxford

German Advisory Group on Economic Reforms in Ukraine (1999a): Monetisation: The Sweet Poison. Kyiv, June, mimeo

German Advisory Group on Economic Reforms in Ukraine (1999b): Why Is the Hryvnia Under Pressure? Kyiv, July, mimeo

German Advisory Group on Economic Reforms in Ukraine (1999c): With a Crawling Peg Into the Year 2000. Kyiv, August, mimeo

Goldstein, Morris and Peter Isard (1992): Mechanisms for Promoting Global Monetary Stability. In: Goldstein et al.: Policy Issues in the Evolving International Monetary System. IMF Occasional Paper, Washington D.C., June

Gros, Daniel and Alfred Steinherr (1999): Banking Reforms in Eastern Europe with Special Reference to Ukraine. In: Siedenberg, Axel and Lutz Hoffmann (eds.) (1999): Ukraine at the Crossroads: Economic Reforms in International Perspective. Physica-Verl., Heidelberg New York

Hartmann, Philipp (1996): The Future of the Euro as an International Currency: A Transactions Perspective. CEPR Research Report, No. 20, London

Helpman, Elhanan, Leonardo Leiderman and Gil Bufman (1994): A New Breed of Exchange Rate Bands: China, Israel and Mexico. In: Economic Policy, October, pp. 259-306

Krause, Gerhard (1997): Calculating PPP Values for Eastern European Currencies. In: Focus Eastern Europe, Frankfurt am Main, November

Kopits, George (1999): Implications of EMU for Exchange Rate Policy in Central and Eastern Europe. IMF Working Paper, Washington D.C., January

Lankes, Hans-Peter and Anthony J. Venables (1996): Foreign Direct Investment in Central and Eastern Europe since 1990: The Changing Pattern of Investments. In: Economics of Transition Vol. 4, pp. 331-47, London

Masson, Paul R. (1999): Monetary and Exchange Rate Policy of Transition Economies of Central and Eastern Europe After the Launch of EMU. IMF Policy Discussion Paper, Washington D.C., July

Mundell, Robert (1961): A Theory of Optimal Currency Areas. In: American Economic Review, Vol. 51, pp. 657-65.

Noyer, Christian (2000): The International Impact of the Euro. Speech delivered on the occasion of a visit to the USA, January

Nuti, Domenico M. (1996): Inflation, Interest and Exchange Rates in the Transition. In: The Economics of Transition, No.1, pp. 137-158

Papaphilippou, Apostolos (1998): What would Monetary Emission Bring to Ukraine? The Myth of the 'Low Monetisation Coefficient' and the Required Policy Responses. In: Ukrainian Economic Trends, Kyiv, October

Rosati, Dariusz (1996): Exchange Rate Policies During Transition From Plan to Market. In: The Economics of Transition, Vol. 4, No.1, Oxford

Temprano-Arroyo, Heliodoro and Robert A. Feldmann (1998): Selected Transition and Mediterranean Countries: An Institutional Primer on EMU and EU Relations. IMF Working Paper, Washington D.C., June

Vakhnenko, Tatyana (2000): State Debt of Ukraine: Current Condition and Evolution. In: Ukrainian Economic Trends, Kyiv, February

Zettermeyer, Citrin (1995): Stabilisation: Fixed Versus Flexible Exchange Rates. In: Policy Experiences and Issues in the Baltics, Russia, and Other Countries of the Former Soviet Union. IMF Occasional Paper, Washington D.C.

17

Fiscal Federalism in Western European and Other Countries: Centralisation or Decentralisation? What Is Better for Economic Growth? Are there Implications for Ukraine?

Ulrich Thießen[1]

1 Introduction

With the adoption of the budget for the year 2000 Ukraine introduced a possibly far reaching but relatively little noticed and little discussed structural change with respect to fiscal federalism:

The share of the revenues of the lower levels of government in the planned consolidated revenues was substantially reduced (Table 17.1)[2]. Simultaneously the transfers from the central government to sub-national governments were raised. However, the net effect is planned to be a substantially lower share of sub-national government revenues in consolidated revenues.

The reduction of sub-national government revenues will also mean a much lower share of sub-national government budgets both in GDP and in the consolidated budget. This is because the consolidated deficit of lower levels of government remains small and thus sub-national expenditures do not deviate much from sub-national revenues.

---

1 The author is grateful for discussions with Herbert Brücker, Wolfram Schrettl, Helmut Seitz, Tatyana Vakhnenko, and Christian Weise. The usual disclaimer applies.

2 Ukraine has three main levels of government (central government, regional governments (oblasts) and local ones (rayons).

Table 17.1[3]
Ukraine: Selected indicators of fiscal federalism, in %

	1999	2000 Plan
Share of revenues of lower levels of government (excluding transfers from the central government) in consolidated government revenues (1)	40.2	24.0
Transfers from the central government to lower levels of government (in percent of GDP)	2.3	2.6
Share of revenues of lower levels of government (including transfers from the central government) in consolidated government revenues (1)	49.4	34.3
Memorandum item: Share of consolidated government revenues in GDP (1)	26.7	25.4

(1) Excluding the social insurance system and own revenues of budgetary institutions.

Source: Budget reports of the Ministry of Finance.

If this planned reduction of the budgets of the lower levels of government materialises permanently, the power of the central government in the redistribution of GDP and in determining government expenditure programmes will most likely increase. In addition, the planned new 'budget code' aims to regulate and define the expenditures local governments are obliged to make. Hence, it appears that discretionary spending decisions on the part of local governments are increasingly being reduced. Overall, the power of the central government concerning decisions that influence economic growth, such as public investment and other expenditure programmes, is most likely increasing, while that of local governments may decline.

Hence, the question arises whether this development, i.e. increasing centralisation of governmental decision making, is good for Ukraine's development, or whether there may be reasons to argue for more decentralisation. The literature presents conflicting views on this issue.

This Chapter attempts to contribute to a (hopefully increasing) discussion of this issue, by looking at the experience of Western European countries where a wide variety of fiscal decentralisation exists. However, in an attempt to increase the validity of the findings the sample of Western European countries is enlarged by

[3] All Tables from 17.2 see in Appendix

several other high-income countries and several developing countries whose large land size is similar to Ukraine's.

The Chapter is organised as follows: Section 2 provides a brief overview of the main theoretical arguments for and against fiscal decentralisation. Section 3 outlines the applied growth framework and estimation strategy. Section 4 presents and discusses the estimation results and Section 5 concludes.

2 The case for and failures of fiscal decentralisation

In this Chapter, fiscal decentralisation connotes the (legal) power of sub-national governments to raise tax revenues and decide on spending programmes on their own all within legal criteria. It should be noted that there is no formalised theory on the relationship between fiscal decentralisation and economic growth. This may reflect conflicts inherent in fiscal decentralisation.

2.1 The case for fiscal decentralisation

2.1.1 The 'diversification hypothesis'

The 'diversification hypothesis' (or 'decentralisation theorem') maintains that uniform levels of public goods and services across jurisdictions will generally be inefficient (Oates, 1972, 1977). In a simple model of only two communities each of which has a different demand for a single public service being offered, and with immobile individuals, no economies of scale in the production of the public service, and that no spill-over effects from one community to the other, *a uniform level of public services offered in each community is inefficient*. This is because marginal benefits and marginal costs of the public service differ, due to different demand schedules in both communities. Resources can be saved without making anybody worse off by diversifying government outputs in accordance with local demands. Hence, the 'Pareto' efficiency can be raised through fiscal decentralisation. According to this model, the larger the variance in people's demands for public goods, the larger the benefits of decentralisation tend to be. In other words, local government outputs need to be differentiated according to local tastes and circumstances but this requires discretion of local governments over spending programmes, i.e. fiscal decentralisation.

Introducing mobility of people into the Oates model causes incentives for individuals to move to the community that is perceived as supplying the best combination of public service and local tax rate. By so doing, individuals contribute to efficient resource allocation. This is also the main thrust of the famous Tibout (1956) model.

However, freedom for local communications to decide on public spending and taxation themselves inevitably results in inequitoes. In addition, relaxing the restrictive assumptions of the above models such as no spill-over effects and no economies of scale makes apparent the need for central government intervention. However, this very erodes fiscal decentralisation (Prud'homme, 1994, 1995) making clear a basic conflict inherent in fiscal decentralisation.

Nevertheless, Oates (1993) argued that the thrust of the basic case for fiscal decentralisation (greater allocative efficiency) should also apply to a dynamic framework of economic growth. It could be expected that centrally determined policies consider regional and local conditions in the provision of public goods and services less well than locally determined policies, for instance regarding infrastructure and education. Economic development and growth might therefore be promoted if local authorities have input into such policy decisions.

2.1.2 The 'Leviathan restraint hypothesis'

Fiscal decentralisation may act as a constraint on the behaviour of revenue-maximising governments (Brennan/Buchanan, 1980). To the extent that governments behave as revenue-maximisers, horizontal and vertical competition among different levels of government may contribute to containing the size of their budgets and thus restrain the overall size of the public sector. Fiscal decentralisation may thus prevent an oversupply of public goods and services and/or 'x-inefficiency' in the public sector.

2.1.3 The 'productivity enhancement hypothesis'

Fiscal decentralisation implies a transfer of responsibility associated with accountability to sub-national governments. This may provide incentives for them to not only consider local preferences of residents (as in the Oates model) but to search for innovations in the production and supply of public goods and services. Production costs and prices of public goods and services could thus be lower and their quality better than in a uniform approach to providing public goods and services. In addition, fiscal decentralisation relieves the central government from many tasks. Thus, the latter may be able to better concentrate on efficient production of those public goods and services for which it still bears responsibility (ideally goods and services with large spill-overs among communities and/or substantial economies of scale in production).

2.1.4 Political arguments

Increasingly the economics literature acknowledges democracy as a factor of importance for long term economic growth. Political integration of minority groups, competition of governments, containment of vested interests, well defined property rights, transparency in public transactions all tend to promote the development of markets and may better be guaranteed by a democratic than by an autocratic system.

For transition countries it has been shown that economic reform and democracy (proxied by the civil liberties index constructed by Freedomhouse) are highly positively correlated (EBRD, 1999, p. 113). An empirical analysis of the political aspects of reform in these countries does not support the traditional view that concentration of political power, limited political competition and even rapid implementation of reforms enhances the prospects for successful and sustained economic reforms (EBRD 1999, Chapter 5). This analysis argues that *more political competition and less concentration of political power promote economic reform* by weakening the influence of vested interests on public policy. Fiscal decentralisation may imply less concentration of political power. It also may contribute to a better integration into society of ethnic and other minorities (especially in the local or regional context), which may reduce tensions in countries with regional ethnic diversities, thus stimulating economic activity.

2.2 Shortcomings of fiscal decentralisation

The problem with fiscal decentralisation is that it causes some important shortcomings, which require central government intervention. This intervention, of course, erodes fiscal autonomy, responsibility and accountability of sub-national governments. The case for fiscal decentralisation may be further weakened because of problems with practical implementation.

2.2.1 Variance of incomes among households and regions produces inequities under fiscal decentralisation

The Oates model showed that fiscal decentralisation breeds social inequity: Incomes and tax bases are unevenly distributed among jurisdictions and regions. Wealthier communities and regions are attempting to fend off low-income households. Thus, there needs to be a centralised redistribution policy.

2.2.2 Macro-economic stabilisation

In order for a country to be able to smooth out macro-economic fluctuations it must at least preserve the option to intervene quickly on the macro-economic level, especially through fiscal policy. For sub-national governments, however, there may be few incentives and/or possibilities to act counter-cyclically, in a co-ordinated fashion and symmetrically regarding recession and boom periods.[4] Also,

---

4 It is generally agreed that the power of sub-national governments to borrow should be strictly limited and that bailouts of sub-national governments by the central

fiscal decentralisation may change the income elasticities of revenues of the different government levels such that stabilisation becomes more difficult. (If, for instance, the relatively income elastic and productive income tax and VAT revenues were to accrue to sub-national governments, the stabilisation task for the central government would become more difficult). Also, macro-economic stabilisation under fiscal decentralisation may be inhibited whenever spending and revenue decisions of lower levels of government do not conform to stabilisation goals.

As stressed by Tanzi (1995) the stabilisation task in many countries (especially transition countries) refers not only to counter-cyclical actions, but especially to fiscal adjustments needed to eliminate structural (chronic) fiscal imbalances. However, structural imbalances may be worsened by fiscal decentralisation: One example for this is when one government level grants an exemption to a tax, the revenue of which is in large part received by another level of government. Thus, tax-sharing arrangements may cause perverse incentives.

Fiscal decentralisation may contribute to predatory and unpredictable taxation (such as in Russia, see Zhuravskaya, 1999) promoting shadow economic activities. Furthermore, effective and timely co-ordination among the different government levels may be difficult to implement, thus hindering stabilisation.

2.2.3 Quality of governments and of local democracy

If at the central government level there is a lack of quality of whatever kind (e.g. lack of knowledge, corruption) causing inefficiencies, then decentralisation could, in principle, be a remedy. However, it appears unreasonable to assume that local governments would be less affected by these problems. On the contrary, in general it can be argued that central governments achieve higher quality levels. They can attract more qualified people because of better career opportunities and salaries (Prud'homme, 1994). In addition, local democracies may offer less effective control by elected officials than occurs at the central level, because officials at the local level are closer to the people and therefore possibly more susceptible to personal influence. If the quality of government declines with the level of government, then decentralisation could increase inefficiencies. If the quality at all government levels is high, decentralisation might not be needed, because the central government could then speedily collect and process all the information necessary to achieve those efficient results that are expected from decentralisation.

---

government should be avoided. Obviously, this inhibits expansionary policies on the part of sub-national governments.

2.2.4 Low per capita income level

There are fixed costs involved with running and controlling sub-national administrations under decentralisation regime. In low-income countries these fixed costs could consume such a large share of the total funds available, that decentralisation might seem difficult to justify (Prud'homme, 1995). The point that there appears to be a positive correlation between income level and fiscal decentralisation has also been made by Bahl and Linn (1992, pp. 391-393): "Decentralisation more likely comes with the achievement of a higher stage of economic development". The authors argue that there is a relatively high threshold level of economic development at which fiscal decentralisation becomes attractive. Such a threshold level can be explained not only with the fixed costs of decentralisation but also by the fact that at a relatively low per capita income level, the demands for public goods and services may be concentrated on very few goods and have a small variance. Thus, at a low-income level it may not be difficult for a central government to have all information necessary to make the right decisions regarding local public goods production. With a rising income level, or starting at a certain minimum income level, the demands for public goods and services increase and so does their variance, i.e. the preferences of people become more heterogeneous. Hence, economic advantages from diversification of outputs within local jurisdictions emerge, and thus possibly also from fiscal decentralisation.

2.2.5 Small size of the country

If a country and/or its population are relatively small, the outlooks of all its inhabitants might be relatively homogeneous. Hence, differences in individual preferences for public goods and services may not be pronounced, thus reducing the potential gains from decentralisation. In addition, the fixed costs, which decentralisation implies may not be warranted.

2.2.6 Scarcity of good local taxes

It is clear that decentralisation requires that sub-national governments have their own revenue sources. From the perspective of the expected benefits arising from competition and accountability of sub-national governments these revenue sources should be determined by the sub-national governments themselves. From the perspective of securing a 'good' tax system that provides for equity, little distortions, low administrative costs, income elastic revenues, etc. the revenue sources need to be determined at the national level. As a compromise the traditional Musgrave (1959) view is still widely shared. This view holds that since of the three main functions of a government (i.e. allocation, redistribution and stabilisation) only the allocation function may be shared by different levels of government, its financing should rely – to the maximum extent possible – on the benefits-received principle in order to preserve fairness and economic efficiency. However, available sources for taxes, fees and surcharges are scarce, and in general they do not yield sufficient revenue and their administration can be costly and difficult (McLure, 1995; Tanzi, 1995). Hence, revenue sharing is indispensable in financing sub-national governments but this reduces the latter's fiscal autonomy, responsibility and accountability and has the mentioned drawbacks for stabilisation.

2.2.7 Low degree of urbanisation

The local governments of rural areas are faced with a poorly diversified tax base and democratic controls may function less well (Prud'homme, 1994). Hence, a rising degree of urbanisation may facilitate decentralisation and vice versa.

2.2.8 Few goods and services are truly 'public'

The idea of efficiency gains through fiscal decentralisation is based on the assumption that a government needs to supply goods and services, which are 'public' (non-excludable, non-rival). However, there are few goods and services that qualify for the strict definition of being public: basic education and health care, waste disposal services, utilities, security, prisons, etc. all could and sometimes are supplied by private companies. The activity of these private companies could be subject to governmental supervision to maintain minimum quality standards. Hence the question arises, whether instead of decentralisation a superior form of improving efficiency in supplying these goods and services could be simply to encourage their private supply. Equity aspects and positive externalities could be considered by introducing vouchers, issued by the central government to consumers, that allow a minimum consumption per capita at no direct cost to the consumer (McLure, 1995). Consumers would use the vouchers for their basic needs and thus decide directly and not via the local democracy on the types and quality of services they want to consume. Equity and regional equalisation aspects could very well be safeguarded by this approach, especially when combined with means testing.

However, there may also be drawbacks to this approach: It is the central government that would have to decide on the goods and services that can be obtained with the vouchers. But the central government is farther away from consumers than local governments. Misuse of the vouchers and difficulties with means testing could be other problems.

To sum up, important determinants of fiscal decentralisation are[5]:

---

5 Panizza (1999) tests for the sign and significance of some of these determinants of fiscal decentralisation (income per capita, ethnic fractionalisation, country size, and the level of democracy). Using different estimation methods and a large set of

- the quality of the central and local governments;
- the quality of local democracy;
- income differentials between households and regions;
- per capita income;
- size of the country;
- the degree of urbanisation or local and regional differences in the diversification of tax bases;
- diversity of ethnic groups;
- presence of true public goods and services.

When theoretical considerations yield ambiguous results, empirical analysis becomes even more important. Given the vagueness of outcomes of theoretical analyses of fiscal decentralisation, the case for and against it ultimately hinges on empirical evidence as to whether it promotes economic performance.

3 Analytical background and estimation proceedings

3.1 Analytical background

With the rise of the theoretical endogenous economic growth models effects of economic policies on the growth process became explicitly recognised. In addition, human capital was introduced in the production function as a separate production factor. The growth accounting equation was modified to either include human capital separately or to replace raw labour by effective labour. With human capital counted separately, the growth accounting equation becomes:

$$y = \beta_1 k + \beta_2 h + \beta_3 l + \beta_4 a, \qquad (17.1)$$

where y is the rate of growth of real GDP, k is the rate of growth of physical capital, h is the rate of growth of human capital, l is the rate of growth of raw labour, a is the rate of growth of overall efficiency in combining capital (physical and human) and raw labour, and β_i is the elasticity of economic growth with respect to argument i.

countries, he finds for the period of about 1975 through 1985 that all these four determinants are positively correlated with fiscal decentralisation.

In endogenous growth models one or several of the right-hand side variables in equation (17.1) are made dependent on one or several variable(s) of interest, in particular policy variables. Usually, the steady-state growth rate in these models depends positively on the variable(s) of interest. Thus economic growth can be higher than in traditional neo-classical growth models. The growth rate can be larger than the sum of the exogenous rates of population growth and technical progress. The capability of these theoretical models to account for the potentially powerful effects of government policies on economic growth inspired extensive empirical work on these effects. Yet, there is still no consensus theoretical model to guide empirical work on growth.

Two basic estimation approaches are employed in this empirical work: First, growth equations are specified such that in addition to the independent variables suggested by traditional neo-classical growth theory (i.e. initial per capita income level, population growth and the share of physical-investment in GDP), variables are included that represent human capital investment, government policies and political factors (e.g. Levine and Renelt, 1992; Barro and Sala-i-Martin, 1992; Barro 1997). Variables that represent government policies include the share of government consumption expenditures in GDP, measures of the degree of openness of the economy, of the level of public infrastructure, of macro-economic stability (inflation, domestic credit growth, standard deviation of inflation, and domestic credit growth), etc. However, this approach is associated with interpretation difficulties, because it implicitly assumes that the independent variables included in the growth regression affect economic growth only through variables that are not included. For instance, when estimating a growth regression that includes measures for k, h and l in equation (17.1) and a variable that represents a particular macro-economic policy, it is implicitly assumed that this variable does not affect economic growth through its impact on k, h, and l but solely through its impact on the productivity residual a. However, macro-economic policies and fiscal decentralisation affect growth, in particular via investment in physical and human capital.

A two step method that avoids this interpretation problem and allows identification of the channels through which macro-economic policies affect economic growth was applied by Fischer (1993) on the basis of a proposal by Elias (1992): First, run regressions where the growth rate is dependent only on the policy variables of interest. Second, run regressions of the change in both the supply of production factors and the productivity residual on the macro-economic variables of interest.

In this Chapter, both approaches are used since the interpretation problem associated with the first approach may become less serious when additional evidence from the second approach is used.

3.2 Estimation proceedings

3.2.1 Country sample

The sample includes 17 Western European countries (i.e. the member countries of the European Union plus Norway and Switzerland). However, to improve the statistical robustness, nine additional countries with a relatively large country size and different income levels were also included (see Appendix Table 17.2).

3.2.2 Indicators of fiscal decentralisation

Several indicators of fiscal decentralisation were employed. Since this study presents both pure cross-sectional regressions (using averages of the annual data covering the period 1975-1995) as well as pooled cross-sectional (panel) regressions (covering the period 1981-1995), there are two types of indicators. Those, which are available as time series can be used in both regressions. Those, which are available only as period averages, can be used in the pure cross-sectional regressions.

The share of sub-national government expenditures in consolidated government expenditures is the best known indicator of fiscal decentralisation (indicator A in Table 17.2, denoted IFDA in the regressions). This indicator is available on an annual basis since about the 1970s, although surprisingly even for some advanced industrial countries there are considerable gaps (the Appendix describes these gaps and the methods used to fill some of them).

Two additional indicators of fiscal decentralisation have been found in the political science literature (indicators B and C in Table 17.2): However, these two indicators are average values for the last three decades approximately, and are not available as time series. Thus they can be used only in pure cross-sectional regressions and not in panel regressions.

A fourth indicator was constructed to test for a non-linear (hump-shaped) relationship between economic performance and fiscal decentralisation (denoted A' in Tables 2 and 3 and IFDA' in the regressions): For the pure cross-sectional regressions this indicator was obtained by simply transforming the period averages of indicator A such that low and high values become low values whereas medium values of indicator A become high values (Appendix Table 17.3).[6] In the pooled cross-sectional regression non-linearities in the effects of fiscal decentralisation on economic growth, capital formation and productivity were estimated using a

6 This method is borrowed from Calmfors and Driffill (1998). They suggested it in the context of an analysis of the relationship between the degree of centralisation of wage bargaining and unemployment and proposed a hump-shaped relationship between this degree and real wages and unemployment.

spline function of indicator IFDA. The function breaks at shares of 30 and 45 percent of sub-national government expenditures in consolidated expenditures. The resulting three indicators are denoted FDL for 'low degree of fiscal decentralisation', FDM for 'medium degree of fiscal decentralisation', and FDH for 'high degree of fiscal decentralisation'.

Table 17.2 (see Appendix) presents correlation coefficients between the indicators A, B, C, and A' of the sample countries (i.e. indicators of the average degree of fiscal decentralisation during the past three decades or so) on the one hand, and the per capita income level of 1998 (measured in US-Dollars) and the average real per capita growth rate during the past three decades, on the other hand. Fiscal decentralisation, as measured by the indicators A, B and C, is positively correlated with the income level. (Note that in contrast to indicators A and B, indicator C rises with increasing centralisation). A relatively high, positive correlation is found for Western Europe, especially if Luxembourg is excluded.

However, the correlation between these measures of fiscal decentralisation and average per capita growth rates is negative for Western Europe while positive for other countries. The correlation between fiscal decentralisation and economic growth is particularly high and positive for the low-income countries in the sample (which are middle-income countries in World comparison).

These first impressions from Table 17.2 suggest the following. First, that indeed the income level needs to be considered when examining growth effects of fiscal decentralisation. Second, taken at face value, the simple correlation coefficients from Table 17.2 would suggest that middle-income countries could reap more benefits from fiscal decentralisation for their growth and income performance than high-income countries! For high-income countries the chances for economic growth may rise when moving from a low or high degree of fiscal decentralisation towards a medium degree. Growth regressions may shed more light on these questions.

3.2.3 Specification

Limited specifications are used for both the pure cross-sectional growth regressions and the panel regressions so as to focus on a few key factors. Nevertheless, the specifications are consistent with a large number of endogenous growth models. The pure cross-sectional per capita growth regressions use a set of independent variables, which are always included. These are the initial level of real GDP per capita in 1970 (RGDP70) from Summers, Kravis and Heston (1980) to consider the (conditional) convergence hypothesis, the average annual rate of population growth (GPOP), the average annual gross investment share of GDP

(INVGDP), and the initial secondary-school enrolment rate in 1970 (SEC70) from Unesco as a proxy for the ratio of human capital investment to GDP.[7]

Variables representing the degree of fiscal decentralisation are the average annual indicator IFDA, its transformation IFDA' (to test for a hump-shaped relationship), and the indicators B and C from the political science literature. These four variables are denoted FD variables, and they are used alternately. Period averages of the annual values of the proxy for self-reliance of sub-national governments (SR) and of the annual changes of this variable (CHSR) are included to test for Oates' hypothesis that increasing self-reliance promotes economic growth.

Also a dummy variable is included as a proxy for financial support granted by the European Union to Greece, Ireland, Portugal and Spain (DEU4). These countries received substantial transfers from the European Union during the period considered and this may have influenced their economic growth. Finally, to consider the hypothesis that structural rigidities are so pronounced in many countries that domestic and/or external disturbances have a relatively long lasting impact on economic growth, the average annual change in the unemployment rate (CHUER) is included as a proxy for such disturbances. In the very long run the impact of the change of the unemployment rate disappears, however. Thus, the estimated pure cross-sectional specification has the following general form:

$$\begin{aligned} GYP_i = {} & \alpha + \beta_1 \, RGDP70_i + \beta_2 \, GPOP_i + \beta_3 \, INVGDP_i \\ & + \beta_4 \, SEC70_i + \beta_5 \, CHUER_i + \beta_6 \, DUE4_i \\ & + \beta_7 \, FD_i + \beta_8 \, SR_i + \beta_9 \, CHSR_i + \epsilon_i , \end{aligned} \tag{17.2}$$

where GYP is the average annual growth rate of GDP per capita, FD is either IFDA, IFDA', B or C. The subscript i is indexing the country.

The equation was estimated using averages over for the period 1975-1995 for up to 26 countries. The expected signs of the estimated coefficients are as follows: β_1 is expected to be positive if there is evidence for conditional convergence (i.e. if countries with relatively low initial income tend to grow faster than other countries after controlling for differences in the rates of investment in physical and human capital, population growth and technical progress). The expected effect of population growth on per capita economic growth (β_2) is negative. The effects of investment in physical capital and of past investment in human capital (β_3 and β_4) are clearly positive. To the extent that due to structural rigidities of the economies disturbances may have long lasting adverse effects on economic growth, β_5 is expected to have a negative sign. β_6 is expected to be positive if this dummy

---

7 In the estimations the initial school enrolment ratio was found to have a higher significance than the average school enrolment ratio over the considered period. This could be explained with lags between completion of education and its appropriate use as a production factor.

coefficient captures the effect of grants from the EU and if these grants are used as intended, i.e. for improvements of the physical and institutional infrastructure of the recipient countries. Finally, the signs of major interest in this study β_7, β_8 and β_9 are not clear because theory suggests that fiscal decentralisation may have positive and negative influences on economic growth. In addition, it is not clear, a priori, whether there are non-linear effects of fiscal decentralisation.

Turning to the panel growth regressions, initial income is replaced by the real per capita growth rate of the previous year. However, in preliminary estimations this variable was generally not significant and its inclusion did not raise but lowered the explained variation of per capita growth. It was therefore dropped from most of the estimated panel equations. Nevertheless, to account for (conditional) convergence effects, a dummy variable was included for countries with relatively low income. In regressions with data for the Western European countries, a dummy is included for fife countries with relatively low initial income, i.e. Greece, Ireland, Italy, Portugal, and Spain (denoted DEU5). Note, however, that four of these five countries, namely Greece, Ireland, Portugal, and Spain received substantial net transfers from the European Union during much of the considered time period and, thus, this dummy is likely to capture at least two effects: potential (conditional) convergence effects and effects of financial support granted by the European Union. In the regressions with data for the full sample a dummy for European and non-European countries with relatively low initial income is included (denoted DLI).[8] Preliminary estimations also showed that the gross investment share of GDP was insignificant, and in some cases even had the wrong sign. Therefore, the growth rate of real gross fixed capital formation was used instead.[9] Also included in the panel regressions are the secondary school enrolment ratio as a proxy for investment in human capital, the change in the unemployment ratio as a proxy for macro-economic disturbances, and, of course, measures of fiscal decentralisation. The latter are the share of sub-national government expenditures in consolidated expenditures (IFDA) and, alternatively, the three categories of fiscal decentralisation (low, medium and high fiscal decentralisation) to test for non-linear effects. In addition, the variables SR and CHSR are also included. The general form of the estimated panel regressions thus is:

$$GYP_{i,t} = \alpha + \beta_1 GYP_{i,t-1} + \beta_2 GPOP_{i,t} \qquad (17.3)$$

$$+ \beta_3 GKAP_{i,t} + \beta_4 SEC_{i,t} + \beta_5 CHUER_{i,t}$$

$$+ \beta_6 DUE5_{i,t} + \beta_7 DLI_{i,t} + \beta_8 FD_{i,t}$$

---

8 These countries are Greece, Ireland, Italy, Portugal, Spain, Argentina, Brazil, Korea, New Zealand, and South Africa.

9 Under the assumption that real capital stock depreciation is a relatively stable share of real gross investment, the latter is highly positively correlated with real net investment and thus also with the change in the real capital stock.

$$+ \beta_9 \, SR_{i,t} + \beta_{10} \, CHSR_{i,t} + \in_{i,t},$$

where GKAP is the annual growth rate of real gross fixed capital formation as a proxy of the growth rate of the real capital stock, SEC is the annual secondary school enrolment ratio, and DEU5 and DLI are dummy variables as explained above and used alternately. FD represents the indicators of fiscal decentralisation, i.e. either the share of sub-national government expenditures in consolidated government expenditures (IFDA) to test for linear effects of fiscal decentralisation, on the one hand, or the indicators FDL, FDM, and FDH to test for non-linear effects, on the other hand. The subscripts i and t are indexing the country and time period.

The equation was estimated for the period 1981 through 1995. The expected signs for β_1 and β_2 are negative, for β_3 and β_4, positive, for β_5, negative, for β_6 and β_7, positive. The signs for β_8, β_9 and β_{10} are not clear a priori.

Based on the growth accounting framework, two additional panel regressions were estimated to examine the channels through which fiscal decentralisation may influence economic growth: Firstly, capital formation was examined and, secondly, total factor productivity growth (the Solow residual).

Capital formation is specified as a function of macro-economic policy variables, including measures of fiscal decentralisation, of macro-economic disturbances (cyclical effects) and of a dummy variable to capture catch-up effects of countries with relatively low initial income, and additionally in the Western European context, potential effects of grants provided by the European Union to member countries with relatively low incomes. Macro-economic policy variables include the fiscal balance as a share of GDP (denoted FBGDP), the inflation rate (denoted GCPI), and uncertainty of economic agents with regard to macro-economic stability, which is proxied by the standard deviation of domestic credit for overlapping five year periods (denoted STDDC). The same measures of fiscal decentralisation as in the previous equation are used. Macro-economic disturbances are proxied, as before, by the change in the unemployment rate (CHUER). Those regressions that are estimated with data for the Western European countries include a dummy variable for the four countries that received substantial grants from the European Union (DEU4). The regressions estimated with data for all sample countries include a dummy for countries with relatively low initial income (DLI). Thus, the estimated equations have the general form:

$$\begin{aligned} GKAP_{i,t} = \alpha &+ \beta_1 \, GKAP_{i,t-1} + \beta_2 \, FBGDP_{i,t} \\ &+ \beta_3 \, GCPI_{i,t} + \beta_4 \, STDDC_{i,t} + \beta_5 \, CHUER_{i,t} \\ &+ \beta_6 \, DUE4_{i,t} + \beta_7 \, DLI_{i,t} + \beta_8 \, FD_{i,t} \\ &+ \beta_9 \, SR_{i,t} + \beta_{10} \, CHSR_{i,t} + \in_{i,t}, \end{aligned} \tag{17.4}$$

where the dummy variables (DEU4 and DLI) are used alternately. As before, FD represents either the indicator IFDA or the indicators FDL, FDM, and FDH. The expected signs of the estimated coefficients are $\beta_1 > 0$, $\beta_2 > 0$, to the extent that the potential crowding out effect of budget deficits prevails, β_3, β_4, and $\beta_5 < 0$, since inflation, uncertainty and disturbances are likely to inhibit capital formation, and β_6 and $\beta_7 > 0$, because of catch-up effects and due to the effects of the grants provided by the European Union. Again, the effects of the measures of fiscal decentralisation β_8, β_9, and β_{10} are unclear.

Finally, panel equations are estimated to examine the relationship between fiscal decentralisation and total factor productivity growth. Total factor productivity growth (RES) was calculated for the sample countries as a Solow residual.[10] Independent variables included are the lagged unemployment rate (UER) as a measure of cyclical effects on productivity growth, dummy variables for Western European countries and for other countries with relatively low income to capture potential catch-up effects and effects of European Union grants, and the indicators of fiscal decentralisation. Hence, the general form of the estimated equations is:

$$RES_{i,t} = \alpha + \beta_1 RES_{i,t-1} + \beta_2 UER_{i,t-1} + \beta_3 DUE4_{i,t} \qquad (17.5)$$
$$+ \beta_4 DLI_{i,t} + \beta_5 FD_{i,t} + \beta_6 SR_{i,t}$$
$$+ \beta_7 CHSR_{i,t} + \epsilon_{i,t} \, .$$

The expected signs are: $\beta_1 > 0$, $\beta_2 < 0$, β_3 and $\beta_4 > 0$. The signs of β_5, β_6 and β_7 are unclear.

4 Estimation results

4.1 Pure and pooled cross-sectional growth equations

Table 17.4 (see Appendix) presents the pure cross-sectional regressions for the twenty-year period 1975-1995. The variables that are always included in the regressions have in almost all cases the expected sign and are in general highly significant. There is strong evidence for (conditional) convergence since initial

---

10 Assuming a constant labour share of income of 0.65 the residuals were calculated as: $RES_{it} = GDPR_{it} - 0.35\ GKAP_{it} - 0.65\ GLAFO_{it}$, where GDPR is the growth rate of real GDP, GKAP is the growth rate of the real capital stock, and GLAFO is the growth rate of the labour force, i = 1, ...26; t = 1981-1995. Note that the underlying assumptions of this procedure (constant factor shares, no consideration given to the quality of factor inputs etc.) are very restrictive, which is necessitated by data constraints.

income (RGDP70) lowers the per capita economic growth rate. Investment in physical and human capital are positively related to per capita economic growth while population growth tends to lower per capita growth. This latter relationship is, however, not obtained in all estimated equations and thus ambiguous. The considered twenty-year period was characterised by a trend of rising unemployment rates in many countries reflecting deep-seated structural rigidities. These have been very costly in terms of per capita growth, as indicated by the estimated coefficients of the variable CHUER. The estimated coefficient of the dummy variable for four 'low' income Western European countries (DEU4) is in most cases significant and positive. It suggests that even when controlling for convergence effects, per capita growth in these countries was on average almost half a percentage point higher than in the other Western European countries. Hence, it appears that EU grants to these countries indeed had a positive impact on growth.

In the pooled cross-sectional regressions presented in Table 17.5 (see Appendix), the initial income variable is replaced either by dummy variables for countries with relatively low income (DEU5 and DLI) or by the growth rate of real per capita GDP, lagged one period. In addition, the investment to GDP ratio is replaced by a proxy for the growth rate of the real capital stock, and the secondary school enrolment ratio of 1970 is replaced by the annual secondary school enrolment ratio. In contrast to the variables population growth and capital stock growth, the school enrolment variable is not significant in any of the estimated panel equations (Table 17.5), and in some cases even has an unexpected negative sign. Apparently, the addition of the time series dimension to the cross-sectional dimension causes a break down of the significance of this regressor. This result has also been found in other empirical growth studies. One major reason for this may be that there is a considerable time lag between completing education and the contribution of educated labour to production and economic growth. Given that this study focuses on the relationship between fiscal decentralisation and economic growth, no attempt has been made to redefine this proxy variable for human capital.

The variables of main interest in this study are the fiscal decentralisation indicators. The share of sub-national government expenditures in consolidated government expenditures (IFDA) is not significant in the growth regressions for European countries (equations 17.2a and 17.2d, Table 17.4). However, this indicator is significant for the whole sample (Equations 17.2g and 17.2j). But this significance disappears and the IFDA coefficient for European countries even becomes negative when adding the time series dimension data, i.e. when estimating panel regressions (equations 17.3a and 17.3e, Table 17.5).[11] Apparently, the time series relation between fiscal decentralisation as measured by

---

11 Due to data constraints the pooled cross-sectional regressions presented in Table 5 use the time period 1981 through 1995.

indicator IFDA and growth (the effect of changes in the fiscal decentralisation measure on growth within each country over time) was negative in Western Europe during the period considered.

The same result was obtained when using the indicators B and C of fiscal decentralisation from the political science literature. These indicators can be used only in the pure cross-sectional regressions and they are significant only in the regressions with data for European countries. They indicate that higher decentralisation is associated with lower per capita growth in Western Europe (not shown in Table 17.4). This corresponds to the negative sign of the IFDA variable found in the panel regression 3a for Western European countries. So far then the impression is that at least for Western Europe, the relationship between fiscal decentralisation and economic growth may even be negative.

Substantial further insight can, however, be gained by testing for a non-linear relationship between fiscal decentralisation and economic growth. This requires use of the transformed indicator IFDA' instead of indicator IFDA in the pure cross-sectional regressions. In the panel regressions the spline function of fiscal decentralisation needs to be substituted for indicator IFDA (with fiscal decentralisation broken into the three categories FDL, FDM, FDH).

Equations 17.2c and 17.2e, Table 17.4, show that for Western European countries the indicator IFDA' is significant and positive, suggesting that indeed the relationship between fiscal decentralisation and economic growth may not be linear. Rather, it appears that a medium degree of fiscal decentralisation is positively related to per capita economic growth. By contrast, when estimating pure cross-sectional regressions where all countries in the sample are included, the indicator IFDA' is barely significant but IFDA is (equations 17.2g and 17.2j in Table 17.4 need to be compared with equations 17.2h and 17.2k). This suggests that for non-European countries in the sample there is a positive association between fiscal decentralisation and per capita economic growth. The pooled cross-sectional regressions (Table 17.5) confirm this: Equation 17.3c shows that for Western European countries the variable FDM (medium degree of fiscal decentralisation) has a slightly larger estimated coefficient than the variables FDL (low degree of fiscal decentralisation) and FDH (high degree of fiscal decentralisation). In other words, in Western Europe, a medium degree of fiscal decentralisation was associated with a slightly higher per capita growth rate than either a low degree or high degree of fiscal decentralisation.

For the full sample it is found, however, that with an increasing degree of fiscal decentralisation, the per capita growth rate tends to increase (equation 17.3f). Splitting the sample into one group that includes 9 countries with relatively low income and another group that includes 12 countries with relatively high income shows that these two country groups differ with regard to the existing relationship between fiscal decentralisation and economic growth. For the country group with relatively low income the association between fiscal decentralisation and growth strengthens substantially as fiscal decentralisation rises (equation 17.3j, Table 17.5). The higher the decentralisation category, the higher becomes both its estimated coefficient and its significance. By contrast, for the country group with relatively high income the medium category of fiscal decentralisation (FDM) has both a larger estimated coefficient and higher significance than the other two categories (equation 17.3k, Table 17.5).

Regarding the relationship between the measure of self-reliance of sub-national governments (SR) and its change (CHSR), on the one hand, and economic growth, on the other hand, the evidence from pure cross-sectional regressions (Table 17.4) suggests that both variables are negatively related to economic growth throughout. However, when adding the time series dimension to the pure cross-sectional dimension (Table 17.5) the estimated coefficient of the change of the self-reliance variable (CHSR) becomes positive and in some cases significant (equations 17.3h and 17.3k, Table 17.5). This finding provides support for Oates' (1995) claim that increasing self-reliance of sub-national governments on their own revenues is beneficial for economic growth.

However, these results do not yet shed light on the channels through which fiscal decentralisation and increasing self-reliance of sub-national governments may effect economic growth. This is the goal of the following two Sections.

4.2 Capital formation panel equations

Table 17.6 shows the panel regressions of capital formation. Lagged capital stock growth (GKAP (-1)), the inflation rate (GCPI), the proxy for macro-economic disturbances (CHUER) and the dummy variables (DEU4, DLI) have the expected signs and are in general highly significant. Interestingly, the estimated coefficients of the variables fiscal balance as a share of GDP (FBGDP), inflation (GCPI), and macro-economic uncertainty (STDDC), are larger and more significant for the group of relatively wealthy countries (equations 17.4a- 4c, and 17.4h) than for the group of countries with relatively low income (equation 17.4g).

The association between capital formation and fiscal decentralisation is similar to the one between per capita growth and fiscal decentralisation. For Western European and high-income countries the relationship does not appear to be linear (the IFDA variable is not significant). For Western European countries it is the medium category of fiscal decentralisation that has the largest estimated coefficient (equations 17.4b and 17.4c), i.e. growth of the real capital stock tends to be larger in countries with a medium degree of fiscal decentralisation than in countries with either a low or high degree of decentralisation. Taken at face value, the estimated coefficients of the fiscal decentralisation variables FDL, FDM, and FDH for Western European countries suggest the following: After controlling for the influence on capital stock growth of macro-economic policies (fiscal balance, inflation), of uncertainty, and of macro-economic disturbances, the capital stock grew at least 0.4 percentage points per year faster in countries with a medium degree of fiscal decentralisation than in countries with either a low or high degree of decentralisation. Given that the average annual growth of the estimated real capital stock for the 17 Western European countries during 1975-1995 was about 2.5%, this is a considerable difference. The finding that a medium degree of fiscal decentralisation is associated with higher capital stock growth also holds for the group of 12 wealthiest countries in the sample (equation 17.4h). For these countries it is estimated that a medium degree of fiscal decentralisation may raise annual capital stock growth by even more than 1 percentage point. However, for the group of 9 countries in the sample with relatively low per capita income (equation 17.4g), the estimated coefficients of the three categories of fiscal decentralisation and their significance increase with increasing decentralisation.

Turning to the self-reliance indicators (SR and CHSR), Table 17.6 shows that the signs are as expected, but in most cases the indicators are not significant at the 5 percent level. However, in the regression for all countries for which these data are available the change of the self-reliance ratio (CHSR) is significant at the 10 percent level (equations 17.4d and 17.4e). Overall, the evidence appears to support the hypothesis of a positive association between increasing self-reliance of sub-national governments and capital formation.

These results provide explanations for the estimated relationships between per capita economic growth and fiscal decentralisation discussed in the previous Section: Increasing fiscal decentralisation in low-income countries is on average statistically significantly associated with higher per capita economic growth through higher capital formation. With regard to high-income countries and Western European countries the medium category of fiscal decentralisation is estimated to have the largest positive impact on capital formation. Hence, the growth regressions for these countries showed that a medium degree of fiscal decentralisation is associated with higher economic growth than either a low or high degree of fiscal decentralisation.

4.3 Total factor productivity panel equations

Finally, the relationship between total factor productivity growth and fiscal decentralisation needs to be examined. The regressions of total factor productivity growth are shown in Table 17.7. Obtaining a satisfactory statistical fit proved to be difficult. The explained portion of the variation in total factor productivity growth is relatively low. However, the results confirm the impression gained in the previous estimations that the income level needs to be considered when examining the relationship between fiscal decentralisation and economic performance. Table 17.7 suggests that in countries with relatively low income, the association between fiscal decentralisation and growth of total factor productivity becomes stronger on average as fiscal decentralisation increases (equation 17.5c).

In other words, in these countries a higher degree of fiscal decentralisation is on average statistically significantly associated with higher total factor productivity growth. By contrast, regarding wealthy countries and the group of Western European countries the opposite is found, i.e. a lower degree of fiscal decentralisation is associated with higher total factor productivity growth (equations 17.5a, 17.5b, and 17.5d).

Interestingly, in these regressions the dummy for the four Western European countries that received substantial net transfers from the European Union proved insignificant. This may suggest that these transfers had little influence on total factor productivity growth. The growth promoting effect of these transfers was thus mainly the result of their positive influence on capital formation.

The self-reliance indicators (SR and CHSR) did not prove to be significant regressors in the total factor productivity growth regressions. This would suggest that the positive association between increasing self-reliance of sub-national governments and economic growth – which was found in the panel growth regressions – needs to be explained with the positive impact of increasing self-reliance on capital formation.

5 Concluding remarks

The foregoing empirical analysis suggests that for countries with relatively low incomes, the association between fiscal decentralisation and economic growth and its determinants (capital formation and total factor productivity growth) become stronger as fiscal decentralisation increases. With regard to Western European countries and high-income countries the estimations suggest a hump-shaped relation between fiscal decentralisation, on the one hand, and growth and capital formation, on the other hand.

Regarding the relation between economic performance and the reliance of sub-national governments on their own revenue sources (own taxes and shared taxes) to finance their expenditures, there is empirical evidence suggesting that capital formation is positively related to increasing self-reliance.

However, this evidence refers to a limited group of non-transition countries and to a certain time period. Therefore it can serve as an illustration only.

But what may be said about Ukraine's particular case? The criteria for the choice of fiscal decentralisation derived in the theoretical part of this Chapter (Section 2) may be briefly examined:

It was argued that for very low-income countries fiscal decentralisation may be less attractive due to the fixed costs it produces and due to relatively low and homogeneous demand for public goods and services in these countries. On account of data restrictions, very low-income countries were not included in the above empirical analysis so that the regression results cannot be used as evidence against this argument. Nevertheless, the fixed cost argument does not appear to apply to Ukraine (the existence of lower levels of government has never been questioned) and it may also be questionable whether the demand for public goods and services is relatively homogenous in Ukraine. Other potential theoretical arguments against fiscal decentralisation, that were mentioned above, are:

- poor quality of the local governments and of local democracy;
- large income differentials between households and regions;
- low degree of urbanisation, i.e. little diversified tax bases in the regions.

Indeed, supporters of fiscal centralisation in Ukraine could raise these arguments. However, supporters of decentralisation may raise the following counter arguments:

The quality of local governments may not be worse than that of the central level, and the quality of local democracy may not be worse than that at the national level.

The problems of relatively large income differentials between Ukraine's regions and of little diversification of some regional tax bases could be alleviated by way of an improved system of tax sharing and transfers. Ideally, sharing could provide a relatively stable source of revenue to sub-national governments (e.g. sub-national governments as a group would receive a fixed share of the relatively stable VAT revenues), while providing incentives for them to diversify and increase their local tax base and local economic growth. Such a system of incentives would require that the share of a given sub-national government in both shared tax revenues and transfers depend on the following indicators: population, average income, incidence of poverty and actual tax revenues compared to potential tax revenues (i.e. fiscal effort). To reduce arbitrariness, a formula-based approach would be preferred. [12]

Three important conditions for the success of such a system need to be emphasised: First, revenues from shared taxes and transfers should not be the primary source of income for sub-national governments (mainly because these revenue sources contradict self-autonomy and accountability of sub-national governments). Rather the major part of the sub-national governments' revenues should come from taxes and fees, which they are entitled to raise themselves (under the restriction that the applied tax rates may not exceed moderate ceilings). Second, the central government needs to define national quality standards for the

---

12 An independent advisory council together with a representative body of all levels of government could be charged with the task of defining potential tax revenues and choosing a formula.

goods and services provided by sub-national governments. Third, sub-national government finances need to be regularly audited by an independent agency (such as the national accounting chamber, which would be required to publish reports).

Finally, the problem of relatively large income differentials between individual households might be used as an argument against fiscal decentralisation, because far-reaching autonomy of sub-national governments in a situation of pronounced income inequality could cause unacceptable inequities. But it is not questioned that fiscal decentralisation requires effective central government policies particularly regarding income redistribution, as for instance:

- The central government needs to determine quality standards for goods and services supplied by sub-national governments (education, health care, water supply etc.). These standards must be met in all regions. The required financing must be secured by a transparent system of tax sharing and transfers;
- The central government should determine that the incidence of poverty becomes an important factor in the formula that determines transfer payments to sub-national governments;
- Instead of subsidising selected enterprises and certain private goods and services, the central government could make cash payments or issue vouchers to low-income households so as to provide targeted income support.

In fact, in may be argued that the failure of the central government to implement a transparent and consistent redistributive policy prevents the expected benefits of fiscal decentralisation to materialise. Considerable subsidies are granted to enterprises (mainly in the form of lost tax revenues and lost dividends on the part of the central government), several goods and services are subsidised (e.g. energy, communal services, bread etc.) while some goods are implicitly highly taxed due to import restrictions and other regulations that serve the interest of a few producers (e.g. sugar). On balance the relatively wealthy households are likely to benefit from these policies more than low-income households.[13] But sub-national governments often oppose the cutting of these subsidies and sometimes also of privatisation for fear that low-income households will not be compensated for the resulting welfare loss.[14] Indeed sub-national governments are sometimes entangled in a non-transparent net of relations with enterprises to the detriment of efficient resource allocation. Hence, a prerequisite for improving the functioning of local governments appears to be to provide for a credible funding of the (existing) nation-wide housing programme for low-income households. Then it

---

13 In judging this, one also has to consider that about 25% of consolidated government revenues come from the value-added-tax and excises which are regressive taxes.

14 See also Bird and Wallich, p. 151.

could be expected that objections of sub-national governments to cut subsidies and to privatise might lessen.

In sum, for fiscal decentralisation to contribute to better resource allocation and economic growth the central government has to meet certain prerequisites. Since the government's existing catalogue of structural reforms includes the fulfilment of some of these prerequisites (e.g. implementation of a consistent redistribution policy, introduction of a transparent system of tax sharing and transfers, improvements of the auditing of sub-national government budgets etc.), it could be argued that the envisaged policy of increasing fiscal centralisation should be reconsidered.

References

Bahl, Roy W. and Johannes F. Linn (1992): Urban Public Finance in Developing Countries. New York

Barro, Robert J. and Xavier Sala-I-Martin (1992): Convergence. In: Journal of Political Economy, Vol. 100, No. 2, pp. 223-251

Barro, Robert J. (1997): Determinants of Economic Growth: A Cross-country Empirical Study. Cambridge/Mass.

Bird, Richard (1994): Decentralising Infrastructure: For Good of For Ill? World Bank Policy Research Working Paper No. 1258, Washington D.C.

Bird, Richard, Caroline Freud and Christine Wallich (1994): Decentralisation of InterGovernmental Finance in Transition Countries. In: Comparative Economic Studies, Vol. 36, No. 4, pp. 149- 160

Borjas, G. (1995): Ethnicity, Neighbourhoods and Human Capital Externalities. In: American Economic Review, Vol. 85, pp. 365-390

Brennan, G. and J. Buchanan (1980): The Power to Tax: Analytical Foundations of a Fiscal Constitution. Cambridge/U.K.

Calmfors, Lars and John Driffill (1988): Bargaining Structure, Corporatism and Macroeconomic Performance. In: Economic Policy, Vol. 6, pp. 14- 61

Elias, Victor J. (1992): Sources of Growth. San Francisco

European Bank for Reconstruction and Development (1999): Transition Report 1999, London

Fischer, Stanley (1993): The Role of Macroeconomic Factors in Growth. National Bureau of Economic Research. Working Paper No. 4565, Cambridge/Mass., December

Grossman, Gene and Elhanan Helpman (1990): Comparative Advantage and Long-Run Growth. In: American Economic Review, Vol. 80, pp. 796-815

Holzmann, Robert (1997): Pension Reform, Financial Market Development, and Economic Growth: Preliminary Evidence from Chile. International Monetary Fund Staff Papers, Washington D.C., Vol. 44, No. 2, pp. 149-178

International Monetary Fund: Government Finance Statistics Yearbook. Washington D.C., various issues

International Monetary Fund: International Financial Statistics. Washington D.C., various issues

Leijphart, Arend (1999): Patterns of Democracy, Government Forms and Performance in Thirty-Six Countries. New Haven and London

Levine, Ross and David Renelt (1992): A Sensitivity Analysis of Cross-Country Growth Regressions. In: American Economic Review, Vol. 82, No. 4, pp. 942-963

McLure, Charles Jr. (1995): Comment on Fiscal Federalism and Decentralisation: A Review of Some Efficiency and Macroeconomic Aspects, by Vito Tanzi. In: Michael Bruno and Boris Pleskovic (editors): Annual World Bank Conference on Development Economics 1995. World Bank, Washington D.C., pp. 317-322

Musgrave, Richard A. (1959): The Theory of Public Finance, New York

Oates, Wallace E. (1993): Fiscal Decentralisation and Economic Development. University of Maryland, Working Paper No. 93-94, May

Oates, Wallace E. (1994): The Potential and Perils of Fiscal Decentralisation. University of Maryland

Oates, Wallace E. (1995): Comment on 'Conflicts and Dilemmas of Decentralisation', by Rudolf Hommes, In: Bruno, Michael and Boris Pleskovic (editors): Annual World Bank Conference on Development Economics 1995. World Bank, Washington D.C., pp. 351-353

Oates, Wallace E. (1977): An Economist's Perspective on Fiscal Federalism. In: Wallace E. Oates (editor): The Political Economy of Fiscal Federalism. Lexington, Toronto, pp. 3-20

Panizza, Ugo (1999): On the Determinants of Fiscal Centralisation: Theory and Evidence. In: Journal of Public Economics, Vol. 74, pp. 97-139

Prud'homme, Rémy (1994): On the Dangers of Decentralisation. World Bank Policy Research Working Paper, No. 1252, Washington D.C.

Prud'homme, Rémy (1995): Comment on 'Conflicts and Dilemmas of Decentralisation' by Rudolf Hommes. In: Michael Bruno and Boris Pleskovic (editors): Annual World Bank Conference on Development Economics 1995. World Bank, Washington D.C., pp. 354-359

Romer, Paul (1986): Increasing Returns and Long-Run Growth. In: Journal of Political Economy, Vol. 94, October, pp. 1002-1037

Summers, Robert, Irving B. Kravis, and Alan Heston (1980): International Comparisons of Real Product And Its Composition: 1950-77. In: Review of Income and Wealth, pp. 19-66

Tanzi, Vito (1995): Fiscal Federalism and Decentralisation: A Review of Some Efficiency and Macroeconomic Aspects. In: Michael Bruno and Boris Pleskovic (editors): Annual World Bank Conference on Development Economics 1995. World Bank, Washington D.C., pp. 295-316

Tiebout, Charles M. (1956): A Pure Theory of Local Expenditures. In: Journal of Political Economy, Vol. 64, pp. 416-424

United Nations, UNESCO: Statistical Yearbook, Paris, various issues

Villanueva, Delano (1993): Openness, Human Development, and Fiscal Policies: Effects on Economic Growth and Speed of Adjustment. International Monetary Fund, Working Paper, Washington D.C., July

World Bank: World Development Indicators. Washington D.C., forthcoming

Zhuravskaya, Ekaterina (2000): Incentives to provide public goods: Fiscal Federalism Russian style. In: Journal of Public Economics, Vol. 76, No. 3, pp. 337-368

Appendix

Table 17.2
Income level, growth performance, and fiscal decentralisation of selected Western European and other countries

Country	Income level (GNP per capita in US-Dollars 1998)	Growth performance during 1970-1998 (average annual growth rate of real per capita GDP)	Indicator A of fiscal decentralisation 1)	Indicator B of fiscal decentralisation 2)	Indicator C of fiscal decentralisation 3)	Indicator A' of fiscal decentralisation 4)
Western European countries:						
Luxembourg	43386	5) 2.07	16.5	1.0	0.79	9
Switzerland	40080	1.25	58.2	5.0	-1.53	3
Norway	34330	3.05	38.0	2.0	-0.08	23
Denmark	33260	2.01	56.9	2.0	0.49	5
Austria	26850	2.61	33.5	4.5	-0.37	26
Germany	25850	1.64	46.2	5.0	-1.79	11
Sweden	25620	1.54	42.3	2.0	-0.06	15
Belgium	25380	2.26	12.8	3.2	0.19	7
France	24940	2.06	17.9	1.3	0.36	11
Netherlands	24760	2.70	31.1	3.0	0.33	23
Finland	24110	6) 2.58	44.3	2.0	0.46	13
United Kingdom	21400	2.07	29.3	1.0	1.4	17
Italy	20250	2.27	26.4	1.5	0.01	15
Ireland	18340	3.95	7) 30.0	1.0	0.76	21
Spain	14080	2.47	7) 23.0	3.0	-0.23	13
Greece	11650	2.24	7)8) 4.2	1.0	0.64	1
Portugal	10690	3.49	7) 8.4	1.0	0.61	3
Other selected high income countries:						
Japan	32380	2.97	40.5	2.0	-1.11	19
USA	29340	2.03	50.9	5.0	-1.62	7
Australia	20300	1.95	50.2	5.0	-0.99	9
Canada	20020	2.00	68.5	5.0	-1.22	1
New Zealand	14700	1.07	11.3	1.0	2.16	5
Selected relatively advanced middle income countries:						
Argentina	8970	0.89	37.3	-	-	26
Korea, Rep.	7970	5.92	41.8	-	-	17
Brazil	4570	2.50	38.3	-	-	21
South Africa	2880	0.02	30.0	-	-	19

1) Average share of Government expenditures of lower levels of Government in total Government expenditures during 1975 through 1995. The following shorter periods had to be used for countries whose data are insufficient: Belgium: 1978-95, Greece: 1972-81, Italy: 1985-89, Portugal: 1987-95, Korea: 1976-78, New Zealand, 1978-81 and 1992-98, Brazil: 1975-94, Japan: 1972-74.
2) Classification on the basis of the political organisation in which the activities of Government are divided between regional Governments and the central one. The index rises with increasing fiscal decentralisation. The classification is based on an analysis of the period 1971-1996. See: Arend Lijphart (1999): Patterns of Democracy. Government Forms and Perfomance in Thirty-Six Countries. New Haven and London, p. 313.
3) Classification on the basis of the political and democratic organisation of the country. Note: Contrary to indicators A and B this indicator rises with increasing centralisation! See: Manfred Schmidt (1997): Demokratietheorien. Opladen, p. 245.
4) Indicator A adjusted so that medium values of fiscal decentralisation are transformed into high values whereas low and high values of fiscal decentralisation are transformed into low values. See table 3 for further explanations.
5) 1996.
6) During 1990-1993 Finland experienced a deep recession costing almost 10 percent of GDP. It was mainly caused by external shocks. Eliminating this effect and raising Finland's income accordingly, Finland's rank on this income scale would rise by about 5 places. Hence, without the recession the country's income level would continue to be very close to the other Scandinavian countries. Traditionally, this country group is characterised by a very high degree of fiscal decentralisation.

Table 17.2 (cont.)
Income level, growth performance, and fiscal decentralisation of selected Western European and other countries

Correlation coefficients:							
Correlation between the income level and the indicators of fiscal decentralisation.				Correlation between growth performance and the indicators of fiscal decentralisation			
Indicator A	Indicator B	Indicator C	Indicator A'	Indicator A	Indicator B	Indicator C	Indicator A'
1	0	-0.28	0	-0.38 4)	-0.42	0.46	0
excluding Luxembourg:							
1	1	-0.48	0	-0.42 4)	-0.46	1	0
0	0	-0.70	1	0	0	-0.74	1
1	-	-	0	1	-	-	-0.56

7) During the time period considered, several peripheral countries of the European Union (EU) received substantial net transfers from the EU. Since these transfers have been used to a large extent for infrastructure investment and adaptation of the recipient countries' institutional structure to EU standards they are likely to have had a positive impact on economic growth. Using the data provided by the Government Finance Statistics Yearbook of the IMF, these transfers have been particularly large in the cases of Ireland and Portugal. For instance, during the first half of the 1990s these two countries received annual average net transfers from the EU of about 1 percent and 1.8 percent of their GDP, respectively. According to other sources Ireland received annual net transfers from the EU of up to 7 percent of its GNP in the early 1990s. The positive impact of the transfers on economic growth needs to be considered in a comparison of growth rates of Western European countries. Without this impact the GDP growth rates of the recipient countries may have been lower.
8) Per capita growth of GNP since GDP series are not available over the entire period.
Sources: Income level: World Bank, World Development Report 1999/2000 and World Development Indicators; Growth performance: International Financial Statistics, International Monetary Fund.
Indicators of fiscal decentralisation:
Indicators of fiscal decentralisation: Indicator A: Calculated from Government Finance Statistics Yearbook, International Monetary Fund.
Indicator B: Lijphart, Arend (1999): Patterns of Democracy, Government Forms and Perfomance in Thirty-Six Countries, New Haven and London, p. 313.
Indicator C: Schmidt, Manfred (1997): Demokratietheorien, Opladen, p. 245.

Table 17.3
Derivation of indicator A' of fiscal decentralisation to test for a nonlinear relationship (a hump shaped relation) between economic growth and the degree of fiscal decentralisation:

	Indicator A	Ranking	Indicator A' 1)
Canada	0.684	1	1
Switzerland	0.582	2	3
Denmark	0.569	3	5
United States	0.509	4	7
Australia	0.502	5	9
Germany	0.462	6	11
Finland	0.443	7	13
Sweden	0.423	8	15
Korea	0.418	9	17
Japan	0.405	10	19
Brazil	0.383	11	21
Norway	0.380	12	23
Argentina	0.373	13	26
Austria	0.335	14	26
Netherlands	0.311	15	23
Ireland	0.300	16	21
South Africa	0.299	17	19
United Kingdom	0.293	18	17
Italy	0.257	19	15
Spain	0.230	20	13
France	0.179	21	11
Luxembourg	0.165	22	9
Belgium	0.128	23	7
New Zealand	0.112	24	5
Portugal	0.084	25	3
Greece	0.042	26	1

1) Starting with the lowest and highest values of indicator A these are given a value of one. The next lowest and highest values of indicator A are given higher values and this procedure is continued up to the medium range values of indicator A which receive the highest values. This transformation of indicator A allows to test for a hump shaped relationship between economic growth and fiscal decentralisation, i.e. whether a medium degree of fiscal decentralisation is more likely to be positively related to economic growth than either a relatively low or high degree.

Source: Authors's calculations.

Table 17.4

Cross-sectional growth regressions: Dependent variable: Average annual growth rate of real GDP per capita during 1975 through 1995 1)

Equation	Constant	RGDP70	GPOP	INVGDP	SEC70	CHUER	DEU4	IFDA	IFDA'	SR	CHSR	R2 adjusted	F-statistic	Number of observations
17 Western European countries														
(2a)		-0.022	-0.32	0.08	0.02	-0.01	0.005					0.99	12056.0	17
		(-2.37)*	(-3.88)*	(4.50)*	(4.65)*	(-5.39)*	(4.09)*							
(2b)		-0.021	-0.35	0.09	0.01	-0.01	0.004	0.004				0.99	9432.2	17
		(-2.17)'	(-3.91)*	(3.80)*	(1.42)	(-5.41)*	(2.75)*	(0.90)						
(2c)		-0.023	-0.21	0.07	0.01	-0.01	0.004		0.03			0.99	411.9	17
		(-1.83)'	(-2.22)'	(3.38)*	(2.24)*	(-4.34)*	(2.18)'		(4.42)*					
(2d)		-0.018	-0.16	0.10	0.01	-0.01	0.004	0.006		-0.012	-0.10	1.00	5918916	17
		(-2.13)'	(-1.42)	(5.39)*	(1.51)	(-6.22)*	(2.34)*	(0.96)		(-2.75)*	(-2.86)*			
(2e)		-0.015	0.04	0.09	0.01	-0.007	0.003		0.02	-0.014	-0.06	0.98	116.1	17
		(-2.07)'	(0.28)	(7.13)*	(2.37)*	(-5.16)*	(1.80)		(2.82)*	(-3.42)*	(-1.83)			
25 countries 2):														
(2f)		-0.037	-0.30	0.13	0.01	-0.02						0.99	430.5	25
		(-4.93)*	(-2.89)*	(10.86)*	(3.14)*	(-4.84)*								
(2g)	-0.007	-0.038	-0.005	0.17	0.01	-0.01		0.015		-0.02	-0.25	0.99	548.7	25
	(-2.12)'	(-4.86)*	(-0.04)	(11.54)*	(3.71)*	(-9.21)*		(6.71)*		(-7.80)*	(-5.55)*			
(2h)	-0.019	-0.020	0.254	0.20	0.02	-0.01			0.018	-0.02	-0.24	0.99	412.6	25
	(-3.34)*	(-2.56)*	(2.68)*	(9.28)*	(8.10)*	(-6.74)*			(1.97)'	(-7.38)*	(-4.95)*			
All 26 countries:														
(2i)	-0.018	-0.036	-0.52	0.18	0.01							0.99	2224.3	26
	(-4.28)*	(-5.24)*	(-4.54)*	(12.52)*	(3.27)*									
(2j)	-0.02	-0.02	-0.34	0.21	0.02			0.012		-0.02	-0.15	0.99	255.0	26
	(-4.72)*	(-2.56)*	(-1.47)	(11.45)*	(2.89)*			(5.74)*		(-6.16)*	(-6.07)*			
(2k)	-0.028	-0.041	-0.19	0.21	0.02				0.01	-0.02	-0.15	1.00	11927.8	26
	(-4.81)*	(-0.54)	(-1.01)	(10.0)*	(5.20)*				(1.44)	(-4.82)*	(-3.22)*			

1) Variable definitions are:
RGDP70: Real income in 1970 from the Summers, Kravis, Heston (1980) income table; DEU4: Dummy variable for four European countries that received considerable net transfers from the European Union which may have influenced their growth rate, i.e. Greece, Ireland, Portugal and Spain
GPOP: Average annual growth rate of the population during 1995-95; INVGDP: Average annual share of gross investment in GDP during 1975-95,
SEC70: Secondary school enrollment ratio in 1970, SEC: Average school enrollment ratio during 1975-95;
CHUER: Average annual change of the unemployment rate during 1975-95; IFDA: Indicator of fiscal decentralisation A from table 2.
IFDA': Indicator of fiscal decentralisation A' from table 2; SR: Self-reliance ratio: Average share of own revenues of lower levels of government in their total revenues during the period 1975-95, CHSR: Average change of the self-reliance ratio during 1975-95.
2) All countries listed in table 2 excluding South Africa due to missing unemployment data.
Note: GLS method (with cross section weights) is used. T-statistics in parentheses, * indicates significance of the respective variable at the 95 percent probability level or higher.
' indicates significance at the 90 to 95 percent probability level.
Source: Own calculations

Table 17.5
Pooled cross-sectional growth regressions: Dependent variable: Annual growth rate of real GDP per capita 1)

							Dummy variables	
Equation	Constant	GDPR(-1)	GPOP	GKAP	SEC	CHUER	DEU5	DLI
16 Western European countries (Europe 17 excluding Greece):								
(3a)	0.02		-0.60	0.13	0.002	-0.004	0.005	
	(3.04)*		(-15.68)*	(10.59)*	(0.48)	(-4.70)*	(2.52)*	
17 Western European countries:								
(3b)	0.016		-0.59	0.11	0.001	-0.005	0.004	
	(3.13)*		(-15.14)*	(10.11)*	(0.24)	(-6.08)*	(2.53)*	
(3c)			- 0.59	0.11	-0.001	-0.005	0.004	
			(-16.74)*	(10.09)*	(-0.18)	(-5.99)*	(1.81)'	
15 Western European countries (Europe 17 excluding Greece and Portugal):								
(3d)			- 0.61	0.14	-0.001	-0.004	0.005	
			(-17.40)*	(10.60)*	(-0.21)	(-4.13)*	(2.44)*	
22 countries (full sample from table 2 except Greece, Japan, Korea, South Africa):								
(3e)	0.015		-0.61	0.14	0.003	-0.006		0.003
	(2.99)*		(-16.49)*	(12.42)*	(0.60)	(-6.81)*		(1.77)'
25 countries (full sample except South Africa):								
(3f)			-0.60	0.13	0.003	-0.007		0.006
			(-15.67)*	(11.94)*	(0.74)	(-7.79)*		(2.87)*
26 countries (full sample):								
(3g)			-0.67	0.18	0.003			0.003
			(-14.66)*	(20.80)*	(0.62)			(1.79)'
21 countries (full sample except Greece, Portugal, Japan, Korea, South Africa):								
(3h)			-0.61	0.14	-0.0001	-0.005		-0.004
			(-18.08)*	(13.39)*	(-0.02)	(-6.28)*		(-1.87)'
6 non-European countries (Australia, Canada, USA, Argentina, Brazil, South Africa):								
(3i)			-1.32	0.20	0.025			
			(-4.09)*	(7.94)*	(1.39)			
9 countries with relatively "low" per capita income (Greece, Ireland, Portugal, Spain, Argentina, Brazil, Korea, South Africa):								
(3j)		0.07	-1.50	0.13	-0.004			
		(1.19)	(-7.46)*	(8.51)*	(-0.43)			
12 countries with highest per capita income 2):								
(3k)		-0.10	-0.55	0.1	-0.004	-0.009		
		(-2.11)*	(-14.36)*	(6.18)*	(-0.48)	(-5.86)*		

1) Annual data for the period 1981 through 1995 using 17 Western European countries and 9 other countries. Variable definitions: GDPR (-1): Per capita real GDP growth rate lagged one period: GPOP: Growth rate of the population: GKAP: Growth rate of real gross fixed capital formation used as a proxy for growth of the real capital stock: Gross fixed capital formation is deflated using the producer price index, or, if not available, the CPI, in order to obtain real gross investment. Under the assumption that real capital stock depreciation is a relatively stable share of real gross investment, the latter is highly positively correlated with real net investment and thus also with the change of the real capital stock, since real net investment equals the change in the real capital stock. SEC: Annual secondary school enrollment ratio; CHUER: Annual change of the unemployment rate: DEU5 and DLI are dummies to consider the "convergence" hypothesis: DEU5: Dummy for five European countries wih relatively "low" initial income, i.e. Greece, Ireland, Portugal, Spain and Italy: DLI: Dummy for European and non-European countries with relatively low "initial" income, i.e. Greece, Ireland, Italy, Portugal, Spain, Argentina, Brazil, Korea, New Zealand, South Africa. IFDA: Indicator of fiscal decentralisation, see footnote 1, table 17.2. IFDL, IFDM, IFDH are indicators of fiscal decentralisation which allow to test for non-linear effects of fiscal decentralisation using a spline function. The function breaks at the values 0.3 and 0.45 of indicator A in table 17.2: FDL ("low fiscal decentralisation") is the value of fiscal decentralisation when indicator A is 30 percent or less. FDM ("medium fiscal decentralisation") is the value of fiscal decentralisation when indicator A is between 30 and 45 percent.

Table 17.5 (cont.)
Pooled cross-sectional growth regressions: Dependent variable: Annual growth rate of real GDP per capita 1)

Fiscal decentralisation variables								Number of
IFDA	FDL	FDM	FDH	SR	CHSR	R2 adjusted	F-statistic	Observations
-0.006						0.70	96.1	241
(-0.89)								
						0.69	113.6	255
	0.017	0.018	0.013			0.70	84.0	255
	(3.25)*	(3.13)*	(2.38)*					
	0.018	0.018	0.014	-0.001	0.04	0.72	67.0	234
	(2.60)*	(2.37)*	(1.78)'	(-0.14)	(1.62)			
0.002						0.69	125.1	331
(0.41)								
	0.0134	0.0158	0.0163			0.66	103.3	375
	(2.81)*	(3.32)*	(3.58)*					
	0.012	0.013	0.015			0.63	111.9	390
	(2.56)*	(2.65)*	(3.07)*					
	0.020	0.022	0.021	-0.006	0.05	0.83	168.0	312
	(3.55)*	(3.56)*	(3.49)*	(-1.37)	(2.24)*			
	0.014	0.038	0.021	-0.026	0.06	0.57	18.2	93
	(0.76)	(2.19)*	(1.14)	(-1.38)	(0.56)			
	0.026	0.031	0.063			0.71	56.3	135
	(3.04)*	(3.31)*	(5.87)*					
	0.021	0.024	0.021	0.0006	0.11	0.72	51.9	180
	(2.19)*	(2.32)*	(2.05)*	(0.08)	(2.26)*			

FDH ("high fiscal decentralisation") is the value of fiscal decentralisation when indicator A is above 45 percent. SR: Self-reliance ratio of lower levels of Government, measured by the share of their own revenues relative to their total revenues; CHSR: Change of the self-reliance ratio. Note: GLS method is used (cross section weights). T-statistics in parentheses: * indicates significance of the respective variable at the 95 percent probability level or higher: ' indicates significance at the 90 to 95 percent probability level. The countries considered are those shown in tables 2 and 3 with the following exceptions due to insufficient data: IFDA could not be constructed for Greece, Japan and Korea: CHUER is missing for South Africa: SR and CHSR are not available for Greece, Portugal, Japan, Korea, New Zealand.

2) Austria, Belgium, Denmark, Finland, France, Germany, Luxembourg, Netherlands, Norway, Sweden, Switzerland, USA.

Source: Own calculations.

Portugal, Lux. Italy, Switzerland, New Zealand : iffa 81-95 missing panel data completed by judgement: ifdl, m, h possible

Greece: assuming ifdl, because of data up to 1981; but iff no data and not possible to complete even with judgement

Japan and Korea: data only available for early 1970s with rising iff index in about the medium range: from then on no data on iff: we assume Japan ifdm (medium range): Korea ifdh (high range).

in sum: iffa missing for Greece, Japan, Korea.

ifdl, ifdm, ifdh constructed for all 26 countries

Table 17.6

Pooled cross-sectional regressions: Capital formation as a function of macroeconomic policy variables and external factors 1)

Equation	Constant	GKAP(-1)	FBGDP	GCPI	STDDC	CHUER	DEU4	DLI	IFDA	FDL	FDM	FDH	SR	CHSR	R2 adjusted	F-statistic	Number of observations
16 Western European countries:																	
(4a)	0.063	0.19	0.15	-0.41	-0.09	-0.04	0.04		-0.01						0.56	45.4	241
	(4.75)*	(3.70)*	(1.45)	(-4.45)*	(-2.12)*	(-10.45)*	(3.60)*		(-0.46)								
17 Western European countries:																	
(4b)		0.17	0.17	-0.34	-0.08	-0.04	0.05			0.055	0.06	0.052			0.54	38.7	255
		(3.22)*	(1.58)	(-3.41)*	(-2.04)*	(-10.78)*	(4.08)*			(6.01)*	(7.03)*	(5.78)*					
15 Western European countries (excluding Greece and Portugal):																	
(4c)		0.18	0.22	-0.48	-0.05	-0.04	0.04			0.041	0.045	0.031	0.35	0.16	0.61	36.3	229
		(3.45)*	(1.90)'	(-5.60)*	(-1.33)	(-10.4)*	(3.32)*			(2.64)*	(2.50)*	(1.64)	(1.51)	(1.64)			
21 countries (full sample except Greece, Portugal, Korea, Japan and New Zealand):																	
(4d)		0.15	0.063	-0.008	0.002	-0.04'		0.027	0.007				0.044	0.19	0.51	40.7	307
		(3.12)*	(0.67)	(-2.68)*	(0.42)	(-12.93)*		(2.47)*	(0.31)				(2.98)*	(1.88)'			
21 countries (full sample except Greece, Portugal, Korea, Japan and New Zealand):																	
(4e)		0.138	0.16	-0.008	0.002	-0.042		0.024		0.021	0.029	0.021	0.018	0.19	0.510	32.9	307
		(2.97)*	(1.56)	(-2.64)*	(0.42)	(-12.94)*		(2.18)*		(1.57)	(1.77)'	(1.29)	(0.82)	(1.89)'			
26 countries (full sample):																	
(4f)		0.4	0.13	-0.01	0.003			0.015		0.014	0.026	0.023			0.23	17.6	390
		(8.93)*	(1.37)	(-2.84)*	(0.89)			(1.48)		(1.64)	(3.49)*	(3.34)*					
9 countries with relatively "low" income (Greece, Ireland, Portugal, Spain, Argentina, Brazil, Korea, New Zealand, South Africa):																	
(4g)		0.3	0.0003	-0.01	0.004					0.014	0.029	0.098			0.27	9.2	135
		(3.92)*	(0.001)	(-3.22)*	(1.07)					-0.85	-1.23	(4.43)*					
12 countries with highest per capita income 2):																	
(4h)		0.16	0.2	-0.45	-0.07	-0.044				0.048	0.061	0.048	0.012	0.27	0.58	28.5	180
		(2.64)*	(1.69)'	(-3.61)*	(-1.48)	(-10.00)*				(2.27)*	(2.52)*	(2.01)*	(0.41)	(1.26)			

1) Dependent variable: GKAP, proxy for the growth rate of the real capital stock, see table 5. FBGDP: Fiscal balance as a share of GDP. GKAP(-1): Proxy for the growth rate of the real capital stock lagged one period; GCPI: Inflation (growth rate of the CPI), STDDC: Standard deviation of domestic credit growth as a proxy for uncertainty of financial variables on the part of economic agents. The standard deviation is calculated for overlapping five year periods where the last 4 years, the current year and the following year are considered; other variable definitions: see tables 4 and 5

Note: GLS method is applied (with cross section weights) using annual data for the period 1981 through 1995 for the same countries as explained in table 4

T-statistics in parentheses, * indicates significance of the respective variable at the 95 percent probability level or higher,

' indicates significance at the 90 to 95 percent probability level

2) Austria, Belgium, Denmark, Finland, France, Germany, Luxembourg, Netherlands, Norway, Sweden, Switzerland, USA. (Japan excluded due to missing data).

Source: Own calculations.

Table 17.7

Pooled cross-sectional regressions: Total factor productivity growth and fiscal decentralisation 1)

Equation	RES (-1)	UER (-1)	DE4	FDL	FDM	FDH	SR	CHSR	R2 adjusted	F-statistic	Number of observations
17 Western European countries:											
(5a)	0.3	-0.0008		0.016	0.012	0.003			0.18	14.8	255
	(5.18)*	(-2.86)*		(4.99)*	(4.01)*	(0.97)					
15 Western European countries:											
(5b)	0.34	-0.0008		0.016	0.011	0.003	-3.3 E-05	-0.007	0.25	13.3	229
	(5.96)*	(-3.21)*		(3.59)*	(2.27)*	(0.55)	(-0.005)	(-0.24)			
8 countries with relatively "low" income (Greece, Ireland, Portugal, Spain, Argentina, Brazil, Korea):											
(5c)	0.12	-0.001	0.016	0.005	0.011	0.018			0.1	3.6	121
	(1.39)	(-2.97)*	(2.28)*	(0.85)	(1.51)*	(2.46)*					
15 countries with highest per capita income 2):											
(5d)	0.29	0.0003		0.011	0.006	0.003			0.14	10.2	225
	(4.66)*	(-0.71)		(2.62)*	(2.33)*	(0.98)					

1) Total factor productivity is the Solow residual (RES). Due to data constraints it is calculated assuming a constant labour share of 0.65, i.e.: RESit = GDPRit - 0.35 GRKAPit - 0.65 GLAFOit , where GLAFO is the growth rate of the labour force, i = 1, ... 26; t = 1981-1995.

2) Austria, Belgium, Denmark, Finland, France, Germany, Italy, Japan, Luxembourg, Netherlands, Norway, Sweden, Switzerland, United Kingdom, USA.

Note: GLS method is applied (with cross section weights) using annual data for the period 1981 through 1995 for the same countries as explained in table 5, footnote 1). T-statistics in parentheses; * indicates significance of the respective variable at the 95 percent probability level or higher; ' indicates significance at the 90 to 95 percent probability level.

Source: Own calculations.

Maps

Ukraine in Europe

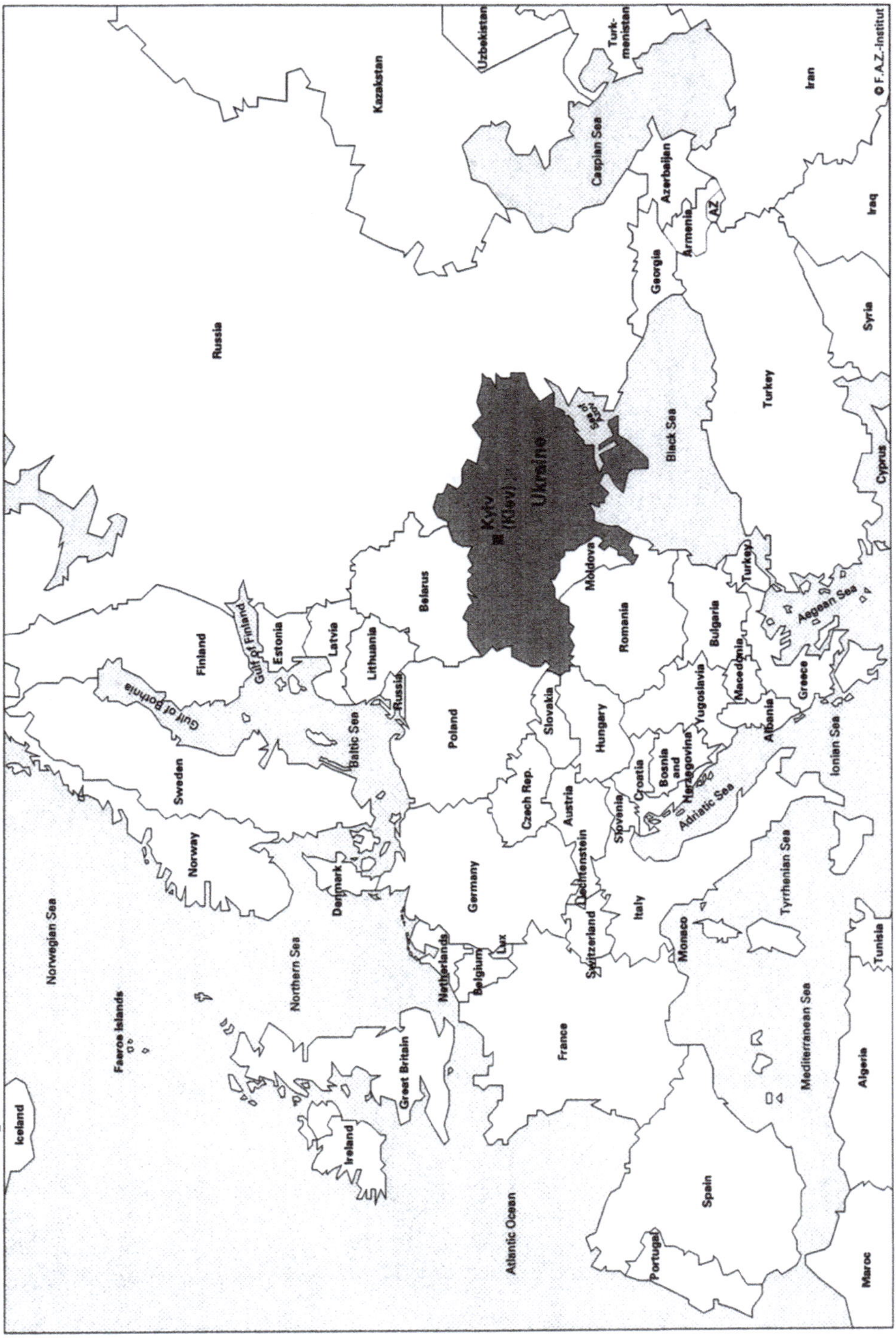

Ukraine: Administrative map

Ukraine: Economic map

Statistical Annex

Macroeconomic Indicators for Ukraine 1992-1999

	1992	1993	1994	1995	1996	1997	1998	1999
Macroeconomic development								
GDP, real (% change, yoy)	16.8	-14.2	-23.0	-11.8	-10.0	-3.2	-1.9	-0.4
Gross industrial output (% change, yoy)	-6.4	-7.6	-27.2	-11.5	-5.1	-2.0	-1.67	3.14
Agricultural output (% change, yoy)	-8.3	1.5	-17.0	-3.9	-9.0	-2.0	-9.8	-5.7
Capital investment (% change, yoy)	-36.9	-10.3	-25.0	-35.0	-22.0	-7.5	6.1	2.9
Inflation rate (CPI in %, Dec./Dec.)	2,100	10,255	401	182	40	10	20.0	19.2
Sector shares (in % of GDP)								
Industry	44.6	27.6	35.0	34.6	31.0	28.4	29.8	33.2
Construction	7.5	7.2	7.4	7.7	6.7	5.9	5.6	5.2
Agriculture	20.6	18.4	14.3	14.9	13.3	13.9	13.7	12.8
Trade	6.5	10.1	7.3	5.9	6.4	9.1	8.7	9.0
Services and other	20.8	36.7	36.0	36.9	42.6	42.7	42.2	39.8
Foreign Trade								
Exports of goods and services (bn. USD)	11.3	8.6	10.2	12.7	15.5	15.4	17.62	16.23
Imports of goods and services (bn. USD)	11.9	11.1	12.7	15.3	19.8	19.6	18.83	15.24
of which: energy imports (as a % of total imports)	n.a.	49	44	45	48	45.89	40.36	44.87
Current account deficit (bn. USD)	0.62	0.85	1.40	1.52	1.18	1.29	1.3	-0.83
Foreign debt (bn. USD)	3.51	4.21	7.17	8.14	9.2	9.6	11.48	12.44

Sources: MinStat Ukraine, MinEcon Ukraine, World Bank, EU-TACIS

Suggested Reading

I Policy, History, Culture

Alexandrova, Olga (1997): Die Partnerschaft NATO-Ukraine. Berichte des Bundesinstituts für ostwissenschaftliche und internationale Studien, Köln

Hawrylyshyn, Bohdan (1997): Ukraine: Recent Past, Current State, Future Prospects. In: European Space, Baltic Space, Polish Space, No. 2, pp. 221-234

Holowaty, Serhij (1993): Ukraine. In: Weidenfeld, Werner (Hrsg.): Demokratie und Marktwirtschaft in Europa, Gütersloh, pp. 239-252

Kuzio, Taras (1999): Contemporary Ukraine - Dynamics of Post-Soviet Transformation. Armonk, NY, Sharpe, Vol. XXI

Lüdemann, Ernst (1997): Die Auseinandersetzung mit der kommunistischen Vergangenheit in der Ukraine. Berichte des Bundesinstituts für ostwissenschaftliche und internationale Studien Nr. 39, Köln

Malinovska, Olena (1996): Migration und Migrationspolitik in der Ukraine nach 1991. Berichte des Bundesinstituts für ostwissenschaftliche und internationale Studien Nr. 42, Köln

Motyl, Alexander J. (1993): Dilemmas of Independence: Ukraine After Totalitarism. Council on Foreign Relations Press, Vol. XV, New York

Ohliger, Rainer and Rainer Münz (1999): Die Ukraine nach der Unabhängigkeit: Nationsbildung zwischen Ost und West. Berichte des Bundesinstituts für ostwissenschaftliche und internationale Studien, Köln

Ott, Alexander (1997): Wer hat die reale Macht in der Ukraine? Berichte des Bundesinstituts für ostwissenschaftliche und internationale Studien, Köln

Ott, Alexander (1999): Die unterschiedlichen außenpolitischen Positionen der ukrainischen Elite. Berichte des Bundesinstituts für ostwissenschaftliche und internationale Studien, Köln

Potichnyi, Peter J. (1997): Formation of Political Parties in Ukraine. Berichte des Bundesinstituts für ostwissenschaftliche und internationale Studien, Köln

Salmon, Benedikt (1997): Die ukrainischen orthodoxen Kirchen 1997. Berichte des Bundesinstituts für ostwissenschaftliche und internationale Studien, Köln

Sasse, Gwendolyn (1998): Die Krim: regionale Autonomie in der Ukraine. Berichte des Bundesinstituts für ostwissenschaftliche und internationale Studien Nr. 39, Köln

Sundakov, Alex (1999): Transition Crisis: Is Crisis Management Delaying Transition? In: Siedenberg, Axel and Lutz Hoffmann (eds.) (1999): Ukraine at the Crossroads: Economic Reforms in International Perspective. Physica-Verl., Heidelberg New York, pp. 111-118

Van Zon, Hans, Andre Batako and Anna Kreslavska (1998): Social and Economic Change in Eastern Ukraine: The Example of Zaporizhzhia. Ashgate Publishing Limited

Wittkowsky, Andreas (1997): Fünf Jahre ohne Plan: die Ukraine 1991-96: Nationalstaatsbildung, Wirtschaft und Eliten. Hamburg

Wittkowsky, Andreas (1997): Ukrainian Simulations in the Transitional Period. Deutsches Institut für Entwicklungspolitik, Berlin, Dezember

Wittkowsky, Andreas (2000): The Ukrainian Disease: Rent-seeking, the Debt Economy,and Chances to Harden Budget Constraints. Deutsches Institut für Entwicklungspolitik, Berlin, April

Yekelchyk, Serhy (1998): The Making of a 'Proletarian Capital': Patterns of Stalinist Social Policy in Kiev in the Mid-1930s. In: Europe-Asia Studies, No. 50, pp. 1229-1244

II Eureopean Integration

Dunn, John F. (1995): The Situation in Ukraine and Its Implications for the European Union's Common Foreign and Security Policy. CEPS Working Document No. 92, Brussels, 1995

Europäischer Rat (1998): Gemeinsame Strategie 1999 für die Ukraine. Europa-Dokumente No.68/69, Luxembourg

Kempe, Iris, Wim van Meurs and Barbara von Ow (1999): Die EU-Beitrittsstaaten und ihre östlichen Nachbarn (The EU Accession States and Their Eastern Neighbours). Gütersloh, Verl. Bertelsmann-Stiftung

Ponomarenko, Anatolij (1999): Die europäische Orientierung der Ukraine: Dekret des Präsidenten der Ukraine über die Strategie der Integration der Ukraine in die Europäische Union: Partnerschaftsabkommen zwischen der EU und der Ukraine. Zentrum für Europäische Integrationsforschung, ZEI-Discussion Paper No. 39, Bonn

III The Real Economy: Structural Aspects of Transformation

Aghion, Philippe and Simon Commander (1999): On the Dynamics of Inequality in the Transition. In: The Economics of Transition, Vol. 7, No. 2, pp. 275-298

Akimova, Iryna (1998): Promyshlennoye proisvodstvo: rynochnaya orientatsiya i strateghii rasvitiya. Bisnes Inform, Kharkiv

Akimova, Iryna and Gerhard Schwödiauer (2000): Restructuring of Ukrainian Enterprises after Privatization: Does Ownership Structure Matter? In: Atlantic Economic Journal, March

Åslund, Anders and Georges de Ménil (eds.) (2000): Economic Reform in Ukraine – The Unfinished Agenda. M.E. Sharpe, New York

Banian, King (1999): The Ukrainian Economy Since Independence. Studies of Communism in Transition, Cheltenham

Blanchard, Olivier Jean (1999): The Economics of Post-Communist Transition. Oxford

Bofinger, Peter, Simon Commander, Fabrizio Coricelli, Evgeniy Gavrilenko, Barry. W. Ickes, Dalia Marin, Jan A. Poser, Monika Schaffer and Volkhart Vincentz: The Non-Cash Economy in CIS: In quest of policy recommendations. In: Economic Systems, Vol. 24, Issue 1, 2000, pp. 51 - 98

Buck, Trevor (1999): Corporate Governance and Employee Ownership in an Economic Crisis: Enterprise Strategies in the Former USSR. In: Journal of Comparative Economics: The Journal of the Association for Comparative Economic Studies, Vol. 27, No. 3, pp. 459-474

Clement, Hermann (1999): Wirtschaftsentwicklung in ausgewählten mittel- und osteuropäischen Ländern 1998/99. Arbeiten aus dem Osteuropa-Institut, München

Commander, Simon and Mark Schankerman (1997): Enterprise Restructuring and Social Benefits. EBRD, Working Papers No. 22, London

Commander, Simon and Christian Mumssen (1999): Understanding Barter in Russia. EBRD Working Paper No. 37, London

Cornelius, Peter and Patrick Lenain (1997): Ukraine: Accelerating the Transition to Market. Proceedings of an IMF/Work Bank Seminar, Washington D.C.

Cramon-Taubadel, Stephan von and Ludwig Striewe (1999): Die Transformation der Landwirtschaft in der Ukraine: Ein weites Feld, Kiel, Vauk-Verl.

Djankov Simeon (1999): Ownership Structure and Enterprise Restructuring in Six Newly Independent States. In: Policy Research Working Paper No. 2047,World Bank

Dobczansky, Jurij (1998): Ukrainian Economic Literature in the Library of Congress, 1992-1998: A Selected Bibliography. In: Ukrainian Economic Review, Vol. 3, pp. 183-202

Egorov, Igor (1995): The Transformation of R&D Potential in Ukraine. In: Europe-Asia Studies, Vol. 47, No. 4, pp. 651-668

Egorova, Victoria and James M. Otto (1998): Restructuring the Ukrainian Coal Industry. In: Resources Policy. Vol. 24, No.3, pp. 157–166

Estrin, Saul and Adam Rosevear (1999a): Enterprise Performance and Corporate Governance in Ukraine. In: Journal of Comparative Economics: The Journal of the Association for Comparative Economic Studies, Vol. 27, No. 3, pp. 442-458

Estrin, Saul and Adam Rosevear (1999b): Enterprise Performance and Ownership: The Case of Ukraine. In: European Economic Review, Vol. 43, pp. 1125-1136

European Bank for Reconstruction and Development (EBRD): Transition Report. London, yearly issues

Gray, Cheryl (1996): In Search of Owners: Lessons of Experience with Privatization and Corporate Governance. Policy Research Working Paper No. 1595, World Bank

Hansen, John and Diana Cook (1999): Economic Growth with Equity – Which Strategy for Ukraine? World Bank Discussion Paper No. 408, Washington D.C.

Hansen, John and Vira Nanivska (eds.) (1999): Economic Growth with Equity – Ukrainian Perspectives. World Bank Discussion Paper No. 407, Washington D.C.

Havrylyshyn, Oleh (1997): Economic Reform in Ukraine. In: Macroeconomic Stabilization in Transition Economies, Cambridge, pp. 281-310

Hirschhausen, Christian R. von (1998): Industrial Restructuring in Ukraine Seven Years After Independence: From Socialism to a Planning Economy? In: Communist Economies & Economic Transformation, Vol. 10, No. 4, pp. S. 451 - 465

Hoffmann, Lutz and Axel Siedenberg (eds.) (1997): Aufbruch in die Marktwirtschaft: Reformen in der Ukraine von innen betrachtet. Frankfurt/Main, Campus.

Horn, Manfred (1999): Energy Demand Until 2010 in Ukraine. In: Energy Policy, Vol. 27, No. 12, pp. 713-726

Kaufmann, Daniel (1997): The Missing Pillar of a Growth Strategy for Ukraine: Institutional and Policy Reforms for Private Sector Development. Harvard Institute for Internat. Development, Development Discussion Paper No. 603, Cambridge/Mass

Konings, Jozef and Patrick Paul Walsh (1999): Disorganization in the Process of Transition: Firm-level Evidence from Ukraine. In: The Economics of Transition, Vol. 7, No. 1, pp. 29-46

Konings, Jozef, Patrick Paul Walsh and Larisa Krivenko (1999): Theoretical-Methodological Concepts of Market Strategy of a Firm in the Process of Integration of Ukraine into the EU. In: Osteuropa-Wirtschaft, Vol. 44, No. 4, pp. 392-402

Leshchenko, Larisa and Valerij Ravenko (1999): Privatization and Restructuring in Ukraine. In: Paul Hare, Judy Batt, Martine Cave and Saul Estrin: Reconstituting the Market: The Political Economy of Microeconomic Transformation, London, Harwood Academic press

Lukas, Zdenek (1999): Agriculture in Transition: Widening Gap Between the CEECs and Russia and Ukraine. Forschungsberichte des Wiener Instituts für Internat. Wirtschaftsvergleiche, Wien

Lunina, Inna A. and Christian R. Hirschhausen (1998): Restrukturizatsiya ugolnoy promyzhlennosti: evropeyskiy opyt i situatsiya v Ukraine. In: Voprosy ekonomiki, Vol. 70, No. 5, pp. 90 - 102

Marin, Dalia and Monika Schnitzer (1999): Disorganisation and Financial Collapse. Münchener wirtschaftswissenschaftliche Beiträge, No. 99-14

Mirucki, Jean (1999): A Visibility Analysis of the Scientific Production of Ukrainian Economists: 1969–94. In: The Journal of Socio-Economics, Vol. 28, No. 2, pp. 185-196

Opitz, Petra (1999): Neslushniy chas dlya deregulatsii? – Prichini zanepadu restrukturizatsii energetichnoho sektory Ukrainii. In: Ekonomist, No.6, June

Ritzen Jo, William Easterly and Michael Woolcock (2000): On 'Good' Politicians and 'Bad' Policies: Social Cohesion, Institutions, and Growth. In: Policy Research Working Paper No. 2448, World Bank

Schulze, Eberhard (1999): Eigentumsverhältnisse landwirtschaftlicher Betriebe und Unternehmen in Rußland und in der Ukraine: Befragungsergebnisse aus den Regionen Nowosibirsk und Shitomir. IAMO (Institut für Agrarentwicklung in Mittel- und Osteuropa), Discussion Paper No. 18, Halle/Saale

Siedenberg, Axel and Lutz Hoffmann (eds.) (1999): Ukraine at the Crossroads: Economic Reforms in International Perspective. Physica-Verl., Heidelberg New York

Thede, Sighelm (1999): Die Entwicklung der Unternehmensstrukturen in der Ukraine. In: Osteuropa-Wirtschaft, Vol. 44, No. 3, pp 241-256

Thießen, Ulrich (2000): Zum wirtschaftspolitischen Reformschritt der Ukraine und zur Konditionalität der westlichen Hilfe. Deutsches Institut für Wirtschaftsforschung/DIW – Diskussionspapier Nr. 192, Berlin

Thießen, Ulrich (2000): Ukraine: Beschleunigt sich der Reformprozeß nach dem Regierungswechsel? In: DIW-Wochenbericht, Deutsches Institut für Wirtschaftsforschung/DIW, Berlin, Vol. 67, Nr. 4/5, pp. 43-53

Thomas, Steve (1999): Economic and Safety Pressures on Nuclear Power: A Comparison of Russia and Ukraine Since the Break-up of the Soviet Union. In: Energy Policy, Vol. 27, No. 13, pp. 745-767

USAID (1999): Small and Medium Enterprises. Baseline Survey, Kyiv, December

VanAtta, Don (1998): Household Budgets in Ukraine : A Research Report. In: Post-Soviet Geography and Economics: Formerly Post-Soviet Geography, Vol. 39, No. 10, pp. 606-616

Vincentz, Volkhart and Wolfgang Quaisser (1998): Wachstumsfaktoren in Transformationsländern. Arbeiten aus dem Osteuropa-Institut München

Weller, Stephan (1998): Absatz- und Bezugssysteme in der ukrainischen Landwirtschaft: Heutige Situation und Entwicklungsmöglichkeiten. Fachverl. Koehler, Giessen

Warzynski, Frederic (2000): The Causes and Consequences of Managerial Change in Ukraine and the Complimentary of Reforms. LICOS Discussion Paper No. 88, Leuven

Wiener Institut für Internat. Wirtschaftsvergleiche (1999): Countries in Transition 1999: Bulgaria, Croatia, Czech Republic, Hungary, Poland, Romania, Russia, Slovak Republic, Slovenia, Ukraine. Bratislava, GOYA (WIIW handbook of statistics)

Wittkowsky, Andreas (1998): Die Unterstützung langsamer Transformationsländer: Ansätze und Erfahrungen in der Ukraine. Deutsches Institut für Entwicklungspolitik/DIE, Berlin

IV Financial and Fiscal Aspects

Bofinger, Peter, Heiner Flassbeck and Lutz Hoffmann (1997): Orthodox Money-Based Stabilization (OMBS) Versus Heterodox Exchange Rate-Based Stabilization (HERBS): The Case of Russia, the Ukraine and Kazakhstan. In: Economic Systems, Vol. 21, No. 1, pp. 1-33

Clement, Hermann und Michael Knogler (1998): Entwicklung und Reform des Finanzsektors in der Ukraine: die wirtschaftliche Entwicklung 1996/97. Arbeiten aus dem Osteuropa-Institut No. 205, München

Evstigneev, Vladimir R. (1998): Estimating the Opening-up Shock: An Optimal Portfolio Approach to Would-be Integration of the C.I.S. Financial Markets. In: Review of Economies in Transition, Vol. 6, pp. 23-61

Janssen, Volker (1996): External Financial Assistance and Structural Blockades: The Case of Ukraine. In: Transformation Strategies and the Role of Economic Assistance to Central and East Europe, Leipzig, pp. 97–10

Kaufmann, Daniel and Aleksander Kaliberda (1996): An 'Unofficial' Analysis of Economies in Transition: An Empirical Framework and Lessons for Policy. Harvard Institute for Internat. Development, Development Discussion Papers No. 558, Cambridge/Mass.

Kravchuk, Robert S. (1998): Budget Deficits, Hyperinflation, and Stabilization in Ukraine 1991–96. In: Public Budgeting & Finance, Vol. 18, No. 4, pp. 45-70

Sochan, Peter (1998): The Banking System in Ukraine. In: Russian & East European Finance and Trade: A Journal of Translations, Vol. 34, No. 3, pp. 70-93

Vakhnenko, Tatyana (1998): Vremya gosudarstvennogo dolga: teoreticheskiy aspekt. In: Ekonomika Ukrainy: politiko-ekonomicheskiy zhurnal Ministerstva Ekonomiki Ukrainy, No. 3, pp. 21-30

Vincentz, Volkhart (1998): Währungskrisen und Verschuldung Osteuropas: Gutachten unter dem Titel: Kontinuierliche Berichterstattung zu den Auswirkungen der Transformation auf die Beziehungen Deutschlands mit Osteuropa. Osteuropa-Institut München

Tables

Graphs

The Authors

Iryna Akimova, Ph.D.: Director of the Institute for Economic Research and Policy Consulting, Kyiv, founded by the Ukrainian Government and the German Advisory Group on Economic Reforms with the Ukrainian Government. Associate Professor of Economics at the Kharkiv State Polytechnic University. Teaching and research in macro-economics, and economic reforms in transition countries. Particular focus on corporate restructuring development of the small business sector in Eastern Europe.

Dieter Biehl, Dr.rer.pol.: Director of the Institute of Structural Research at the Universität Frankfurt/Main, Professor emeritus of Public Economics. Managing Editor of the Journal Public Finance/Finances Publiques. Research and publications in public economics, European integration and regional development.

Herbert Brücker, Dr.rer.pol.: Research Associate at the German Institute for Economic Research (DIW), Berlin. Specialises in international and institutional economics. Previous positions at the German Institute for Development Policy (DIE), Berlin, and the Universität Frankfurt/Main.

Charles Clover: Kyiv Correspondent with the Financial Times. Graduated with an MA from Johns Hopkins SAIS, and from the University of Wisconsin at Madison. Fulbright Scholarship in Jordan.

Stephan von Cramon-Taubadel, Dr.sc.agr.: Professor of Agricultural Policy at the Universität Göttingen, and member of the German Advisory Group with the Ukrainian Government in Kyiv. Editor-in-Chief of Agricultural Economics. Research in agricultural trade, agricultural policy analysis, and quantitative methods of agricultural market and price analysis. Education at McGill University, the University of Manitoba, and the Universität Kiel.

Mirosław Gronicki, Dr.: Chief economist at CASE (Center for Social and Economic Analysis) in Warsaw, Chief economist at BBG bank. Research and teaching in macroeconomics and econometrics. Extensive applied research in transition economics in Poland and Ukraine. Research and teaching at the University of Pennsylvania, Gdansk University, Charles University in Prague. Education and graduated in economics at Gdansk University.

Bohdan Hawrylyshyn, Dr.és.sc.écon., Dr.h.c.: Chairman of the International Centre for Policy Studies and of the International Management Institute, Kyiv. President of the Ternopil Academy of National Economy and Foundation Vidrodgenia. Advisor to the Chairman of the Parliament and the Prime Minister of Ukraine. Member of the Club of Rome and the Academy of Science of Ukraine. Former director of the International Management Institute, Geneva.

Christian von Hirschhausen, Dr.rer.oec.: Research Associate at the German Institute for Economic Research (DIW), Berlin, and member of the German Advisory Group with the Ukrainian Government in Kyiv. Specialises in structural and competition policy and enterprise reform. Previous positions at the UN (New York), École des Mines de Paris, University of Colorado (Boulder), and the Technische Universität Berlin.

Lutz Hoffmann, Dr.sc.pol.: Former President of the German Institute for Economic Research (DIW), Berlin, Professor emeritus of Economics at the Freie Universität Berlin and joint head of the German Advisory Group with the Ukrainian Government in Kyiv. Past appointments as advisor to the Prime Minister of Malaysia, at the World Bank, as Director at UNCTAD (Geneva) and as head of a group advising the President and Government of Kazakhstan.

Ryszard Kokoszczyński, Dr.: Deputy Governor of the National Bank of Poland since 1998, Assistant Professor at the Department of Economics, Warsaw University. Research and teaching in macro-economics, monetary economics and policy, and banking in transition economies. Education at Warsaw University and the Institut für Weltwirtschaft at the Universität Kiel.

Gerhard Krause: Former member of the German Advisory Group with the Ukrainian Government in Kyiv. Currently a member of the International Bilateral Relations Division at the European Central Bank, dealing with policy issues arising with accession countries, especially focusing on exchange rate strategies. Formerly staff member of Deutsche Bank Research (Frankfurt/Main) and of Creditanstalt Investment Bank (Vienna). Education at the Universität Wien, the University of Lexington (USA) and the IECS/IEP in Strasbourg (France).

Felicitas Möllers: Analyst at Deutsche Bank Research/Emerging Markets (Frankfurt/Main) and member of the German Advisory Group with the Ukrainian Government in Kyiv. Particular concentration on banking reform and foreign investment. Former assistant to the management of Deutsche Bank in Leipzig and assistant to Georg Krupp, member of the Board of Managing Directors of Deutsche Bank in Frankfurt/Main. Educated at the Universität Freiburg/Br. and at MIIT Moscow, graduated in economics from the Universität Kiel.

Arkady Moshes, Ph.D. (history): Section Head for Security of the Central Eastern Europe and the Baltic Sea Regions at the Institute of Europe, Russian Academy of Sciences (Moscow). Specialised in Russian relations with Ukraine, Belarus and the Baltic States, and developments in the Baltic and Black Sea regions. Author of "Domestic Political Developments and Foreign Policy of Ukraine in 1991-1995" (in Russian) and "Overcoming Unfriendly Stability: Russian-Latvian Relations at the End of the 1990s".

Petra Opitz, Dr.rer.oec.: Research Associate at the German Institute for Economic Research (DIW), Berlin, and member of the German Advisory Group with the Ukrainian Government in Kyiv. Particular concentration on deregulation and corporate restructuring in Eastern Europe. Formerly with the Institute for Economics at the Universität Oldenburg, the International Centre for Conversion (Bonn), the Freie Universität Berlin and the Academy of Sciences (Berlin).

Wolfgang Quaisser, Dr.sec.agr.: Research Associate at the Institute for Eastern European Studies (Munich). His work focuses on foreign trade in transition countries and the eastern enlargement of the EU. Numerous publications on the economies of Central and Eastern Europe, especially Poland. Education at the Universität Gießen (agriculture) and the Universität Frankfurt/Main (research projects in the Department of Economics). Previous positions as visiting Professor of Economics at Portland State University and Research Fellow of the Alexander von Humboldt Foundation (Feodor-Lynen Programme).

Klaus Schneider: Senior official in the External Relations Department of the European Commission (Brussels). Since 1982 he has been involved in the development of relations between the EU and Eastern European countries, in particular the former Soviet Union, and later the New Independent States. He specialised in contractual relations with Russia, Ukraine, Moldova and Belarus. He is now retired from the Commission.

Andrew Seton: Director for Ukraine, European Bank for Reconstruction and Development, Kyiv. Formerly Director of Deutsche Morgan-Grenfell in charge of Eastern European/FSU corporate and project finance and Head of the New York Office of Morgan-Grenfell. Various positions in trade and project finance with Morgan-Grenfell. Education at Oxford University, MA, M.Phil.

Ludwig Striewe: Research Associate at the Institute of Agricultural Economics of the Universität Göttingen, and member of the German Advisory Group with the Ukrainian Government in Kyiv. Research on agricultural market policies, rural financial markets in Ukraine, European market and structural policies. Education at the Universität Kiel and the Wageningen Agricultural University (Netherlands), graduated in agriculture and obtained a European Master of Agricultural Economics.

Ulrich Thießen, Dr.rer.pol.: Research Associate at the German Institute for Economic Research (DIW), Berlin, and member of the German Advisory Group with the Ukrainian Government in Kyiv. His work concentrates mainly on macro-economic analysis, especially on monetary, fiscal and external economic policy. Formerly economist with the IMF in Washington D.C.

Christian Thimann, Dr.rer.pol.: Head of the International Bilateral Relations Division of the European Central Bank, dealing with policy issues arising with central banks outside the EU. Particular focus on central banks in EU accession countries and countries in Eastern and South-Eastern Europe. Formerly staff member at the IMF. Education at the Universität Bonn, the London School of Economics, and the Universität München.

Volkhart Vincentz, Ph.D.: Research Associate at the Institute for Eastern European Studies (Munich) and member of the German Advisory Group with the Ukrainian Government in Kyiv. Work focuses on foreign trade in the countries of the former Soviet Union and the effects of the division of labour between Eastern and Western Europe. Numerous publications on the economies of the Soviet Union and Russia. Doctorate at Boston University.

Index

GPSR Compliance

The European Union's (EU) General Product Safety Regulation (GPSR) is a set of rules that requires consumer products to be safe and our obligations to ensure this.

If you have any concerns about our products, you can contact us on ProductSafety@springernature.com

In case Publisher is established outside the EU, the EU authorized representative is:

Springer Nature Customer Service Center GmbH
Europaplatz 3
69115 Heidelberg, Germany

Batch number: 10725973

Printed by Printforce, the Netherlands